The Tanner Lectures on Human Values

# THE TANNER LECTURES ON HUMAN VALUES

## 14
## 1993

Kornai, Kohl, Hill, Havel, Nozick, Taylor,
Baltimore, Sagdeev, Diamond

Grethe B. Peterson, *Editor*

UNIVERSITY OF UTAH PRESS
Salt Lake City

Copyright © 1993 University of Utah Press
Copyright © 1993 Václav Havel

All rights reserved
ISBN 0-87480-418-3
ISSN 0275-7656

∞ This symbol indicates books printed on paper
that meets the minimum requirements of
American National Standard for Information Services —
Permanence of Paper for Printed Library Materials,
ANSI A39.38–1984.

THE TANNER LECTURES ON HUMAN VALUES
was composed in Intertype Garamond with Garamond Foundry display type
by Donald M. Henriksen, Scholarly Typography, Salt Lake City.

*THE TANNER LECTURES ON HUMAN VALUES*

The purpose of the Tanner Lectures is to advance and reflect upon scholarly and scientific learning that relates to the entire range of human values.

To receive an appointment as a Tanner lecturer is a recognition of uncommon capabilities and outstanding scholarly or leadership achievement in the field of human values. The lecturers may be drawn from philosophy, religion, the humanities and sciences, the creative arts and learned professions, or from leadership in public or private affairs. The lectureships are international and intercultural and transcend ethnic, national, religious, or ideological distinctions.

The Tanner Lectures were formally founded on July 1, 1978, at Clare Hall, Cambridge University. They were established by the American scholar, industrialist, and philanthropist, Obert Clark Tanner. In creating the lectureships, Professor Tanner said, "I hope these lectures will contribute to the intellectual and moral life of mankind. I see them simply as a search for a better understanding of human behavior and human values. This understanding may be pursued for its own intrinsic worth, but it may also eventually have practical consequences for the quality of personal and social life."

Permanent Tanner lectureships, with lectures given annually, are established at nine institutions: Clare Hall, Cambridge University; Harvard University; Brasenose College, Oxford University; Princeton University; Stanford University; the University of California; the University of Michigan; the University of Utah; and Yale University. Other international lectureships occasionally take place. The institutions are selected by the Trustees.

The sponsoring institutions have full autonomy in the appointment of their lecturers. A major part of the lecture program is the publication and distribution of the Lectures in an annual volume.

The Tanner Lectures on Human Values is a nonprofit corporation administered at the University of Utah under the direction of a self-perpetuating, international Board of Trustees. The Trustees meet annually to enact policies that will ensure the quality of the lectureships.

The entire lecture program, including the costs of administration, is fully and generously funded in perpetuity by an endowment to the University of Utah by Professor Tanner and Mrs. Grace Adams Tanner.

Obert C. Tanner was born in Farmington, Utah, in 1904. He was educated at the University of Utah, Harvard University, and Stanford University. He has served on the faculty of Stanford University and is presently Emeritus Professor of Philosophy at the University of Utah. He is the founder and chairman of the O. C. Tanner Company, manufacturing jewelers.

GRETHE B. PETERSON
*University of Utah*

## THE TRUSTEES

**JAMES J. DUDERSTADT**
*President of the University of Michigan*

**DAVID PIERPONT GARDNER**
*President Emeritus of the University of California*
*President Emeritus of the University of Utah*

**THE REV. CAROLYN TANNER IRISH**
*Washington, D.C.*

**GERHARD CASPER**
*President of Stanford University*

**ANTHONY LOW**
*President of Clare Hall, Cambridge*

**O. DON OSTLER**
*Chief Executive Officer, O. C. Tanner Company*

**JACK W. PELTASON**
*President of the University of California*

**CHASE N. PETERSON**
*President Emeritus of the University of Utah*

**NEIL L. RUDENSTINE**
*President of Harvard University*

**BENNO C. SCHMIDT, JR.**
*President of Yale University*

**HAROLD T. SHAPIRO**
*President of Princeton University*

**ARTHUR K. SMITH, CHAIRMAN**
*President of the University of Utah*

**OBERT C. TANNER**
*Professor Emeritus of Philosophy at the University of Utah*

**LORD WINDLESHAM**
*Principal of Brasenose College, Oxford*

## CONTENTS

The Tanner Lectures on Human Values ................. v

The Trustees ........................................ vii

Preface to Volume 14 ................................ ix

János Kornai     I. Market Socialism Revisited ......... 1
                    II. The Soviet Union's Road to a Free Economy: Comments of an Outside Observer ................ 42

Helmut Kohl     (Lecture at the University of California, Berkeley) ......................... 69

Christopher Hill     The Bible in Seventeenth-Century English Politics ................... 85

Václav Havel     (Lecture at the University of California, Los Angeles) ..................... 109

Robert Nozick     Decisions of Principle, Principles of Decision ...................... 115

Charles Taylor     Modernity and the Rise of the Public Sphere ..................... 203

David Baltimore     On Doing Science in the Modern World.. 261

R. Z. Sagdeev     Science and Revolutions .............. 307

Jared Diamond     The Broadest Pattern of Human History.. 351

The Tanner Lecturers ................................ 391

Index to Volume 14 .................................. 399

*PREFACE TO VOLUME 14*

Volume 14 of the Tanner Lectures on Human Values includes lectures delivered during the academic year 1991–92.

The Tanner Lectures are published in an annual volume. A general index to Volumes I through V is included in Volume V; beginning with Volume VI, each volume has its own index.

In addition to the Lectures on Human Values, Professor Tanner and the Trustees of the Tanner Lectures have funded special international lectureships at selected colleges and universities which are administered independently of the permanent lectures.

# I
## *Market Socialism Revisited*

Delivered at
Stanford University
January 18, 1991

# II
## *The Soviet Union's Road to a Free Economy: Comments of an Outside Observer*

Delivered at
Leningrad University
June 13, 1991

*JÁNOS KORNAI*

THE TANNER LECTURES ON HUMAN VALUES

JÁNOS KORNAI is Head of the Department, Institute of Economics, the Hungarian Academy of Sciences, and Professor of Economics at Harvard University. He received a Doctor of Economics degree from the Karl Marx University of Economics, Budapest, in 1961 and a Doctor of Sciences degree from the Hungarian Academy of Sciences in 1965. A Fellow and former President of the Econometric Society, he is also an honorary member of the American Academy of Arts and Sciences, a foreign member of both the Royal Swedish Academy and the Finnish Academy of Sciences, and a member of the Hungarian Academy of Sciences. From 1972 to 1977 he served as Vice Chairman for the United Nations Committee for Development Planning. His numerous published works in English include *Overcentralization in Economic Administration* (1959), *Anti-Equilibrium* (1971), *Growth, Shortage and Efficiency* (1982), *The Road to a Free Economy* (1990), and *Vision and Reality, Market and State* (1990).

I

INTRODUCTION: DELIMITATION OF THE SUBJECT[1]

The great transformation taking place in Eastern Europe, the Soviet Union, and China has revived the discussion about market socialism.[2] Since this study does not cover the whole issue, I would like to begin by delimiting the subject examined and briefly noting the methods of approach.

1. Initial conditions have a strong effect on any formation that actually occurs in history. Where did it start from before reaching its present state? Because of the differing circumstances in which the genesis occurred, it is worth distinguishing clearly between two subject-areas. One is market socialism as a system to replace capitalism, and the other market socialism as a system to replace old-style, Stalinist, prereform socialism or, as I call it in my works, classical socialism.[3]

The subject of this study is the development and operation of market socialism during the process of reforming the socialist sys-

---

[1] The Soviet Union and Yugoslavia still existed when the lecture was delivered. This written text uses the terminology current at that time. I owe thanks for valuable observations particularly to Eric Maskin and John M. Litwack, the discussants of my lecture in Stanford, and to all who commented on the first draft, above all Zsuzsa Dániel, Mária Kovács, and Carla Krüger. Exclusive responsibility for any errors in the study is the author's, of course. I am grateful to Brian McLean and Julianna Parti for their excellent translation. I take this opportunity of expressing thanks to the Tanner Foundation for the honor of their invitation, and also to Kenneth J. Arrow and Partha Dasgupta for preparing the discussions on the lecture and for the inspiring conversations I had with them and other Stanford colleagues.

[2] Almost every book and study discussing the reforms, particularly in the first stage of the changes, mentions the concept of market socialism. Market socialism is the main topic of some major pieces of writing; I pick out here the ones that had a thought-provoking effect on me while I was working on this study: P. Bardhan (1990), W. Brus and K. Laski (1989), A. de Jasay (1990), D. Lavoie (1985), J. Le Grand and S. Estrin (1989), G. E. Schroeder (1988), and G. Temkin (1989).

[3] The concept of "classical socialism" is clarified in more detail in my book *The Socialist System* (1992).

tem.⁴ I do not discuss at all the other problem of market-socialist-style reform of capitalism.

Of course the two sets of problems overlap, since both of them entail thoroughly weighing the same value choices and the same instruments. But when it comes to practical conclusions and normative proposals they hold only in a specific context. What is true in the framework of reform socialism does not necessarily apply to the reforms of capitalism or vice versa. History does not move like a pendulum; having swung one way, it does not return to its original state. Explanations in which the unidirectional, "whence-and-whither" nature of history is ignored can easily lapse into serious fallacies.

2. Influential ideas tread a long path from their first formulation in theory to their realization in practice. For simplicity's sake, three stages in this path are distinguished here.

*The vision:* This may be a utopia presented in an outline form,⁵ or a normative model of pure theory. The series of the latter was opened by E. Barone ([1908] 1935); an outstanding work is the study by Oscar Lange (1936–37). Ideas related to Lange's can be found in the works of F. M. Taylor (1929) and A. Lerner (1946).⁶ Because of its outstanding significance for the history of theory, the Lange model will be returned to regularly in subsequent parts of this study.

---

⁴ A terminological observation is needed. The term "socialism" in this study, as in my other works, denotes actual socioeconomic systems marked by the monopoly rule of the Communist party. While I am aware of the importance to adherents of socialist ideas of clarifying whether these systems merited the name "socialism," I use it in a value-free sense. It is what the countries concerned called or still call themselves, and I have abstained from renaming them.

⁵ On the concept of vision, see J. A. Schumpeter (1954), R. Heilbroner (1990), and J. Kornai (1986a).

⁶ Formalization of the Lange-Taylor-Lerner models is dealt with in several works; I would stress the classic work of K. J. Arrow and L. Hurwicz (1960), E. Malinvaud's model (1967), and, of the most recent literature, the studies by I. Ortuno-Ortin, J. E. Roemer, and J. Silvestre (1990).

*The blueprint:* This can appear in a variety of forms, for instance as the practical proposals of reform economists,[7] the political declarations of leaders, or resolutions on reform passed by a Communist party and government in power in a socialist country.

*Realization:* This covers what actually goes on in the economy, the de facto rules of the game, and the attitudes and behavioral regularities of the actors in the system.

Although the first stage is very important, it is not discussed here in all its details. The main subject of this study is political and economic history, not intellectual history, and so attention is centered on the blueprint and realization.[8] Although I admit the relevance of utopias and pure theoretical models, I would like to point out to Western readers that the practical experience of what took place in the socialist countries cannot be ignored even in the debate at the "visionary" level. The old ideas must be reconsidered in the light of the new evidence.

3. A whole range of countries went through a stage in which certain ingredients of market socialism were applied. Changes pointing in this direction occurred from 1949 onward in Yugoslavia and from 1953 in Hungary. Certain elements of market socialism appeared much later in Poland, the Soviet Union, China, and Vietnam. It is not possible here to discuss the matter country by country. Although there were appreciable differences between the specific formations that came into being in each country and its pace of historical development, an attempt will be made to formu-

---

[7] A few pioneering works are mentioned, grouped by countries. *Yugoslavia*: B. Kidric (for the works he wrote in the 1950s, see his 1985 volume); *Hungary*: Gy. Péter (1954a, 1954b), J. Kornai ([1957] 1959); *Poland*: W. Brus ([1961] 1972); *Czechoslovakia*: O. Sik (1966); *Soviet Union*: E. G. Liberman ([1962] 1972), *China*. Y. Sun ([1958–61] 1982).

[8] When Hayek (1935) took issue with the adherents of market socialism during the famous debate in the 1930s around the article by Oscar Lange, he stepped out of the realm of pure theoretical models by also bringing forward practical counterarguments that belong, according to the terminology of this study, to the blueprint stage.

late general statements. A common *prototype* will be outlined for each blueprint and for each practical realization. A prototype blueprint consists of a compression of thousands of political speeches, party programs, proposals submitted to the authorities, and resolutions passed by the state. A prototype realization is a generalized image of common practice, intended to describe what goes on in the offices of finance ministers or chief executives of state-owned firms and what are the characteristic tendencies in the economy.

The prototypes of both kinds result from a high degree of abstraction. They omit the less essential, ad hoc features and are intended to reflect the fundamental characteristics of market-socialist reforms. Neglecting the differences between countries, they focus on the properties in *common*.

This study sheds light on the problems posed by market socialism from various angles. The first part approaches the matter mainly from the point of view of *political economy*, and the second from the point of view of *philosophy*. The latter examines both the epistemological-methodological and the ethical-political aspects.

1. BLUEPRINT AND HISTORICAL REALIZATION: THE VIEWPOINT OF POLITICAL ECONOMY

1.1 *The Blueprint*

The main features of the prototype blueprint can be summed up as follows:

1. The political monopoly of the Communist party must be maintained. Some degree of political liberalization may occur: *glasnost'* may develop, that is, a higher degree of honesty in the provision of political information and greater tolerance for alternative views; there may be more openness in relations with the West. But no fundamental change in the political structure is permissible.

I propose to make a sharp distinction between two stages. In the first of these a *reform* of a market-socialist character takes place, while the Communist party's monopoly of power basically remains. The point of departure for the second stage is a *revolutionary* change in the political sphere, when the monopoly of the Communist party is broken and parliamentary democracy develops after free, multiparty elections. At that point the system commences the *transition* from socialism toward a capitalist market economy. The issues of this transition are extremely important, of course, but they are outside the scope of this study. Occasional references are made to the problems of the transition, but the subject here is the reform socialism associated with the names of Tito in Yugoslavia, Kádár in Hungary, Deng Xiaoping in China, Rakowski in Poland, and Gorbachev in the Soviet Union.

2. The predominance of public ownership must be maintained. Except in Yugoslavia's case, this means the predominance of state ownership. The specific characteristics of Yugoslav development cannot be dealt with here in detail, and the discussion that follows is concerned with state ownership. The observations, however, are applicable to Yugoslavia's case as well.

An important — perhaps the most important — component in the economic changes at the stage of historical realization is the evolution of the formal and informal private sector. Although it provides a relatively small proportion of production, it plays a big part in improving supply to the public and introducing property relations that conform with the market economy. But the idea of developing the private sector does not appear in the *blueprint* for market socialism before the actual transformation begins. The blueprint exclusively prescribes a renovation of the conditions under which state-owned firms operate. So in the rest of this study the remarks on market socialism refer exclusively to the state sector.

3. The relative share of decisions made at central level must diminish radically in favor of decentralized decisions made at local-government or more frequently enterprise level.

A similar idea is expressed by another formula. A state-owned firm is linked vertically with its superior authorities and horizontally with its sellers and buyers. In the blueprint, the vertical links remain but the horizontal links are radically reinforced.

4. The main indicator of success for a firm is profit. The incentives for managers are to be tied to profits, and profit-sharing is to be introduced for the firm's workers.

5. The range of instruments available to the center must alter. Direct commands, the main instrument so far, should give way to indirect instruments or "economic levers." The blueprint's drafters assume that if firms are profit-maximizing, their actions can be influenced by changes in interest and exchange rates, taxes, subsidies, and specific prices. Centrally set prices and other financial parameters are to be strings pulled by the center to which firms will react like puppets.

6. The prototype blueprint does not clarify the kind of prices it seeks to introduce. Prices set by a decentralized process will reflect the market situation. But on what principles will centrally decided prices be set, including wages, interest rates, and exchange rates? The blueprint *fails* to say these must be market-clearing prices.

7. The economy must be opened up to relations with the capitalist world. The international credit market must also be entered, and it is worth raising loans from capitalist governments, banks, and firms in order to advance socialist development.

Let us look briefly at the best-known vision, the Lange model. The prototype blueprint is akin to it in aiming to operate profit-maximizing state-owned firms with a high degree of autonomy. It shares its aim of using central prices and financial levers to influence firms' decisions, but clearly departs from Lange theory in not stating firmly that market-clearing prices will be introduced.

The most important difference is that the blueprint contains a far richer set of rules. Pure theory can abstract away many important factors. Not so practice, which *must* settle all problems of choice one way or another. The prototype blueprint outlines many features of the system ignored in Lange's work and the theoretical controversy on market socialism in general.

That is not a shortcoming of the Lange model or the debate on it. Richness of detail cannot be expected in an intellectual construct belonging to the realm of pure normative theory. But it is not a mere shortcoming, but a fatal fallacy to take the theoretical model too seriously, so to speak, and treat it as a blueprint.[9]

In fact, even the blueprint falls far short of the complexity of reality, disregarding several considerations that prove highly important in practice. These will be returned to later.

The leitmotiv running through the seven attributes listed is that a new *Third System* must be created. This is to differ from the prereform, Stalinist classical socialism, but also from capitalism.[10] It is considered not a transitory stage that leads from socialism to capitalism, but a separate social formation, a lasting and robust new system.

## 1.2 *The Economic Performance*

In many features, if not in its entirety, the blueprint was applied for varying periods in the countries listed in the introduction. But it must be added that the historical realization differed from the blueprint in several respects, developing many characteristics that the drafters of the blueprint had not foreseen. Before turning to these departures, let us take a quick look at the economic performance produced by the blueprint's application. There is an ample body of empirical literature on the subject, and works discussing the issues of the transition to a market economy usually summarize the earlier period's economic successes and failures as well.[11] Rather than going into detail or presenting statistics, just a few of the main characteristics will be emphasized here.

[9] This Oscar Lange himself never did.

[10] This Third Road idea is well reflected in the following quotation from Gorbachev: "What alternatives are before us? . . . One is to maintain the command-administrative system, the strict planning, and the commands in culture as well as the economy. The other . . . suggests reverting to capitalism. Can we take either of these roads? No, we reject them. . . ." (*Pravda*, November 26, 1989).

[11] See, for instance, the articles of D. Lipton and J. Sachs (1990a, 1990b) and G. W. Kolodko (1991) on Poland, the article by J. Kornai (1986a), and the OECD

- Signs of slowdown had appeared before the reform began and were among the motives for breaking with the old command economy. The market-socialist reforms at most bring a measure of temporary revival; they do not halt the downturn permanently. The economy arrives at a point of stagnation, and later, in fact, an absolute contraction of production sets in. If appreciable growth does appear in any sectors, as it did, for instance, in Chinese farming for a good many years, it is due not to the realization of the market-socialist blueprint at all, but to de facto privatization, which falls outside the original market-socialist blueprint, as mentioned earlier.
- The stagnation or decline in GDP is accompanied by stagnation or decline in real consumption. Once again, the only countervailing force is the evolution of the private sector, which helps to improve supply and living conditions.
- Severe disequilibria are caused. Classical socialism is a chronic shortage economy, with distorted relative prices, but quite a stable general price level. Market-socialist reform is accompanied in most countries by a new, more complex problem: the "shortage-cum-inflation" syndrome. A grave and growing budget deficit develops, becoming one of the main factors fueling the growing inflation, which develops into open hyperinflation in some countries. In others the inflation is artificially repressed and a huge monetary overhang is created.
- There is no significant improvement in efficiency and factory productivity. Nor are there any tangible results in goods quality, innovation, or technical advance.
- The share of foreign trade conducted with capitalist countries increases, but the performance in this field is again poor. There is a deficit in trade with the capitalist market. Foreign debt rises and certain countries reach the brink of insolvency.

---

report (1991) on Hungary, and the joint IMF, IBRD, OECD, and EBRD report (1990) on the Soviet Union.

If the blueprint was meant to create a Third System, it certainly did not prove its economic superiority over the First, modern capitalism. Nor can clear conclusions be drawn from a comparison with the Second System, classical socialism. On the one hand there are benefits. Although state-owned firms do not turn into real profit-maximizing economic units, some impression on the mentality of managers is made by the market-economic rhetoric, coupled with a few actual measures. They learn to pay more heed to financial indicators and buyer requirements. (This eases the later, real transition toward a market economy after the great political changes have taken place.) The main factor tending to improve the economic situation is the development of the formal and informal private sector. Perhaps most importantly of all, life becomes more tolerable, mainly because there is a measure of political liberalization and human rights are asserted more easily. On the other hand there are serious negative consequences, primarily for the macroeconomic equilibrium. Take, for example, East Germany, Czechoslovakia, and Romania, three countries whose political leaders stubbornly resisted all market-socialist reform, and compare them with Yugoslavia, Hungary, Poland, and the Soviet Union, which took the market-socialist road for varying periods. The macrosituation on the eve of the postsocialist transition is clearly worse in the second group than in the first: the budget deficit is greater, inflation faster (or the combination of shortage and inflation more acute), and foreign debt higher. The market-socialist experiments led to a situation in which the leadership lost control.

The economic leadership fails to understand what is happening. Repeated promises of an improvement cannot be kept, and this leads to frustration and protests from the general public. Since the reform has been coupled with political liberalization, the discontent takes open forms: demonstrations and protest meetings take place, and new parties opposed to the Communist party are organized. The old political system disintegrates.

So what has gone wrong with the market-oriented reform?

One view is that the original blueprint is basically a good one, but it has one or two shortcomings that need rectifying. "Reform the reform."

Another view is that the blueprint was wrongly implemented. The blueprint is in order, but it has not been applied in a consistent way because the bureaucrats and other conservative forces have sabotaged it.

In my view these factors are only a small part of the explanation. The main proposition in this study is that *the blueprint of market socialism is doomed to failure.* Although classical socialism causes great suffering and operates inefficiently, it is at least coherent. Combined with the "requisite" degree of brutal repression, it is viable and robust. The market-socialist reform, on the other hand, is not capable of becoming a robust system. In fact it is only its predecessor, classical socialism, in the process of falling apart. The subsequent sections of this study advance arguments in favor of this proposition, grouped under the following themes: the role of the state and politics; property rights and the soft budget constraint; social discipline; and exit, entry, and natural selection.

The causal explanation for the failure is far from exhaustive. Several important issues are missing: for instance, the problem of prices and the related problem of information, mainly because they have been adequately covered in other works. In my view, however, the phenomena to be examined are among the main factors explaining the failure.

## 1.3 *The Role of the State and Politics*

The authors of the Lange model and the purely theoretical ideas related to it do not refer specifically to a particular theory of the state. But some underlying tacit assumptions can be discerned, and these are not merely naive, but ultimately quite false. The theory assumes that the state will be content to perform three modest functions: (1) to determine the market-clearing prices, (2) to enforce the profit-maximization rule for state-owned firms, and (3) to perform some redistribution of personal incomes. The theory disregards the real nature of any modern state, let alone such an exceptionally powerful state as the one that operates under the socialist system.

The prototype blueprint is not so naive as the utopian pure theory. On the contrary, its axiomatic point of departure is a special form of state, the party-state. It postulates that on the one hand the Communist party's political monopoly is to remain, and on the other the market will coordinate a substantial proportion of the economic processes. Yet these two postulates cannot be satisfied together, because each precludes the realization of the other. That is the biggest flaw in the blueprint.

Let us look at the modern reformulation of market socialism in the light of contract theory and the so-called principal-agent model.[12] This suggests there is a specific kind of *contract* between the state-center and the manager of a state-owned firm, with the center as principal and the manager as agent acting on its behalf. Western theoretical economists today are often found to draw the following conclusion: the experiments in market socialism so far have failed because the terms of the contract were wrong. With a better contract, the market-socialist system will work.

To counter this view, the main thesis put forward in the previous section can be rephrased like this. It is *impossible* to devise and enforce any contract between the state-center (as it actually exists in these countries) and the managers of firms (those actually operating in these countries) that would ensure an efficient allocation of resources. Let me draw attention to the qualifiers in parentheses. A contract between an imaginary principal and an imaginary agent is quite irrelevant to the subject of this study. Let me repeat for the sake of emphasis: our concern is with actual

[12] An overall view of this promising new line of research is provided by O. Hart and B. R. Holmström (1987) and J. E. Stiglitz (1987).

organizations and actual persons whose actions are dictated by their real natures and circumstances.

I hope that further research will produce an exact formulation of this assertion. In terms of strict logical proof, this assertion can only be rated as a conjecture for further research to prove or disprove. It can, if you like, be classed as a bold conjecture, as can the other assertions in this study. But the intuition rests on clear observation of a plain fact: thousands of highly intelligent, well-intentioned people in all the countries that experimented with market socialism were unable to hammer out and consistently implement a contract that was guaranteed to operate efficiently.

Here are a few arguments to support the conjecture.

1. It is a false assumption to expect any government (let alone an individual dictator or a politburo as a collective dictator under a Communist-dominated political system) to maximize the social-welfare function. It is even doubtful whether any other well-defined utility function can be assumed. If there is an ultimate objective at all, it is to maintain the power of the political rulers, not further the welfare of society. The real motives are described more precisely, in fact, by saying that Communist leaders have multiple objectives. To mention just a few, these include fulfilling their deeply entrenched ideological obligations; in the case of smaller countries, faithfully serving the master-country, the Soviet Union; increasing their military might; accelerating growth in the shortest time possible; and, alongside all these, improving the population's standard of living, of course. It is an elementary truth to empirical political scientists that no politician ever has a consistent order of preferences. Unless stupid or stubborn, he or she will improvise, always adjusting to the contingencies, putting one thing first today and another tomorrow.

Since state ownership places the machinery of the whole economy in the hands of politicians, it is naive to expect that production can ever be "depoliticized." On the contrary, it will invariably be subject to the ever-changing political winds. Important though efficiency, growth, technical advance, and so on remain as tasks, they can be easily pushed into second place if the day-to-day considerations of politics so require: for instance, if politicians give popularity priority over other tasks or need to extract more revenue for military purposes.

No politician wants to "sign a contract." They do not like to state their goals plainly, because it ties their hands and limits their room for maneuver. They do not want to be absolutely faithful to any kind of commitment or contract. They prefer flexible action adjusted ad hoc to the changing circumstances.

Even under modern capitalism, the business sphere primarily governed by criteria of profit and efficiency is never separated perfectly from the political sphere moved by considerations of power, but the separation goes quite a long way. The Communist monopoly of political power and predominant state ownership preclude that separation altogether.

2. Another approach is to look at *roles* instead of *objectives*. Capitalist owners basically fulfill one role: they behave as owners. In this role they primarily seek to enhance their income and the value of their property. The state, however, particularly the socialist state, has several concurrent roles. Apart from drawing income from its property, it performs the following other functions:

- legislator, setting the rules for the economy;
- police officer, enforcing the law;
- judge, arbitrating in cases of conflict;
- allocator, redistributing wealth and income;
- insurer, providing a cushion against risks, a dispenser of social security, and a paternalistic benefactor;
- union official, defending workers from managerial abuse.

Conflict between these roles is inevitable. In a democratic constitutional state they are separated, but market socialism, arising under the conditions of Communist power, conserves a political and governmental structure that combines these functions in a totalitarian party-state, instead of separating them.

The role of judge needs special mention. A contract between the state-center and a firm's manager is inevitably incomplete. If it covered every possible detail, it would be hopelessly complex and opaque, and its observance extremely expensive to check. But if the contract between the state-center and the manager fails to cover every detail, legal disputes may arise. Who adjudicates? There is no judicial independence in a totalitarian state. "Plaintiff," "defendant," and "judge" are all dependent on the party and all subordinate to the upper levels of the party-state bureaucracy.

3. Mention was made under point 1 of an individual fictional politician, but in fact every political leadership in existence is a coalition, and that applies under a one-party system as well. Within the coalition there are factions and power struggles. Any coalition is temporary and fragile. So whatever contract is drawn up between the state-center and the management of a firm, its enforcement and the conditions under which it can be renegotiated are subject to the power struggle. There is no stability and persistency, only capricious volatility. Even if the members of the coalition agree with the firm's management on the terms of their relations (the "contract") at a given time, its enforcement remains subject to monetary future configurations of power in the coalition.

4. Market socialism assumes that the bureaucracy exercises self-restraint. (Party apparatchiks are to be understood as included in the bureaucracy as an aggregate term; the members of the party apparatus are not just members of the bureaucracy, they are its core.) However great the bureaucracy's power, it is expected to refrain from using it and leave the decisions to the management of the firm and the market agreements between buyers and sellers.

This assumption rests on a vain hope. In fact the temptation is almost irresistible. If power gets into the hands of power-hungry people, they will use it. Moreover, it has become the tradition and routine for them to do so in the period of classical socialism. Both the bureaucrats and the citizens are used to that, and it is sometimes actually demanded even by those over whom the power is exercised. If there is a shortage of a product or service, for instance, the authorities are expected to intervene and organize an administrative distribution.

Oscar Lange's model sought to confine itself to two simple rules. The prototype blueprint intended the bureaucracy to have much greater power, but it set limits, saying where the role of the bureaucracy was to end and the role of the market to begin. But in reality the bureaucracy constantly oversteps the bounds with millions of interventions. Microregulation prevails.

The leadership under reform socialism appeals time and again to the bureaucracy to assist instead of obstructing the process of reform. This proves to be absurd, since the situation contains an innate contradiction. The bureaucracy cannot "assist," because its very existence is a basic obstacle to market-socialist reform.

The growth of the bureaucratic apparatus is not easy to halt, and a reduction is more hopeless still. Once a position in the bureaucracy has come into being, it is extremely difficult to abolish it. Far from falling, the number employed by the party-state and total spending can sometimes even rise during the experiments with market socialism.

There is a struggle going on around the reform, a struggle for power, prestige, influence, and privilege. The more autonomy individuals gain and the more scope there is for voluntary contracts between individuals, the less power bureaucrats are left with. So it is in their own interest to resist.

## 1.4 *Property Rights and the Soft Budget Constraint*

A return can be made here to an issue mentioned earlier, the principal-agent relation and the "contract" between the principal and the agent. The following argument is often used to defend the concept of market socialism.

Ownership has been separated from control under modern capitalism. The owners of a large joint-stock company are a large number of shareholders, while control is concentrated in the hands of the senior executives. The former constitute the principal and the latter the agent. If this works well under capitalism, why should it not work well under market socialism, even though the owner is the state (or the government representing it)? After all, the output of General Motors is presumably no smaller than Albania's or Mongolia's.

This argument rests in my view on a false analogy, the criticism following from the ideas introduced in the previous section.

The *objectives* of the owners are radically different. In the first place, shareholders in General Motors seek financial gain in the short and long term, whereas the government under market socialism has complex motives that are ultimately subordinate to political goals.

The *instruments* in the hands of the owners are also different. The shareholders of General Motors can dispense financial rewards and penalties, with dismissal as the ultimate sanction; they do not have a KGB. A totalitarian party-state has countless administrative and ideological instruments available to it, though they have weakened since the classical socialist period.

So *the situation of the agent* differs fundamentally under the two sets of contractual circumstances. A General Motors manager has an exit: he or she can quit. (To stick with the U.S. car industry, Lee Iacocca left Ford after conflicts with Henry Ford, the main shareholder, and went to the rival firm of Chrysler as chief executive.) There is no real exit for a company manager under market socialism, since ultimately there is just one employer, the state. (Staying with the same analogy, it is like being able to move from Buick to Pontiac, but not escape from General Motors altogether.) Wherever managers go they are accompanied throughout life by a personnel file. Instead of jobs being allocated by a competitive labor market, top executives are assigned to them by a strongly centralized, ubiquitous network of personnel departments controlled by the party and secret police. A quarrel with the centralized bureaucracy can badly damage or even ruin a manager's career prospects, while good connections in the party and other branches of the bureaucratic apparatus open up a wide range of other careers, as a party functionary, for instance, a high-ranking official, or a diplomat.

This situation decides the motivation of the subordinate agent in the principal-agent relationship. The key trait is loyalty to superiors, not business success or concern for customers. A manager is a bureaucrat, a member of the *nomenklatura*.

A simple conclusion can be drawn: *there is no real decentralization without private ownership*. This well-known proposition was first emphasized strongly in the works of Mises and later expounded in more detail by the "property-rights school."[13] The practical experience of the socialist countries supplies new and convincing evidence to support the old truth. The experiments in applying market socialism confirm that the survival of state ownership inevitably conserves a high degree of centralization.

Let us look at the various property rights more closely.

(a) *Income*. The residual income of a capitalist joint-stock company, after deduction of expenses and taxes, clearly belongs to the shareholders. Though there are institutional owners as well, a high proportion of the shares are held by individuals with direct *personal interests*. With a firm under market socialism this income flows into the state treasury, which is quite *impersonal*. Even if part of the residual income is passed to the managers under various incentive schemes, the proportion is uncertain and the subject of constant negotiation.

(b) *Alienation*. Property rights in a capitalist joint-stock company are transferable, whereas the ownership of a market-socialist firm is inalienable: its sale is precluded by legal constraints.

---

[13] See L. von Mises ([1920] 1935), and also A. A. Alchian (1965, 1974) and A. A. Alchian and H. Demsetz (1972). The position is summarized concisely in the title of W. G. Nutter's study (1968): "Markets without Property: A Grand Illusion."

(c) *Control*. A substantial part of this shifts from the center to the management of the firm, but the rights are not clearly separated, since the center continues to exercise control in a variety of ways. The line dividing the provinces of the superior state organizations and the firm's managers at any time depends on negotiation.

A clear, plain assignment of property rights is lacking. The key to grasping the situation is to see how every decision is based on ad hoc negotiations between the upper levels of the bureaucracy and the managers of the firm. The relative bargaining positions are uncertain. The superior bureaucratic authorities combine strength and weakness: strength in possessing the instruments of state power and weakness in being unable to resort to extreme instruments of terror. But the firm's managers are strong and weak too: strong in that they can resort to blackmail — "our output is vital in the shortage economy"; "we cannot dismiss our workers" — but weak because their careers depend on their superiors' grace and favor.

This is the context in which the syndrome of *soft budget constraint* emerges.[14] As mentioned before, the blueprint states profit to be the main indicator of a firm's success, but this is not taken seriously. With the prevailing political structure and predominance of state ownership there must be softness of the budget constraint. The state cannot let down an insolvent firm; it must bail it out. This conclusion can be drawn directly from what has been said about relations between the party-state and a state-owned firm.

Private ownership is an essential requirement for a hard budget constraint. Private owners can be left to their fate; it is their problem, not the state's. Softening of the budget constraint is the result of deep state involvement, since the state bears ultimate responsibility for the fate of the firm.

---

[14] This concept was introduced in my work *Economics of Shortage* (1980); for a more detailed explanation see my 1986b article and chapters 8 and 21 of the 1992 book.

## 1.5 Social Discipline

The bargaining that permeates society ties in with another noteworthy problem: social discipline.

Any complex process of coordination demands a measure of discipline. There must be a combination of positive and negative incentives, the carrot and the stick.

Discipline is needed at work to ensure full use of working hours, obedience to technological imperatives, and cooperation between the various phases of work.

Discipline is needed in pay or wages can become divorced from performance, which has harmful micro- and macroeconomic effects.

Discipline is needed in finance. Among the many facets of this multiple requirement is that persistently loss-making firms must be wound up, since their survival merely contributes to social costs.

Classical socialism rested on commands, mandatory planning instructions, and a brutal enforcement of obedience. There were rewards for discipline and loyalty to the party and the state, but harsh penalties for violations of discipline.

Capitalism applies market discipline mainly by economic means. Work discipline is reinforced by refined pay schemes, and most of all by the threat of dismissal and unemployment. Wage discipline is ensured by the self-interest of the owners, since extra pay unjustified by performance ultimately comes out of their pockets. Financial discipline in the business sphere is enforced primarily by the hard budget constraint: a firm that gets into difficulties will not be rescued by the state with tax breaks or subsidies, or with soft loans from the banking system.[15]

Under the reform pointing toward market socialism, the discipline of the command economy is lifted without true market discipline being applied. Softness is not confined to the budget con-

[15] Certain symptoms of the soft budget constraint syndrome appear in modern capitalism due to various factors: there are rescues of insolvent firms and even whole sectors. How inevitable this is and to what extent it brings an erosion of financial discipline, along with all the detrimental consequences known from the experience of the socialist countries, is a matter of debate.

straint; all the other forms of discipline slacken too. Superiors and subordinates connive to flout the law. Inspectors turn a blind eye to laxity and indiscipline. Laws and rules lose their prestige.

The breakdown of discipline is also to blame for the low efficiency at microlevel, and on a macrolevel it is the main contributor to the macrotensions — the wage spiral, excess state spending, and the practice of wantonly distributing credit and never demanding its repayment. All these phenomena ultimately bring about inflation, monetary overhang, and indebtedness.

## 1.6 Entry, Exit, and Natural Selection

In the discussion of market socialism to this point, the composition of the firms sector was taken for granted. In fact the multitude of firms is not constant, and the regularities governing entry and exit, birth and death, are extremely important.

One of capitalism's great virtues is the freedom of entry into all areas where it is unimpeded by monopolies. Opportunity is the mother of enterprise. The entrepreneur in Schumpeter's sense pools his or her talents with the financial resources of the lender.[16] Loan capital may come from various sources. The financial backing for the enterprise is provided by a competitive banking sector and a decentralized capital and money market.

Market socialism differs little from classical socialism in this respect. Entry is governed by bureaucratic decisions. The foundation of firms is the bureaucracy's task and privilege. There are strong monopolistic tendencies: why create rivals for oneself? Competition and the right of free entry are inseparable, and they are just what market socialism lacks.

The situation is similar on the exit side. With a hard budget constraint, a loss-making firm cannot survive. This applies invariably to the normally small and medium-sized firms in the non-

---

[16] "Capitalism is that form of private property economy in which innovations are carried out by means of borrowed money," writes Schumpeter (1939: vol. 1, p. 223).

corporate sector. Here the exit rate is very high, amounting to 20–30% of firms a year in many countries. The proportion is far lower in the corporate sector, but a similar selection effect operates there through the mechanism of corporate takeovers. If the earlier management was incapable of drawing the maximum profit from the firm, the potential new owners hope for new profitmaking opportunities by taking over control of the shares, and this is usually accompanied by aggressive dismissal of the previous management.

These strict principles of selection fail to apply in an economy with a soft budget constraint. There is a bureaucratic redistribution of profits, which are taken from strong firms and given as assistance to weak ones. The state has sunk investments in an existing firm, and so it has a vested interest in its survival.[17] Exit is relatively rare, and when it does occur it is by an arbitrary bureaucratic decision.

The overall effect of the entry-exit rules set is that no rivalry occurs. A brief return must be made to an issue mentioned several times before: Can an effective "contract" be made between the state-center and a firm's manager? To the counterarguments advanced so far another can be added. For the "principal" (in this case the state-center) to gauge performance by the "agents" (in this context the managers of firms), it must be able to compare firms. But that requires free entry and competition, which makes a real comparison with winners and losers, not just paper assessments.[18]

Without free entry and without exit by the losers in the competition, the "creative destruction" that Schumpeter deemed so important cannot occur. Once the production structure has formed, it is frozen. That is one more reason for the low efficiency and weak performance.

---

[17] This mechanism is formalized and its negative results graphically shown by M. Dewatripont and E. Maskin (1990). The effect of the phenomenon on innovation is analyzed by Y. Qian and C. Xu (1991).

[18] Although this study does not deal with the issue of prices, it must be mentioned here that the comparative reports on paper of firms' performances are useless in any case because distorted and irrational prices are used to compile them.

To sum up, there are various arguments to support this study's main proposition that the failure of market socialism is not due to weaknesses in the blueprint or in the way it is implemented. Given certain fundamental features of the sociopolitical system—namely, the survival of the Communist party's political monopoly and the predominance of state ownership — the quest for a truly efficient economy is hopeless. There is a built-in instability, and the experiment sooner or later breaks down.

## 2. Learning by Disappointment: The Epistemological and Ethical Viewpoint

### 2.1 *Understanding the Process of Understanding*

Some of the arguments against market socialism put forward in this study were known a good while before the present collapse of the Eastern European system. Reference was made earlier to Mises, Hayek, and the exponents of the "property-rights school," whose writings advance numerous objections still valid today. Why did the warnings fall on deaf ears in Eastern Europe? Why did reform politicians and reform economists not take the critics' words to heart? A broader problem lies behind these questions. What are the constraints on enlightenment and rational argument?

Some autobiographical elements appear in this part of the study; introspection contributes to the analysis. I envy those who never change their *Weltanschauung* from the moment they start to ponder the great issues of life to the day they die. No doubt this is not rare in relatively stable societies, but it is hardly possible in the troubled region of Eastern Europe. Many people, even those who tried to serve the same set of fundamental ethical principles throughout their lives, have come to change their philosophy, perhaps more than once, under the influence of disturbing experiences and dramatic changes in their social environment.

One side of people's lives is the history of their opinions. What doctrines did they subscribe to and when? In what period (if ever) were they faithful Marxists? When did they become adherents of reform, perhaps of market socialism itself, and when did they abandon hope of reforming the socialist system (assuming they went through that stage as well)? The discussion here does not cover the way *individuals* differ in the pace at which they go through the process of faith, disappointment, and enlightenment. The question I am interested in is what induced *large groups* of reform politicians and reform economists to devote themselves to the cause of market socialism. What drew them to it and what repelled them from it? The concern in this part of the study, as in the first, is not with individual cases, but with a *prototype* history of ideas: an intellectual movement and the general formulae of moral and political conviction that inspired it.

The question remains topical, because the idea has not been dispelled. It still influences many people despite the historical failure; the greater the difficulties encountered in the transition from socialism to capitalism, the greater the influence of market-socialist ideas tends to become.

## 2.2 *The Struggle with Marxism*

The reform politicians and reform economists of Eastern Europe were brought up in the Marxist intellectual tradition, with *Das Kapital* as their bible. Acceptance of market socialism is quite alien to the spirit of Marxism. Marx recognized the high degree of organization and efficiency *inside* the factory in a capitalist economy, but he emphasized that complete anarchy reigned on the market connecting the factories.[19] According to this concept, the market is a poorly operating, blind coordination mechanism based on *ex post* reactions to signals. So it must be replaced in the superior socialist society by conscious planning tuned to *ex ante* signals.

Nor was the market attacked merely by the spread of rational arguments. There was indoctrination that delved deep into the

---

[19] ". . . the most complete anarchy reigns among . . . the capitalists themselves," Marx writes in *Capital* ([1867–94] 1978: chapter 51, p. 1021).

metarational, emotional realm, inducing prejudices against the market. A true Marxist views the market with suspicion and contempt. The need to free humanity from its market fetters is one reason why private property must be eliminated.

Overcoming these prejudices requires a great effort of will. Many formerly dogmatic Marxists never manage to overcome them entirely, an example being the frequent fulminations against "speculators," "profiteers," and "black-marketeers" even during the reform.

Despite this antipathy, market socialism seemed to many Communist politicians inclined toward reform to be a necessary concession. They wanted to retain the earlier structure of power, the political monopoly of the Communist party, because that for a Leninist was the prime consideration.[20] And they also wanted to retain the predominance of state ownership. These two attributes of socialism had more than an instrumental value in the Communist system of values, more than a purpose in terms of some other, ultimate aim like the welfare of the people or human happiness. They themselves possessed an intrinsic value, being absolutely indispensable characteristics for a system worthy of the name "socialist." So market socialism seemed to be a promising combination of socialism and capitalism: a dominant role is assigned to the fundamental socialist attributes in the power structure and property relations, and a little injection of capitalism is administered: some influence of the market on coordination. The new combination will improve efficiency without abandoning socialism.[21] As

---

[20] Stalin quotes Lenin's statement that "the question of power is the fundamental question of the revolution," adding himself: "The seizure of power is only the beginning. . . . The whole point is to retain power, to consolidate it, and make it invincible" (1947: p. 39).

[21] As an illustration, a quotation from Gorbachev: "In short: the advantages of planning will be increasingly combined with the stimulating factors of the socialist market. But all of this will take place within the mainstream of socialist goals and principles of management" (1987: p. 91). A later statement: "The superiority of the market has been demonstrated on a world scale . . . it is really the regulated market economy which allows us to increase national wealth. . . . And, of course, state power is in our hands" (*Izvestia*, July 11, 1990).

long as politicians and economists retain their belief in this combination, they can be classed as *naive reformers*.

The reform camp broke up into conflicting groups as it became increasingly clear that *the alternatives were mutually exclusive*. There could *either* be socialism with Communist party rule and predominant state ownership *or* a genuine market economy.

2.3 *Compatibility with Walrasian Thinking*

Let us turn to another intellectual current: Walrasian economics.²² Several groups must be considered here: (1) economists in Eastern Europe who were converts from Marxism to contemporary Western economic ideas; (2) again in Eastern Europe, a small number of economists, mainly of the older generation, who never went through a Marxist phase; and (3) Western economists who had an interest in market socialism.

The great attraction of Lange-type normative theories is the neat way they fit into the Walrasian tradition and combine nicely (on an intellectual plane, not in reality) with certain socialistic ideas such as a more equitable distribution of income through redistribution by the state. Even the ownership question can be ignored. What really matters is not ownership, but correctly setting the rules and drawing up the contracts with managers, which in turn assures the right motivation and rational prices.

The shortcomings of this view have been outlined in the first part of this study. The Walrasian model, along with most of its later variants including the Lange-type model, is a marvelous piece of intellectual machinery placed in a sociopolitical vacuum. It is a construction that lacks *a positive theory of politico-socioeconomic order* as a foundation. Walrasian economics and its more recent theoretical, mathematical-cum-economic kin like game theory, contract theory, and organization theory are very powerful tools for

²² The term "neoclassical" is intentionally avoided here in order to leave open the question of whether the Austrian school (including von Mises and Hayek, who have an outstanding role in connection with the subject of this study) belong inside or outside the neoclassical school.

analysis. Analysts using them can arrive at sharp and relevant results, so long as the work is based on the right social theory. But they can reach misleading conclusions if their work is grounded on a false social theory, irrespective of whether their points of departure in social theory are spelled out or just implicit in the construction of the model.

The word "vacuum" has been used because the Lange model lacks, among others, the following attributes required by a more complete theory:

- understanding of the sociopolitical environment of the actors and the institutions that influence their behavior;
- incorporation of the state, as an endogenous constituent of the system, in the overall theory of the economy;
- an explanation of how the preferences of decision makers and the changes in these preferences, the decision-making routines, and the political and social constraints on human actions are determined by the social circumstances and by the extent to which the social situation explains the goals of individuals and groups.

The Austrian school certainly offers a richer explanation of these attributes of the socioeconomic order than sterile application of Walrasian theory, but it is still not rich enough. Much can be learnt from Marx if the explanatory theory of the economic order is being examined (although Marx and Hayek are admittedly strange bedfellows. Economists should make far greater use of the accumulated knowledge offered by modern sociology, political science, social psychology, and history. All this knowledge is required in order to reach the right normative conclusions.

There is nothing wrong with the tools of the Walrasian school, or, more widely, with the analytical methods of the neoclassical school, so long as they are treated with care and circumspection. But there are dangers in using them in an easygoing way because they tempt people to employ the wrong *research strategy*. Research should never *start* with formal analysis. The right questions must be put to start with; sound assumptions and sound conjectures must be devised. An erroneous strategy holds fewer dangers when the research is into "small" questions, especially if they can be compared with observable, repeatedly occurring facts. In that case it is simple to confront theory with praxis, which acts as a safeguard against serious error. An erroneous strategy becomes more dangerous in the case of "big" and rarely repeated issues, and more dangerous still, in fact positively fatal, with never-repeated future events of vast import like the transformation of whole societies. Starting the analysis "in the middle," with precise formalization but without very carefully weighing all the relevant political, sociological, and psychological assumptions and implications, can be very harmful indeed.

To add a personal note here, these ideas inspired me to write the book *Anti-Equilibrium* (1971). In retrospect I can see I was too harsh in my rejection of some analytical instruments that can actually do good service if they are used with sufficient precaution. I was not sufficiently confident in the Walrasian school's powers of rejuvenation, whereas prominent members of it have made great progress in expanding its range of tools and improving the realism of its models since then. Yet I still feel there was an element of justice in my bitter reproaches at that time. When I wrote the book, very widespread use was made of the narrow-minded, technique-oriented research strategy just outlined — starting research "in the middle" of the cognitive process by devising a formal model. Paucity of knowledge about the real workings of society often led to false positions. I might add that this approach is none too rare today. The artificial barrier and mutual mistrust between "institutionalists" and "analytical" economists still persists, damaging the usefulness of both approaches.

So far as I can see, the intellectual convenience of combining Walrasian thinking with socialistic principles of distribution still has an effect on the thinking of many economists. My request to my colleagues is to face up to Eastern European experience, especially the political, social, and psychological aspects of it; this may induce them to reexamine their adherence to the concept of market socialism.

### 2.4 Three Fallacies

Closely related to the issue discussed in the previous section are three fallacies with which I would like to take issue.

1. Schumpeter's pioneer theory of the role of the entrepreneur is highly relevant to the subject of this study, market socialism.[23] (See section 1.6 above on the role of entry, exit, and natural selection.) When the Walrasian normative theory was devised, the question was evaded of how "creative destruction" would occur in a Lange economy: elimination of obsolete technology and organization and introduction of revolutionary new products, technologies, and forms of organization.

Schumpeter later drew some far-reaching conclusions from his earlier theory and other observations on the future of capitalism and socialism.[24] Let me try, with a little simplification, to sum up his line of thinking. The main role in modern capitalism is played by large corporations, including monopoly firms. These have become bureaucratized to a great extent. The role of the entrepreneur has weakened. The bureaucratic monopoly firm is capable of taking over the entrepreneur's function, primarily in innovation. If that is the case — capitalism itself has become bureaucratic — and if Lange has proved anyway that market socialism is viable and efficient, it is best to acknowledge that socialism will replace capitalism. This is foreseeable, and even if it is not glad tidings, there is no need to oppose it.

This prophecy of Schumpeter's has been a subject of controversy ever since.[25] I am convinced that Schumpeter's reasoning here is erroneous.

---

[23] See J. A. Schumpeter ([1911] 1968).

[24] J. A. Schumpeter ([1942] 1976).

[25] See, for instance, the volume published for the 40th anniversary of the appearance of *Capitalism, Socialism and Democracy*, ed. A. Heertje (1981).

First, the analysis of modern capitalism given by Schumpeter is biased and exaggerated. Luckily, the "entrepreneur" of Schumpeter's earlier works has not disappeared from the world of contemporary capitalism at all. On the contrary, it is often the entrepreneurs as battering rams for innovation who induce large corporations to innovate after all in spite of their indolent tendencies. Think, for example, of the role played in revolutionizing the computer industry by the founders of Microsoft or Apple, or other initially small ventures, in relation to the near-monopoly IBM. Strong bureaucratic tendencies have certainly arisen, and the role of the state has grown to a large extent. But those like myself, who know from personal experience what *real* bureaucratization of a system means, may be better placed to appreciate that the process of bureaucratization has not gone very far. Modern developed capitalism has basically remained a decentralized, competitive, private market economy.

Second, market socialism in real life did not fulfill the expectations of Lange or the later Schumpeter, as the first part of this study set out to show. Fifty years after the appearance of Schumpeter's book, its prophecy has been refuted by history. Instead of socialism replacing capitalism, capitalism is regaining lost territory that classical socialism ruled for a long time and the market-socialist experiments could only occupy temporarily.

2. Some reform economists familiar with contemporary Western theory favor the idea of market socialism for the following reason. They realize the various shortcomings in the operation of an unrestrained private market economy. The list is well known: the problems of externalities, public goods and monopolies, the income distributional troubles, and so forth. They are also aware of the many drawbacks of planning and overcentralized state control. The former they like to call market failures and the latter planning failures.

Now market socialism offers the prospect of a nice *complementarity*, with planning and the market coexisting peaceably side by side, each curbing the other's excesses. While the central authorities make corrective interventions when the market errs, the market and the partial degree of decentralization prevent the state from becoming excessively bureaucratic.[26]

No such nice complementarity materialized under the market-socialist reforms in Eastern Europe. The market failures persisted: the harmful externalities (air and water pollution, environmental damage, congestion), the monopoly position of vast state-owned firms, and the unjust distribution of income. At the same time, the market failed to gain vigor because it was throttled by the bureaucracy, which intervened even where the market had not failed.

3. There are a great many illusions about the potentials of "system design" and "system engineering." Some think they can be applied on a national scale, not just in a particular firm or smaller sector. The optimal schemes of organization and rules of operation must be thought out methodically. Once a wise and benevolent government possesses them, it will see they are implemented successfully.

That is not what happens in practice. Rules are only effective if they are compatible with the nature of the government and society concerned. Otherwise the implant will be rejected. The necessity for compatibility and coherence among the elements in a system is clearly recognized, but a detailed explanation is still lacking. Promising though the mathematical and economic researches into the compatibility of incentives are, they are still only in the initial stages of exploring the problem. They remain for the time being insufficiently associated with the nonformalized empirical studies of society's functioning and human behavior.

A high proportion of social institutions come into being by *evolution*. Again there is a process of natural selection. A large number of mutations occur, with some of the new institutions and rules that arise proving viable, while others disappear. One of the

[26] This idea also appeared in my book *Anti-Equilibrium* (1971: pp. 334–43).

innate weaknesses of market socialism is that it is an artificial construct, a constructivist creature, to use Hayek's term.[27] Nor is it merely that the theoretical model and later the blueprint were artificial, for it also imposed a great many governmental interventions on people.

As an illustration, let me refer to one of the problems discussed in the first part of the study. Market socialism rests on the assumption that firms will behave *as if* they were profit maximizers. If that is so, they can be stimulated to do what the center wants by well-calibrated subsidies, tax concessions, administrative prices that ensure a high profit margin, and credit at concessionary interest rates. At the same time, firms can be dissuaded in a similar way from actions the center opposes by well-calibrated taxes, the setting of prices unfavorable to the firm, and deterrent interest rates. True, but to exert this influence, each bureaucratic agency builds up its own system of incentives and deterrents. Toward the end of the Hungarian experiment with market socialism, state-owned firms were subject to restraint or inducement from some 200 types of special taxes and subsidies. The outcome was for the impact of any scheme to be canceled out by the others. The firm failed to react like an obedient puppet when all its strings were pulled from various directions because they were tangled up. This also meant the profit motive ceased to apply, because the financial impact of market success and failure was cushioned by the tailor-made taxes, subsidies, and other interventions in prices and the firm's financial affairs. Instead of a natural environment of free contracts, the firm operated in an artificial setting of bureaucratic decrees.

The arguments against such artifacts do not imply that the state and political movements should be passive bystanders observing the evolution of society. Their activity is required, so long as it reinforces existing healthy trends that arise in a natural way and does not impose artificial constructs on society.

[27] See L. von Mises (1981) and F. A. Hayek (1960, 1989).

## 2.5 The Democratic Choice of an Economic System

That brings us to the question of *choice* of a system. A distinction was drawn in the introduction between seeking to introduce market socialism instead of capitalism and seeking to introduce it instead of classical socialism. All politicians and economists have a self-evident right to recommend market socialism as a replacement for capitalism or a way of reforming it, if that is what they believe, provided they seek to do so by democratic, parliamentary means. A party proposing to introduce market socialism may stand in the elections, and if it wins it can put the necessary legislation through in accordance with the democratic constitution. The fact that I would not vote for such a party myself is irrelevant to my argument — I fully recognize the legitimacy of forming such a party and of its political activity.

But the question of "whence and whither" must be raised again in the case of Eastern Europe. The idea of market socialism did not gain ascendancy through a free competition of ideas. What happened was that the group which had happened to gain power in the Communist party embraced this idea and then imposed it on society. Although the methods used were less brutal than the earlier confiscation of the factories and mass collectivization, the introduction was nonetheless made by government decree. Once again it was a question of "forced happiness." The ruling group considers this will be good for the people, so let them have it.

For a long time many reform economists did not even consider this side of the matter. It seemed to be self-evident that the ruling elite of the party-state should decide. The elite had to be convinced (or its membership altered) for the idea of reform to prevail. One of the greatest shortcomings in the market-socialist blueprint is its failure to enquire whether this is really what the people want.

It is still too early to make general predictions. Majorities were won in the Hungarian, German, and Polish elections by parties that rejected market socialism and sought to introduce a private market economy. What happens in the elections in the other countries which have turned to parliamentary democracy remains to be seen. My guess is that if any party comes out clearly in favor of market socialism, it will fail in free elections to win the majority required to apply its ideas.

This line of argument, by the way, strongly backs up another cardinal point of departure in this study: the sharp difference between the initial positions in the East and in the West. Those in a developed Western country who favor market socialism are normally racked by ethical and political dilemmas. They would like to retain the efficiency of the market economy, but they also demand a more equitable distribution of income and taxation — greater equity. Rightly or wrongly, they hope that some form of market socialism will produce a better compromise between these conflicting sets of values. The tacit assumption behind this line of thinking among Western economists is an axiomatic acceptance of democracy and respect for human rights, including the right to private property.

The debate in the East was about something else; relatively less attention was given to the dilemma of "efficiency versus equity." For a long time the opposing sides merely argued about which kind of socialism was more efficient, taking as axiomatic the absence of democracy, the one-party system, and the harder or softer kinds of totalitarianism. Once this axiom was questioned and doubt cast on the legitimacy of the political structure, it marked the beginning of the end for the system.

## 2.6 *The Tutors: Disappointment and Trauma*

From introspection, and also from conversations with friends and colleagues, I can state that those who at some stage in their lives changed their opinion on the subjects discussed in this study were not influenced to do so by books or articles. Thinking is strongly affected by metarational factors: values, sentiments, prejudices, and hopes. These act like gates, or at least like filters, either receiving certain influences or rejecting them. The soul and intellect of an individual are either open to an idea or closed to it.

I read Mises and Hayek thirty years ago and rejected their objections to market socialism. Later I read them again in a different frame of mind, and suddenly I became receptive to their arguments. The resistance was gone from my old self, the "naive reformer" who took certain axioms of Eastern European socialism as unquestionable and merely sought greater decentralization instead of overcentralization.

What changed many of our minds was a series of political traumas and disillusionments. With professional experts like economists, the decisive blow was not dealt in many cases by negative experiences in their own areas of competence. Revision of their professional opinions might have come later. First, the foundations of their *philosophy of life* collapsed, usually under the influence of some earthshaking event: the sight of Russian tanks in Badapest, Prague, or Afghanistan, or the experiences related by a friend on being released from prison. Once this enlightenment has happened, suddenly or gradually, as a result of a psychologically searing experience, the mind immediately opens to the rational arguments as well. A passion to read and reread is aroused. Works whose ideas had bounced off the walls of prejudice suddenly appear convincing. More superficially or more deeply, people plow up the layers of their own thinking, revising their philosophies and their professional principles. This tilling of the soil is needed before an economist who has had a blind faith can start thinking seriously about professional issues like free entry and market-clearing prices.

This kind of retrospection is a painful process that teaches modesty and intellectual humility. But a little pride can also be taken in remembering that we had the strength at least to struggle with our own prejudices, to open the intellectual gates and to help others to open theirs.

But while admitting the moral virtue in such a gradual awakening, one has to ask whether it was worth painfully seeking the answer to a few very difficult questions if that answer was already known. I am sure it was; there was sense and value in the search.

This ties in with the limits of predictive force in the social sciences, a matter that was touched upon in section 2.3 above and must be returned to here. The social sciences are capable of giving comparatively reliable predictions only for "small," frequently recurring events. No firm prediction can be given *by scientific means* for "large," nonrecurring events. The warnings of a Mises or a Hayek about market socialism are brilliant guesses, but they are not scientifically proved *ex ante*. A vision was confronted by a guess, not a scientific proposition by a scientific repudiation of it. An *ex post* position has now been reached; a large enough body of knowledge has accumulated for assertions to be proved. The economists of countries where an experiment was made in applying market socialism are now in a position to make statements based on firsthand experience. Reports from eyewitnesses and victims have special weight in any trial. It is not the same thing to debate about market socialism in London or Chicago in the 1930s as to debate about it in Budapest, Warsaw, or Moscow today. The second debate has the special weight; it is greater, richer, and in many ways more convincing than the debate in the 1930s.

I spoke just now about the limits of rational convictions and the prejudices that obstruct ideas. But that does not mean people should be left to themselves to go through their own process of learning and disillusionment. The problem still remains. It is still on the agenda where the socialist system persists, which is no small part of the world, including, for instance, China and Vietnam, two countries where experimentation with market socialism continues on a nationwide scale.

In addition, a special rearguard action is being fought to defend market socialist ideas in the postsocialist countries where parliamentary democracy has been introduced. This curious notion, which might be called "anti-Bolshevik market socialism," can be summed up like this: "The Communists could not cope with the state-owned firms. Now we, as the successors in power to the Communists, will show we are capable of managing the state sector well, however large it may be." So state ownership is retained over a far wider sphere than is economically justified, bureaucratic centralization is reintroduced into the management of the state sector, and executive appointments to it are made on political instead of professional grounds. These are phenomena familiar from the period of the socialist system, and their effect will be as damaging now as it was under the leadership of the Communist party.

So the problem continues, which is why it is worth continuing to deal with it. Perhaps there are enough enlightened or potentially enlightened people by now who will listen to what those who have been through the experiments in market socialism have to say. I would like to hope that the experience in Eastern Europe will make it easier for them to avoid the blind alleys and choose the right path.

## REFERENCES

Alchian, Armen A. 1965. "Some Economics of Property Rights." *Il Politico*, 30(4), 816–29.

———. 1974. "Foreword." In *The Economics of Property Rights*, ed. E. G. Furuboth and S. Pejovich, pp. xiii–xv. Cambridge, Mass.: Ballinger Publishing Company.

Alchian, Armen A., and Harold Demsetz. 1972. "Production, Information, Costs, and Economic Organization." *American Economic Review*, Dec., 62(5), 777–95.

Arrow, Kenneth J., and Leonid Hurwicz. 1960. "Decentralization and Computation in Resource Allocation." In *Essays in Economics and Econometrics*, pp. 34–104. Chapel Hill: University of North Carolina Press.

Bardhan, Prahab. 1990. "Some Reflections on Premature Obituaries of Socialism." *Economic and Political Weekly* (India), February 3, 259–62.

Barone, Enrico. [1908] 1935. "The Ministry of Production in the Collectivist State." In *Collectivist Economic Planning*, ed. F. A. Hayek, pp. 245–90. London: Routledge and Kegan Paul.

Brus, Wlodzimierz. [1961] 1972. *The Market in a Socialist Economy*. London: Routledge and Kegan Paul.

Brus, Wlodzimierz, and Kazimierz Laski. 1989. *From Marx to Market: Socialism in Search of an Economic System*. Oxford: Clarendon Press.

Dewatripont, Michel, and Eric Maskin. 1990. "Credit and Efficiency in Centralized Economies." *Discussion Paper*, no. 1512. Cambridge, Mass.: Harvard Institute of Economic Research, Harvard University.

Gorbachev, Mikhail S. 1987. *Perestroika*. New York: Harper and Row.

Hart, Oliver, and Bengt R. Holmström. 1987. "The Theory of Contracts." In *Advances in Economic Theory: Fifth World Congress*, ed. T. Bewly, pp. 71–155. Cambridge: Cambridge University Press.

Hayek, Friedrich A. (ed.) 1935. *Collectivist Economic Planning*. London: Routledge and Kegan Paul.

———. 1960. *The Constitution of Liberty*. London: Routledge, and Chicago: Chicago University Press.

———. 1989. *Order — with or without Design*. London: Centre for Research into Communist Economies.

Heertje, Arnold (ed.) 1981. *Schumpeter's Vision: Capitalism, Socialism and Democracy after Forty Years*. New York: Praeger.

Heilbroner, Robert. 1990. "Analysis and Vision in the History of Modern Economic Thought." *Journal of Economic Literature*, Sept., 28(3), 1097–1114.

IMF, IBRD, OECD, EBRD. 1990. "The Economy of the USSR: Summary and Recommendations." A study undertaken in response to a request by the Houston Summit, Washington, D.C.

Jasay, Anthony de. 1990. *Market Socialism: A Scrutiny: "This Square Circle."* London: Institute of Economic Affairs.

Kidric, Boris. 1985. *Sabrana Dela* (Collected Works). Belgrade: Izdavacki Centar Komunist.

Kolodko, Grzegorz W. 1991. "Polish Hyperinflation and Stabilization 1989–1990." *Most*, 1(1), 9–36.

Kornai, János. [1957] 1959. *Overcentralization in Economic Administration*. Oxford: Oxford University Press.

———. 1971. *Anti-Equilibrium*. Amsterdam: North-Holland.

———. 1980. *Economics of Shortage*. Amsterdam: North-Holland.

———. 1986a. "The Hungarian Reform Process: Visions, Hopes and Reality." *Journal of Economic Literature*, Dec., 24(4), 1687–1737.

———. 1986b. "The Soft Budget Constraint," *Kyklos*, 39(1), 3–30.

———. 1992. *The Socialist System: The Political Economy of Communism.* Princeton: Princeton University Press, and Oxford: Oxford University Press.

Lange, Oscar. 1936–37. "On the Economic Theory of Socialism." *Review of Economic Studies*, Oct. (1936), Feb. (1937), 4(1, 2), 53–71, 123–42.

Lavoie, Don. 1985. *Rivalry and Central Planning: The Socialist Calculation Debate Reconsidered.* Cambridge: Cambridge University Press.

Le Grand, Julian, and Saul Estrin (eds.) 1989. *Market Socialism.* Oxford: Clarendon Press.

Lerner, Abba P. 1946. *The Economics of Control.* New York: Macmillan.

Liberman, Evsey G. [1962] 1972. "The Plan, Profit and Bonuses." In *Socialist Economics*, ed. A. Nove and D. M. Nuti, pp. 309–18. Middlesex: Penguin Books.

Lipton, David, and Jeffrey Sachs. 1990a. "Creating a Market Economy in Eastern Europe: The Case of Poland." *Brookings Papers on Economic Activity*, 75–133.

———. 1990b. "Privatization in Eastern Europe: The Case of Poland." *Brookings Papers on Economic Activity*, 2, 293–333.

Malinvaud, Edmond. 1967. "Decentralized Procedures for Planning." In *Activity Analysis in the Theory of Growth and Planning*, eds. E. Malinvaud and M. O. L. Bacharach, pp. 170–208. London: Macmillan, and New York: St. Martin's Press.

Marx, Karl. [1867–94] 1978. *The Capital.* London: Penguin.

Mises, Ludwig von. [1920] 1935. "Economic Calculations in the Socialist Commonwealth." In *Collectivist Economic Planning*, ed. F. A. Hayek, pp. 87–130. London: Routledge and Kegan Paul.

———. 1981. *Socialism.* Indianapolis: Liberty Classics.

Nutter, Warren G. 1968. "Markets without Property: A Grand Illusion." In *Money, the Market and the State*, ed. N. Beadles and L. Drewry, pp. 137–45. Athens: University of Georgia Press.

Organization for Economic Co-operation and Development. 1991. *OECD Economic Surveys: Hungary 1991.* Paris: OECD.

Ortuno-Ortin, Ignacio, John E. Roemer, and Joaquim Silvestre. 1990. "Market Socialism." Davis: University of California, manuscript.

Péter, György. 1954a. "Az egyszemélyi felelős vezetésről" (On Management Based on One-Man Responsibility). *Társadalmi Szemle*, Aug./Sept., 9(8–9), 109–24.

———. 1954b. "A gazdaságosság jelentőségéről és szerepéről a népgazdaság tervszerű irányításában" (On the Importance and Role of Economic Efficiency in the Planned Control of the National Economy). *Közgazdasági Szemle*, Dec., 1(3), 300–324.

Qian, Yingyi, and Chenggang Xu. 1991. "Innovation and Financial Constraints in Centralized and Decentralized Economies" (mimeo). Cambridge, Mass.: Department of Economics, Harvard University, manuscript.

Schroeder, Gertrude E. 1988. "Property Rights Issues in Economic Reforms in Socialist Countries." *Studies in Comparative Communism*, Summer, 21(2), 175–88.

Schumpeter, Joseph A. [1911] 1968. *The Theory of Economic Development: An Inquiry into Profits, Capital, Credit, Interest and Business Cycles.* Cambridge: Harvard University Press.

———. 1939. *Business Cycles: A Theoretical, Historical and Statistical Analysis of the Capitalist Progress.* New York: McGraw-Hill.

———. [1942] 1976. *Capitalism, Socialism and Democracy.* New York: Harper and Row.

———. 1954. *History of Economic Analysis.* New York: Oxford University Press.

Sik, Ota. 1966. *Economic Planning and Management in Czechoslovakia.* Prague: Orbis.

Stalin, Josef V. 1947. *Problems of Leninism.* Moscow: Foreign Languages Press.

Stiglitz, Joseph E. 1987. "Principal and Agent." Entry in *The New Palgrave: A Dictionary of Economics*, ed. J. Eatwell, M. Milgate, and P. Newman, vol. 3, pp. 966–72. 4 vols. London: Macmillan, and New York: Stockton Press.

Sun, Yefang. 1982. "Some Theoretical Issues in Socialistic Economics," originally published in the period 1958–61. In *Social Needs versus Economic Efficiency in China*, ed. K. K. Fung. Armonk: M. E. Sharpe.

Taylor, Fred M. 1929. "The Guidance of Production in a Socialist State." *American Economic Review*, March, 19(1), 1–80. Reprinted in *On the Economic Theory of Socialism*, ed. B. E. Lippincott. Minneapolis: University of Minnesota Press, 1938.

Temkin, Gabriel. 1989. "On Economic Reform in Socialist Countries: The Debate on Economic Calculation under Socialism Revisited." *Communist Economies*, 1(1), 31–59.

# II

## 1. Introduction[1]

The transition to a market economy is an incredibly difficult task. The job can only be done and the great problems that arise can only be resolved in each country by those living *in* the society concerned. It is inevitable that the situation can be understood only to a limited extent by an *outsider*. That warns me to be modest; no one can be sure whether his advice is applicable or points in the best possible direction. I immediately state this emphatically at the outset, but I shall not add repeated warnings and reservations to my proposals later. To all the recommendations in my lecture the general comment applies that they must be taken critically; Soviet economists must formulate their own views on the basis of their own far greater local knowledge.

I am not a "Sovietologist." In trying to grasp the Soviet Union's problems and the choices before it, I draw on two kinds of sources.

---

[1] This lecture was given shortly before the city's name was changed to St. Petersburg. Apart from the city reverting to its old name since then, the Soviet Union has ceased to exist and many other great changes have occurred in the political and economic fields.

The text here is the written form of the lecture delivered orally in June 1991, with nothing altered. It is easy to be wise or at least wiser after the event, but I feel I must take responsibility for the lecture given then even in retrospect. A comparison of the proposals made then with the actual course of events may be instructive — it will certainly be worth me or someone else undertaking such a comparison later.

I am grateful to the Tanner Foundation for the honor of being invited to deliver the first Tanner Lecture in the Soviet Union. This provided a forum at which I could express my ideas and proposals before noted Soviet economists and a chance for me to become acquainted with the views and problems of my Soviet colleagues during a whole series of conversations.

I also owe thanks to the rector of Leningrad University, Professor S. L. Merkuriev, and his colleagues for organizing the meetings and for their kind hospitality.

I express my gratitude to Brian McLean and Julianna Parti for their precise and fluent translation.

As a Hungarian I have studied all that has happened in my own country at close quarters. Hungary is small by comparison with the Soviet Union, but it can rightly be considered a laboratory where some very important experiments were conducted. In this respect it has moved far ahead of the Soviet economy in recent decades. The first hesitant, interrupted, and mercilessly suppressed experiments aimed at a radical transformation of society took place in the period 1953–56. Dismantling of the old-style command economy then recommenced in 1968. Finally came the great political turning point in 1989, with the formation of the institutions of political democracy, followed by free elections and an open, declared transition toward the kind of market economy in which private ownership will become the dominant property form. I think a thorough familiarity with Hungary's historical experience is very instructive for all countries seeking to advance in a similar direction.[2]

Another part of my knowledge comes from the fact that I have specialized in comparing economic systems. I deal primarily with the comparison of East and West, capitalism and socialism. This I do not do merely by studying professional literature and statistics. Half my time in the last decade has been spent in the socialist world (more recently the postsocialist world) and the other half in the capitalist world. One of my workplaces is the Hungarian Academy of Sciences and the other Harvard University. This "commuter" life-style has enabled me to gain experience of both systems *from within*, by living under them.

In 1989, before the completion of the political change and the free elections, I wrote a book about Hungary called *A Passionate Pamphlet in the Cause of Economic Transition*. This later appeared in English in a somewhat expanded form as *The Road to a Free*

---

[2] Works on the history of the Hungarian economic reforms available in English include L. Antal (1979), T. Bauer (1983), I. T. Berend (1990), P. Hare, H. K. Radice, and N. Swain (1981), J. Kornai (1983, 1986, [1989] 1990a), J. M. Kovács (1990), G. Révész (1990), and L. Szamuely (1982, 1984).

*Economy* (1990). I was delighted that the book also became available to readers in Russian.[3] My belief is that much of the book's message also applies to the Soviet Union's case, when adjusted, of course, to the conditions here. This lecture is connected with the book. I sum up its content briefly, adding a few ideas inspired by experience gained since it was written.[4] I would like to emphasize particularly the proposals I consider of prime importance from the point of view of Soviet practice at present.

The lecture consists of two main parts. The first two sections contain warnings: they discuss which are the blind alleys that should be avoided in my opinion. The remaining sections of the lecture present my proposals.

2. REFORM SOCIALISM

I draw a distinction between two "prototypes" of the socialist system. To make them more graphic, I attach the names of party leaders to the two types. One is *classical socialism*: the socialism of Stalin and Brezhnev (Soviet Union), Mao Zedong (China), Honecker (East Germany), Husák (Czechoslovakia), and Ceausescu (Romania). The other is *reform socialism*: the socialism of Tito (Yugoslavia), Kádár (Hungary), Deng Xiaoping (China), and Gorbachev (Soviet Union).[5]

---

[3] The book appeared in Russian on three occasions: first in a limited exclusive edition, then in four installments in the very widespread and popular periodical *EKO*, and finally in a large edition from the publishers Ekonomika (1990b).

[4] A great influence on my ideas was exerted by the experiences of the Polish stabilization, and in connection with these the conversations I had with Professor Jeffrey Sachs, to whom I would like to express my thanks here. I learned much from the first radical programs of the Soviet transition, which are generally associated with the names of A. Shatalin and G. Yavlinsky, with several other Soviet and foreign economists also taking part in the elaboration of them. See the so-called Shatalin Plan under Working Group (1990) and edited by G. Allison and G. Yavlinsky (1991). The proposals put forward in the lecture conform with other stabilization programs to a large extent, but differ from them on a few essential points.

[5] In this section of the Leningrad lecture I dealt with issues dissected in much more detail in my study "Market Socialism Revisited," published in this volume. In this written text I have made some radical cuts in the ideas presented orally at

Within each prototype there are many variants that show different specific characteristics from country to country, and within each country at various times. A "prototype" is a theoretical construct that disregards the detailed differences between these variants and emphasizes their common characteristics.

The reform is an effort to combine socialism and capitalism to some extent. The idea is for the following facets of classical socialism to remain: (1) the ruling role of the Communist party, but somewhat mitigating the repression and allowing a degree of freedom for alternative views; (2) the pervasive role of state control and the subordination of the economy to the bureaucracy; (3) the predominance of state ownership. The following elements of capitalism should concurrently appear: (4) market coordination as the main (or one of the major) integrators of the economy — this embraces far-reaching decentralization, a high degree of autonomy for the firm, and partial liberation of prices; (5) the development of the private sector, although confined within very narrow limits.

Reform socialism's adherents hope that this combination will unite all the real (or perceived) advantages of socialism and capitalism. They intend it not as a temporary state but as a lasting, robust Third System or Third Road that will sooner or later prove its superiority over the First, capitalism, and the Second, classical socialism.

The market-socialist experiments undoubtedly scored some notable achievements, primarily in transforming the thinking of economic leaders. In places where the economy went through the stage of reform, managers have a better understanding of what is meant by profit and loss, a contract between buyer and seller, and adjustment to demand. Trade and financial, scientific, and scholarly relations with the West expanded, which had an effect on production inside the country as well. In this respect countries

---

much greater length at the time, in order to avoid duplication. However, a degree of overlap between the two cannot be avoided.

where a period of reform socialism began well before the political turning point have better starting positions in the transition to a market economy than countries jumping straight from the classical system onto the road of capitalist development.

I repeat that the reform had useful consequences, but it failed to attain its fundamental objectives; it was incapable of convincing and permanent good economic results.

There is no real market without the autonomy of the firm, and that can be guaranteed only by private ownership. State ownership is compatible with a market economy, but only where confined within relatively narrow limits and where the various forms of private ownership — for example, individual enterprises and joint-stock companies — account for the overwhelming majority of production.

So long as the predominance of state ownership remains, the head of a firm is basically dependent on the party and the state bureaucracy; appointment, promotion, and dismissal are in their hands, and on them depend his or her power, prestige, and financial privileges. While that is the case, it is far more worthwhile to pay attention to the bureaucracy's wishes than to the buyers'. Nor do the party apparatus, the ministries, and the other authorities respect the autonomy of the firm in any case; they intervene in its life in thousands of ways.

So the *microeconomy* did not gain a truly market-economic character. This connects with several unfavorable *macroeconomic* phenomena. There is a runaway in nominal wages. Although the firm is not really autonomous, its partial independence is enough to produce a reckless rise in wages divorced from productivity growth. The banking system distributes loans irresponsibly and does not insist on them being repaid. In fact credit becomes one of the main instruments for salvaging firms on the brink of financial ruin. Fiscal discipline loosens. On one side there is a growth in subsidies to loss-making production and exports and in price subsidies for various consumer goods and services. Meanwhile there is unjustifiably generous financing of state investments that yield a poor return or an actual loss. Huge sums are consumed in maintaining the armed forces and further rearmament. On the other side there is laxity in collecting state revenues. The ever greater discrepancy between expenditure and revenue raises the budget deficit, which is covered by taking up foreign loans or printing money, that is, by inflationary means.

Three dangerous macrodisequilibria appear: a chronic, worsening shortage, accelerating inflation, and growing indebtedness. These three problems appear in differing proportions in each country and period. The threefold problem used to be called the "Polish syndrome," because that is where it arose in its most extreme form. But Poland has embarked on radical changes since then. These days it is more apposite to call it the "Soviet syndrome," for it is here in this country that the three negative phenomena are developing in parallel and in combination to the most oppressive degree.

*Perestroika* brought an end to the brutal oppression of classical socialism, but it also loosened its tight discipline and coherence. Meanwhile it proved unable to create a true market discipline in its place, for which laws passed by a legitimate parliament and market competition would have been required. What is needed are real private owners who take costs and profit seriously because they affect their own pockets and who cannot rely on the state invariably bailing them out of any financial trouble.

The market-socialist experiment that has taken place in the Soviet Union so far has been incomplete and inconsistent, since it was unbacked by radical change, either on the political scene or in property relations. It is a system that falls between two stools: it is not viable socialism (because it cannot operate permanently without firm repression and limitation of civil liberties) and it is not a modern capitalist market economy either. Failure is inevitable.

## 3. THE ROMANTIC THIRD ROAD

Market socialism, as mentioned before, is itself an attempt of a Third Road kind; it has been tried out in several countries, including the Soviet Union, and it did not work. However, there is another intellectual trend one might call the Romantic Third Road which has never been tried out anywhere. It appears only in writing, or more frequently in conversation, mainly among writers, politicians, and social scientists. There are also some economists whose ideas can be placed here.

Although the trend is not uniform, I shall try to pick out a few common traits in their ideas.

All kinds of socialist systems ruled by the Communist party must be rejected — not just classical socialism, but socialism that experiments with market reforms as well. Capitalism must be dismissed as well, including its modern Western forms, because the profiteering, commercialism, and degenerate morality that flourish under it are repulsive.

So what kind of society must be aimed at? The answers vary according to the roots and outlook of the respondent:

• There must be a return to the pure and natural life of the village.

• A truly communal life must be created. This entails communal ownership. A great many versions of this are put forward in the discussions: the village community, the peasant community, genuinely, voluntary cooperative ownership, and so on.

• Although it can be considered a version of the previous item, special mention must be made of the idea that worker communities must be established and ownership of the factories given to them. To this is connected the demand for workers' self-management.

There should be direct relations between producers and consumers; the profiteers and speculators of commerce must be eliminated.

- There should be discipline, but it should rest on tradition, on the commandments of religion. Some people want an autocratic ruler — a king or a tsar — to impose order in accordance with age-old tradition. Others oppose autocratic rule, rejecting the idea of discipline based on respect and coercion. Their ideas come close to the old and more up-to-date forms of anarchism and anti-étatism, advocating a voluntary discipline complemented by a kind of "direct democracy" that avoids the forms of modern Western parliamentarianism and the multiparty system.

I am afraid that the list just given is too orderly. In reality there is a tangle of ideas that are unclarified and emotionally inspired rather than rationally ordered.

Let me try without prejudice to assess these views. In fact the only view that I reject on *ethical* grounds is autocratic rule: discipline is not worth it *at that price*. Liberty and human rights are things of such value that they cannot be subordinated to other desires — for instance, the demand for order and discipline.

All the other aspirations are not repugnant in themselves to my mind; I respect people's desire for honesty, community life, and liberation from bureaucracy and profiteering. My prime objection is a pragmatic one: we seem to be presented only with a collection of desires, not with a realistic constructive program. The First System was not imposed on people by the force of the state. There was no politburo or government to declare in earlier centuries: "Let there be capitalism." The capitalist market economy developed by evolution as the combined outcome of millions of voluntary individual decisions. Although the state promotes this evolution with its laws and apparatus, the capitalist economy is basically built up "from below"; the entrepreneurs decide about accumulation and the expansion of production.

The position was different with the Second System, which was established by the force of the state. Each of its institutions was brought into being "from above."

Adherents of the Third System need to consider: Why do the forms and patterns of behavior they favor not appear on a mass scale and come to predominate? And if people do not choose this Third Road even in places where there has been freedom of choice so far, why do they expect people to choose precisely this in our region? Or if people do not choose it of their own accord, should it be the system imposed upon them at this time?

Churchill said that democracy was a bad system, but no one had yet found a better one. The same can be said of the capitalist market economy: it is a bad system, but no one has yet discovered anything better. There are many versions of it: the individualistic North American and the more egalitarian Scandinavian models differ from each other, but both form a capitalist market economy. This system too could do with fundamental repairs through reforms, but however much it is repaired, it will be far from perfect. The *real choice* is between the socialist system that has existed hitherto and the Western type of market economy. The choice must be made without illusions: the socialist system cannot really be repaired, and the capitalist system will have many repulsive attributes even in its repaired form. Yet basically we must choose these days the relatively better of the two. Third Road views are an effort to sidestep that choice, but I do not believe they offer a road that can be followed or an alternative that can be realized.

### 4. Reform and Revolution

Having explored the two blind alleys, let us turn to the road that leads to a free economy. A short clarification of terms is required first of all, concerning the distinction between reform and revolution. There are many different current definitions, but for my part I use the following in this lecture and my other works: While reform yields important changes, it retains the fundamentals of the system concerned. Revolution, on the other hand, changes the fundamentals radically, so bringing about a *change of system*.

So the distinction between reform and revolution in this vocabulary is *not* whether it takes place slowly and steadily or explosively and rapidly. A reform may be swift and a revolution may be gradual. Moreover, the distinction is *not* that a reform is peaceful and a revolution violent and bloody. The process of reform may also be induced by bloody uprisings, and those impeding it may use violence against the reformers; a revolution, on the other hand, may take place without bloodshed. The difference lies in how superficial or deep the change is. To use a Hegelian expression here, revolution brings a qualitative change.

Applying these definitions, it can be stated that *perestroika* was not a revolution but a reform, despite the many assertions to the contrary in the Soviet debates on the matter. What is now required in this country is a real revolution, a change in the fundamental characteristics of the system. If that does not occur, the problems will worsen and the crisis will continue and in fact deepen.

It is clear from these definitions that what I advocate is the need for a revolution, not an explosive rapidity of change. I am not recommending an uprising or any other violent action. The more smoothly and peaceably it takes place, the better. In terms of my value judgments, the most attractive solution is the kind of "velvet revolution" that took place in Prague. Revolution in my vocabulary means this and only this: radical events that make no concessions and consistently alter the bases of the system are required. It means "only" this, but it is no small thing, of course. The country's citizens need a new system if they want to prosper.

The title of my 1990 book contains the expression "free economy," not simply market economy, because the former is more comprehensive and contains more elements. Let me briefly sum up the main criteria for a free economy.

• A political system with free competition of ideas, freedom of speech, freedom of the press, freedom of assembly, and freedom of association. These freedoms contain in themselves the abolition of the one-party system, freedom for alternative parties to organize, and free parliamentary elections.

- An economic system that guarantees the right of free enterprise and freedom of entry into economic life.
- Freedom of property belongs among the liberties that need to be respected. Private property must be protected; legal guarantees must be given that it will not be confiscated. The economy must be led toward property relations in which private ownership is the predominant property form.
- The role of the state must be reduced, with the authorities subject to control by the law, parliament, and publicity.
- The market must be the main (although not the exclusive) coordinator of the economic processes.

5. THE NEW POLITICAL ERA: DEMOCRATIC CONSENSUS

An essential condition for solving the economic problems is a fundamental change of the *political* system. I am an economist, but I have to underline that the primary problem is political and not economic.

I make no comment on the present situation or on what will happen in the coming days. I do not feel competent to do so. I shall describe instead a hypothetical political situation, the beginning of a *new political era*. The main factors would be the following.

1. Several parties form and compete with each other. A fair election campaign takes place, followed by a fair multiparty election. A new legitimate parliament gets down to work. A new government is formed and can count on strong parliamentary support.

2. A satisfactory solution is found between the federative organizations and the republics, which the latter accept. Viable cooperation develops among the republics. The division of spheres of authority, rights, and obligations is clearly defined. It may be that several republics secede. It can be assumed that most of the present territory of the Soviet Union will continue to form a common economic area in the future.

3. An agreement is reached on the role of the army, which comes under civilian supervision.

4. Reconstruction and the program of transition toward a free economy receive widespread support. A consensus develops, in two senses. On the one hand there is overwhelming majority support in parliament for the economic program, and on the other it receives support from both the employees and the employers, the latter including the entrepreneurs of the private sector as well.

From now on I shall call the political position summed up in those four points the *democratic consensus*.

The government of the democratic consensus would have political, legal, and moral grounds for addressing the people like this: We want to open a new chapter in the country's history. We cannot promise that life for everyone will improve swiftly or markedly. Great difficulties can be expected, with much suffering for many people. But we are capable of leading the country toward a better system under which growth along a better path will begin in a few years, bringing an improvement in the economic situation.

I regard what I have just outlined as a historic, nonrecurrent opportunity, but not as a *prognosis*, for it is by no means certain that the situation will really develop in this way. What I have put forward is a *desire*: this is how I would like to see the political situation for this long-suffering people develop. Although a great deal of trouble and deprivation would still accompany this desired situation, it would entail relatively less suffering than any other and bring a resolution of the economic crisis relatively sooner.

There is a historic, nonrecurrent opportunity, but this opportunity can be missed. The situation may become far worse: bloody conflicts may break out, the changes may be held up, and the troubles may be aggravated by domestic political strife and the lack of agreement between the interested parties. The painful but vital measures may be deferred by a leadership that shrinks from the sacrifices and tries to prevaricate instead. Measured in historical terms, this will only delay the radical turn, not take the edge off it, but procrastination that continues for several years is undesirable because it will demand sacrifices that might have been avoided.

The rest of the lecture sums up the economic tasks ahead, to each of which a label is attached.

Some of the proposals are *conditional*. This means that their feasibility is strongly dependent on the political situation; for them to succeed completely, a democratic consensus must develop.

The other proposals are *unconditional*. Even if a democratic consensus fails to develop, there is still a good chance of implementing them and they will still contribute to improving the economic situation.

This categorization also shows that I am not arguing for an "all-or-nothing" strategy. I am not claiming that *either* the optimal political conditions are achieved, in which case everything can be accomplished, *or* the position on the political front is worse than desired, in which case everything is hopeless. A great many useful changes can be made in either case, but a new political era will be required for a real breakthrough.

My proposals are grouped under three themes: (1) macrostabilization and liberalization, (2) the transformation of property relations, and (3) social welfare policy.

I have not tried to make my proposals "original" in an academic sense: I do not come up with some hitherto secret magic cure for all the ills. Economists have been debating these matters in other parts of the world for a long time. On most of them there is no general agreement, but I would like at least to convey to my Soviet colleagues which of the alternative views I subscribe to myself.

## 6. Macrostabilization and Liberalization

I am convinced of the need for a large-scale package of measures for stabilizing and liberalizing the Soviet economy.[6] This is

---

[6] This idea was proposed for the Hungarian economy in my book ([1989] 1990a). Practical implementation of the stabilization package for the Polish economy

absolutely necessary: in my view it is impossible to set the Soviet economy to rights without one.

The expression "shock-therapy" is widespread in this context. It is a very unfortunate expression, and to the extent that a name can do damage this one has certainly done so by scaring many people away. The expression was taken from psychiatry, where the shock itself is thought to have a healing effect. In economic stabilization, however, it has nothing of the kind. To stick to the medical analogy, the shock is not the actual therapy, because it is an undesirable but in some cases inescapable side-effect. If the job can be done without administering a "shock" to people, that is all to the good. It is worth aiming to minimize the upheaval and pain.

In fact I employ a medical metaphor in my own writings, advocating surgery for stabilization. This, in my view, is a better way of conveying that this is a quick, radical intervention, to be preceded by presurgical treatment and followed by after-care.

The expression "package" conveys that it consists of a set of measures closely dependent on each other. If single measures were divorced from the package and introduced by themselves, the effect would be doubtful or perhaps even positively detrimental. It is a condition for success that the measures be introduced at about the same time, or condensed into a short period, and harmonized with each other in detail.

The main components of the package, in my view, should be the following:

1. Elimination of the state budget deficit. This in itself is a complex task, of which only a few elements will be noted here.

Numerous steps must be taken toward eliminating subsidies (both price subsidies and subsidies to loss-making firms). Even if

---

is associated primarily with L. Balcerowicz. A great influence on the Polish stabilization package was exerted by the work of J. Sachs; the ideas and early experiences on this are summarized in his articles written jointly with D. Lipton (1990a, 1990b). Many other economists support this strategy. See, for example, O. Blanchard et al. (1991) and S. Fischer and A. Gelb (1990).

all subsidies cannot be eliminated in a single stage, a large-scale partial dismantling of subsidies must be accomplished straight away in the first stage and a clear timetable worked out for complete elimination of them.

Another vital measure is a drastic cut in military spending.

At the same time, tax revenues must be raised. Sooner or later it will be necessary to devise an up-to-date tax system that includes value-added tax and personal income tax. However, I feel the first step should be to standardize turnover taxes and raise their average rate.

Under no circumstances can the budget deficit be covered anymore by credits from the central bank, since that fuels inflation. If the measures listed prove insufficient, foreign or domestic loans will be necessary.

2. A tight, restrictive monetary policy is required, with tight control on credit. If the banking system continues to distribute credits indiscriminately, the stabilization will be gravely endangered.

3. Care must be taken to ensure wage discipline. It is extremely important for the employees and the unions representing them to behave in a self-restrained and responsible way. This was one of the things I was thinking of when I talked about the need for the democratic consensus. But it must be added that the fate of the stabilization cannot be entrusted exclusively to voluntary self-restraint. Punitive taxes, using an appropriate fiscal formula, must be levied on firms that fail to impose wage discipline, causing nominal wages to run away by comparison with the trend in productivity.

4. All prices must be freed. The chance of certain firms abusing their monopoly position must be prevented by antimonopoly legislation and adequate state supervision.

5. The ruble must be drastically devalued. An exchange rate must be set that corresponds realistically with the market conversion rate between hard currencies and the ruble and can then be sustained over a longer period.

Stabilization of shaken currency invariably entails changing every price, every exchange rate and interest rate, every wage, and the nominal value of every quantitative index at once. There must be some "fixed point" to hang onto. For this the literature on stabilization uses the expression "nominal anchor"; it is something to which the tossing ship of the economy can be chained. A wide variety of economic quantities may appear as applicants in various kinds of stabilization — for instance the money supply, the average wage level, or a fixed foreign exchange rate. I share the view of other economists that the best candidate for nominal anchor during the process of stabilization in Eastern Europe and the Soviet Union today is a predetermined foreign exchange rate. This will concurrently lighten task no. 4, the liberalization of prices. At least for products and services that are items of foreign trade on the world market, the starting point for the calculation must be the world-market price multiplied by the stable foreign exchange rate. The domestic price may differ from this due to the relations between supply and demand, but it is a calculation from which a start can be made, so that the new price system need not be conjured out of thin air.

6. When and how the domestic currency should be made convertible is a matter of debate. My proposal, in agreement with many other economists, is that the first stabilization package should already contain substantial steps toward convertibility, even if all the complex criteria for it cannot be satisfied immediately in every respect. I would draw special attention to two interrelated measures. One is to legalize private foreign exchange dealings. It is needless and dangerous to force them underground. The public should be able to place foreign exchange in their possession as deposits in foreign exchange accounts without restriction or enquiries into the source of the money. The other measure required is an undertaking from the state banking system to convert foreign exchange without limitation at the stable foreign exchange rate.

This is just what turns this rate into an "anchor." Everyone understands — state-owned firms, the private sector, individuals, and foreign business people — that the money has a stable value, because they can always obtain hard currency for domestic money at the fixed exchange rate.

There are numerous conditions to satisfy, of course, before convertibility can be applied in reality, not just declared. Some of them will be mentioned later, but there is another condition that ties in with task no. 5 above — the correct foreign exchange rate. It is hard to gauge the figure. If a "miss" cannot be helped, it is better to undervalue the domestic currency than overvalue it. Let imports be a trifle too costly and exports unrealistically profitable; though this places a greater burden on the public, it enhances the stabilizing effect.

7. A final very important task is to liberalize foreign trade, including imports. Foreign goods flowing into the country improve the supply, while the competition encourages domestic producers to perform better. What is more, foreign prices are imported along with the foreign goods; as mentioned earlier, this is highly important in a situation where a previously absurd and irrational system of prices has to be replaced swiftly with a realistic system of market prices.

There is a whole range of requirements for the success of the stabilization surgery.

Above all there must be painstaking preparation. The partial measures must accord with each other; careful calculations must be used to work out the harmony between a few of the most important macroindices.

Prime importance attaches to creating the requisite political conditions, the state referred to earlier in this lecture as democratic consensus. Among the factors behind inflation are inflationary expectations; in other words, the participants in the economy expect the inflation to continue. This expectation is a self-fulfilling prophecy. It must be dispelled and replaced with a new expectation, so that the public, the firms, and the economic leaders believe the situation will change and inflation will be curbed. For such a belief to take hold, the words of politicians and the promises of the government must gain credibility, which is not something created by command; it must be based on political legitimacy and trust. Without such trust, credibility, and consensus, the stabilization program will crumble away under the effect of obstruction and a crisis of confidence.

Also required from the outset is at least a minimal private sector. There must be in operation a formal and informal private sector able, in the weeks of the changeover, to plug the gaps left by the state sector in the supply to the general public and deliver the main staple articles from the producer to the consumer. This will be returned to later.

Reserves are required. On the one hand there must be reserves of goods, above all stocks of foodstuffs that appear in the stores in the first hours of the stabilization operation and engender confidence in a better future. On the other hand there must be foreign exchange reserves to ensure that convertibility can be maintained. These also allow quick auxiliary imports to be made if there are problems with supply.

The stabilization operation must rest fundamentally on the country's own resources, but it is desirable to have substantial Western aid to lighten the burden. The most favorable forms for this assistance are contributions to a stabilizing foreign exchange reserve and to goods stocks in the form of import credits.

Even if all these conditions are satisfied and the government decides to perform the stabilization surgery, there will still be an enormous upheaval. It can then be expected (after an initial surge of price rises) that the currently rising rate of inflation will be curbed, and also that one of the gravest chronic ailments of the socialist system — shortage — will be overcome in wide areas of the economy. But great difficulties must be awaited nonetheless: a fall in production in numerous sectors and the appearance of unemployment that continues to grow for some time. Even when accomplished, the stabilization achievements will be very hard to defend.

Unfortunately there are other possible scenarios that cannot be ignored: many of the conditions listed may be lacking. I fear it is impossible here to give any simple prescription. If certain elements in the package summed up under the seven heads above are introduced individually (or slowly), they may well do more harm than good. Economic politicians cannot be given a blank check inviting them to set about any of the seven tasks they fancy, at any pace or in any order, just so as to get things under way. That would be a dangerous game that could discredit the stabilization plans altogether.

But I do not say either that it is a case of "all or nothing." To take just two examples, any progress in reducing the budget deficit or curbing the supply of credit can be beneficial. All an adviser can do is to weigh the advantages and drawbacks of single partial measures on a case-by-case basis. The Soviet Union today is at any rate in a situation where no partial measure can substitute for a large and drastic package of measures.

## 7. Transformation of Property Relations

The main direction of the changes is clear: it is toward building an economy in which the majority of social production derives from enterprises in private ownership. Let me say a few words first of all about the ultimate position.

It can be expected that the private sector will not be an absolute ruler, any more than it is in developed Western countries. A smaller share of the firms will remain in public (state or municipal) ownership. It is still too early to decide exactly where the line will be drawn. That will emerge from the competition between the various property forms, with attention being paid to international experience. Here again, the will of the public must be exerted through parliament; what is to remain in state ownership and what is to be privatized must be decided by legislation.

As in advanced capitalist countries, the private sector will not present a uniform picture. Small, medium-sized, large, and even gigantic firms will operate side by side. There will certainly be an increase in the relative weight of small and medium-sized firms, because production in the Soviet economy, as in the other socialist countries, has been excessively concentrated.

Private firms of various types in terms of their legal form will exist side by side: joint-stock companies in which all or most of the shares are in private hands and listed on the stock exchange, limited-liability companies (companies not listed on the stock exchange), personal enterprises, and so on. It is worth remembering that — with the United States and Britain as exceptions — the joint-stock companies listed on the stock exchange in most developed countries account for only the smaller proportion of aggregate production, in spite of their large role.

The transition cannot achieve this terminal situation in a short period. On this matter I take issue with many of my Western and Eastern European colleagues, who urge "rapid privatization." Let there be no misunderstanding — I too want the process to take place as soon as possible. But a desire is one thing and a realistic chance of attaining it another. The government may decide about convertibility or the foreign exchange rate and having made up its mind accomplish it in a short space of time. But the government cannot decide to "introduce capitalism"; it cannot appoint entrepreneurs by decree. The word itself sheds light on the matter: private enterprise assumes that people undertake risky investment voluntarily in the hope of making a profit. Once they have done so, some of them will go bankrupt, while others accumulate wealth and expand their undertakings. In other words this is an *evolutionary* process that wise government measures can speed up and stupid measures or indifference can slow down. Whatever the case, it will take several years to run its course.

To use the qualification mentioned earlier, development of the private sector is an unconditional task, unlike macrostabilization, which is a conditional task (at least in its most advantageous, "packaged" form). Turning immediately to the partial tasks, most of them can be embarked on at any time, even if some of the conditions for a democratic consensus are lacking. And it would be a good idea if some of the energies currently expended on political battles were transferred to these tasks instead. That is not to deny, of course, that radical political change and the creation of a democratic consensus would greatly boost the development of the private sector as well.

Let us list the component tasks:

1. The "legal infrastructure" for the operation of the private economy must be created. Here are a few examples of the legislation indispensably required: a law on contract, a company law, a law on foreign investment, a bankruptcy law, a banking law, and a labor law. Even if these subjects have been covered by earlier laws and decrees, the legislation must be redrafted in line with the requirements of a modern market economy.

2. It is desirable for the changes in the law to be accompanied by a reeducation of public opinion. Appreciation and respect for private property and business undertakings must be developed and prejudices overcome. Here a great deal depends on the politicians and on the press and television.

3. Private business activity was largely banned earlier, and even since the beginning of the reforms private enterprise has only been permitted under exceptional circumstances within narrow limits. A significant part of the private sector has been forced underground and been operating as a "second economy." It is time to change the proportions of what is permitted, what is restricted, and what is banned. The point of departure should be freedom to pursue all private activity; "free enterprise" should become a fundamental right. This right can then be restricted, but only where important public interests dictate. The restrictions should be laid down in carefully drafted legislation, not subject to the whims and ill-will of bureaucrats.

4. It follows from the previous points that harassment of private entrepreneurs by the police, the authorities, and the political organizations must cease. The private sector cannot be expected to accumulate unless it feels that its property is totally secure.

5. The foundation of private enterprises must be encouraged. Apart from moral and political inducements, they need credit on favorable terms; the state should lighten the credit system's task by offering guarantees for these "start-up" loans; it should also give tax concessions for private investments.

6. Great importance attaches to what is known in several Eastern European countries as "small-scale privatization." This covers the sale of stores, restaurants, small hotels, small factories, vehicles, housing, and agricultural smallholdings to private owners, either individuals or partnerships. I have only mentioned transactions that could be entered into by a buyer with a relatively small stock of capital. Special long-term credit and repayment schemes must be devised and generous finance must be made available for small-scale privatization.

In many cases it is justified to break up a large state-owned firm into smaller parts, thus making it amenable to small-scale privatization. It is not right to do this, of course, where advantages of mass production, the economies of scale provided by a large factory, would be lost. But as mentioned before, the socialist economy is excessively concentrated; the size of many gigantic firms is economically unjustified. Breaking them up into smaller units will have a beneficial effect.

Tasks 5 and 6 are closely connected. A new private firm may in fact start life by buying an asset owned by the state, or a private firm that has come into being by some other means may purchase state property at a later stage in its development as a way of expanding its factory.

7. The property rights in large state-owned firms that (a) it is not advisable to retain in state ownership, (b) it is not desirable to break up into smaller units, and (c) are economically viable

must be transferred into private hands. There is a lot of debate about the most effective way of doing so.

The main instrument in my view should be to transform these firms into joint-stock companies and *sell* their shares. The buyer may be either domestic or foreign. It can prove useful for managers and employees to take part in the privatization program; it is worth encouraging them to take up a percentage of the shares by offering suitable credit schemes, for instance. Once the market economy has normalized, a significant proportion of the general public will be willing to hold some of the savings in the form of shares. Equity will also be purchased by various large institutions (e.g., insurance companies and private foundations).

Many people support the idea of a *free* distribution of shares, either to the employees of the firms concerned or to the whole population through a system of coupons or vouchers. For my part I do not feel this is an expedient solution to the problem. At most I would give property free of charge to certain institutions (for instance, decentralized pension funds) as a way of supplying them with initial operating capital. A detailed account of the arguments for and against would exceed the bounds of this study, and so I shall merely draw my Soviet colleagues' attention to the literature on the subject.[7] In any case correct planning of Soviet privatization will be made easier by having the early experiences in Eastern Europe available by the time it comes onto the agenda. The strategies chosen differ from country to country: Germany and Hungary have basically opted for sales, while free distribution on a mass scale is being prepared in Czechoslovakia and Poland. It will be instructive to compare the results.

8. All the tasks mentioned so far tie in with a forceful development of the financial sector. There is a need for decentraliza-

---

[7] I put my own position in my 1992 article. To my knowledge, the idea of a free transfer of property rights was first advanced in an article by J. Lewandowski and J. Szomburg (1989); see also R. Frydman and R. Rapaczynski (1990) and D. Lipton and J. Sachs (1990b).

tion of the banking system and for the development of private pension funds and insurance companies (alongside the social security system). A modern market economy includes a great many other kinds of financial institutions such as investment and mutual funds, venture capital funds that can finance high-risk new undertakings, financial institutions specializing in housing investments, and so on.

While emphasizing the multiplicity of the paths and instruments, I would like to pick out from the many partial tasks one that I consider to be the most important of all: *the evolution of a new middle class*, the emergence of a million entrepreneurs on a small and medium scale. By entering the private sector, this new stratum, along with its employees, whose earnings will normally become appreciably higher as well, can become a bulwark for the new system in the cities and the countryside alike. I would measure the speed of the transition primarily by the rate at which this stratum grows. The degree to which the growth of this entrepreneur stratum is promoted also constitutes one of the major measures of economic success for the new democratic governments.

## 8. Social Welfare Policy

All active participants in the new democratic political era must strive from the first day to accomplish the tasks of the transition in a humane way. This too is among the "unconditional tasks"; whether the conditions favoring the changes emerge or not, all believers in the new democratic political order and an efficient market economy must do everything they can in their own field to alleviate the grave problems and suffering that accompany the transformation of society.

Politicians can win popularity with populist rhetoric at most for a time, until it emerges that they are doing nothing to help with the problems. I do not want to disguise the fact that implementation of the program outlined in the earlier parts of this lecture is accompanied by sacrifices of many kinds. Production in many sectors falls, producing unemployment. Relative prices and wages are readjusted, reducing the real income of many people. Masses of people will be afflicted by the freed prices and raised taxes and compensated for them only in part. As the real market becomes dominant in the economy, insecurity increases as well in many respects: businesses fail and jobs are no longer secure. All this happens at a time when the country is down at heel, its reserves exhausted.

So what is the minimum that can and must be ensured even under these circumstances?

First of all, unemployment must be openly recognized as a permanent concomitant of life. That means setting up a system of unemployment benefits, after responsible consideration of the country's financial potentials, augmented by better organization of labor exchanges and retraining schemes.

Apart from that, a welfare system must be developed to give at least temporary help to those of the needy whose reintegration takes time and permanent support to those incapable of helping themselves.

Under socialism there were large, cumbersome, overcentralized systems of redistribution in operation; these allocated housing and dispensed health care and pensions. There is a great need for decentralization in this area, and also for private institutions to take part in the provision alongside the institutions of the state. But the transformation must be accomplished in a way that does not cause a further trauma to people already shaken during the stabilization process. A gradual, very tactful approach is needed here.

I notice social welfare policy being relegated into the background in many Eastern European countries, which impedes the development of the democratic consensus. I sincerely hope that my Soviet friends will learn from this experience and try to avoid committing the same error.

The need is not just for new state regulations and new institutions, but for a new public morality. Too great a role was played in our earlier lives by a state that was both repressive and paternalistic; people expected it to take care of them. With the advent of the market economy, the idea of individual liberty and autonomy becomes the center of the system of values. The chief commandment for all active people is to help themselves, not wait idly for the state to decide instead of them and do something on their behalf. But this prime imperative should be complemented by another: that society must assist those in need of help, both by voluntarily and spontaneously organized solidarity and by state means.

## REFERENCES

Allison, G., and G. Yavlinsky (eds.). 1991. "Window of Opportunity: Joint Program for Western Cooperation in the Soviet Transformation to Democracy and the Market Economy." Cambridge: Joint Working Group of Harvard University, and Moscow: Center for Economic and Political Research, manuscript.

Antal, László. 1979. "Development — with Some Digression: The Hungarian Economic Mechanism in the Seventies." *Acta Oeconomica*, 23(3–4), 257–73.

Bauer, Tamás. 1983. "The Hungarian Alternative to Soviet-Type Planning." *Journal of Comparative Economics*, Sept., 7(3), 304–16.

Berend, Iván T. 1990. *The Hungarian Economic Reform*. Cambridge: Cambridge University Press.

Blanchard, Oliver, et al. 1991. *Reform in Eastern Europe*. Cambridge: MIT Press.

Fischer, Stanley, and Alan Gelb. 1990. "Issues in Socialist Economy Reform." *Working Paper WPS 565*. Washington, D.C.: World Bank.

Frydman, Roman, and Andrzej Rapaczynski. 1990. "Markets and Institutions in Large Scale Privatizations." In *Economic Research Report*, pp. 90–420. New York: New York University.

Hare, Paul, Hugo K. Radice, and Nigel Swain (eds.). 1981. *Hungary: A Decade of Economic Reform*. London and Boston: Allen and Unwin.

Kornai, János. 1983. "Comments on the Present State and Prospects of the Hungarian Economic Reform." *Journal of Comparative Economics*, 7(3), 225–52.

———. 1986. "The Hungarian Reform Process: Visions, Hopes and Reality." *Journal of Economic Literature*, Dec., 24(4), 1687–1737.

———. [1989] 1990a. *The Road to a Free Economy: Shifting from a Socialist System: The Example of Hungary.* New York: W. W. Norton.

———. 1990b. *Put' k svobodnoi ekonomike: Strastnoe slovo v zaschitu ekonomicheskih preobrazovanii* (The Road to a Free Economy). Moscow: Ekonomika.

———. 1992. "The Principles of Privatization in Eastern Europe." *De Economist* (forthcoming).

Kovács, János Mátyás. 1990. "Reform Economics: The Classification Gap." *Daedalus*, Winter, 119(1), 215–48.

Lewandowski, Janusz, and Jan Szomburg. 1989. "Property Reform as a Basis for Social and Economic Reform," *Communist Economies*, 1(3), 257–68.

Lipton, David, and Jeffrey Sachs. 1990a. "Creating a Market Economy in Eastern Europe: The Case of Poland." *Brookings Papers on Economic Activity*, 1, 75–133.

———. 1990b. "Privatization in Eastern Europe: The Case of Poland." *Brookings Papers on Economic Activity*, 2, 293–333.

Révész, Gábor. 1990. *Perestroika in Eastern Europe: Hungary's Economic Transformation, 1945–1988.* Boulder: Westview Press.

Szamuely, László. 1982. "The First Wave of the Mechanism Debate in Hungary (1954–1957). *Acta Oeconomica*, 29(1–2), 1–24.

———. 1984. "The Second Wave of the Economic Mechanism Debate and the 1968 Reform in Hungary." *Acta Oeconomica*, 33(1–2), 43–67.

Working Group formed by a joint decision of Mikhail S. Gorbachev and Boris N. Yeltsin. 1990. "Transition to the Market, Part 1: The Concept and Program." The Shatalin Plan. Moscow, Arkhangel's koe: Cultural Initiative Foundation, August, manuscript.

*HELMUT KOHL*

THE TANNER LECTURES ON HUMAN VALUES

Delivered at

University of California, Berkeley
September 13, 1991

HELMUT KOHL studied law, social and political science, and history at the Universities of Frankfurt and Heidelberg, and received a Ph.D. degree in 1958. He joined the Christian Democratic Party (CDU) in 1947, was later Chairman of the CDU, Rhineland-Palatinate, for six years, and in 1964 became a member of the CDU national executive. He served as Prime Minister of Rhineland-Palatinate from 1969 to 1976, then as Leader of the Opposition in the German Bundestag from 1976 to 1982. Since 1982 he has been Federal Chancellor of the Federal Republic of Germany.

I

Thirty-one years ago the University of California honored one of my predecessors, Konrad Adenauer, the first chancellor of the Federal Republic of Germany. Never before in history, Konrad Adenauer said then during his visit to California, had a victorious nation helped the defeated to such an extent as the American people had aided the Germans. At that time our country was still divided, and an end to this division was not in sight.

Today I am here to thank you for everything that the American nation has done for the good of Germany. For decades the American people have defended freedom in Europe. Germany owes the recovery of its unity in freedom not least to the untiring commitment of America and its presidents for more than four decades, from Harry S Truman to George Bush.

Ronald Reagan rightly assessed the historic opportunity for German unity at a very early stage when he called out in front of the Brandenburg Gate during his visit to Berlin in June 1987: "Mr. Gorbachev, tear down this wall."

In three weeks' time, on October 3, the dream of Germany's freedom and unity will have been reality for exactly one year. I thank George Bush for his assistance. The recovery of political unity in free self-determination for us Germans coincided with the end of the East-West conflict, at the focus of which the Germans had been for over forty years.

Today we jointly face the new challenges of securing political, economic, social, and ecological stability in those European countries which have after decades liberated themselves from the yoke of Communist tyranny and want to establish a liberal economic and social order.

Probably nobody in the West is more familiar than we Germans are with the terrible legacy of the Communist rulers: an uncompetitive and moribund economy, dilapidated towns and villages, transport links in a disastrous state, and a highly polluted environment. But above all the tyranny left deep wounds in the hearts of the people. The people in the eastern part of Germany must now gain faith in themselves and each other as well as confidence in life under a new, liberal system.

Optimism and a pioneering spirit are the decisive prerequisites for the success of the reconstruction work ahead of us. Even more than economic factors, it was this creative spark that passed from America with the Marshall Plan to Europe and Germany over forty years ago. The Marshall Plan was the American response to an epochal challenge. Today we can build on that encouraging example.

## II

I know that here in California, too, my country's major scientific institutions enjoy special esteem. You will appreciate that first and foremost I would like to mention my alma mater, Heidelberg. President Bush's reference to "partners in leadership" should also apply to science and technology in the future. Let us work jointly to attain this goal.

An important step toward scientific and technological partnership has been made by Americans and Germans in the form of the successful international institute of computer science here at Berkeley. This example should be emulated in other scientific fields and at other locations.

California's great intellectual affinity with European culture is now as detectable as when Berkeley was founded 123 years ago. But looking out on the ocean always reminds one of the opposite coast. Just as I visualize the familiar images of America and its cities when standing on Europe's Atlantic coast, the view of the Pacific conveys a picture of the forces of attraction between California and the East Asian region from Japan to Singapore. Where else than here in California is the visitor made more aware of the interlinkage and interdependence of the world's three main economic and industrial centers: North America, Europe, and East Asia?

### III

As a united and sovereign country, Germany has acquired greater responsibility in Europe and worldwide. We know that we can live up to this responsibility only together with our American and European friends. For us Germans, being partners in leadership means assuming our share of responsibility in the family of free nations. We are willing to do so. In Western burden-sharing, we are ready to play a part commensurate with our economic and political potential. German policy must prove its worth above all in the following fields.

First: now that the two parts of my country which were separated for over four decades have been politically united, we must also achieve economic, social, and cultural unity. We can solve the economic and social problems in a few years. But over forty years of division — and this is the real problem facing the Germans — have become deeply embedded in the hearts and minds of the people. We need patience, compassion, and mutual understanding to heal those wounds.

Second: in Europe we seek not only economic but also political union as a precondition for our future. Europe must in future be more than a deluxe free-trade area.

Third: German-American friendship and close partnership between Europe and America are decisive prerequisites for Europe and America succeeding, through joint efforts, in coping with the global tasks of the future.

Fourth: the establishment of stable democracies and of a social market economy in the reformist countries of Central, Eastern, and Southeastern Europe and political and economic restructuring in the Soviet Union and its republics call for our joint support. This is in the European and American interest; it is in our common interest.

Fifth: we want to contribute toward a peaceful order worldwide founded on the rule of law, respect for human rights, the right of nations to self-determination, and a common commitment to the integrity of Creation as entrusted to humanity.

## IV

For us Germans, one of the most urgent tasks on the agenda for the 1990s is to eliminate the disastrous legacy left by over forty years of communism in the GDR. Reconstruction in the eastern federal states is a pioneering task in two respects. It is a pioneering task because it is unprecedented in history. It is also a pioneering task because its success is of great importance far beyond my country's borders. It will be a source of hope and encouragement for the Hungarians, Poles, Czechs and Slovaks, for the Romanians and Bulgarians, for the Albanians, and not least for the peoples of Yugoslavia, the Baltic states, and the Soviet Union.

All of them face far more difficult starting conditions than the Germans in the former GDR. The conditions for a fresh start in eastern Germany are favorable. The western federal states have for almost nine years now been characterized by an excellent economy and an outstanding investment climate. The economic upswing there is undiminished, with growth during the first six months of this year amounting to $4\frac{1}{2}\%$ compared with last year. It is true that the weaker economic situation of our partners is making itself felt in Germany. Nonetheless, experts forecast growth in excess of 3% for the year as a whole. Together with Japan we thus still head the league of industrial nations.

In the new federal states a change for the better is in sight. Not least because of the high demand from the eastern federal states, Germany has become a kind of economic locomotive. Under numerous programs we are making available in the $2\frac{1}{2}$ years from mid-1990 to the end of 1992 the equivalent of over $100 billion for reconstruction in the new federal states. Many experts believe that the economy there will pick up by the end of this year. What we need now above all is private investment — and I hope it comes from the United States, too. Never before have there been such attractive conditions in Germany to encourage investors from all over the world.

The speed of structural change is best illustrated by the increased pace of privatization in the new federal states. By the end of July, 3,000 former state enterprises had been transferred to new owners. They will invest over DM 70 billion in the coming years. Potential investors from the United States are now able to obtain information from an agency set up in New York specifically for this purpose.

Of course, we are confronted with large problems, and we have no reason to conceal them. But every day I see that the people who are now free want to work and to use the opportunities afforded by freedom. My message to you is this: we shall make it. I am certain that in a few years' time the regions of the former GDR will be flourishing.

V

For us Germans, the momentous change that we have all been witnessing since the autumn of 1989 bears out a policy whose foundations were laid by Konrad Adenauer in the 1950s. Now as then, our policy is based on the conviction that German unity and European unification are two sides of the same coin. We want the free and united Germany to be part of a free and united Europe.

Following German reunification, Germany is dedicating itself in a special manner and with all its strength to continuing the process of European unification. In his famous speech at Zurich in 1946, Winston Churchill already spoke of a "United States of Europe." We Germans associate that term with the vision of a federal Europe. En route to that goal we shall complete by the end of next year a large single market in Europe encompassing 340 million people — an area without borders for people, goods, and services. In the next few months the tracks will be laid for the period after 1992: our aim is that the heads of state or government of the European Community should sign two treaties in December establishing a uniform timetable for the Economic and Monetary Union as well as the Political Union.

A European Political Union must, inter alia, lay clear-cut foundations for a common foreign and security policy. In future this will also include a common defense policy. Let me make two things absolutely clear in this context:

1. My government does not want to weaken the tried-and-tested Atlantic Alliance in any way. NATO will remain a decisive prerequisite of our common security.

2. I also strongly oppose any considerations that run counter to the principle of indivisibility of our common security and would ultimately erode the transatlantic security linkage.

But the experience we are now gaining shows that Europe must at last speak with one voice in foreign and security affairs. The importance of this is illustrated by the civil war in Yugoslavia, the Gulf war, and the events in the Soviet Union. Only if it speaks with one voice can the European Community ultimately play a role in Europe and worldwide commensurate with its economic weight and political responsibility.

This responsibility will increase as the Community gains in size. We are making every effort so that the negotiations on association agreements between the European Community and Hungary, Poland, and Czechoslovakia are completed as quickly as possible. Accession to the Community must also be open to those three countries, once appropriate conditions exist there. Europe includes not just Paris, London, and Berlin, but also Warsaw, Prague, and Budapest — and naturally Vienna and Stockholm as well.

## VI

Germany and the European Community will remain closely linked to the democracies of North America. We want to expand this partnership. Europe needs America, but let me also add this: America needs Europe. I have already referred to the common cultural assets of the Old and New Worlds. I am firmly convinced that cultural exchange in the fields of literature and the fine arts, music, and films will gain further importance. Cultural bonds will thus become the source of new and multifaceted artistic achievements.

It is important to speak of economic aspects, but we should not forget that we must also reach people's hearts. Man cannot live by bread alone. Cultural and scientific cooperation is just as essential as economic and security cooperation.

The economic dimension of our relations will acquire greater prominence. Europe as an economic area will become all the more important for the United States, the more Europe merges and the larger the European Community becomes. Alongside North America and East Asia, the European Community will be one of the three centers of the world economy.

For us Germans in the heart of our continent, the role and responsibility of the United States and Canada in and for Europe continue to be of vital importance for peace and security. The North Atlantic Alliance remains the indispensable security link between Europe and North America. This includes the guaranteed presence of substantial North American forces in Western Europe and on German soil in the future, too.

Let me add a personal remark: I come from a region of Germany, the Palatinate, where a particularly large number of American soldiers and their families live — in good-neighborliness with the local population. The human contacts that have evolved there cannot be overrated in terms of their significance for friendship between our two peoples.

Even after the end of the East-West conflict we cannot dispense with the capability to protect peace and our common freedom effectively. This is the mission of the Bundeswehr and of the troops of our American and European allies.

## VII

Just under a month ago, on August 21, the citizens of the Soviet Union achieved a great victory for democracy, freedom, and justice. Their resistance caused the coup to fail. This was exactly twenty-three years after freedom had been crushed by tanks in Prague. August 21, 1991, will go down in history as a belated triumph for the people who had then tried to stop those tanks. Thus not only Stalin has been overcome in the USSR, but also Marx and Lenin since August 21.

What event could bring this home to us more clearly than the ban on the political activities of the Communist party of the Soviet Union? I am certain that the fundamental reforms will take place even faster in the future. The people in Moscow, Leningrad — the old and new St. Petersburg — and many other regions in the Soviet Union deserve our respect for their courage and firmness. This particularly applies to President Boris Yeltsin of the Russian Republic, without whose courage the coup would hardly have failed so quickly.

The unanimous condemnation of the coup by the free democracies of the West helped considerably to force the perpetrators to give up. During the coup numerous heads of state or government assured President Yeltsin of their support.

We Germans associate with Mikhail Gorbachev the memory of the turning point that made it possible to achieve German unity in agreement with all our friends and European neighbors. I am therefore personally grateful to him. When we met in the Caucasus in July 1990, he acknowledged for the first time the right of the Germans to decide for themselves on their membership in an alliance. Our decision was clear. It was a decision in favor of the West, in favor of NATO and a future at the side of free nations.

After the failed coup in the Soviet Union, the tracks were laid for extensive democratic renewal. Historic changes resulted above all for the three Baltic republics. Estonia, Latvia, and Lithuania, which had been forcibly annexed by Stalin acting in collaboration with Hitler, have regained their freedom. In reestablishing diplomatic relations on August 28, the Federal Republic of Germany also gave expression to the desire to resume the tradition of peaceful relations reaching far back into the Middle Ages.

Despite all our delight and satisfaction at the historic victory of freedom and democracy, the motto now cannot be "business as usual." Not least we owe this to the men and women who lost their lives during the days of that Russian "August Revolution."

The recent developments give rise to the conclusion that the Western nations must now jointly provide swift and extensive aid to the Soviet Union so that it can progress further toward democracy and a market economy. The emerging union and the republics must now develop a self-contained economic program. Only in this way can a reliable framework be established for effective — and additional — Western assistance. The dialogue by the West with the Soviet Union and the provision of assistance will take account of the new distribution of powers between the union and the republics.

This year's economic summit in London already paved the way for the integration of the Soviet Union into the world economy. We must now quickly implement the decisions taken there. I myself shall make every effort to ensure that this dialogue soon leads to tangible results for the sake of the people in the Soviet Union.

In providing aid for the Soviet Union and the reformist countries of Central, Eastern, and Southeastern Europe, my government has time and again pressed for fair international burden-sharing. This major task cannot be left to a few in Europe. All industrial nations should participate in accordance with their potential because democratization and economic reorientation in those countries are in the interest of the entire world. Freedom, democracy, and the rule of law are a contribution toward peace not just for Russia, but for the whole world, for each of us.

Since 1989, the Federal Republic of Germany has supported the reform process in Central, Eastern, and Southeastern Europe with over DM 90 billion, over DM 60 billion of this going to the Soviet Union alone. At present, we are thus providing 56% of all Western aid to the Soviet Union and 32% of Western assistance to the countries of Central, Eastern, and Southeastern Europe. With this we have reached the limits of our potential. We cannot solve this problem on our own. Naturally, we shall participate in further multilateral efforts.

However, financial assistance alone is not sufficient. There is a prospect of lasting success only if we actually achieve new, comprehensive economic partnership, open still further our markets for those countries, and support them extensively in reorganizing their social and economic systems.

The conflict in Yugoslavia is a source of great concern for us. In view of the large-scale military activity of the last few weeks and the terrible pictures that we see daily, the main priority is to ensure that the use of force is stopped immediately without qualification. When dialogue and harmonious coexistence are no longer possible we must, in line with our understanding of the right to self-determination, consider the question of recognizing under international law those republics which no longer wish to belong to Yugoslavia. Historical experience shows that a state cannot be held together with tanks. The international community, particularly the Europeans, will continue to work toward a peaceful solution on the basis of the Charter of Paris.

## VIII

The completion of Germany's internal unity and the exceptional challenges posed by the far-reaching changes in Europe demand major exertions on our part. But we Germans want to live up to our responsibility as a large democracy and industrial nation. We are therefore also willing to make our contribution toward solving global problems.

The great poverty in Third World countries, the diseases, hunger, and environmental destruction in large parts of the world, as well as oppression — we must not be indifferent to any of these things. Our moral duty of solidarity with our fellow beings demands this, as do our common sense and our awareness of interdependence and responsibility for each other.

We must therefore continue to pursue a development policy which actively supports the poorest and weakest and above all helps them to help themselves. We realize that the successful use of our resources depends on the basic political, economic, and social conditions in Third World countries. We expect respect for human rights, democratic structures based on the rule of law, and a social, ecologically orientated market economy. Above all, scarce resources in the Third World must not be wasted by disproportionately high spending on armaments.

It remains crucial that we give our partners in the Third World an opportunity to earn funds for their development through equitable trade. In other words, we the industrial nations must open our markets still further. In this context, too — and not least in view of the transatlantic relationship — the GATT Uruguay Round is of vital importance. As a major trading nation we Germans — and this also applies to the European Community as a whole — have a special interest in open world markets.

We Germans have achieved economic success since the war not least by consistently rejecting protectionism. Free world trade alone holds the key to our future. All of us, including the Europeans and Germans, must therefore contribute at the GATT negotiations toward a solution which produces balanced results. Of course, this also applies to our American friends.

An area which similarly calls for global efforts is that of environmental protection. This will be a particularly important subject at the next economic summit in Munich. In the past few years I have on numerous occasions suggested that environmental protection be linked to the debt problem. For example, cancellation of the debt of Third World countries should, inter alia, be made dependent on the funds thus released being used for specific environmental measures. The destruction of tropical rain forests and the hole in the ozone layer over the Antarctic concern people in America just as in Europe. The danger of changes in the world's climate hits a vital nerve of all peoples without distinction. We therefore need universal partnership in environmental matters.

The last few years have seen splendid headway being made by the ideals of freedom, democracy, and the rule of law. But in many parts of the world people are still arbitrarily arrested, humiliated, tortured, and murdered. They deserve our solidarity.

America and Germany are united in the goal of fashioning a world in which there is more freedom, peace is more secure, and our national environment is protected and conserved more effectively. We want to do so jointly.

## IX

Allow me finally to say a few personal words to the students here. This is a good opportunity for me to speak to young Americans.

When I entered this auditorium just now, I recalled the days when I was eighteen or twenty years old. That was 1948/50. The Deutschmark had just been introduced. Our country had been destroyed to an extent inconceivable to many today. We were not only materially finished, but also morally at rock bottom. The disgraceful Nazi crimes were fresh in the minds of people.

As I said at the beginning of my lecture, the Americans were the first to extend their hand to us in partnership and then friendship. Inspired by this spirit and driven by the energy of the people we achieved the reconstruction of our country — just as we shall achieve it in the eastern federal states in the next few years.

At that time we young Germans, as pupils and students, had a dream: that of regaining German unity and building a United States of Europe. There have been many setbacks, much pessimism, and a great deal of skepticism along this road. Yet we accomplished German unity and have advanced substantially toward the unification of Europe. In a few years' time we shall also fully attain this goal.

I regard this as the fulfillment of a dream. In the 1990s, at the end of a century which has seen so much death, suffering, and misery, we have the opportunity jointly to build a better world.

Yours is the time now coming. Those who are at present eighteen, twenty, or twenty-two years old have the opportunity to take part in shaping the next century. Remember the experience gained by the generation of your parents and grandparents: peace and freedom, democracy, and the rule of law are the indispensable prerequisite for personal happiness, too.

This is your opportunity. God bless you.

# The Bible in Seventeenth-Century English Politics

CHRISTOPHER HILL

The Tanner Lectures on Human Values

Delivered at

University of Michigan
October 4, 1991

JOHN EDWARD CHRISTOPHER HILL was educated at Balliol College, Oxford, where he was a Brackenbury Scholar in Modern History. He was a Fellow of All Souls College, Oxford, from 1934 to 1938, a Fellow and Tutor in Modern History for twenty-seven years at Balliol, and a Master of Balliol College from 1965 to 1978. A foreign member of the American Academy of Arts and Sciences, he is the author of numerous books on seventeenth-century English history, including *Puritanism and Revolution* (1958), *Intellectual Origins of the English Revolution* (1965), *God's Englishman: Oliver Cromwell* (1970), *Milton and the English Revolution* (1977), and most recently *A Nation of Change and Novelty: Radical Politics, Religion and Literature in 17th-Century England* (1990).

The Bible has always been a potentially revolutionary book. There were fierce conflicts over the establishment of the canon for the early Christian church, as it transformed itself from a popular underground organization to the state church of the Roman Empire; and today the Bible is crucial to the liberation theology of Latin America. Countless radicals in between have turned to the Bible to support their cause.

In England in 1381 our first anti-poll-tax rebels asked

> When Adam delved and Eve span,
> Who was then the gentleman?

The couplet was repeatedly quoted by rebels — from Edward VI's reign to the 1640s. In Shakespeare's *Henry VI* Jack Cade said, "Adam was a gardener," and his followers wanted the magistrates to be "labouring men." When the second grave-digger in *Hamlet* asked if Adam was a gentleman he was recalling the same rhyme.

Throughout the Middle Ages the Bible was kept in Latin, readable only by the clergy and a very few exceptional laymen. Translation into the vernacular was forbidden. The English version was made by Wyclif's followers, the Lollards, almost simultaneously with the Peasant's Revolt of 1381, was a prohibited document. It circulated in manuscript at underground discussion groups of peasants and artisans, from the late fourteenth century to the Protestant Reformation of the early sixteenth century.

The invention of printing, and the rapid increase of literacy among the laity in the sixteenth century, led to new versions, following the example of Luther's German Bible. John Foxe the Martyrologist thought that the coincidence in time of the Reformation and the spread of the printing press was a divine miracle. Many of the earlier translators were burned, including William

Tyndale, whose superb version of the 1520s underlies all subsequent English translations. If Tyndale had survived to become a bishop in Edward VI's reign we should all have heard more of his translation.

The accident of Henry VIII's quarrel with the papacy in the 1530s made him suddenly permit publication of the Bible in English: though he was careful to insist that it should not be read by anyone below the rank of gentleman or lady and that it should not be discussed in unauthorized assemblies. But this attempt to abolish "diversity of opinions" was of no avail once the Bible was available in English. Resistance to the brief restoration of Catholicism under Mary showed that hundreds of ordinary men and women were prepared to suffer martyrdom for the faith which they believed they had found in the Bible. The Marian Martyrs came almost exclusively from the poorer classes; wealthy believers were able to escape into exile. But whilst many hitherto Protestant clergy and gentry conformed under Bloody Mary, the constancy of the humbler sufferers under persecution, glorified in Foxe's *Book of Martyrs*, established a myth and testified to the reality of a core of convinced Protestants in England. When Elizabeth succeeded Mary it was natural and necessary for her to clasp the English Bible to her bosom in a public demonstration of her devotion to it.

Under Elizabeth, the popular version was the Geneva Bible, produced by Marian exiles and sold in deliberately cheap, pocketable editions. It quite eclipsed the official "Bishops' Bible" in popular estimation and sales. Two specialties of the Geneva Bible, and a reason for its popularity, were its woodcut illustrations and its extensive marginal notes. The latter glossed the text in a radical, Calvinist, sense — as contrasted with the unadorned text of the official Bible used in all parish churches. James I particularly disliked the Geneva Bible. The point of the Authorized Version, published under his auspices in 1611, was to get rid of all marginal commentary and to leave the Bible to be interpreted by authorized parsons of the Church of England established in every parish, and by the seventeenth century assumed to have sufficient education to be able to cope with this task.

One of the popular aspects of what we call Puritanism was its emphasis on household religion, in which the father of the family expounded the sacred text to his wife, children, servants, and apprentices. In many parishes "lecturers," freelance preachers hired by town corporations or financed by public subscription, offered a theology more popular with their congregations than that supplied by the officially appointed vicar or rector. The hierarchy always disliked the popular element in the appointment of lecturers and tried to discourage them. Archbishop Laud for a few years in the 1630s was successful in suppressing them altogether. In discussions of sermons the Geneva marginal notes must have been very useful to those who lacked a university education: popular preachers expected their congregations to have their Bibles handy. The Geneva Bible was prohibited under Laud: Milton and Bunyan used both the A.V. and the Geneva Bible.

The Bible was not only read on Sundays, when all were legally compelled to attend their parish church. Men, women, and children encountered it on all sides — in the ballads they bought and sang and in their daily surroundings. Where today we would have wallpaper and paintings on the walls, almost all houses had hangings to keep out draughts and to cover up the rough surfaces. These often took the form of "painted cloths," representing Biblical scenes. Biblical texts were painted on walls and posts in houses. All walls were covered with printed matter — illustrated ballads and broadsides, again often on Biblical subjects. "Godly tables," printed especially for decorating walls, were described as "most fit to be set up in every house": they regularly contained texts from the Bible as well as prayers and instructions to "godly householders." Most of the population would first encounter both print and the Bible with such decorations.

So the Bible was omnipresent in houses. But houses include alehouses, which with churches were the main centres of community life. Their walls too had painted texts and painted cloths and were covered with ballads, broadsides, and "godly tables." Men and women who had never opened a Bible would be well acquainted with many of its stories and texts. Several generations of children in the sixteenth and seventeenth centuries grew up in an environment suffused with the new print culture and the Bible in English. "The people of the Book" could come to know it well without reading it.[1]

In consequence almost everybody in the sixteenth century and most in the seventeenth accepted that the Bible was the authoritative source of all wisdom — on politics and economics as well as on what we should today call religion. Opening the Bible at random was a favourite way of asking for divine guidance. When English sailors had lost contact with the Dutch fleet in 1653, a prayer-meeting in the flagship opened the Bible, and II Chronicles XX.16 gave them the answer. Biblical phrases could convey more than appeared on the surface, as in Thomas Hobbes's apparently innocent remark "the apostleship of Judas is called his bishopric," to which he carefully gave Acts I.20 as a reference. The cry "To your tents, O Israel!" was the title of a pamphlet published just before the outbreak of civil war; the phrase was used again as the conclusion of a near-Digger pamphlet in 1648, *Light Shining in Buckinghamshire*. There was no need to remind people that this cry had been the prelude to successful rebellion against the king. (I Kings XII.16; II Samuel XX.1).

The Bible was central to the political discussions which accompanied civil war: both sides appealed to its text. The Bible — and especially the New Testament—is fairly consistently in favour of obedience to the powers that be, who are ordained of God. But in the Old Testament there are few good kings. When James I tried to produce Biblical support for monarchy he was reduced to quoting the warnings of the prophet Samuel trying to persuade the

---

[1] I owe these two paragraphs to Tessa Watt's most useful book, *Cheap Print and Popular Piety, 1550–1640* (Oxford University Press, 1991), chapters 4–6.

Israelites not to choose a king. Samuel listed the dreadful things a king would do to his subjects: James cheerfully cited this as a call for absolute obedience even to the worst of kings.

Bad kings in the Old Testament were mostly those who introduced idolatry. Since radical Protestants equated popery with idolatry, they made much of this point. Nimrod, allegedly the founder of monarchy, was described by Milton as a rebel who disrupted the "free equality, fraternal state" which preceded his rule.

The Old Testament had other attractions for people in the seventeenth century. A continuing theme is the extermination of the previous inhabitants of the Promised Land by the Chosen People who invaded it. The brutality with which this conquest was accompanied is not often emphasized. Moses, after a military victory over the Midianites, instructed his troops to kill all the men and women prisoners except virgins, whom they might "keep alive for yourselves" (Numbers XXXI.14–18). The unconcern with which Old Testament prophets advocated the slaughter of the heathen inhabitants seemed to justify the self-righteousness with which seventeenth-century English settlers extirpated the native inhabitants of Ireland — Papists, no better than heathens — and New England settlers on occasion massacred American Indians.

The most revolutionary Biblical concept was that of the millennium. In times of crisis throughout the Middle Ages it had been assumed that the end of the world and judgment day were at hand. But by the seventeenth century a consensus among Protestant scholars interpreting the Biblical prophecies seemed to have agreed that the 1650s were a probable date for the Second Coming of Jesus Christ and the millennium. We recall Milton's phrase of 1641 — "shortly-expected king." This was a heady notion, especially for less educated persons than Milton. As the date approached, the English civil war could easily be seen as the prelude to the last times depicted in Revelation.

One necessary condition was the overthrow of Antichrist. Protestants identified the pope as Antichrist, and in the 1630s there were widespread suspicions of an international Papist plot against England's Protestant independence, in which Charles's Queen Henrietta Maria and his first minister, Archbishop Laud, were involved. In the civil war the royalists were labelled "the Antichristian party."

The concept of the covenanted Chosen People, which runs through the Old Testament, was taken over by English millenarians. From the days of Elizabeth England was a "beleaguered isle," surrounded by hostile Catholic powers. The forward-looking party among Elizabeth's advisers — Leicester, Walsingham, Drake, Sir Philip Sidney — aspired to lead European Protestants in a crusade against the papal Antichrist and Spain: Elizabeth showed no enthusiasm for such a policy, James and Charles even less, on good financial grounds. But others were eager, for a whole variety of reasons.

Such a campaign, as the sea-dogs well realised, might lead to the conquest of "new worlds, for gold, for praise, for glory," as Ralegh put it." [2] Plunder-trade with America and the Far East and the slave trade from Africa were open to any state which possessed a powerful enough navy. Gain and godliness were in an alliance which seems to us more uncomfortable than it apparently seemed to contemporaries. The attempts of James and Charles to come to terms with the great Catholic powers — Spain and France — by marriage alliance and political agreement seemed to convinced Protestants a shameful betrayal of the duty of a covenanted nation. A significant literature in the 1620s and 1630s cried out against this betrayal and insisted that God would turn against his Chosen People if they turned away from him. The idea that God was leaving England loomed large in the minds of many of the early emigrants to New England, where they expected to set up a Bible Commonwealth. When England and Scotland signed the Solemn League and Covenant in 1643, it was designed not only to

[2] Walter Ralegh, "The 11th and last book of the Ocean to Scinthia," in *Poems*, ed. A. M. Latham (London: Routledge and Kegan Paul, 1951), p. 27.

be a military alliance against Charles I but also to be "an encouragement to the Christian churches groaning under or in danger of the yoke of Antichrist" to join in a struggle for liberation.

There was always an inextricable link between the religious duties of the covenanted nations and their economic interests. John Pym was treasurer of the Providence Island Company, an outpost for plundering Spanish America, as well as leader of the Long Parliament and a convinced Puritan. Under Oliver Cromwell, when Parliamentary supremacy had enabled England to build up the strongest navy in Europe, the whole power of the state was put behind the attempt to break Spain's monopoly of South and Central America and the Dutch monopoly of Far Eastern trade, as well as to suppress piracy in the Mediterranean. Charles I had forbidden English merchants to trade in the Mediterranean, because he could give them no protection against pirates: and so he frustrated the switch to exporting the light New Draperies which would compensate for loss of Baltic and North German markets for heavier English cloths. Under Cromwell Admiral Blake suppressed the pirate base in Algiers; England annexed Dunkirk, from which pirates had sacked English shipping even in the Channel. Economic policies, clearly; but rank and file participants in Cromwell's Western Design in 1655 said they were engaged in extending the kingdom of Christ. I fear they believed it. Marvell's poems about Oliver Cromwell glorify his naval aggression against antichristian Spain, in a millenarian spirit; Dryden's *Annus Mirabilis* after the restoration continued to boost the new commercial foreign policy, but no longer in religious terms.

In the millenarian atmosphere of the revolutionary decades, utopian thinking about the forthcoming millennium was rife. But the price of utopia was eternal vigilance. When the civil war failed to usher in Christ's kingdom, when it led indeed to disastrous divisions among the Parliamentarians which enabled Charles I to launch a second civil war in 1648, there was much heartsearching among the saints. Who was to blame? How had the

Chosen Nation fallen short of its responsibilities? The answer was found in Numbers XXXV.33: "blood defileth the land: and the land cannot be cleansed of the blood that is shed therein, but by the blood of him that shed it." Many others texts supported the idea that if the land was not purged of blood guiltiness by identifying and punishing the offender, the nation as a whole (including not least the Parliamentarian Army) would remain responsible, liable to divine retribution.

The answer found among the saints, especially in the Army, was that Charles I was the Man of Blood.[3] For the first civil war Parliamentarians had blamed evil councillors rather than the king; but that evasion of the issue no longer carried conviction now that the imprisoned king, with no councillors about him, had unleashed the bloodshed and misery of a second civil war. Was there to be no end? First the rank and file, then the leadership anxious to maintain Army unity, convinced themselves that Charles I, the Man of Blood, must be brought to justice, in obedience to Biblical injunctions. This belief helped the generals and their supporters to summon up the audacity to commit so unprecedented an action. There was no *legal* justification for regicide. But the declared will of God must override mere human laws. "We will cut off his head with the crown on it," declared Oliver Cromwell.[4]

Regicide was driven on by a group of Biblically inspired enthusiasts. Many believed that the time had come for the rule of the saints pending the Second Coming of King Jesus. "The saints shall judge the world," said George Fox, later the Quaker leader; "whereof I am one," he added.[5]

The democratic republican Levellers, more secular-minded, drew back from regicide, and one effect of the king's execution

---

[3] This paragraph is based on the pioneering work of Patricia Crawford, "Charles Stuart, That Man of Blood," *Journal of British Studies*, 16 (1977); see also Elizabeth Tuttle, *Religion et idéologie dans la révolution anglaise, 1647–1649* (Paris: Edition L'Harmattan, 1989).

[4] R. W. Blencowe (ed.), *Sydney Papers* (London, 1825), p. 237.

[5] G. F. and J. N[ayler], *Sauls Errand to Damascus* (1654), pp. 10–11.

was to weaken Leveller influence with the separatist congregations and the rank and file of the Army. The beneficiaries were the generals, but only at the price of serious divisions among the radicals which ultimately led to their defeat. So the Bible can be held responsible for regicide, for the triumph of Oliver Cromwell and the generals, and for the ultimate failure of the Revolution. In 1660 the throne came to be occupied not by King Jesus but by Charles II, the Merrie Monarch.

A persistent Old Testament theme is the struggle against idolatry, into which the Chosen People were always liable to relapse under the influence of the heathen natives whom they had subjugated. This was closely analogous to still surviving Catholic sentiments in England, associated with shrines and holy places, as Old Testament idolatry had been associated with groves and high places. In the Elizabethan Book of Homilies (sermons to be read by all ministers incapable of writing their own) the longest was that against idolatry. "The nature of man," it said, "is none otherwise bent to worshipping of images (if he may have them and see them) than it is bent to whoredom and adultery in the company of harlots." The great Puritan Richard Sibbes agreed: "naturally all men are idolaters before conversion."[6] All Papists are idolators, which is why they cannot be tolerated. The kings of Israel and Judah lapsed into idolatry, often under the influence (or alleged influence) of foreign (heathen) wives. The parallel with Charles I's Queen Henrietta Maria was irresistible, and was often drawn.

With the collapse of censorship in 1640 there was a printing explosion. Ninety times as many books and pamphlets were published in 1642 as had been in 1640; the number of newspapers rose from 0 before 1640 — when they were illegal — to over 700 by 1645. Pamphlets and newsbooks did not reach only the literate: they were read aloud in alehouses, in marketplaces, and in the Army. It is difficult to grasp the significance of this sudden revolu-

[6] *Complete Works*, ed. A. B. Grosart (Edinburgh: James Nichol, 1862–64), vol. 2, p. 386.

tion. One aspect of it has perhaps not been sufficiently emphasized. After 1640 *anyone* could get into print who could persuade a printer that there was money in his or her idea. For the first time in English history significant numbers of persons ( including women) who had no university education, often no grammar school education even, could publish their thoughts. Demand was insatiable.

So reading matter was no longer monopolized by people with a shared classical education who assumed that discussion must be conducted according to formal rules, starting from a syllogism. The new writers were oblivious to all that. Cobbler How's *The Sufficiency of the Spirits Teaching without Humane-learning*, published in 1640, was a manifesto. He argued that while learning might be useful to scholars, lawyers, and gentlemen, uneducated men were more desirable than scholars in the pulpit, since the Spirit's teaching was all that mattered for understanding "the mind of God." All men should read the Bible and decide for themselves, not as the learned told them. So the Bible liberated the hitherto inarticulate, whose views on politics and morality were not necessarily those of their social superiors.

In the next twenty years 20,000 or so books and pamphlets were published, the majority of which were by authors who were "illiterate" in the eyes of academics. The rules of logic which structured academic controversy were ignored. University scholars treated the newcomers with contempt, and this in its turn fuelled opposition to the universities as such; the whole classical curriculum and the conventions of academic argument were called in question. Indeed, were universities of any use at all?

Men like Gerrard Winstanley stressed proudly that they got their ideas not from books, or from other men, but direct from God, from the Bible, or from common sense. Common sense told Winstanley that co-operation was better than competition, and so a communist society better than a competitive one. Writers like Cobbler How, the Leveller leaders Lilburne, Walwyn, and Wildman, the Ranters Clarkson, Coppin, and Salmon, the Quakers Fox and Nayler, and many, many others, could beat the academics at their own games. Many of those I have named were important opinion-formers. They were supported by university men like William Dell, who joined in the attack on academic education. "Antichrist chose his ministers from the universities," Dell said.

It was a significant turning point in English intellectual life. In the short run the Bible triumphed over the classics and logic; in the long run neither side won. But the universities never recovered their monopoly of correct thinking; the ultimate victor was laicization. John Bunyan was still deeply hurt by academic sneers at him for daring to preach and write without a proper education. He consoled himself with the thought that God's own "are not gentlemen. . . . cannot with Pontius Pilate, speak Hebrew, Greek and Latin." When it came to prose style he could beat them all. The uneducated laity had broken through into opinion-forming and — with Bunyan — into literature.

Liberation of the press made possible publication of new interpretations of Biblical myths. The democratic implications of Adam the gardener were emphasized. "We may see Adam every day walking up and down the street," Winstanley said. The story of the apple was only a legend, at which the devils laughed in *Paradise Lost*: for Winstanley it was allegorically true of all men and women. Traditionally the stories of Cain and Abel, Esau and Jacob, had been used to illustrate the inscrutability of God's will in predestinating some to eternal life, others to damnation: God loved the trickster Jacob but hated simple-minded Esau. For Levellers and especially for Winstanley the younger brothers Abel and Jacob stood for the oppressed classes in society, tyrannized over by their elder brothers, who would ultimately be overthrown. Primogeniture was a target for Leveller and Digger attack because of its tendency to concentrate property in the hands of the eldest son to the detriment of younger sons and daughters. This was a grievance affecting younger sons of the gentry as well as of yeomen and peasants. The fact that David and Solomon, like Abel and Jacob and Joseph, were younger sons was emphasized: so too were the self-made men who rose to prominence in the Bible — David, Gideon, Samson.

There were two views of Samson in the seventeenth century. According to one interpretation he was a violent man whose claims to divine support were unfounded, and he died a reprobate in the useless destruction of the Philistines. The other interpretation saw him as a predestined saint, who fell into temptation and sinned, but who suffered, repented, and was given divine strength to seize his opportunity to destroy God's enemies — the Philistine aristocracy and priests. The former view — Samson the terrorist — was by and large that of conservatives; the latter — Samson the freedom-fighter — was that of the radicals, including Milton in *Samson Agonistes*. Some modern critics still defend the conservative view.

Another multifaceted myth is that of the wilderness, in which the Israelites, on their way from Egypt to the Promised Land, languished for many years. The wilderness is neither as bad as the lands of captivity nor as good as the still unreachable Zion. It became a potent consolatory symbol for men like William Sedgwick and William Erbery. The saints "are in a wilderness, in a desolate barren estate," Sedgwick said in 1648 as he awaited the time when the saints would judge the world. "Satan and wicked men have reigned long, but they shall reign no longer." God will shine forth, significantly, "in those that are the lowest of the people." [7] Erbery — like Milton — thought that the church had been in the wilderness since the time of the Apostles and that the saints would be "bewildernessed" until the Second Coming, which Erbery awaited with growing despair. Only "after the fall of Rome shall there be new heavens and new earth." [8]

[7] Sedgwick, *Some Flashes of Lightnings of the Sonne of Man* (1648); *A Second View of the Army Remonstrance* (1649), p. 15.

[8] *The Testimony of William Erbery* (1658), sig. (a); cf. p. 65. Both passages are by John Webster, editor of this posthumous collection of Erbery's works. A not unfair summary of Erbery's views is given in Thomas Edwards's *Gangraena* (1646), part I, p. 78, part II, pp. 89–90.

Many sectaries followed the Bible in contrasting the wilderness of the world with the garden of the church, separated by its hedge of discipline and doctrinal orthodoxy. An analogy was the enclosure of land from the waste. This was relevant to the English enclosure movement and to the colonization of Ireland and North America. It was the duty of the saints to bring the earth under cultivation and to bring the heathen into the church. Here was justification not only for enclosure and eviction in England but also for expropriation of the natives in Ireland and New England. Radical Protestantism was strong among the Elizabethan sea-dogs and among colonizers of Ireland and New England.

Some radicals reacted against the heavy Old Testament Biblicism of traditional Puritans, perhaps disliking the vengeful cries of Old Testament prophets calling for extermination of the heathen. They put new emphasis on the sceptical subversiveness of Jesus of Nazareth, his questioning of accepted shibboleths. William Walwyn specialized in this line of approach, but Milton, Gerrard Winstanley, and Clement Writer pursued the same line of thought. Arguing against the orthodox who attacked the radical Family of Love, Walwyn asked them innocently, "What family are you of, I pray?" [9]

Conflicting interpretations of Biblical stories and of the lessons to be drawn from them led to an intensification of Biblical scholarship and growing doubts about the absolute infallibility of the Bible as a guide to action in all spheres of life. Under Elizabeth, Ralegh, Hariot, and Marlowe called traditional Bibliolatry in question in their "school of atheism." At a time when exploration and trade expansion were bringing English merchants into contact with different civilizations and religions, it is perhaps no accident that Ralegh and Hariot were enquiring explorers and colonizers and that Marlowe had a wider historical and geographical imagination than any other Elizabethan dramatist — as witness *Tambur-*

---

[9] *The Writings of William Walwyn*, ed. J. R. McMichael and B. Taft (Georgia University Press, 1989), p. 79: *The Power of Love* (1643).

*laine* and *Faustus*. Such awareness surfaced after 1640. In 1649 the Koran was translated into English.

I quote words attributed to Walwyn: "the Scripture is so plainly and directly contradictory to itself" that he could not believe it to be the Word of God.[10] It was a historical document to be interpreted just like any other. Winstanley made great use of Biblical myths, but thought that whether there were such happenings as the Gospel narrative tells us "it matters not much." [11] Ranters like Abiezer Coppe and Joseph Salmon also distinguished between "the history" and "the mystery." Some Ranters were said to believe that the Bible "hath been the cause of all our misery and divisions, . . . of all the blood that hath been shed in the world." [12] Thomas Tany publicly burned the Bible to make the point.

The Worcestershire clothier Clement Writer produced serious works denying the infallibility of the Bible because of its many errors and contradictions. "The Scriptures report the miracles; can the miracles reported by the Scripture confirm that report?" [13] The most impressive summing up of this sceptical scholarship was *The Rusticks Alarm to the Rabbies*, published by the ex-Baptist Quaker Samuel Fisher in 1660. Protestants, he said, had believed that "all would be unity itself among them" once they had replaced the traditions of the church by the text of the Bible; he might have been referring to Milton's *Areopagitica*, published in the more hopeful year 1644. But in fact, Fisher continued, "dark minds diving into the Scripture divine lies enough out of it to set whole countries on fire." The Bible, he declared, was read too

---

[10] [Anon.], *Walwins Wiles* (1649), in *Leveller Tracts*, ed. W. Haller and G. Davies (New York: Columbia University Press, 1944), p. 298.

[11] Winstanley, *The Law of Freedom and Other Writings* (Cambridge: Cambridge University Press, 1983), p. 232: *Fire in the Bush* (1650).

[12] My *The World Turned Upside Down* (Penguin ed.), p. 262.

[13] Writer, *Fides Divina* (1657), *passim*; *An Apologetical Narration* (2nd ed., 1658), pp. 62, 78.

much and quoted too often. We must "turn to the light and Word within." [14]

Fisher's huge tome was published too late to be publicly discussed in England: strict censorship of books of that sort was restored with Charles II. But he was read by Spinoza, and through Spinoza the attitude toward the Bible of Fisher and his predecessors in England passed into the European Enlightenment.[15]

Later in the century, from a more radical Protestant angle, M.M. (M. Marsin or Mercin) also dealt cavalierly with the text of the Bible. Its statements, she said, should be divided into two kinds: doctrinal, which are binding on Christians; and historical, which are of interest but of no binding authority. Among the latter is St. Paul's instruction to the Corinthians that women should not be allowed to preach. This was because St. Paul had lost his temper with some Corinthian women and is of no general significance. Immediately following this, M.M. hinted that when God sentenced all women to subjection to men because of Eve's transgression he too may have overreacted — just like St. Paul. She doesn't actually say that, but it seems to me to be implicit in the way she puts it. Women found their subordination "intolerable," she added.[16] We have come far. Now the Bible is used to subvert traditions hitherto supported by the Bible.

Consideration of the literary importance of the Bible is too vast a subject, but it must be mentioned. Popular Biblical drama helped to spread Protestant propaganda, from John Bale onward. It helped early London theatres to win audiences, though once the novelty had worn off it yielded to more secular plays in face of

---

[14] *The Rusticks Alarm*, in Fisher, *The Testimony of Truth Exalted* (1679), pp. 440–41.

[15] R. H. Popkin, "Spinoza, the Quakers and the Millennium, 1656–1658," *Manuscrito*, 6 (Brazil, 1982); "Spinoza and the Conversion of the Jews," in *Spinoza's Political and Theological Thought*, ed. C. De Deugd (Amsterdam, 1984).

[16] M.M., *Good News to the Good Women* (1700), pp. 14–16. I am deeply indebted to Tim Hitchcock of the Polytechnic of North London for introducing me to M.M.

Puritan hostility to the stage. Milton's *Samson Agonistes* was never intended to be acted. Sixteenth- and seventeenth-century ballads, madrigals, and lute songs draw heavily on Biblical themes, now newly available in the vernacular. Translations and paraphrases of the Psalms formed a significant literary genre from Wyatt to Milton, preparing the way for metaphysical poetry and the poetry of meditation. The paradoxes of the Bible — comparing the kingdom of heaven to a mustard seed, referring the sluggard to the ant, contrasting the lilies of the field with Solomon in all his glory, welcoming home the prodigal son with the fatted calf, declaring that the poor shall inherit the earth, that wisdom is folly and folly wisdom, and that death is the crown of life — these are startling effects of constrast which delighted those who eagerly read Donne and his followers.

> Nor ever chaste unless you ravish me.
> Created sick, commanded to be sound.
> Here in dust and dirt, oh here
> The lilies of his love appear.
> [Christ came] leaping upon the hills to be
> The humble king of you and me.

The "double heart" of the metaphysical poets derives from Psalm XII.2 and the Epistle of James I.8. The paradoxical element in the Bible fitted the conflicts and contradictions of a society in transition such as England in the late sixteenth and early seventeenth centuries. The Song of Songs, because it was held to be an allegory for the love affair between Christ and his church, gave a new respectability to erotic poetry: few were the poets who did not try their hand at paraphrasing it. Paraphrase of other books of the Bible led on to a spate of Biblical epics, a tradition which culminated in *Paradise Lost* and *Paradise Regained* and faded away in the mock epics *Absalom and Achitophel* and Samuel Pordage's retort, *Azariah and Hushai*.

We miss much that is significant in Elizabethan and Jacobean literature if we ignore the Bible. Royalist theorists applied the text "Touch not mine anointed" to kings, whereas in fact — as was recalled in the revolutionary decades — the Bible applies it to believers, who are not to be molested by political authorities. Shakespeare nearly always uses the phrase ironically in relation to divine right theories. The usurper Richard III described himself as "the Lord's anointed." The king who uses the famous phrase "such divinity doth hedge a king" is the usurping regicide Claudius in *Hamlet*. Whenever Richard II makes a particularly eloquent speech about "the balm" which "not all the water in the rough rude sea can wash . . . from an anointed king," we know that something dreadful is just about to happen to him, until finally "with mine own tears I wash away my balm."

Boys and girls learnt to read from the Bible; then they went on to Biblical chapbooks, ballads, and madrigals. Biblical epics based on stories from the Old and New Testaments provided reading matter for the eagerly curious newly literate, a gap which was ultimately to be filled by the novel. The Bible offered an easy fund of stories for literary hacks to draw on until the material had been exhausted. Then Defoe took over.

Since I have emphasized radical use of the Bible for innovatory purposes, perhaps I may suggest some areas in which the Bible was not a source of innovation but of defence of the status quo.

What to us seems the most serious constraint of the Bible on seventeenth-century radical reformers is its attitude toward women. It reinforced the pressures working against equality of the sexes — the household economy, the long tradition of excluding women from public and professional life and from equal education. It is an unfortunate fact that the sacred texts of the three great religions — Judaism, Islam, and Christianity — date from the heyday of patriarchy. There are surviving traces in the Old Testament of prepatriarchal female warrior leaders who recall Boadicea in pre-Roman Britain. There are prophetesses. But the patriarchs dominate.

"Thou shalt not covet thy neighbour's wife, nor his ox, nor his ass, . . . nor anything that is his" ran the tenth commandment:

a wife is a piece of property, of livestock. Wives could be repudiated. The Bible says nothing against women coveting their neighbours' husbands: husbands were not property to be owned or stolen. Similarly the command in Exodus "thou shalt not suffer a witch to live" proved fatal to many a poor old woman and was a real obstacle to the slow emergence of a rational attitude to accusations of witchcraft.

St. Paul told wives to submit themselves to their husbands and to keep silent in church. If they had problems, they must ask their husbands in the privacy of their homes. One argument for the inferiority of women was that the Bible said God created Adam before he created Eve. But this was being challenged. A Tory defender of women's rights, Mary Astell, in 1706 asked whether men who used this text ever noticed that God created the animals before he created Adam. What should we conclude from that?[17]

Christ's "Ye have the poor always with you" (Matthew XXVI.11) seemed to countenance the institutionalization of poverty in the Elizabethan poor law and to accept its inevitability: "the poor" rather than "poor people." Racialism too — Columbus, we are told, got from the Bible his attitude toward the Indians whom he met in America: servitude was the necessary fate of all the descendants of Ham. The consequences could hardly have been worse, or more lasting. The analogy between Old Testament and Irish or Indian "heathenism" seemed to authorize forcible suppression in both cases. The Bible had a strong delaying effect on the emergence of an antislavery movement.

The same is perhaps true of theories of toleration. There is much intolerance in the Old Testament: Roger Williams observed that "persecutors seldom plead Christ, but Moses."[18] Walwyn

---

[17] Mary Astell, *Reflections upon Marriage*, in *The First English Feminist*, ed. Bridget Hill (Aldershot: Gower/Temple Smith, 1986), p. 76.

[18] Quoted by D. M. Wolfe, *Milton in the Puritan Revolution* (New York: Nelson, 1941), p. 33.

was most unusual in declaring, "The Word of God is express for toleration." [19] Those who advocated toleration in England wanted it not on abstract general principles but as a means of establishing unity against an enemy. For radical Protestants that enemy was international Catholicism, against which all who rejected the pope could be united, even if they did not accept the national church; but for many members of that church peaceful papists seemed less dangerous than radical sectaries. Toleration was from this point of view an aspect of foreign policy. So long as the Thirty Years War continued, and a Papist invasion of England (or Ireland) seemed a real possibility, radical Protestants strongly opposed toleration for Papists. Throughout the period one group remained beyond the pale of toleration: those who denied the existence of God. This was thought to preclude a recognition of rewards and punishments in the afterlife, regarded as a necessary prop of the unequal social order. This consideration should be borne in mind when we comment — as we must — on the absence of evidence for open atheism in the seventeenth century.

De facto the hegemony of the Bible ended with the English Revolution in which it had played so large a part. In 1657 an M.P. was jeered at for citing "a Scripture to confirm what he said." [20] The fact that Thomas Hobbes quoted the Bible so extensively (657 times in *Leviathan*, and as often again in his other political works) [21] confirmed many in the growing belief that you could prove anything by judicious selection of Biblical texts. Whether or not it was Hobbes's intention, political theory was henceforth argued primarily in non-Biblical terms. The point can be made from a different angle in relation to James Harrington. In his *Oceana* (1656) the argument is primarily secular, with

[19] Walwyn, *Toleration Justified and Persecution Condemned* (1646), in *Writings of William Walwyn*, p. 170.

[20] *Diary of Sir Archibald Johnston of Wariston*, vol. 3, *1655–1660*, ed. J. D. Ogilvie (Scottish History Society, 1940), p. 71.

[21] This is the estimate of Wolfgang Palaver, in *International Hobbes Association Newsletter*, new series, 10 (November 1989), 24–31.

occasional Biblical allusions. But in later writings defending *Oceana* he made a case for saying that his utopia was entirely Biblical. This was certainly an afterthought, intended to reconcile the then dominant godly to his schemes. But the popularity of Harringtonianism in the century after 1660 owed nothing to this *ex post facto* Biblicism.

The Bible was used in the 1640s, especially by lower-class sectaries, to subvert traditional orthodoxies accepted by those whose opinions mattered. In the 1640s and 1650s radicals defended very different moralities — Leveller egalitarian democracy, Digger communism, Ranter free love. The impossibility of reaching agreement led to Biblical criticism and ultimately scepticism about the authority of the Bible. How right Henry VIII had been to try to restrict Bible reading, and especially discussion of the Bible, to the upper classes!

Restoration of monarchy and the Church of England in 1660 established and enforced a new consensus among those whose opinions mattered. But the latter had learnt a lot. They now recognized the dangers of attributing absolute authority to a Bible whose interpretation was contentious. Lady Brute in Vanbrugh's *The Provoked Wife*, when confronted with the Biblical command to return good for evil, retorted simply by saying "that may be a mistake in the translation."

Vanbrugh's play and Mary Astell's and M.M.'s treatises all appeared in print, interestingly, after the ending of censorship in 1695. By the end of the century the Bible had ceased to be the centre of intellectual discussion. It continued to be of the greatest importance for belief and conduct during the next two centuries, especially among dissenters. But it never again reached the peak of unimpeachable authority which it attained between the first appearance of the printed Bible in English and the defeat of the Biblical revolution in the mid-seventeenth century.

Historians who try to argue that the English Revolution had no long-term causes or consequences have not reflected sufficiently on this fact. Religion did not cause the Revolution, nor was the Bible a casualty of it. But the absolute sovereignty of the Bible was a victim of the wide-ranging political, social, and intellectual revolution which overthrew the traditional monarchy with its Star Chamber and High Commission, handing control of the state over to Parliament and taxpayers who set England on the path of colonial and commercial imperialism, which by the end of the century had made her top nation — though by then English aggression was no longer justified in the name of overcoming Antichrist. The Revolution also established greater freedom of religious worship, of the press, and of discussion and so promoted secularism. The Bible could now be treated facetiously *in print*, not only by a dramatist but also by a pious Anglican like Mary Astell. The infallible Bible contributed very largely to making the Revolution — and in the process lost its infallibility.

*VÁCLAV HAVEL*

THE TANNER LECTURES ON HUMAN VALUES

Delivered at

University of California, Los Angeles
October 25, 1991

VÁCLAV HAVEL, Czechoslovak playwright, writer, and politician, was educated at the Academy of Arts, Prague. A former spokesman for the Charter 77 human rights movement, he was imprisoned on several occasions for "subversive" and "antistate" activities, and was sentenced to nine months' imprisonment for incitement and obstruction in February 1989, less than a year before he became President of Czechoslovakia in December 1989. He has been awarded numerous honorary degrees and prizes, including the Austrian State Prize for European Literature 1968, Olof Palme Prize 1989, Frankfurt Book Fair Peace Prize 1989, and the Simón Bolívar Prize 1990, among others. Author of many works, his most recent are *Slum Clearance* (1988), *Letters to Olga* (1989), *Temptation* (1989), and *Disturbing the Peace* (1990).

Mr. President, ladies and gentlemen: I have come to beautiful sunny California from a country where forests are dying, where rivers resemble sewers and drains, where there are places where people are sometimes advised that they should not open their windows, and where you can see on television advertisements for gas masks recommended for children to wear on their way to and from school. I have come to the West Coast of the United States of America from a small country in the center of Europe in which gaps that were once left unplowed between fields were removed so that land is now sliding down, soil is disintegrating and deteriorating, then to be poisoned by chemical fertilizers which, in turn, contaminate the groundwater. Birds that used to live in the fields have nowhere to nest and, consequently, are dying out while agricultural workers are compelled to use chemicals again to combat vermin. I have come from a country that supplies the whole of Europe with a strange export article: sulphur dioxide.

For years I was one of those who criticized all that; now I am one of those who are criticized for all that.

When thinking about what has brought about this horrible condition, and encountering time and again obstacles preventing us from changing it speedily, I always arrive at the conclusion that its root causes are not of a technical or economic nature, but rather of a philosophical nature. That is, I see in the Marxist ideology and the Communist pattern of governing an extreme and alarming example of the haughtiness of modern humanity, which has named itself the master of nature and of the world, the only one who understands them, whom everything has to serve and for whose sake this planet is in existence. Intoxicated by the achievements of the mind, by modern science and technology, people entirely forget that this knowledge has its limits and that beyond these limits there is a great mystery, something higher and infinitely more sophisticated than their own intellect.

I am increasingly inclined to believe that even the term "environment," which is inscribed on the banners of numerous commendable civic movements, is in a way misguided as it is, unwittingly, a product of the same anthropocentrism that has caused the extensive devastation of our earth. The word "environment" somehow tacitly implies that whatever is not human is just something that environs humanity, surroundings inferior to us which we should, in our own interest, tend or care for. I do not think that this is the case. The world is not divided into two types of being, one superior and the other just surrounding the former. The universe, nature, being is one infinitely complex and mysterious metaorganism of which humanity is but a part, even if an original one. Every one of us is a crossroads of thousands of relations, links, influences, and communications — physical, chemical, biological, and other — of which we know nothing. While there would have been no *Challenger* space shuttle without humanity, there would have been no humanity without air, water, and earth, without thousands of incidents which cannot be incidental, and thanks to which there can be a planet on which there can be life. Every one of us is a very special and complex interlacing of space, time, substance, and energy, but nothing more than an interlacing thereof, unthinkable without them and without the order of the universe of which they are dimensions. And none of us knows how a single quiver of a shrub in California influences the state of mind of a miner in the north of Bohemia, and how the miner's state of mind affects the quiver of the Californian shrub. I believe that people will hardly avert the danger of an environmental catastrophe unless they realize that humanity is not the master of being, but only a part thereof — the fact that humans are the only components of being known to us to date that are aware of their being, and even of the fact that it will end one day, does not change anything.

Yet one who has said "A" has to say "B" as well. One who has recognized that we are but tiny particles in a grand physical structure has to realize sooner or later that we are but particles of a grand metaphysical structure as well. We have to realize that we are not related only to the present moment and the present place but also to the world as a whole and to eternity. We have to recognize that we will do a disservice to our immediate, temporary, local, and particular interests if we fail to pay regard to the universal, superindividual, and supertemporal interests. Only those who have a sense of responsibility for the world, toward the world, and before the world are genuinely responsible toward themselves, and for themselves.

The Communist rulers of Czechoslovakia acted according to the concept *après nous le déluge* (after us the deluge). They secured for themselves undisturbed life in positions of power by bribing the whole society with money stolen from future generations, hoping that nobody would notice. Miners in strip mines extracting poor-quality brown coal, which was then improperly burnt in heating plants with no filters, could be satisfied because they could easily buy VCRs. When sitting in front of them, tired from work, and watching video programs they did not notice that their children who joined them had pus in their eyes. But their wives did. While they were glad to see their husbands bringing home fair sums of money, they were beginning to be suspicious about that same money. They were beginning to realize that if they had been getting less and the rest had been invested in more modern and cleaner ways of power generation their children's eyes would not have been constantly irritated. The *après nous le déluge* concept is typical of those who do not feel related to any order other than that of their own benefit. It is a nihilistic concept of those who have forgotten that they are but component parts of the world, not the world's proprietors. It is a concept of those who do not feel related to eternity, who have styled themselves masters of space and time.

I believe that the devastation of the environment brought about by the Communist regimes is a warning to the whole contemporary civilization. I believe that you should read the message coming to you from our part of the world as an appeal to rise in defense against all those who despise the mystery of being, be it cynical business people caring for nothing but the interests of their corporations or left-wing saviors who have fallen for the narcotic of cheap ideological utopias. The former as well as the latter lack what I would call a metaphysical anchor, that is, a humble respect for the entirety of creation and consciousness of our obligation toward it.

It is not my intention to be a mentor to anyone, least of all to teachers and students of this venerable university. Yet I have deemed it my duty to share with you the philosophical experience which I — like many of my fellow citizens — had in the environment I come from. This experience is probably the principal article that we can and should export from my country at this moment.

If I were to embody that experience in one simple sentence I would probably phrase it as follows: if parents believe in God their children will not have to wear gas masks when going to school and will not have pus in their eyes.

Thank you for your attention.

*Decisions of Principle, Principles of Decision*

ROBERT NOZICK

THE TANNER LECTURES ON HUMAN VALUES

Delivered at

Princeton University
November 13 and 15, 1991

ROBERT NOZICK, currently Arthur Kingsley Porter Professor of Philosophy at Harvard University and past Chairperson of the Philosophy Department, was educated at Columbia College and Princeton University. He is a member of the Council of Scholars of the Library of Congress, a Fellow of the American Academy of Arts and Sciences, and a Senior Fellow of the Society of Fellows at Harvard. He is also a member of PEN, America, and the Author's Guild. He was a cultural advisor to the U.S. Delegation to the UNESCO Conference on World Cultural Policy held in Mexico City in 1982, and has made several television programs for public broadcasting, serving as host and interviewer. He is the author of numerous books and articles, including *The Examined Life* (1989) and *Philosophical Explanations* (1981), which received the Ralph Waldo Emerson Award of Phi Beta Kappa. Professor Nozick received a National Book Award for *Anarchy, State and Utopia* (1974).

1. How to Do Things with Principles

What are principles *for*? Why do we hold principles, why do we put them forth, why do we adhere to them? We could instead simply act on whim or the passion of the moment, or we could maximize our own self-interest and recommend that others do the same. Are principles then a constraint upon whim and self-interest, or is adherence to principles a way of advancing self-interest? What functions do principles serve?

Principles of action group actions, placing them under general rubrics; linked actions are then to be viewed or treated in the same way. This generality can serve different functions: intellectual, interpersonal, intrapersonal, and personal. I start with the intellectual.

*Intellectual Functions*

Consider judicial decision making. In one system, a judge simply decides a case so as to yield what she thinks is the best or right or preferable result in that particular case. Another system of judicial decision involves principled decision: a common law judge is to formulate a principle to fit (most or almost all) past precedents and a range of hypothetical cases and then use this principle to decide the current case. Trying to formulate an acceptable general principle is a *test* of your judgment about the par-

---

These lectures were delivered at Princeton University, where I was a graduate student, and I dedicate them to my teachers there: to Carl Hempel and to the memory of Gregory Vlastos. The first draft of these lectures was written at the Rockefeller Foundation Research Center at Bellagio, Italy, in the summer of 1989. I am grateful to the discussants of these lectures at Princeton, Clifford Geertz, Gilbert Harman, Susan Hurley, and Amos Tversky, and also to Scott Brewer, David Gordon, Christine Korsgaard, Bill Puka, Tim Scanlon, and Gisella Striker, for their very helpful comments and suggestions. Special thanks to Amartya Sen for the many discussions of this material we have had, inside of class and out, and to Laurance Rockefeller for his interest in and generous support of this research project.

ticular case: is there *some* adequate general principle — a principle that gives the right result in all established cases and obvious hypothetical ones — that also yields the result you want in this case? If you cannot find such a principle, reconsider what result you do want in this case.

Such a procedure is a test of a particular judgment on the assumption that any correct judgment is yielded by *some* true acceptable general principle, that true particular judgments are consequences of general principles applied to specific situations. If search fails to uncover an acceptable general principle that yields some judgment in particular, this may be because there is no such acceptable principle, in which case that particular judgment is mistaken and should be abandoned. Or perhaps you have not been astute enough to formulate the correct principle. We have no mechanical procedure to decide which is the explanation.[1]

When you find a general principle or theory that subsumes this case, a principle you would be willing to apply to other cases as well, this particular judgment receives new support. Consider empirical data points $a$, $b$, $c$, $d$. If a straight line is the simplest curve through these, this supports the prediction that another point $e$, also on that straight line, will hold. It is not an easy matter — inductive logicians have discovered — to isolate and explain how a (relatively) simple lawlike statement can group existing data points so that inferences and predictions legitimately can be made about new points. Nevertheless, we do not doubt that data can support the hypothesis that a law holds and also support a prediction that a new point will accord with that law. Similarly, the simplest principle that covers acceptable normative points $a$, $b$, $c$, $d$ also will support an additional judgment $e$ (that

---

[1] A weaker assumption would maintain not that *every* correct judgment is yielded by an acceptable principle but that some or most are. Still, finding an acceptable general principle that yields a particular judgment would (tend to) show that judgment was correct. However, failing to find one would not be a conclusive reason for abandoning the judgment, for it might be one of those that stands alone, no consequence of any acceptable principle.

fits this principle) as a correct normative point too. A theorist gains confidence in his particular judgment (or side in a controversy) when he can formulate a general principle or theory to fit it, especially one that is appealing on its face.[2]

Philosophers of science have tried to demarcate scientific laws from accidental generalizations. Accidental generalizations only happen to hold, or to have held, true. From such a generalization — for example, that all the coins in my pocket are dimes — one cannot infer a subjunctive statement such as: if there *were* an additional coin in my pocket now, it *would be* a dime. (Whereas from a scientific law — for instance, that all freely falling bodies fall a distance equal to $\frac{1}{2}gt^2$ — we can infer that if some other object now at rest were in free fall it would travel a distance equal to $\frac{1}{2}gt^2$.) If all previous data fit a given generalization, we can plausibly infer that new data would fit it (and hence predict that new data that *will* be gathered will fit it) *only if* that generalization is of lawlike form and is a candidate for being a law. It is when data fall under a lawlike statement (or arise from several of them) that we can legitimately extrapolate to further cases. The features of a lawlike statement, those aspects that differentiate it from an accidental generalization, constitute our license to travel from given data to predictions or expectations about further data. Similarly for particular normative judgments: what licenses us to travel to a further judgment on the basis of previous ones is the previous ones' all falling under a normative general principle. The

---

[2] Mark Tushnet has argued that in the legal arena the requirement of principled decision constitutes no constraint upon the result a judge can reach; if the previous cases fit a principle (even an established one) whose result the judge wishes to avoid in the present case, this case always can be distinguished from the others by some feature or other. (See "Following the Rules Laid Down: A Critique of Interpretavism and Neutral Principles," *Harvard Law Review*, 96 [1983], 781–827.) However, merely to distinguish the case (at best) allows the new judgment, it does not *support* it. To support it, the judge would have to formulate a new principle, plausible on its face, that fits (most of) the old cases, this new one and some obvious hypothetical ones as well; that is, she would need a principled rationale for the distinction she wishes to make, and for why that distinction should make a difference. It is no easy matter to formulate acceptable principles, much less to do this as frequently as one's desires about new cases would mandate.

features of a normative principle license a subjunctive inference to a new case that steps beyond the indicative instances that happen already to have fallen under it. Principles are transmission devices for *probability* or *support*; this flows from data or cases, via the principle, to judgments and predictions about new observations or cases whose status otherwise is unknown or less certain.

What features enable principles to transmit probability? The following features have been mentioned to distinguish scientific lawlike statements (or nomic universals) from accidental generalizations.[3] Lawlike statements do not contain terms for particular individual objects, dates, or temporal periods — or if they do, these statements can be derived from more general lawlike statements that do not. Lawlike statements contain purely qualitative predicates: stating the meaning of these does not require reference to any *particular* object or spatio-temporal location. Lawlike statements have an unrestricted universality; they are not simply a finite conjunction that was established by examining all cases. Lawlike statements are supported not just by instances falling under them, but also by a linkage of indirect evidence.

These very same features might be what enables a normative principle to license the derivation of new judgments from previously accepted ones. Writers on ethics frequently say ethical principles must be formulated using general terms only, no names of particular persons, groups, or nations. This feature might enable a principle to license an inference to a new case, hence enable new normative judgments to be supported by previous ones. A generalization lacking this feature of non-particularity might be, at best, an accidental one, incapable of transferring support from some data to others. When moral principles are general and do not contain any non-qualitative predicates or particular names, rather than being a specifically *moral* aspect of the principles, this feature might link data or judgments together to support subjunc-

[3] See C. G. Hempel, *Aspects of Scientific Explanation* (New York: Free Press, 1965), pp. 264–72, and Ernest Nagel, *The Structure of Science* (New York: Harcourt, Brace and World, 1961), pp. 47–78.

tive inferences. It would be worthwhile to investigate how much of the "form" of moral principles is necessary for such linkage.

This does not mean these features are tagged onto weaker generalizations to make moral principles that perform inferential functions, any more than such features are tagged onto accidental generalizations to make scientific laws. One can hold that scientific laws and moral principles each hold true apart from any constructions we add or any uses of them we make, that their independent truth is what makes these uses possible. Nevertheless, features such as generality, containing no proper names, no positional predicates, would not be specifically *moral* features, but lawlike ones, necessary for anything to be a law, scientific or moral. In context, not specifically moral features may have moral consequences.

A person may seek principles not only to test her own judgment or give it more support but to convince others or to increase their conviction. To do this she cannot simply announce her preference for a position — she must produce reasons convincing to the others. Reasons might be very particular but also can be general considerations that apply well to a wide range of cases and point to a particular judgment in this instance. If these judgments in the other cases are ones the other person already accepts, then the general reasoning will recruit these cases as evidence and support for the judgment proposed in the present case. Principles or general theories thus have an interpersonal intellectual function, justification to another. Justification by general principles is convincing in two ways: by the face appeal of the principles and by recruiting other already accepted cases to support a proposed position in this case.[4]

In using a judge to illustrate the testing and support function of principles, I have imagined that her purpose is to arrive at the right decision about a particular case and that she treats the past

---

[4] Abstract principled reasoning lends support to a particular position by recruiting other accepted judgments as support, but is this only one particular mode of justification, an abstract and impersonal *male* mode?

decisions as (for the most part) right themselves. That is, I have treated a judge as structurally identical to a moral reasoner who wishes to decide what is right or permissible on this new occasion or situation and who utilizes her knowledge of what is right or permissible in other actual or hypothetical situations to formulate, test, and support a moral principle that yields a result for this situation.

Of course, a judge also is a figure in an institutional structure; principled decisions that fit past cases may have a particular point within that institution. Legal theorists tell us the doctrine of respecting precedents, *stare decisis*, can enable people to predict more exactly the legal system's future decisions and so to plan actions with some confidence about their legal consequences.[5] For this effect, the precedents need not have been decided correctly or be followed with the goal of reaching a right decision; they are followed in order to yield a result that has been expected. Second, principled decisionmaking might be desired to constrain a judge's basis for decision. To be excluded are her personal preferences or prejudices, moods of the moment, partiality for one side in a dispute, or even thought-through moral and political principles that are personal to her. It might be held that a judge's own views, preferences, or even considered views should have no more effect than anybody else's — the judge was not given that institutional position to put her own preferences into effect. A requirement that decisions be principled fittings to past precedents might be a device to *constrain* the effect of such personal factors, limiting their play or crowding them out *altogether*.

However, the analogy to science where the aim is truth and correctness casts doubt upon the last strong claim. Fitting the scientific data is a requirement — here too there is leeway, and different ways a "best fit" can be defined. But this does not uniquely

---

[5] I have not checked to see what empirical studies of people's decisions exist to support this *empirical* claim by the legal theorists, what alternative legal structure functioned as the control, etc.

determine one lawlike statement. An indefinite number of curves can fit any finite set of data points; more than one will be lawlike. Hence additional criteria will be necessary to select which lawlike statement to tentatively accept and use in predicting. These criteria include simplicity, analogy to supported lawlike statements in related areas,[6] fit with other accepted theories, explanatory power, theoretical fruitfulness, and perhaps ease of computation.[7] Merely requiring that a prediction fit the past data according to some lawlike statement does not uniquely determine that prediction. How likely is it, then, that merely requiring that a judge's decision in a new case fit past decisions according to some principle will suffice to uniquely determine that decision? Indeed, we find judges enjoined to utilize additional criteria, including various "formal" ones.[8] We can raise analogous issues about ethics too. Quine holds that the totality of (possible) empirical data does not uniquely determine an explanatory theory. Are correct ethical principles uniquely determined by the totality of correct judgments about particular cases, actual and hypothetical, or does underdetermination reign there? In addition to fitting particular judgments, must a moral principle also satisfy certain further criteria?

There is a connection between using principles as a device for reaching correct decisions and using them to constrain the influ-

---

[6] All of the small number of data points we possess seem to fall on a straight line, but for all related phenomena we have found that a linear relationship does not hold. Perhaps here it is an accident of the particular data we happen to have.

[7] See the list of factors in Thomas Kuhn, "Objectivity, Value Judgment and Theory Choice," in his *The Essential Tension* (Chicago: University of Chicago Press, 1977), pp. 320–39, and W. V. Quine and Joseph Ullian, *The Web of Belief*, 2nd ed. (New York: Random House, 1978), pp. 64–82. The need for such additional criteria may not result just from the finiteness of our data. Quine has claimed that the totality of all possible observations does not uniquely select an explanatory theory. (See his "On the Reasons for Indeterminacy of Translation," *Journal of Philosophy*, 67 [1970], 178–83, and "On Empirically Equivalent Systems of the World," *Erkenntnis*, 9 [1975], 313–28.) It is difficult to determine the truth of this strong claim without an adequate theory of explanation and of what detailed structure the explanatory relation might involve.

[8] See P. Atiyah and R. Summers, *Form and Substance in Anglo-American Law: A Comparative Study in Legal Reasoning, Legal Theory, and Legal Institutions* (Oxford: Oxford University Press, 1987).

ence of undesired or irrelevant factors such as personal preference. We want to decide or judge a particular case by considering all and only the relevant reasons concerning it. A general principle, which forces us to look at other actual and hypothetical cases, can help test whether a reason $R$ we think is relevant or conclusive in this case really is so. Would $R$ be relevant or conclusive in another case? If reasons are general, we can check $R$'s force in this case by considering other cases. Moreover, deciding via a general principle can call our attention to other relevant reasons, ones we have not yet noticed in this case. Looking at another case where feature $R$ does *not* have great force might lead us to notice another feature $F$ that the present case has, and it is $R$ and $F$ together which have great force. (If we hadn't looked at the other case, we might have thought $R$ alone was enough.) Including all the relevant reasons might help to ensure that *only* relevant reasons are used, *if* these fill the space and so crowd out irrelevant ones. And will we really be willing to accept the impact that an irrelevant reason imposed in this case also would have upon other cases and examples? Notice that this use of hypothetical or other actual cases to test a judgment in this case already assumes that reasons are *general*. If we assume that things happen or hold for a reason (or cause) and that reasons (or causes) are general, then a general principle, perhaps defeasible, can be formulated to capture this reason, to explain why an event the scientist studies occurs or why a particular judgment about a case is correct.[9]

Principles can guide us to a correct decision or judgment in a particular case, helping us to test our judgment and to control for personal factors that might lead us astray. The wrongness that principles are to protect us against, on this view, is individualistic — the wrong judgment in *this* case — or aggregative — the wrong judgments in *these* cases which are wrong one by one.

---

[9] It would be interesting to investigate how far the parallel between the structural features of reasons and of causes extends and to explain why this parallelism holds. Do reasons show parallels to phenomena of probabilistic causality?

However, judgments together might have an additional wrong, a *comparative* wrong that occurs when cases that should be decided in the same way are decided differently. It has been held to be a maxim of (formal) justice that like cases should be decided alike; this general maxim leaves open which likenesses are the relevant ones.[10] Principles might function to avoid this injustice or disparity, not simply to get each and every case decided correctly by itself but to get relevantly similar cases decided similarly. But if I see films two weeks in a row, I need not decide which ones to attend on a similar basis. These two similar decisions, then, apparently do *not* count as like cases that must be decided alike. What demarcates the domain within which the maxim of formal justice is to operate? As a moviegoer, I do not see my task in deciding which movie to attend (on either occasion) as that of reaching a *just* decision on that occasion. The issue of comparative injustice arises only in contexts that involve individual justice or injustice, however these latter contexts are marked. If case *A*, calling for a decision of justice, is decided wrongly, that is bad. If now case *B*, relevantly similar, is decided differently — that is, correctly — and if that decision introduces an additional bad into the world, not the result in case *B* itself but the comparative bad of the two cases being decided differently, and this bad stands over and above the badness involved when case *A* was decided incorrectly, then *this* context of justice is a comparative one, invoking the formal maxim of justice.[11] One function of principles, then, may be to avoid this

---

[10] See Herbert Hart, *The Concept of Law* (Oxford: at the Clarendon Press, 1961), pp. 155–59, and Chaim Perlman, *The Idea of Justice and the Problem of Argument* (London: Routledge, Kegan Paul, 1963).

[11] I have said that a necessary condition for invoking the formal maxim of justice is that the context is one in which a just decision is to be reached, but I have not claimed this is a sufficient condition. If there are individual decisions involving justice that do not have that comparative aspect, then a further criterion is needed to mark which contexts involving justice do invoke the formal maxim. In *Anarchy, State, and Utopia* (New York: Basic Books, 1974), chapter 7, I presented a theory of distributive justice, the entitlement theory, which explicitly was not a patterned theory and did not involve comparisons among the holdings of different people. However, that is not to say that the formal maxim would not apply to people's

particular type of injustice, ensuring that like cases will be decided alike. (Whether it would be better to decide both cases wrongly, avoiding the comparative injustice, or to decide one of them correctly, avoiding injustice in that individual case but incurring the comparative injustice, presumably will depend upon particular features of the situation and the cases.)

*Interpersonal Functions*

A principled person can be counted upon to adhere to his principles in the face of inducements or temptations to deviate. Not necessarily in the face of any possible temptation or of extremely great inducement — nevertheless, principles are some barrier to a person's following the desires or interests of the moment. A person's principles of action thus have an interpersonal function, in reassuring others that (usually) he will get past temptations; they also have an intrapersonal function, helping the person himself to get past temptation.

Consider, first, the interpersonal function. When (refraining from) an action is mandated by a person's principles, we can count on it more. Being able to rely to some significant extent upon his behavior, we ourselves can perform actions whose good outcome is contingent upon the principled person's specific behavior. Even were the future to bring him inducements to deviate, we can trust that he will not, and we can rely upon this in planning and executing our own actions. Otherwise we would have to behave differently, for the chance would be too great that this previous behavior would come to naught or to ill. With those personally close to us, we can rely upon their affection and continuing good motivations to produce coordinate actions; with others more distant, we rely upon their principled behavior.

---

holdings arising in accordance with the *same* general principles (of justice in acquisition, transfer, and rectification). Hence, so far as that theory goes, in addition to the injustice of someone's holdings not arising through the operation of those principles, there could be an additional comparative injustice if another's holdings had so arisen (e.g., the first is discriminated against by others who do not let those principles of justice in holdings apply to him).

Such considerations are familiar in discussions of contract law. Contracts enable a person to bind himself to carry out an action, thereby encouraging another to count upon this and thus perform an action which takes her out on a limb that would be sawed off if the first person failed to perform. Since the first person benefits from that second person's action, which would not be performed if the first person had not contractually bound himself to act, this first person is willing in advance to restrict himself to so acting in this case even should his future incentives change. For if his action was left dependent upon the vagaries of future fluctuations, the second person would not perform that complementary action which the first person now wishes her to do.

Principles constitute a form of binding; we bind ourselves to act as the principles mandate. Others can depend upon this behavior, and we too can benefit from others' so depending, for the actions they thereby become willing to do can facilitate our social ease and interactions, and our own personal projects as well.[12] *Announcing* principles is a way to incur (what economists term) reputation effects, making conditions explicit so that deviations are more easily subject to detection. These effects are most pertinent for someone who makes repeated transactions with many people, assuring others that he will act a certain way (in order to avoid diminution of a reputation that serves him in interaction).[13]

These considerations can make a person want to *seem* to others to have particular principles, but why would he actually want to

---

[12] Principles others can count upon our following also might deter them from certain actions rather than inducing them to cooperate. A nation or person with a principle to retaliate against certain offenses, even when that is against his immediate interests, might deter others from such offenses. Announcing such a principle increases the cost of making exceptions in order to ensure that none will be made.

[13] The U.S. government wishes to issue debt and promises not to inflate, but after the debt is taken up by others it will be optimal for the government to inflate — and the others realize this beforehand. Hence the government attempts to commit to rules for managing the currency, to be followed by an agency independent of Congress, rather than leaving itself absolute discretion. See Finn Kydland and Edward Prescott, "Rules Rather Than Discretion," *Journal of Political Economy*, 85 (1977), 473–91.

have them? For most of us, possessing principles may be the most convincing and the least effortful route to seeming to have them, but fiction and real life too abound with skilled deceivers. Suppose a person does want to have a particular principle, and not merely seem to, because this will function most convincingly for others and most easily for himself. *Can* he come to have that principle merely because of its useful interpersonal functions? Mustn't he think the principle is *correct*?

And how reassuring would I find someone's telling me that he believes his holding a principle is indeed necessary to reassure me and others? "But do you hold it," I would wonder, "and how strongly?" If his attitude toward the principle was that it was a reassurance for others, even a very necessary and extremely useful reassurance, wouldn't I wonder about his continuing adherence in the face of monetary temptations or inducements to deviate? What I would want, I think, is for the person to think the principle was *correct* and *right*. Of course, it is not enough that he think this now — his belief must be stable, not subject to overturn by the slightest counterargument or counterinducement. That's what would reassure me sufficiently so that I would run risks whose good outcome was contingent upon his good behavior. And I might be proficient at detecting genuine belief that a principle was correct and be unwilling to run cooperative risks in its absence.[14]

Believing in the correctness of his principles, then, might be a useful trait for a person to have, making possible an expanded range of interactions with others and cooperative activities. This belief could be useful, even if the notion of "correct principles" made no sense at all. For this — let us for the moment suppose — senseless belief, evidenced by the person and detected by others, would be a reliable indicator to them of his future conduct and would lead them to do trusting actions that benefit him too. (Simi-

[14] It would be useful to list and compare what bases other than his accepting principles as objectively valid there might be for reliance upon a person's actions; these might include the other functions of principles which we list whose successful performance does not depend upon a belief in the objective validity of principles.

larly, the belief that certain conduct was divinely prescribed and that all deviations would meet dire punishment might be a useful belief for people to have, whether or not it was true or made any sense at all, provided it guaranteed to others their continuing conduct.) This raises the possibility of a sociobiological explanation not of particular patterns of conduct but of the belief in an objective moral order. Believing in *correctness* might be selected for.

If people are to be assured about my future conduct, it may not be enough for me simply to announce my principles; other people may need to see, upon occasion, that I actually am adhering to these principles. Yet the principles I think most correct or adequate may be difficult for others to observe in operation; those most adequate principles might respond to subtle contextual details, nuances of history or motivation or relationship not known to others or reliably checked by them. "Justice," it is said, "must not only be done but be seen to be done." Yet what if what can be dependably seen and recognized is less complex than (fully) adequate justice requires? The interpersonal function of assuring others that justice is being done or that principles are being followed might necessitate following less subtle and nuanced principles but ones whose applications (and misapplications) can sometimes be checked by others.[15]

Thus, there can be a conflict between fine-tuning a principle to a situation and producing public confidence through the principle. The more fine-tuned the principle, the less easily can its applications be checked by others; on the other hand, beyond a point of coarsening, a principle may fail to inspire confidence, not because it cannot be checked but because *its* applications no longer

[15] David Kreps, *A Course in Microeconomic Theory* (Princeton: Princeton University Press, 1990), p. 763, reports that Robert Wilson argues that publicly held accounting firms who perform external audits of businesses, in order to assure potential investors that the auditors themselves are not suborned by the firms they are auditing, must follow established rules for auditing, rules whose application can be externally checked, even if these practices do not provide the most revealing information about the business's finances. Since the application of these established rules *can* be checked, the auditing firm is able to maintain its reputation as an independent third party.

count as desirable. It has been claimed — the matter is one of some controversy — that women's moral judgments are more finely attuned to situational details and nuances of relationship and motivation than are men's.[16] This difference, *if* indeed it holds, might be due — a statistical generalization — to women's less frequently making (or anticipating making) decisions in a nonfamilial realm where the basis or motives of decision are an object of suspicion. If in some (public) realm assurance must be given to others, anyone in that realm may need to bend (somewhat) to the dictates of what *can* provide assurance, and principles are one such device. Predictions have been made about the moral changes to be effected by women's entering in large numbers into previously male arenas — a good thing for very many reasons — but it is not certain that it will be the arenas rather than the included women who will experience the greater change.

Another person's principles enable me to predict with reasonable (though perhaps not perfect) accuracy some aspects of his behavior and hence lead me to count upon those aspects. For that other person, though, his principles do not seem primarily to be predictive devices; only rarely do people attempt to *predict* their own future behavior — usually they just *decide* what to do. Rather, his principles play a role in producing that behavior; he *guides* his behavior by the principle. My knowing of his principles affects my estimate of the likelihood that he will behave a certain way, my estimate of the probability of his behaving that way; but *for him* the principles affect not (merely) *estimates* of the probabilities but these very probabilities themselves: for him the principles are not evidence of how he will behave but devices that help determine what he will (decide to) do.[17]

---

[16] See Carol Gilligan, *In a Different Voice* (Cambridge, Mass.: Harvard University Press, 1982); see also Bill Puka, "The Liberation of Caring: A Different Voice for Gilligan's 'Different Voice,'" *Hypatia*, 5 (1990), 58–82.

[17] Following the philosophical tradition, I use the term "determine" to mean fix, cause, make happen — as in "determinism" — but notice too the term's estimate/evidential/epistemological side, as in "I haven't yet determined what he's trying to do."

## Personal Functions

It is because principles of behavior have a personal function, apart from issues of social interaction, that they are able to perform and achieve their interpersonal function. This interpersonal function — reassuring others of our behavior in the face of temptations, and hence leading them to choose to act coordinately with our actions — could not arise (as a solution in a coordination game) or be maintained without its basis in the personal matrix. What, then, are the personal and intrapersonal functions of principles and in what ways do they achieve these?

Principles may be one way a person can define her own *identity* — "I am a person with *these* principles" — and principles followed over an extended period are a way a person can integrate her life over time and give it more coherence. Some might say it is good to be principled because that is a way of being consistent. However, actions are not (logically) inconsistent in themselves or among themselves. An action *can* be inconsistent with a principle, and hence derivatively with the other actions that fit that principle. But if one wanted merely to avoid inconsistency, that could be done by having *no* principles at all. Principles do knit one's actions together, though. Through them, one's actions and one's life may have greater coherence, greater organic unity. That may be valuable in itself.

What does it mean to define oneself or one's identity in terms of principles? In that case, should we construe the self as a system of principles? These could include principles for transforming existing principles and for integrating new ones, thus for altering the self too in terms of principles. (Would a person's violating her principles then threaten to destroy her self?) However, continuing goals also would integrate a person's life and actions over time. Why define oneself by principles rather than goals? (Unlike principles, goals can be balanced, traded off against others, etc.) A person who doesn't *define* herself through principles nevertheless might *have* principles, not as an internal component of her identity but as an external constraint upon the actions of a separate distinguishable identity. One thinks of the Kantian themes of self-creation and self-legislation, but if chosen goals can give self-creation, why is self-*legislation* needed? Does this role of principles depend upon controversial Kantian claims about what (and only what) gives rise to autonomous freedom?

These personal functions of principles concern one's life or identity as a whole, or at least extended parts of it. Principles also function for a person, more modestly, at the micro-level. One intrapersonal function of moral principles is connected to our commitment to them. In starting long-term projects there is the question of whether we will stick to them in the future, whether our — as some like to say — future selves will carry them out. Only if the answer is yes might it be worthwhile to begin a particular project, and beginning it might be rational only when we have some assurance it will continue. If my holding something *as a principle* now creates a greater cost for deviating from it in the future — that very same action would have less cost when it is no deviation from a principle — then a project that incorporates a current and longstanding principle will be one I am less likely to abandon; this is not because I have some additional principle to stick to my projects, but because this project embodies a principle I (probably) will continue to have. Just as principles have an interpersonal function of giving assurance to another — she can count on my behavior in planning hers — so too they have the intrapersonal function of enabling me to count on certain behavior from my future self — when he too probably will have that principle. Therefore, I now can reasonably undertake some projects that are only desirable contingent upon certain future behavior by me.

Within the process of a person's decision making, principles might function as an exclusionary or filtering device: in choice situations, do not consider as live options those actions that violate your principles. Principles thus would save decision-effort and calculation time for a creature of "limited rationality." Yet the exclusion need not be absolute; if no sufficiently good action (above a certain level of aspiration) is found among the live options, a previously excluded action might be reconsidered.

*Overcoming Temptation*

The central intrapersonal function of principles I want to focus upon is getting us past temptations, hurdles, distractions, diversions. The psychologist George Ainslie has presented a theory of why we do impulsive behavior that we know is against our long-term interests and of what devices we use to cope with the temptations to such behavior.[18] Before turning to Ainslie's work, some background is useful.

We care less now about a future reward, economic and psychological data show, than we will later when that reward eventuates — we "discount" the future. The current utility to us of receiving a future reward is less than its utility will be when it occurs, and the more distant that reward, the less its current utility. This itself is an interesting phenomenon, and we may wonder about its rationality; in our plans and projects of action shouldn't we value a reward at all times as we would when it occurred? To be sure, we also want to take account of the uncertainty that we will survive until that time or that the reward will occur — each may be less than completely certain. In our present calculations, then, we wish to utilize an expected value, discounting that future reward's value by its probability, but shouldn't the utility of the reward's actually being received remain constant, no matter when the time?

Time preference — the term economists use for a utility-discounting of the future — may be evolution's way of instilling in creatures who could not perform such anticipatory probabilistic

[18] George Ainslie, "Specious Reward: A Behavioral Theory of Impulsiveness and Impulse Control," *Psychological Bulletin*, 82 (1975), 463–96; "Beyond Microeconomics," in Jon Elster (ed.), *The Multiple Self* (Cambridge: Cambridge University Press, 1986), pp. 133–75.

calculations a mechanism to roughly the same effect. Innate time preference may be a rule of thumb that approximates what calculations previously would have yielded, at least with regard to those rewards (and punishments) affecting inclusive fitness; there may have been selection for such time preference.[19] A problem arises, then, for beings with the cognitive apparatus to take explicit account of the uncertainties of a future reward's eventuating and to perform explicitly a probabilistic discounting of the future. If already installed in us is an innate time preference — evolution's attempt to perform the probabilistic discounting for us — and moreover what we explicitly discount in our probabilistic calculations is the (already discounted through time-preference) present value of the future reward, then what takes place will be a *double-discounting*. And surely that is too much. It seems that beings sophisticated enough to realize all this who perform expected-value calculations should utilize current estimates of what the utility of the future reward will be when it eventuates (which then are explicitly discounted by the probabilities), rather than the time-preferenced current discounted values of those future rewards. Otherwise, they should skip the expected value calculations and stick with the evolutionarily instilled time preference.[20] However, if pure time preference is a rational phenomenon in itself, not *simply* an evolutionary surrogate for probabilistic discounting, but if such evolutionary shaping did take place, then the situation is more complicated.

---

[19] Can we use information about people's current degree of time preference to make a rough estimate about the harshness and riskiness of the environment and the life history of the organisms in whom this degree of time preference first evolved? Might we use information about the general shape of the time preference curve to check theories about the domain within which selection operated (e.g., how extensive a class of kin within kin selection)?

There might be features in addition to probabilistic discounting that time preference was selected, in part, to approximate. Susan Hurley (in conversation) mentions possible change of utility due to future changes of preference.

[20] I first discussed the perils of double-discounting in "On Austrian Methodology," *Synthese*, 36 (1977), 353–92.

The curves describing the time-preferenced discounting of future rewards need not be straight lines or exponential; they may be hyperbolic.[21] Ainslie noticed that two such highly bowed curves (as the hyperbolic) can cross, and he traced out the implications of this fact. (See figure 1: the utility of a reward is measured on the $y$-axis; its utility for a person at a given time is measured by the height of its curve at that time. The curve slopes downward to the left because a future reward has a lesser value earlier.) Suppose there are two projects or plans of action leading to different rewards, where receiving the earlier possible reward, the smaller of the two, will thwart receiving the later larger one. A person proceeds along in time staying with the project having the highest utility at that time. In the time interval $A$, the more distant reward has the greater utility; in the time interval $B$, though,

FIGURE 1

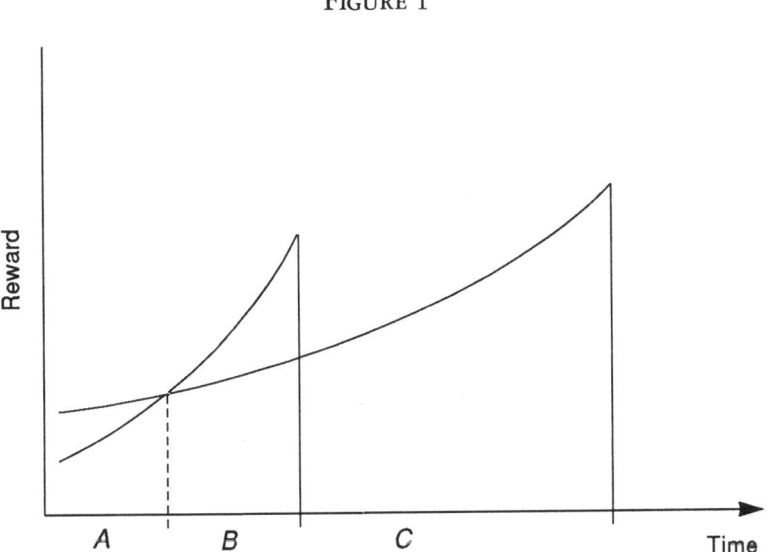

[21] This last shape is a consequence of the "matching law" equations. See Richard Herrnstein, "Relative and Absolute Strengths of Response as a Function of Frequency of Reinforcement," *Journal of the Experimental Analysis of Behavior*, 4 (1961), 267–72.

the nearer reward has the greater utility. Since the larger reward can actually be collected only at the end of the time interval $C$, the person must get through that middle period $B$ without turning to the smaller reward. This presents a problem, because during that middle time interval the prospect of receiving that smaller reward *soon* has greater utility than the prospect of receiving the greater reward later.

Why assume that the person *should* try to get past that intermediate time period; why shouldn't the smaller but more immediate reward be taken?[22] What makes the two periods $A$ and $C$, wherein the larger reward looms largest, the appropriate ones for deciding which choice is appropriate? During them the person will prefer acting to gain the largest reward; during period $B$ she will prefer acting to gain the smaller one — that is, one that is smaller when she gains it than the other one would be when she gained *it*. Where are *we* standing when we say that avoiding the temptation is the better alternative, and why is that standpoint more appropriate than the person's standpoint within the time interval $B$?

Here is a suggestion. The time interval $B$ is not the appropriate benchmark for deciding what the person ought to do because $B$ is not a representative sample of her view of the matter. The time intervals $A$ and $C$ sum to a longer interval. Moreover, when we add her judgments *after* the moment the rewards are to be realized, and graph which rewards seem largest to her *then*, we find that soon after consuming the smaller reward she wishes she had not done this, but after consuming the larger reward (at the end of the time interval $C$), she continues to prefer having chosen that larger reward. I suggest that, often, what makes resisting the temptation and taking the larger reward the preferred option is that this is the person's preference for a majority of the time: *it* is her (reasonably) stable preference, the other is her preference at

---

[22] I thank Amartya Sen for raising this question.

a nonrepresentative moment.[23] (Leaving aside any after-the-fact preferences, if the time interval $B$ lasted for longer than the intervals $A$ and $C$, would it be clear *in that case* that the temptation should be resisted?) Temptations should not always be resisted, only when the desire for the larger reward (including the preference after the fact) is the person's preference for the larger amount of time. This criterion is meant to be defeasible, not conclusive. It does have the virtue of staying close to a person's preferences (though it is not wedded to a particular local preference) in contrast to saying that it simply *is* in the person's interests to resist the temptation or that the relevant criterion is — and resisting temptation serves—the maximization of utility over a lifetime.[24]

Ainslie describes various devices for getting oneself past that intermediate period of temptation. These include taking an action during interval $A$ that makes it impossible to pursue the smaller reward during $B$ (e.g., Odysseus tying himself to the mast); taking an action during interval $A$ (e.g., making a bet with another person) that adds a penalty if you take the smaller reward, thereby altering *its* utility during interval $B$; taking steps during $A$ to avoid noticing or dwelling upon the virtues of the smaller reward during $B$.[25] And — our current topic — formulating a personal general principle of behavior.

A general principle of behavior groups actions; it classifies a particular act along with others — for example, "never eat snacks between meals," "never smoke another cigarette." (I do not, for present purposes, make any distinction between principles and

---

[23] There also is the phenomenon of *regret*, a lowering of current utility due to looking back upon currently undesired past action. Having a tendency toward regret might help one somewhat to get over the temptation during $B$, since during $B$ you can anticipate the lowered utility level during $C$ and also afterward if you take the smaller closer reward now. But will this anticipation feed back sufficiently into the overall utilities during $B$ to affect the choice made then?

[24] For a critical discussion of the single goal of maximizing the total utility over a lifetime, see my *The Examined Life* (New York: Simon and Schuster, 1989), pp. 100–102.

[25] See also Jon Elster, *Ulysses and the Sirens* (Cambridge: Cambridge University Press, 1979).

rules.) We might try to represent the effect of this principled grouping of action within utility theory and decision theory as follows. By classifying actions together as of type $T$, and by treating them similarly, a principle links the utilities of these $T$-actions (or the utilities of their outcomes). It would be too strong to say that because of the principle all $T$-actions must have the same utility; there may be other types and principles that one particular $T$-action falls under while another $T$-action does not, so their utilities may diverge. What a principle sets up is a *correlation* between the utilities of the various actions falling under it. Stating this at the level of preference, when acts of type $T$ are ranked with other actions in a preference ordering, there will be a correlation between the rank orders of the $T$-acts. However, if this correlation were the only effect that adopting or accepting principles had on the utilities of the actions falling under them, then principles would not be of help in getting us past temptations.

The mark of a principle ("never eat snacks between meals," "never smoke another cigarette") is that it ties the decision whether to do an immediate particular act (eating *this* snack, smoking *this* cigarette) to the whole class of actions of which the principle makes it part. This act now stands for the whole class. By adopting the principle, it is as if you have made the following true: if you do this one particular action in the class, you will do them all. Now the stakes are higher. Tying the utility of this act of snacking to the disutility of all those acts of snacking in the future may help you to get through the period $B$ of temptation; the utility for you now of this particular snack is altered. This snack comes to stand for all the snacks, and at this early point the current utility of being thin or healthy later far outweighs the current utility of those distant pleasures of eating; the current disutility of poor health or a poor figure becomes a feature of the currently contemplated particular act of snacking.[26]

[26] In its focus upon a whole group of actions of a certain kind in the personal realm, this may remind some readers of rule utilitarianism in the public realm. How-

But why assume the person will formulate a principle during time period *A* rather than during period *B*? Why won't the person take the snack this time and formulate a principle to always snack or, more generally, a principle to always give in to immediate temptation? But formulating and accepting such a principle (alongside the action of taking the snack now) will not itself bring reward immediately or maximize reward over time. It does generally reduce delay in reward, but during period *B*, facing one particular temptation, do I want to *always* reduce delay for any and every reward? No, for though I am in that *B* period with respect to one particular reward, with regard to many other (pairs of) rewards I am in the *A* period (or the *C* period). With regard to these other more distant pairs of lesser and greater, I do not now want always to take the more immediate one, even though I do now wish to take one *particular* reward (which I am in the *B* period of) that is more immediate. It is because temptations are spread out over time that, at any *one* time, we are in more *A* (or *C*) periods than *B* periods. Hence we would not accept a principle always to succumb to temptation.[27]

By adopting a principle we make one action stand for many others and thereby we change the utility or disutility of this particular action. This alteration of utilities is due to exercising our power and ability to make one action *stand for* or *symbolize* others.

---

ever, our question is how the acceptance of a general principle affects the choice of a particular action that, in the absence of the principle, would not have maximal utility. The comparable question would be how someone with act utilitarian desires who (somehow) decides upon a rule utilitarian principle can manage to put it into effect in particular choice situations.

[27] The proponent of succumbing to temptation may reply, "You are saying that we don't *want* always to succumb to temptation. But you say a principle is the device to get us past what may be our current desire. So perhaps we need a principle to get us past the desire not to always succumb to temptation." Leaving aside the skirting of paradox, a principle is (most easily) adopted during a time period *t* when a contrary desire is stronger than the temptation is during *t*. (The temptation will reach full strength later than *t*.) And there will not be a period when the desire *always* to succumb is not weaker than a contrary desire. (Or if such a temporary period did arise, any principle adopted then soon would be overturned on the basis of a later desire that wasn't just momentary.)

Violating the principle this one time does not necessitate that we always shall violate it; having this snack does not necessitate that we shall become continual snackers. Before we adopted the principle it was not true that doing the act this one time would involve doing it always. Adopting the principle forges that connection, so that the penalty for violating the principle this time becomes the disutility of violating it always. It would be instructive to investigate *how* precisely we are able to do this.

The fact that we can, though, has important consequences. We can so alter utilities (by adopting a principle and making one act stand for others), but we cannot do this too frequently and make it stick. If we violate a particular principle we have adopted, we have no reason to think the next occasion will be any different than this one. If each occasion is the same, and we do it this time, won't we do it on such occasions always? Unless we can distinguish this occasion from the later ones, and also have reasons for believing that this distinction will carry weight with us *later* so that we won't indulge once again by formulating another distinction which again we won't adhere to still later, then doing the action this time will lead us to expect we shall continue to repeat it. (To formulate a distinction that allows this one act yet excludes future repetitions is to formulate yet another principle; we must have more reason to think we shall adhere to that one than to this, or the reformulating will give no credibility to our abstention in the future.) Doing the act this one time, in *this* situation, means we shall continue to do it in the future. Isn't this enough to alter the utility now of doing it this one time, attaching to this particular act now the disutility of all its future repetitions?

We expect that if we do it this one time, we also shall do it repeatedly in the future, but does our doing it this once actually *affect* the future; does it *make* it more likely that we repeat the action? Or does it simply affect our *estimate* of how likely that repetition is? There are two situations to consider. When no principle was adopted previously that excludes the action, doing the action now may have a minor effect on the probability of repetition in accordance with the psychologist's "law of effect": positive reinforcement of an action raises its probability of occurrence in the future. And the estimate of the probability of repetition may be raised somewhat if this action is added to a number of similar ones in the past. When a principle was adopted previously, acting in violation of the principle will raise an observer's estimate and the agent's own estimate too of how likely she is to repeat this particular act. Also, it makes it more likely that she will. The principle has broken down, one bar to the action has been removed; moreover, realizing this may produce discouragement and make the agent less likely to exert effort to avoid the action in the future. (Notice that an action that affects *her estimate* of the probability of similar future actions may then produce discouragement and thereby affect the actual probability of repetition.) Formulating a principle that would constitute an additional bar to the actions it excludes is a way of actually tying the effects of all to the effects of any (previous) one. The more one has invested in a principle, the more effort previously put behind adhering to it, the greater the cost in violating it now. (For how likely is it that you will continue to adhere to another one if you couldn't manage to stick to this one despite so much effort?) Moreover, adhering to the principle this time is a type of action subject to the law of effect; its being positively reinforced makes it more probable that adherence to that principle will occur in the future.

The effects of violating a principle may be more general still, for the probability or credibility of your successfully utilizing *any* principles at all in *any* arena (when faced with a temptation as strong as the one which caused you to succumb this time) may be affected. To be sure, you may try to demarcate and limit the damage to this *one area* but this presents the same problem — one level up — as limiting the damage *within* this area to just *this one* violative action. Deontological principles may have the greatest weight when their violation directly threatens *any* and all principled action in the future: if I violate *this* principle (in this circumstance), how can I believe I will succeed in adhering to any (desirable) principle ever again? Someone might try, in an excess of Kantian zeal, to increase the potential effect of spreading disaster by formulating a (meta-) principle never to violate any principle. But while getting any violation to stand for all might lessen the probability of any given one, the actual consequences of the slightest violation would get dangerously magnified. This is not to say that one violation of a principle, because one act stands for all, discharges a principle so one then can violate it freely and with impunity. One act has the disutility of all, but then so does the next, even if that first act was done. This disutility can be escaped by dropping the principle, not by violating it; however, one then faces the very disutility that adopting the principle was designed to avoid.

Since adopting a principle itself is an action that affects the probability linkages among other actions, some care is appropriate in choosing which principles to adopt. One must consider not only the possible benefits of adherence, but the probability of its violation and what future effects that violation would have. It might be better to adopt a less good principle (when followed) but one easier to adhere to, especially since that principle may not always be available as a credible fall-back if one fails to adhere to the more stringent one. (Also, one wants to adopt a principle sharp enough to clearly mark its violations, so one's future self cannot easily fudge the issue of whether the principle is being followed.) No doubt, a theory of the optimal choice of principles could be formulated, taking such considerations into account.[28]

A principle speaks of all the actions in a group and it makes each present act stand for all. To perform its functions, it must

---

[28] The promulgation of a principle also affects how third parties will carry it out; a designer of principles will take account of how others might distort or abuse them. For a related point about how social theorists such as Marx and Freud should have taken precautions against vulgarization, see my *The Examined Life*, p. 284.

speak of *all* the actions of a certain kind. We do not have principles that say: most Ps should be Qs; or 15% of Ps have to be Qs. Sometimes, though, all we need is to do something some or most of the time (e.g., skipping desserts most evenings, paying most of our bills each month). The way we achieve this through principles is nevertheless to formulate a statement that speaks of "all," "each," or "every," yet is coextensive with the mix we desire. *Each* month, pay most of your bills; *every* week, skip desserts most evenings. A teacher — not myself — whose principle it is not to give very many *A*s grades *every* class on a curve. Thereby, each week or month or class comes to stand for all. Thus, we can explain why principles concern all the members of a class, not just some. (A norm could concern itself with $n$%, where $n$ is not 0 or 100, but a principle cannot.) A principle has certain functions, and to perform these one instance must stand for or symbolize all. The observed "all"-character of principles thus provides support for our view of the functions principles have and the ways they perform them.[29]

Principles may seem crude devices for accomplishing our goals; their universal coverage — giving up *all* desserts, *all* diversions until the task is done — may be more than is necessary to reach the goal. The leeway in what the "all" covers (desserts, weeks) mitigates this somewhat, narrowing the overkill of principles. Still, some will remain. If there were a clear threshold of $n$ repetitions of an action, past which the consequences of continuing that action thwart the goal but before which the goal still can be reached, wouldn't a rational person perform the action precisely $n$ times and then stop? (A more complicated statement is needed if each repetition increases the difficulty of reaching the goal.) No principle would be needed to exclude the $n+1$th action, since that action itself would have bad consequences on balance. This might

[29] An alternative explanation of principles incorporating "all" might propose that principles codify reasons and that reasons are universal (though defeasible); hence principles are too. But why is it that reasons are not "for the most part" but instead are "universal but defeasible," even though the percentages may be the same?

be a theory of (approximately) when the person decides to stop smoking (or gaining weight, etc.), and hence of when she decides to institute a principle. Yet, given temptation, it is a principle that needs to be instituted *then*.

*Sunk Costs*

One method Ainslie mentions for getting past the tempting time interval $B$ is this: *commit* yourself during the earlier interval $A$ to seeking the larger reward during $C$ and during $B$. One mode of such commitment is, during $A$, to invest many resources in the (future) pursuit of that larger reward. If I think it would be good for me to see many plays or attend many concerts this year, and I know that when the evening of the performance arrives I will frequently not feel like rousing myself at that moment to go out, then I can buy tickets to many of these events in advance, even though I know that tickets still will be available at the box office on the evening of the performance. Since I will not want to waste the tickets I have bought, to waste the money already spent on them, I will attend more performances than I would if I left the decisions about attendance to each evening. True, I may not use *all* of these tickets—lethargy may triumph on some evenings—yet I will attend more frequently than if no tickets had been purchased in advance. Knowing all this, I purchase the tickets in advance in order to drive myself to attend.

Economists present a doctrine that all decision making should pay attention only to the (present and) future consequences of various alternative actions. The costs of past investments in these courses of action already have been incurred. While existing resources may affect the consequences of the various actions now open before me — already possessing the ticket I can attend the performance making no additional future payment — and hence be taken into account through these consequences, the mere fact that costs already have been borne to further a certain project should not carry any weight at all as a person makes a decision.

These costs, "sunk costs" as the economists term them, are a thing of the past; what matters now is only the future stream of benefits. Thus, sitting at home this evening, if I now would prefer staying home to going out and attending a performance (for no monetary payment), then the evening at home has higher utility for me than traveling out and attending the performance; therefore I should stay at home. It should make no difference that I already have spent money on the ticket for the performance — so runs the economists' doctrine that sunk costs should be ignored.[30]

This may be a correct rule for the maximization of monetary profits, but it is not an appropriate general principle of decision, for familiar reasons. We do *not* treat our past commitments to others as of no account except insofar as they affect our future returns, as when breaking a commitment may affect others' trust in us and hence our ability to achieve other future benefits; and we do *not* treat the past effort we have devoted to ongoing projects of work or of life as of no account (except insofar as this makes their continuance more likely to bring benefits than other freshly started projects would). Such projects help define our sense of ourselves and of our life.[31]

The particular issue we have been discussing indicates yet another defect in the doctrine of ignoring sunk costs as a general principle of decision. The fact that we do not ignore sunk costs provides one way to get past the temptation during the *B* time interval to choose the smaller but more immediate reward. Earlier, during the time interval *A* when we can clearly see the benefits of the larger but more distant reward, we can sink resources and effort

---

[30] People frequently do not adhere to the doctrine of ignoring sunk costs, as indicated by their decisions when presented with hypothetical choices. On this, see H. R. Arkes and C. Blumer, "The Psychology of Sunk Cost," *Organizational Behavior and Human Decision Processes*, 35 (1985), 124–40. Arkes and Blumer see the people who deviate from the doctrine in the ticket-example as being irrational.

[31] See the Bernard Williams essay in J. J. C. Smart and Bernard Williams, *Utilitarianism: For and Against* (Cambridge: Cambridge University Press, 1973); "Persons, Character and Morality," in Amelie Rorty (ed.), *The Identities of Persons* (Berkeley: University of California Press, 1976).

into achieving that reward, knowing that when the time $B$ of temptation comes, the fact that we do *not* want (and will not want) to have wasted those resources will count for us as a reason against choosing the smaller reward, adding to its disutility. If I know I will be tempted some evening in the future by the smaller immediate reward of comfort (not having to go out into the rain, etc.), yet I also know that now and afterward too I will be happy to have attended all those performances, then I can buy the tickets now, in advance, to spur myself to forgo staying home when that evening arrives.

Everyone sees succumbing to the smaller reward during the time interval $B$ as a problem, an irrationality or an undesirable short-sightedness. The person herself sees it that way — beforehand and later, if not right then — and we see it thus too as we think about it. The economist also sees another type of behavior, the honoring of sunk costs, as irrational and undesirable. But we now see that this latter behavior, anticipated in advance, can be used to limit and check the first type of undesirable behavior (viz., succumbing to the smaller but nearer reward). We can knowingly utilize our tendency to take sunk costs seriously as a means of increasing our *future* rewards. If this tendency is irrational, it can be rationally utilized to check and overcome another irrationality. If someone offered us a pill that henceforth would make us people who *never* honored sunk costs, we might be ill-advised to accept it; this would deprive us of a valuable tool for getting past temptations of the (future) moment. (Might such a tendency to honor sunk costs, which can be adaptive, have been selected for in the evolutionary process?) Since taking sunk costs into account sometimes is desirable (so the economists' general condemnation is mistaken), and sometimes is not, the desirability of taking such a pill would depend upon the comparative numbers of, and stakes within, these two types of situations.

Earlier, I mentioned that the more effort one has put behind adherence to a principle designed to get past temptations of the moment, the greater is the cost in violating it now. It is unlikely that you will manage to stick to another principle if you could not stick to this one despite so much previous effort. Realizing this gives you much reason to hold onto this one — it's the one liferaft in sight — and therefore gives great weight to not violating it in the face of this particular temptation. Groupings of action (in order to avoid immediate temptation) that we have succeeded in following thereby gain a further tenacity. Notice that this involves a sunk cost phenomenon. My reasoning behind sticking to *this* principle, and its associated grouping, involved saying that, if I could not stick to it despite so much previous effort, how could I hope to stick to another? It is only if I *am* someone who honors sunk costs that I will be able to make this argument; only one who thus honors sunk costs would have a reason to adhere now to this current principle for bypassing temptation, rather than succumbing this one time and then formulating a different principle, which too will succumb when its time comes, perhaps on its very first test. It is sunk costs that makes *this* principle the place to take a stand. (Do not argue that these are future-regarding considerations about the future consequences of the two different courses of action — sticking to the present policy vs. succumbing to the temptation and then formulating a new policy — and hence that the person who does not honor sunk costs can go through the same line of reasoning; it is only because of the known tendency to honor sunk costs that one course of action will have, and can be seen to have, significantly different consequences than the other. Otherwise, why think it is less likely that I will adhere to the new principle after violating the old one than that I will continue to adhere to the old principle if I don't violate it now?) Might the known phenomenon of our honoring sunk costs play some role in why we adhere to principles we have just adopted? We now know that if we can manage to adhere to this principle for some time, the fact that we will have invested in it will provide us in the future, as honorers of sunk costs, with reasons to continue to adhere to that principle then — and that may give us some reason now.[32]

To these functions performed by our honoring sunk costs, the economist might reply that, for an otherwise perfectly rational person, honoring sunk costs is not desirable at all; only someone with some *other* irrationality should indulge in it. However, this is not so evident, even leaving aside what was mentioned earlier: commitments made to other persons and past investment in our projects of work and life. For it might be interpersonally useful to have a means of convincing others that we shall stick to projects or aims even in the face of threats that seem to make this adherence work to our future disadvantage — as a way of discouraging their making such threats or carrying them out.[33] This might be useful even if you have no other tendency to irrational behavior, and the others you are trying to convince have none either.[34] However, the theme of countering or fencing in one irrationality with another is worth marking. Can some other things that we think irrational — perhaps weakness of will, self-deception, or fallacies of reasoning — consciously be put to use to thwart or limit still other irrationalities or otherwise undesirable happenings? (And could a total package of such somewhat counterbalancing apparent irrational tendencies even work together better than the *total* package of apparent — when separately considered — rational tendencies?)

---

[32] I owe this suggestion to Susan Hurley, who also asks, in reference to and in parallel to our earlier question about whether we can rely upon someone adhering to a principle when his only reasons for holding it are the benefits to him of our so relying, whether someone can expect to honor costs he has sunk if he will not think he earlier had some independent reason to sink them, a reason other than to get himself to honor them later.

[33] See Thomas Schelling, "The Art of Commitment," in his *Arms and Influence* (New Haven: Yale University Press, 1966), pp. 35–91. See also Schelling's discussion of "the rationality of irrationality."

[34] It also might be a useful trait, especially for the young, to be optimistic about the chances of success of possible projects — otherwise no new and daring things would be tried — yet also to tend to stick to ongoing projects in which significant investment has been made, for otherwise at the first serious difficulty one might turn to another untried project one is still (overly) optimistic about.

Let me mention one other technique a person might use to carry herself over that tempting time interval $B$ where the smaller reward looms so large. She might consider what action she would recommend to another person in that very situation, someone whose well-being she cares about — a child or a friend, for example — and then adopt that advice for herself. Distancing oneself from the situation, looking at the diagram impersonally instead of simply looking ahead from one time point, might be a way to defuse the allure of the otherwise nearer (but ultimately smaller) reward. This procedure requires an ability to look at a situation you are in impersonally and to think the same principle of choice should apply to yourself as to others, that you should do the very same action another should do in that situation. A strong predisposition to such an impartial attitude would be extremely useful in surmounting the $B$ interval of the crossed curves, hence in maximizing a person's total reward. And this very disposition constitutes one component of ethical judgment: applying the same principles to one's own behavior as to others.

There is one function of principles I have not yet mentioned: *drawing the line*. Principles mark a boundary beyond which we will not step — "this is where I draw the line!" — and we think, "If I don't draw it here, where *will* I draw it?" There may be no other obvious place in a gradient of situations, no obvious place within acceptable territory. (Or there may be another acceptable place, but we feel we will not *succeed* in drawing the line there.) This is connected to the earlier mentioned function of principles, getting one past the temptation of the moment, but in this case it is not temptation but rather the *reasoning* of the moment that needs getting past. If I reach *that* point, I will reason that there is no special reason to stop just then, so I had better stop much beforehand, where there *is* a clear line and a *special* one.[35]

---

[35] Thomas Schelling's theory of coordination games might usefully utilize this notion of specialness. In attempting to coordinate with another, I am searching for an action we both will think is special (yet also desirable), and both will realize we

This, I think, is what enables principles to define a person. "*These* are the lines I have drawn." It is these lines that limn/delineate him. They are his outer boundaries. A person in very fortunate circumstances, then, who knows he won't actually get taken very far along any undesirable gradient, may not *have to* draw any specific lines. Thus, in this sense he may not be as well defined as someone in less fortunate circumstances.

*Symbolic Utility*

We have said that by adopting the principle, doing the particular short-sighted action this one time in this situation now *means* we shall continue to do it in the future. This act *stands for* all the others the principle also excludes; doing this one *symbolizes* doing the rest. Is this fact of *meaning, standing for,* and *symbolizing* constituted by the intertwining of the two strands of connection between doing the act now and repeating it in the future that we already have discussed: the way doing it now affects your estimate of the probability of doing it again and the way doing it now alters the very probability of doing it in the future? Or is symbolizing a further fact, not exhausted by these two strands but one that itself affects the utility of alternative actions and outcomes? Symbolizing, I believe, is a further important strand, one that an adequate decision theory must treat explicitly.

Freudian theory explains the occurrence or persistence of neurotic actions or symptoms in terms of the symbolic meaning of these actions or symptoms. Producing evident bad consequences and apparently irrational, these actions and symptoms have an unobvious symbolic significance; they symbolize something else, call it $M$. Yet the mere having of such symbolic meaning alone cannot explain the occurrence or persistence of an action or symptom. We have to add that what these actions and symptoms symbolize —

---

both think it special — not simply striking but special. When there are ten alternatives, nine of them extremely striking, the special one might be the one that isn't — at least at the first level — striking at all.

that is, $M$ — itself has some utility or value (or, in the case of avoidance, disutility or negative value) for the person, and moreover that this utility of the $M$ which is symbolized is imputed back to the action or symptom, thereby giving *it* greater utility than it appeared to have. Only thus can it explain why it was chosen or manifested. Freudian theory must hold not only that actions and outcomes can symbolize still further events for a person, but that they can draw upon themselves the emotional meaning (and utility values) of these other events. Having a symbolic meaning, the actions are treated as having the utility of what they symbolically mean; a neurotic symptom is adhered to with a tenacity appropriate to what it stands for. (I am not aware of a clear statement in the Freudian literature of this equation or of the weaker claim that *some* of the utility of what is symbolized is imputed back to the symbol, despite some such version's being presupposed, I believe, in some Freudian explanations.) Disproportionate emotional responses to an actual event or occasion may indicate their standing for other events or occasions to which the emotions are more suited.[36]

For the symbolic action to get done, *it* must somehow come to have a higher utility than the other actions available to the agent.[37] I have suggested it happens this way: the action (or one of its outcomes) symbolizes a certain situation, and the utility of this symbolized situation is imputed back, through the symbolic connection, to the action itself. Notice that standard decision theory also believes in an imputation back of utility, along a (probabilistic) causal connection. By virtue of producing a particular situation for sure, an action comes to have, to have imputed to it, the utility

---

[36] Once an action or outcome comes to symbolize others, its presence may get taken as evidence for the others or as causes of them, but this is a result of the symbolizing, and not its original fabric (although this evidential or causal role may then reinforce the strength of the symbolic connection).

[37] So a maximizing decision theory would assume. There are other forms of normative decision theory, such as Herbert Simon's "satisficing" theory, but this too would require the action that is done to have, or have imputed to it, a utility above the (shifting) level of aspiration.

of that situation; by virtue of probabilistically producing certain situations, an action comes to have, to have imputed to it, their utilities in the form of an expected utility. What the current view adds is that utility can flow back, be imputed back, not only along causal connections but along symbolic ones.

One mark that it is an action's symbolic connection to an outcome that plays a central role in the decision to do it, rather than the apparently causal connection — I am thinking of cases where the agent does not think the action is itself intrinsically desirable or valuable — is the persistence of the action in the face of strong evidence that it does not actually have the presumed causal consequence; sometimes a person will even refuse to look at or countenance this evidence or other evidence about harmful consequences of the action or policy. (On these grounds, one might claim that certain antidrug enforcement measures *symbolize* reducing the amount of drug use and that minimum wage laws *symbolize* helping the poor.) A reformer who wishes to avoid such harmful consequences may find it necessary to propose another policy (without such consequences) that equally effectively symbolizes acting toward or reaching the goal; simply halting the current action would deprive people of its symbolic utility, something they are unwilling to let happen.

Of course, *according* a particular symbolic meaning to an action $A$ has causal consequences of its own, as it affects which actions we perform, and a purely consequentialist theory can say something about that. It can speak of whether giving such symbolic meaning (or, later, refraining from extinguishing that symbolic meaning) is itself a causally optimal action. However, this will be different than a purely consequentialist (nonsymbolic) theory of the action $A$ itself, and it does not imply that we must assess the according or tolerating of symbolic meaning solely by its causal consequences.

Since symbolic actions often are *expressive* actions, another view of them would be this: the symbolic connection of an action to a situation enables the action to be expressive of some attitude, belief, value, emotion, or whatever. Expressiveness, not utility, is what flows back. What flows back along the symbolic connection to the action is (the possibility of) expressing some particular attitude, belief, value, emotion (etc.). Expressing this then has high utility for the person, and so she performs the symbolic action.[38]

There may not seem to be much difference between these two ways of structuring our understanding of a symbolic action's being chosen. Each will give a different explanation of why a symbolic act is not done. For the first, wherein utility is imputed back to the action along the symbolizing connection, this presents a puzzle. Presumably the symbolizing connection always holds, so that an action of handwashing always symbolizes removing guilt or whatever. Since this situation symbolized, being guilt-free, presumably always has high utility, if utility is imputed back, why won't the action of handwashing always have maximal utility, so that the person will always be doing it? (Apparently, this does happen with some compulsive hand-washers, but not with all, and not with all actions done because of their symbolic meaning.) The expressiveness theory says the possibility of expressing some attitude toward being guilt-free is always present, as a result of the ever-present symbolic connection, but the utility of expressing this may vary from context to context, depending upon how recently one has expressed it, what one's other needs and desires are, and so forth. The utility of expressing that attitude or emotion competes with other utilities. The utility imputation theory will describe this differently. The absolute or relative utility of the symbolized situation can fluctuate for the person; the utility of being guilt-free can actually become less if the person has recently taken steps to alleviate guilt — there now (temporarily) is less to deal with; or the utility of being guilt-free can remain constant while

---

[38] Not that it need always be expressiveness that flows back along the symbolic connection. Perhaps other things may, and these will give rise to new characteristics of the action which themselves have high utility for the agent. The point is that utility is not what flows back.

the utility of other competing goods, such as eating, temporarily rises to become greater than the utility of removing guilt. Each of these structures for understanding symbolic expressiveness will have some utility fluctuate — a slightly different one. What I want to emphasize now is the *importance* of this symbolic meaning, however it is precisely structured.

When utility is imputed to an action or outcome in accordance with its symbolic meaning — that is, when the utility of an action or outcome is equated with the utility of what it symbolically means — we are apt to think this irrational. When this symbolic meaning involves repressed childhood desires and fears, or certain current unconscious ones, this may well result in behavior doomed to be frustrating, unsatisfying, or tormenting. Yet mightn't symbolic meanings based upon unconscious desires also add gratifying reverberations to consciously desired goods? In any case, not all symbolic meanings will be rooted in Freudian material. Many of these others too, however, will look strange to someone outside that network of meanings: recall the dire consequences some people bear in order to avoid "losing face," the deaths people risked and sometimes met in duels to "maintain honor" or in exploits to "prove manhood." Yet we should not too quickly conclude that it would be better to live without any symbolic meanings at all or better never to impute utilities in accordance with symbolic meanings.

Ethical principles codify how to behave toward others in a way that is appropriate to their value and to our fellow-feelings with them. Holding and following ethical principles, in addition to the particular purposes this serves, also has a symbolic meaning for us. Treating people (and value in general) with respect and responsiveness puts us "on the side of" that value, perhaps allying us with everything else on its side, and symbolizes our intertwining with this. (Does it symbolize this to a greater extent than it actually intertwines us, or does a welcomed symbolic connection constitute an actual intertwining?) Kant felt that in acting morally we act as a member of the kingdom of ends, a free and rational legislator. The moral action doesn't *cause* us to become a (permanent) member of that kingdom — it is what we would do as a member, it is an instance of what would be done under such circumstances, and hence it symbolizes doing it under those circumstances. The moral acts get grouped with other possible events and actions and come to stand for and mean them. Thereby being ethical acquires a symbolic utility commensurate with the utility these other things it stands for actually have. (This depends, then, upon these further things actually having utility for the person — a contingency Kant would be loath to rely upon.) There are a variety of things an ethical action might symbolically mean to someone: being a rational creature that gives itself laws; being a law-making member of a kingdom of ends; being an equal source and recognizer of worth and personality; being a rational, disinterested, unselfish person; being caring; living in accordance with nature; responding to what is valuable; recognizing someone else as a creature of God. The utility of these grand things, symbolically expressed and instantiated by the action, becomes incorporated into that action's (symbolic) utility. Thus, these symbolic meanings become part of one's reason for acting ethically. Being ethical is among our most effective ways of symbolizing (a connection to) what we value most highly.

A large part of the richness of our lives consists in symbolic meanings and their expression, the symbolic meanings our culture attributes to things or the ones we ourselves bestow.[39] It is unclear, in any case, what it would be to live without any symbolic meanings, to have no part of the magnitude of our desires depend upon such meanings. What then would we desire? Simply ma-

---

[39] Notice that symbolic meanings might not all be good ones, just as desires or preferences might not be either. The point is that a theory of rationality need not *exclude* symbolic meanings. However, these do not guarantee good or desirable content. For that, one would need to develop a theory of which symbolic meanings and which preferences and desires were admissible, using that to constrain which particular meanings and desires could be fed into the more formal theory of rationality.

terial comfort, physical security, and sensual pleasure? And would no part of how much we desired these be due to the way they might symbolize maternal love and caring? Simply wealth and power? And would no part of how much we desired this be due to the way these might symbolize release from childhood dependdence or success in competition with a parent, and no part either be due to the symbolic meanings of what wealth and power might bring? Simply the innate unconditioned reinforcers evolution has instilled and installed in us, and other things only insofar as they are effective means to these? These had served to make our ancestors more effective progenitors or protectors of related genes. Should we choose this as our only purpose? And if we valued it highly, might we not value also whatever symbolized being an effective progenitor? "No, not if that conflicted with actually being one, and in any case one should value only actually bearing or protecting progeny and relatives, and the effective means to this that evolution has marked out, namely, the unconditioned reinforcers, and also the means to *these*." (Notice, though, that evolution's having instilled desires that serve to maximize inclusive fitness does not mean that it has instilled the desire to be maximally inclusively fit. Males now are not, I presume, beating at the doors of artificial insemination clinics in order to become sperm donors, even though that would serve to increase their inclusive fitness.) But why is actually leading to something so much better than symbolizing it that symbolization shouldn't count at all? "Because that's the bottom line, what actually occurs; all the rest is talk." But why is this bottom line better than all oher lines?

In any case, if we are symbolic creatures — and anthropology attests to the universal nature of this trait — then presumably evolution made us so; therefore the attractive pleasures of symbolization, and symbolic satisfactions too, are as solidly based as the other innate reinforcers. Perhaps a capacity for symbolization served to strengthen other desires or to maintain them through periods of deprivation in reinforcement by their actual objects.

Whatever the evolutionary explanation, though, this capacity, like other cognitive capacities, is not mired in its original adaptive function; it can be employed in other valuable ways, just as mathematical capacities can be employed to explore abstract number theory and theories of infinity, although this was not the function for which they were evolutionarily selected. Once the capacity for symbolic utility exists, it may enable us, for example, to achieve in some sense — that is, symbolically — what is causally or conceptually impossible, thereby gaining utility from that, and also enable us to separate good features from bad ones they actually are linked with, gaining only the former through something that symbolizes only them.

This is not to deny the dangers opened by symbolic meanings and symbolic utilities. Conflicts may quickly come to involve symbolic meanings that, by escalating the importance of the issues, induce violence. The dangers to be specially avoided concern situation where the causal consequences of an action are extremely negative yet the positive symbolic meaning is so great that the action is done nevertheless. (Recall the examples of compulsive hand-washing and drug prohibition.) A rational person would seek an (almost) equally satisfying symbolic alternative that does not have such dire actual consequences. (However, this does not imply that symbolic meanings always should be subordinate to, and come lexicographically after, causally produced outcomes.) Sometimes a symbolic connection will be thought better than a causal one; if an outcome — such as harming someone in revenge — is desired but seen as bad, it may be better for a person to achieve this symbolically than to inflict actual damage.[40] It would be nice to discover a general structural criterion about the kinds of links that establish symbolic meanings that can distinguish the good symbolic meanings from the bad, but perhaps we must simply be vigilant in

---

[40] So should we distinguish cases where the goal is $x$ and someone acts symbolically to achieve $x$ from cases where the goal is a symbolic connection to $x$ and someone acts instrumentally to achieve that?

certain kinds of situations — conflict is one — to isolate and exclude particular symbolic meanings. It may help that many undesirable symbolic meanings are not in equilibrium under knowledge of their causes; if we knew what gave rise to these meanings, or the role they are playing in our current actions, we would not want to act upon them.[41] Some symbolic meanings do withstand these tests, though (e.g., the symbolic meaning of a romantic gesture to the person you love). Perhaps the crucial thing is to stay aware of when meanings and connections are symbolic ones, keeping separate track of these and not treating them (unknowingly) as causally real. This would help with the many Freudian symbolic meanings which, when they enter into conscious deliberation as symbolic, lose their power and impact.[42] (Years ago, this might have helped with those people who devoted their lives to the pursuit of wealth as a "status symbol" but now, in the United States, we find people who knowingly and openly pursue status. Or might they be pursuing status as a wealth symbol?)

Symbolic meaning also is a component of particular ethical decisions. It has been argued that the symbolic meaning of efforts to save a known currently threatened person — a trapped miner, for instance — or of refusing to make those efforts affects our decision in allocating resources to current efforts to save versus accident-prevention measures. (This issue has been termed one of "actual vs. statistical lives".)[43] It also has been argued that the symbolic meaning of feeding someone, giving sustenance, enters into the discussion of the ways in which the lives of direly ill people permissibly may be terminated — turning off their artificial

---

[41] For a discussion of acts in equilibrium, see my *Philosophical Explanations* (Cambridge, Mass.: Harvard University Press, 1981), pp. 348–52.

[42] I thank Bernard Williams for mentioning this example. Williams also points out that some symbolic meanings involve a fantasy that is strictly impossible to realize; and it is unclear how utilities are to be assigned to impossible situations. I would not want to preclude, however, that even incoherent situations might have high utility for us.

[43] See Charles Fried, *An Anatomy of Values* (Cambridge, Mass.: Harvard University Press, 1970), pp. 207–18.

respirator but not halting their food and starving them to death.[44] The political philosophy presented in *Anarchy, State, and Utopia* ignored the importance to us of joint and official serious symbolic statement and expression of our social ties and concern and hence (I have written) is inadequate.[45]

We live in a rich symbolic world, partly cultural and partly of our own individual creation, and we thereby escape or expand the limits of our situations, not simply through fantasies but in actions, with the meanings these have. We impute to actions and events utilities coordinate with what they symbolize, and we strive to realize (or avoid) them as we would strive for what they stand for.[46] A broader decision theory is needed, then, to incorporate such symbolic connections and to detail the new structuring these introduce.

Among social scientists, anthropologists have paid the most attention to the symbolic meanings of actions, rituals, and cultural forms and practices and their importance in the ongoing life of a group.[47] So elaborate is their work that it is somewhat embarrassing to introduce a relatively crude and undifferentiated notion of symbolic meaning. Still, this notion has its uses, not served by nuanced and textured discussions that do not easily connect with formal structures. By incorporating an action's symbolic meaning, its symbolic utility, into (normative) decision theory, we might link theories of rational choice more closely to anthropology's concerns. There are two directions in which such a linkage might go. The first, the upward direction, explains social patterns and struc-

---

[44] See Ronald Carson, "The Symbolic Significance of Giving to Eat and Drink," in Joanne Lynn (ed.), *By No Extraordinary Means: The Choice to Forgo Life-sustaining Food and Water* (Bloomington: Indiana University Press, 1986), pp. 84–88.

[45] See my *The Examined Life*, pp. 286–92.

[46] For a discussion of how some advertising of products utilizes this phenomenon, see my *The Examined Life*, pp. 121–22.

[47] See Raymond Firth, *Symbols: Public and Private* (New York: Cornell University Press, 1973); Clifford Geertz, "Deep Play: Notes on the Balinese Cockfight," in his *The Interpretation of Cultures* (New York: Basic Books, 1973).

tures in terms of individual choice behavior that incorporates symbolic utility. This, the methodological individualist and reductionist direction, is not the one I am proposing here.[48] The second, the downward direction, explains how the patterns of social meanings anthropologists delineate have an impact within the actions and behavior of individuals, that is, through their decisions which give some weight to symbolic utility. (Some anthropologists, as a matter of professional pride, seem not to be concerned with how the cultural meanings they delineate are mediated in individual behavior.)

How does the symbolic utility of an action (or of an outcome) work? What is the nature of the symbolic connection or chain of connections? And in what way does utility, or the possibility of expressiveness, flow through this chain from the situations symbolized to the actions (or outcomes) that do the symbolizing? Notice first that symbolic meaning goes beyond the way in which the adoption of principles makes some actions stand for others. There, an action stood for other things of the same type — other actions — or for a whole group of these, while symbolic meaning can connect an action with things other than (a group of) actions — for instance, with being a certain sort of person, with the realization of a certain state of affairs.

Some useful and suggestive categories have been provided by Nelson Goodman.[49] According to Goodman, $A$ *denotes* $B$ when $A$ refers to $B$; $A$ *exemplifies* $P$ when $A$ refers to $P$ and $A$ is an instance of $P$, that is, is denoted by $P$ (either literally or metaphori-

---

[48] Indeed, given the extent to which symbolic meaning is socially created, maintained, and coordinated, as well as limited by social factors, we might find here a limit to methodological individualist explanations — an important one given the effects and consequences of such meanings. For a symbolic utility might be social not only in being socially shaped, and in being shared, that is, the same for many people in the society, but also in being viewed *as* shared — that being intrinsic to its having that symbolic utility. It is not clear how methodologically individualist explanations might cope with the intricacies involved. In any case, it is not clear what a methodologically individualist account of language would look like.

[49] Nelson Goodman, *Languages of Art* (Indianapolis: Bobbs-Merrill, 1968), pp. 45–95.

cally); *A expresses P* when *A* refers to *P* and *A* has the property *P* figuratively or metaphorically (so that *P* figuratively denotes *A*), and *A* functions as an aesthetic symbol in exemplifying *P*. These relations can be chained together. *A alludes to B* when *A* denotes some *C* and that *C* exemplifies *B*, or when *A* exemplifies some *C* and that *C* denotes *B*. Even longer chains are possible,[50] some of whose links will be figurative or metaphorical. These chains, and others, can connect an action to further and larger situations or conditions, the ones it can symbolically represent or allude to (etc.), and the utility of these larger situations then provides the action itself with a *symbolic utility* that enters into decisions about it. These chains need not be very long; when *A* is in the literal extension of a term *P* and *B* is in that term's metaphorical extension, *A* might have *B* as part of its symbolic meaning. Sometimes an action may symbolically mean something by being our best instantiated realization of that thing, the best we can do.[51]

In what particular way is the symbolic utility (or expressiveness) of an action determined by the utility of that larger situation the chain connects the action to, and by the nature of the chain itself? Do shorter chains transmit more utility/expressiveness from the larger situation to the action itself; is utility/expressiveness lost, the more linkages there are; do different kinds of linkages transmit differing proportions of (or possibilities of expressing) the larger situation's utility? (I am assuming that the symbolic utility of an action cannot be greater than the utility of the larger situation it is connected to by the chain and that it can be less.) Do only some symbolic connections induce the imputation of utility back, and what determines which ones these are? These questions all arise about situations of choice under certainty;

---

[50] Catherine Elgin, *With Reference to Reference* (Indianapolis: Hackett Publ. Co., 1983), p. 143, discusses a particular chain with five links.

[51] Can the symbolic utility of an action be viewed as an *interpretation* of that action, a way of seeing oneself or it a certain way, so that the various modes of interpretive linkage, and full theories of interpretation itself, might enter into the specification of symbolic utility?

further issues arise about choice under risk or uncertainty. Is there a probabilistic discounting along some particular chains; do some kinds of larger situations, even when they are not certain to occur, transmit their full utility back to the action which might yield them? And, of course, the very fact that an action has particular risks or uncertainties associated with it may itself give it a particular symbolic meaning and utility, perhaps connected with being a daring and courageous person or a foolhardy one. Sometimes, though, the presence of probabilities rather than certainty may remove a symbolic meaning altogether. It is *not* the case that a half or a one-tenth chance of realizing a certain goal always itself has half or one-tenth the symbolic utility of that goal itself — it need not symbolize that goal, even partially. Here is another reason why symbolic utilities must be treated as a separate component of a theory of decision and not simply incorporated within existing (causal and evidential) decision theories. For such symbolic utilities do not obey an expected value formula. We might attempt to understand and explain *certain* of the observed deviations from an expected value formula and from the associated axioms of decision theory, by attributing these to the presence of symbolic utilities. I have in mind here the Allais paradox, the certainty effect, certain deviations from Savage's Sure Thing principle, and so forth. There is a symbolic utility to us of *certainty* itself. The difference between 0.9 and 1.0 is greater than that between 0.8 and 0.9, though this difference between differences disappears when each is embedded in larger otherwise identical probabilistic gambles — this disappearance marks the difference as symbolic.[52] A

---

[52] Double-digit inflation has the symbolic meaning of inflation out of control, so there is more concern about a rise from 9% to 10% than from 16% to 17%; if we counted in base eleven the (symbolic) line would be fixed elsewhere. In *Anarchy, State, and Utopia*, I commented on the symbolic meaning of *eliminating* a problem completely, so that there is a greater difference between reducing the number of instances of an evil from one to zero than there is in reducing the number from two to one. There I referred to this as a mark of an ideologue (p. 266); it is better seen as a mark of symbolic meaning.

Notice that the certainty effect, when it occurs, requires measuring utility by a slightly different procedure than the usual one. In the usual procedure, two out-

detailed theory of symbolic utility awaits development. What we can do now is mark a place for it within the structure of a more general theory of decision, a place I shall say more about in the next lecture.

*Teleological Devices*

Principles help you to discover the truth, by transmitting evidential support or probability from some cases to others. Principles also help you to overcome temptation by transmitting utility from some actions to others. Principles are transmission devices for probability and for utility.[53]

---

comes $x$ and $z$ are assigned utility numbers ordered in accordance with the preference between them, and the utility of any third thing $y$ is found in accordance with the archimedean condition. This condition says that when $x$ is preferred to $y$ and $y$ is preferred to $z$, then there is a unique probability $p$ (between zero and one exclusive) such that the person is indifferent between $y$ for sure and an option consisting of a probability $p$ of $x$ and a probability $(1-p)$ of $z$. When the person is fully satisfying all the Von Neumann–Morgenstern conditions there will be no problem, but when the certainty effect occurs, that intermediate certain option $y$ will be assigned a misleading utility. A better procedure might be to measure utility without considering any certain outcomes, by embedding all of the preceding within canonical probability mixtures, for instance, with probability $1/2$. The person then would be asked to find the probability $p$ such that he is indifferent between a $1/2$ chance of nothing and a $1/2$ chance of $y$, and a $1/2$ chance of nothing and a $1/2$ chance of (a probability $p$ of $x$ and a probability $1-p$ of $z$). Thereby we control for the certainty effect. Of course, such a procedure can work only if it is not sensitive to the particular probability, in this example $1/2$, within the canonical probability mixture. It would have to be the case that the same results would be gotten with a wide variety of probabilities within the canonical mixture, perhaps with all but those within epsilon of 0 and 1.

[53] Must all principles transmit only one or the other of these, or can some principles transmit both? Should we speculate that there is *one* thing which all principles transmit, namely $p_i \times u_i$, probability *and* utility? There is no single term within decision theory to denote this weighted sum, $p_i \times u_i$, despite their very frequent travel together *as a unit*. Indeed, formal theories have to institute very particular procedures to disentangle them, procedures that frequently assume they have been successfully disentangled in specific cases and then utilize devices to extend this to situations in general. We might learn something interesting by treating probability and utility as part of one integrated quantity — call it importance — and not separating these components too soon, by investigating what conditions this integrated quantity satisfies. (But isn't there an asymmetry at the beginning between the components, in that importance can be embedded in *probability* mixtures? Do we need to investigate the corresponding possibilities of utility mixtures, which may magnify or diminish the constituent importances? And might a temporal factor be included in the combination to begin with, only later to be abstracted out as a com-

Principles have various functions and effects: intellectual, intrapersonal, personal, and interpersonal. This is not to say they have these effects in every possible situation. A temperature regulatory mechanism will work only within a certain range of temperature; beyond that range it will not be able to bring temperature back and, depending upon its material, it may even itself melt or freeze. Why didn't evolution give us better regulatory mechanisms for body temperature? Given the small probability of such extreme cases' arising, that would be too costly in terms of energy and attendant sacrifice in other functions. A mechanism can perform its function pretty well, well enough, even if it won't work for some of the situations that might arise — similarly for principles.

In order to justify a principle, you specify its functions, and show that it effectively performs that function, and does this more effectively than others would given the costs, constraints, and so forth. We also can ask about the desirability of that function. Why should *anything* do that? A justification will show (or assume) that the function is desirable and does not interfere with other more desirable functions. Fully specified, a justification of a principle $P$ is a decision-theoretic structure, with the principle $P$ occupying the place of an action, competing with specific alternatives, having certain probabilities of reaching certain goals with certain desirabilities, and so on. (Our earlier discussion of factors that would be considered by a theory of the optimal choice of principles would fit into this decision-theoretic, teleological framework.)

A principle can be designed to cope with certain situations or to protect against *particular* dangers, such as giving in to temptations of the moment, favoring one's own interests, believing what one wants to be true. Hence, someone who doesn't face those dangers might not have need for *those* principles. And there might be devices other than principles to cope with such dangers.

---

ponent? Is time-preference primarily a matter concerning probability or utility, or does temporal distance itself constitute a diminution in importance? Does the extension of a utility in time — not its displacement in time — magnify its importance?)

(Might a person cope with favoring her own interests not only through principles, but through empathic interaction with others and imaginative, full projection into their situations?)

We might ask whether the device of general principles itself has its *own* biases or defects. Putting things in terms of decision theory enables us to see principles as devices (that are supposed) to have certain effects — their functions — and hence not only to compare some principles with others, but also to compare principles with other devices. Some goals might be impossible or very difficult for principles to reach, while other means might reach *those* goals more easily.

If one important goal is living together without a conflict so intense that it tears apart and destroys valuable social institutions, then when contending parties strongly put forward incompatible principles there may be no way to resolve that conflict by getting the parties to agree to any third principle, much less to either of the original two. What may be needed is some compromise — but compromise is just what principles are not supposed to do! Hence a leader of an institution or a country may simply try to keep things going, to work out some arrangement to damp down people's fury so that institutional life can continue. To be sure, there may be a principle that recommends doing this, a principle to be applied to all situations of serious principled conflict that threatens to rend and make dysfunctional valuable institutions. However, the particular content of the compromise may simply be determined by what the contending forces, given their respective powers, can manage to live with. That compromise need not itself be determined by principle in the sense that its details are taken to set a precedent for other similar situations. This is not to recommend that political and institutional leaders be unprincipled. Perhaps they are to be principled in their decisions and actions unless in those rare situations where the above-stated principle mandating (unprincipled) compromise comes into effect. (However, looking at the structure of the United States government, there seems to be a different division: some types of decision, those made by the judiciary, are held to require principles, while the details of other decisions, those of the chief executive and legislature, generally are left to the play of various forces, with some oversight by the judiciary to ensure that certain general principles are not violated.) The only point I wish to make here is that the teleological device of principles may not be suited to each and every purpose.

Another reason for thinking that principles of action have a teleological function is this. An actual case, for instance Nazi Germany, may thoroughly refute a principle $P$ that would countenance or allow that. But why wasn't the hypothetical example enough? In 1911 couldn't one say: principle $P$ would allow or even in certain circumstances would require (something like) Nazi Germany. Therefore, $P$ is false, unacceptable, evil.

However, if principles are only supposed to cover the cases that will, would, and could arise, then before the fact, if it is thought such a case is impossible (that the situation, motivations, etc., that would lead to it couldn't arise or succeed it might not be considered a *relevant* counterexample to that or any principle. But once it is discovered that human nature *can* do that — because it *did* — then the principle $P$ which countenances it is refuted.

The consequences of people accepting and acting upon a principle can discredit the principle. "They acted on the principle $P$, and look at the horrendous situation to which that led." Someone else might say that they took the principle too far or took it in a wrong direction — that the principle itself didn't *require* what they did. Nevertheless, the principle $P$ is discredited. When everyone is revolted by the earlier consequences of following $P$, it is difficult for someone to say, "Let's follow $P$ again, but this time in the right way." Why? Is it because $P$ so easily *lent itself* to that way of acting, even when it didn't require it? That's what accepting $P$ leads to when people like people actually are follow it.[54] If a principle is a device for having certain effects, it is a device for having those effects *when it is followed*, so what actually happens when it is followed, not just what it *says*, is relevant in assessing that principle as a teleological device.

But aren't principles also basic truths, which aid our understanding by subsuming instances (à la Hempel) and hence explaining why they hold? Here, again, principles might be considered to be as devices with an *epistemological* function (viz., to produce understanding), and so even here we can ask (decision-theoretically) whether there are other routes to understanding, whether these others are better suited for some contexts or subjects, and so forth.

But mightn't principles be what makes the particular truths true, what gives rise to them — in which case the primacy of principles would be *ontological*? If this does not simply repeat the epistemological function — we understand the particular truths best through principles — and if "giving rise to" is not a temporal relation, and if "makes it true" is not a causal relation, then it is not clear exactly what the ontological thesis claims. Still, this last would not make of principles solely a teleological device, and in any case we need not deny that the formulation of principles (of mathematics, of natural phenomena, of psychology) can bring coherence to these phenomena and depth to our understanding, whether the relation between the phenomena and the principles be ontological, epistemological, or some mixture. Hence, there is a further intellectual function to principles other than the one we began with — the transmission of support and probability — namely, to deepen and unify and make explicit our understanding of what the principles concern. (This will produce tighter relations of support and probability; might these *constitute* rather than result from the increased understanding?) The formulation

---

[54] See my *The Examined Life*, sec. on "The Ideal and the Actual." This also opens the possibility that people who don't want *P* to be followed to a certain result could arrange to have *P* followed to another monstrous result, thereby discrediting it.

of moral principles, thus, could deepen our understanding of moral action or moral facts and phenomena. Here, though, moral principles would have no different a status than physical or psychological ones that describe phenomena but which there is no evident reason to act *on*. It might be said that although correct moral principles hold true — in that they *ought* to be followed — the only way to get them realized, that is, to be true of our actual behavior, is to try to follow them, to act *on them*. This is an empirical claim, one that would require evidence. Perhaps the principles we are able to formulate and follow are so far off what correct moral principles — more complex moral truths — would require that we would better conform to the latter by following routes other than trying to act on principle. It is, after all, an empirical question. In any case, that makes acting on principle, once again, a teleological device.

The Kantian tradition tends to hold that principles function to guide the deliberation and action of self-conscious reflective creatures; hence principles have a theoretical and a practical function. We are creatures who do not act automatically, without any guidance. We could imagine having automatic guidance — would that make principles completely otiose for us? — or, more to the point, acting in a way that doesn't utilize guidance, for instance, at random. (Would acting completely at random suffice to free us from the domain of causality, the function Kant reserves for principles?) Doesn't this show that the purpose of principles is to guide us to something, whatever that is, that we wouldn't reach by acting at random? And doesn't that leave principles as teleological devices? However, Kant also would hold that principles are an expression of our rational nature, constitutive of rationality. To think or act rationally just is to conform to (certain kinds of) principles. Hence it would be a mistake to look only for the extrinsic *functions* that principles serve. If principles are something only a rational agent can formulate and utilize, and if being rational is something we value, then following principles can symbolize and express our rationality. Principles thus might have high utility for us, not because of what their use leads to, but because of what it symbolizes and expresses. To that extent, principles would not be solely teleological devices. But there would remain the question of why we would so value our rational nature, and the acting on principles and reasons which expresses this, if our rational nature serves no further purpose. Why does the buck stop there?

Why are principles so intimately connected with rationality? And why do we value rationality? To speak of something, an action or belief, as rational is to assess the reasons for which it was done or held (and also the way in which the person took account of the reasons *against* doing or believing that). If reasons are, by their nature, general, and if principles capture the notion of acting *for* such general reasons — so that the person is committed to acting thus in other relevantly similar circumstances also — then to act or think rationally you must do so in accordance with principles. But why should we believe or act rationally? One answer would be that we *are* rational, we have the capacity to act rationally, and we value what we are.[55] But if we are to step beyond simple self-praise, mustn't we invoke the functions served by believing or acting rationally? And why must reasons be general? Compare them with their most similar nongeneral relatives. To explain why we should utilize reasons rather than these alternatives, we must again invoke the functions of reasons. Thus, the question turns from one about principles to one about rationality. What are reasons for? What is the function of rationality? Is rationality itself wholly teleological, wholly instrumental?

---

[55] For some critical reflections on the view that we are free when our actions are determined self-consciously by a law of reason, which is a principle constitutive of our essential nature, see my *Philosophical Explanations*, pp. 353–55.

## II. Decision-Value

*Newcomb's Problem*

Newcomb's Problem is well known and I shall just describe it briefly here.[56] A being in whose power to correctly predict your choices you have great confidence is going to predict your choice in the following situation. There are two boxes, B1 and B2; box B1 contains $1,000 and box B2 contains either $1,000,000 ($M) or nothing. You have a choice between two actions: (1) taking what is in both boxes; (2) taking only what is in the second box. Furthermore, you know and the being knows you know (etc.) that if the being predicts you will take what is in both boxes, he does not put the $M in the second box; if the being predicts you will take only what is in the second box he does put the $M in the second box. First the being makes his prediction, then he puts the $M in the second box or not, according to his prediction, then you make your choice.

The problem is not only to decide what to do, but also to understand precisely what is wrong with one of the two powerful arguments that conflict. The first argument is this: if you take what is in both boxes, the being almost certainly will have predicted this and will not have put the $M in the second box and so you will almost certainly get only $1,000, whereas if you take only what is in the second box, the being almost certainly will have predicted that and will have put the $M into the second box and so you will almost certainly get $M. Therefore, you should take only what is in the second box. The second argument is this: the being already has made his prediction and has already either put the $M into the second box, or has not. The $M is either already sitting in the second box, or it is not, and which situation obtains is already

---

[56] The problem was thought of by William Newcomb, a physicist, told to me by a mutual friend, and (with Newcomb's permission) first presented and discussed in Robert Nozick, "Newcomb's Problem and Two Principles of Choice," in N. Rescher et al. (eds.), *Essays in Honor of C. G. Hempel* (Dordrecht, Holland: Reidl, 1969), pp. 114–46.

fixed and determined. If the being has already put the $M in the second box, then if you take what is in both boxes you will get $M + 1,000, whereas if you take only what is in the second box you will get just $M; if the being has not put the $M in the second box, then if you take what is in both boxes you will get $1,000, whereas if you take only what is in the second box you will get no money at all. In either case, whether the $M has been placed in there or not, you will receive more money, $1,000 more, by taking what is in both boxes. (Taking what is in both boxes, as it is said, *dominates* taking only what is in the second.) Therefore, you should take what is in both boxes.

Since 1969 when I first presented and discussed this problem, there has been much detailed investigation and illuminating theorizing about it.[57] In my initial essay, I distinguished those conditional probabilities that mark an action's *influencing* or *affecting* which state obtains from mere conditional probabilities that mark no such influence, and I suggested that when it conflicts with the dominance principle the principle of maximizing conditional expected utility should not be invoked if its conditional probabilities were of the second (nonaffecting, noninfluencing) sort. I supported this by intuitive examples. (These, because of an attempt to incorporate a certain reflexivity, are somewhat more complicated than examples others discussed afterward.) Linked genetic predispositions to a disease and to a career choice should not, I argued, lead someone to avoid one career since this raises the estimate of her chances of getting the disease — whether she actually does have that genetic makeup or will actually get the disease is not *influenced* or *affected* by the career choice. It did not occur to me to utilize this theme for the full and systematic development of competing versions of decision theory, causal and evidential,

---

[57] For a selection of articles until 1985, and a bibliographical listing of others, see Richmond Campbell and Lanning Sowden, *Paradoxes of Rationality and Cooperation: Prisoner's Dilemma and Newcomb's Problem* (Vancouver: University of British Columbia Press, 1985).

with their differing versions of the expected utility principle and even their differing versions of the dominance principle.[58]

The traditional principle of maximizing expected utility treats the expected utility of an action $A$, $EU(A)$, as the weighted sum of the utilities of its (exclusive) possible outcomes, weighted by their probabilities which sum to 1.

$EU(A) = \text{prob}(O1) \times u(O1) + \text{prob}(O2) \times u(O2) + \ldots + \text{prob}(On) \times u(On), = \text{SUM } (i=1, \ldots, n) \text{ prob}(Oi) \times U(Oi)$.

A more adequate principle, noticing that the outcomes need not be probabilistically independent of the actions, specifies the expected utility as weighted not by the simple probabilities of the outcomes, but by the conditional probabilities of the outcomes given the actions—call this the evidentially expected utility of $A$, $EEU(A)$.[59]

$EEU(A) = \text{prob}(O1/A) \times u(O1) + \text{prob}(O2/A) \times u(O2) + \ldots + \text{prob}(On/A) \times u(On), = \text{SUM } (i=1, \ldots, n) \text{ prob}(Oi/A) \times U(Oi)$.

[58] On causal decision theory, see Allan Gibbard and William Harper, "Counterfactuals and Two Kinds of Expected Utility," in Hooker, Leach, and McClennen (eds.), *Foundations and Applications of Decision Theory* (Dordrecht, Holland: Reidl, 1978), pp. 125–62; David Lewis, "Causal Decision Theory," *Australasian Journal of Philosophy*, 59 (1981), 5–30; J. H. Sobel, "Circumstances and Dominance in a Causal Decision Theory," *Synthese*, 63 (1985).

Nor did I notice the possibility of specific situations where the states were probabilistically independent of the actions yet causally influenced by them — Gibbard and Harper's Reoboam example — which should have marked a fourth row in the three-rowed chart on p. 132 of my original article.

[59] On the maximization of conditionally expected utility, though not the term "evidential utility," see my 1963 Princeton University doctoral dissertation, *The Normative Theory of Individual Choice* (since published: New York: Garland Press, 1990). See p. 232: "The probabilities that are to be used in determining the expected utility of an action must now be the conditional probabilities of the states given that the action is done. (This is true generally. However when the states are probability-independent of the actions, the conditional probability of each state given that one of the actions is done will be equal to the probability of the state, so the latter may be used.)" There also the formula for conditional expected utility was stated for the cases of the two particular actions being discussed there, though not the general formula for variable action. The general formula is presented in Richard Jeffrey, *The Logic of Decision* (New York: McGraw Hill, 1965).

The issues that concern us in this book all arise when the probabilities, conditional or otherwise, subjective or objective, are sharply defined. Other issues have led some to formulate theories using probability intervals (see, for example, Isaac Levi, *Hard Choices* [Cambridge: Cambridge University Press, 1986]); how exactly the views stated here might be restated within such frameworks is a question for investigation.

The causal decision theorists too use not simply the unconditional probability of the outcome but a probability relating the outcome to the action, this time not simply the conditional probability, $\text{prob}(Oi/A)$, but some causal-probabilistic relation indicating direct causal influence; the corresponding formula with these causal probabilities states the causally expected utility of act $A$, $\text{CEU}(A)$.

Despite these and other technical elaborations — backtracking subjunctives, explicit incorporation of tickles and meta-tickles, the ratifiability of decisions, and so forth — and despite attempts to show the problem is irremediably ill-defined or incoherent[60] — the controversy continues unabated. No resolution has been completely convincing.

Newcomb's Problem is a complicated one, other cases involve still further complications, the reasoning seems quite compelling on *all* sides — and we are fallible creatures. It would be unreasonable to place absolute confidence in any one particular line of reasoning for such cases, in any one particular principle of decision.[61]

The amount in the first box, the $1,000, has received little attention.[62] If the dominance argument — the second argument

---

[60] Attempts to reject the problem as ill-formed, ill-defined, or impossible in principle include Isaac Levi, "Newcomb's Many Problems," *Theory and Decision*, 6 (1975), 161–75; J. L. Mackie, "Newcomb's Paradox and the Direction of Causation," *Canadian Journal of Philosophy*, 7 (1977), 213–25; William Talbott, "Standard and Non-standard Newcomb Problems," *Synthese*, 70 (1987), 415–58. For a defense of the problem against many such criticisms, see Jordan Howard Sobel, "Newcomblike Problems," *Midwest Studies in Philosophy*, 15 (1990), 224–55.

[61] Some years ago, in a graduate seminar several students, particularly David Cope, queried how anyone could be certain either of causal or of evidential decision theory, given the strong arguments on both sides. I am grateful for this discussion, for it set me along the following train of thought. (However, Howard Sobel writes me to say that things are not symmetrical, for it is only the causal theorists who have tried not only to produce arguments on their own side but to diagnose the [purported] errors of the opposing arguments, in line with the desideratum I proposed in my original article.)

[62] An exception is J. Howard Sobel, who in "Infallible Predictors," *Philosophical Review*, 92 (1988), 3–24, closes the paper by considering "a limit Newcomb Problem" in which the amount in the first box is increasing from $1,000 to (almost) $1 million. However, Sobel does not also consider the situation of reducing

above — is correct, then you will be better off taking what is in both boxes even when the amount of money in the first box is much smaller, $1 for example, or even one cent or a 1/10,000th chance of one cent. However, few of us would choose both boxes in such a case, granting *no* force to the other argument that if we take only what is in the second box we are almost certain to get $M. On the other hand, if the first argument above is correct and is understood as an expected utility argument (with the embedded conditional probabilities not needing to express any influence), then the amount of money $X$ in the first box could be much larger than $1,000 yet the person would still choose to take only what is in the second box. Let us assume that the probability of the being correctly predicting your action (for each choice you might make) is .99. Where $u$ denotes the utility function, the expected utility of taking only what is in the second box is $.99u(\$M)$, while the expected utility of taking what is in both boxes is $.99u(X) + .01u(\$M+X)$. If we suppose that the utility of money is linear with its amount in this range, then this expected utility of taking what is in both boxes is $u(X) + .01u(\$M)$. In this case, the expected utility of taking what is only in the second box will be greater than the expected utility of taking what is in both boxes if $.99u(\$M)$ is greater than $u(X) + .01u(\$M)$ — that is, if $.98u(\$M)$ is greater than $u(X)$. On the assumption that utility is linear with amount of money, then, the person will choose to take only what is in the second box whenever the amount in the first box is less than $980,000. So, for example, in a choice problem having the same structure as Newcomb's Problem but where the first box contains $979,000 (and the second box, as before, contains $M or nothing), the person would not take the contents of both boxes but only what is in the second box. No doubt, the utility of money is not

---

the $1,000 in the first box to almost nothing. In Kenneth MacCrimmon and Stig Larsson, "Utility Theory: Axioms versus 'Paradoxes,'" in Maurice Allais and Ole Hagen (eds.), *Expected Utility Hypothesis and the Allais Paradox* (Dordrecht, Holland: Reidl, 1979), p. 393, the consequences of varying the amount in the second box, though not in the first, are considered.

linear with its amount in this range, but this is no great distortion for our purposes — it is the utility of $M+X$ that will be proportionally less than its monetary amount. The general point holds nevertheless: for very large amounts of money in the first box, $900,000 for example, provided the being is highly accurate in his predictions, a proponent of the first argument would take only what is in the second box. Few of us, however, would feel comfortable following the first argument in this case, granting *no* force to the other argument that we are better off in either case taking what is in both boxes.

By varying the amount of money in the first box we can make people extremely uncomfortable with their otherwise favored argument for choice in Newcomb's initial problem. People who initially chose both boxes are unwilling to follow the dominance argument when the amount in the first box is lowered to $1; people who initially chose only the second box are unwilling to follow the expected utility argument (with conditional probabilities that do not mark influence) when the amount in the first box is raised to $900,000. This suggests that no one has *complete* confidence in the argument he or she follows for Newcomb's initial example — no one is willing unreservedly and across the board to apply the reasoning that seems to move him or her in that case.

A person might have differing amounts of confidence in various principles of decision (and their associated arguments). For the moment we can restrict ourselves to just the two principles of maximizing (conditionally) expected utility, as these are formulated by causal decision theory and by evidential decision theory. These differing amounts of confidence might be represented by degrees of confidence between zero and one inclusive that sum to one; or by degrees that do not sum to one, leaving open the possibility that both of the principles are incorrect for a given case; or by confidence-weightings that are not degrees between zero and one. For some particular person, let $Wc$ be the weight he or she gives to the expected utility principle of causal decision theory, and let $We$ be the weight he or she gives to the expected utility principle of evidential decision theory. Let $\text{CEU}(A)$ be the causally expected utility of act $A$, the utility of that act as it would be computed in accordance with (some favored one of the versions of) causal decision theory; let $\text{EEU}(A)$ be the evidentially expected utility of act $A$, the utility of that act as it would be computed in accordance with evidential decision theory. Associated with each act will be a decision-value $DV$, a weighted value of its causally expected utility and its evidentially expected utility, as weighted by that person's confidence in being guided by each of these two kinds of expected utility.

$$DV(A) = Wc \times \text{CEU}(A) + We \times \text{EEU}(A).$$

And the person is to choose an act with maximal decision-value.[63]

I suggest that we go further and say not merely that we are uncertain about which *one* of these two principles, CEU and EEU, is (all by itself) correct, but that both of these two principles are legitimate, and each must be given its respective due. The weights, then, are not measures of uncertainty but measures of the legitimate force of each principle. We thus have a *normative* theory which directs a person to choose an act with maximal decision-value.

A maximizer of decision-value, if he gives nonzero weights to $Wc$ and $We$ will be led to shift his choice in Newcomb's Problem: from one box to two when the amount in the first box is raised sufficiently; from two boxes to one, when the amount in the first box is lowered sufficiently. Such changes are predictable for maximizers of decision-value. (Thus, the theory of maximizing $DV$ has testable, qualitative, behavioral consequences, at least for those who conform to that normative theory.)

---

[63] If less than complete confidence in one principle leads to following a combination of them, what happens if one does not have complete confidence in this combination? If there is a determinate other principle that one has *some* confidence in, then, insofar as the argument depends only upon actual degrees of confidence, it seems that other principle should also be included in the weighting.

There are many different mathematical structures that would give CEU and EEU a role, but the *DV* formula is especially simple and it would be premature to look now at anything more complicated. The weighted *DV* structure, all by itself, of course, does not give anyone much guidance. How great should the weights be? Must a person use the same weights in all decision situations, or might the weights vary for different types of decision situation, or more systematically according to where a decision situation falls along some dimension *D*—the further to the left the more plausible the use of one of the decision criteria (and hence the greater weight it receives), the further to the right the more plausible the use of the other one? I would welcome a theory to specify or restrict the weights, just as I would welcome a theory to specify or restrict prior probabilities within a Bayesian structure and one to specify or restrict the substantive content of preferences within the usual ordering axioms. Still, in each case the general structure can be illuminating.

That some weight is to be given to both factors, CEU and EEU, means that EEU will receive some weight even in decisions about cases where there is no causal influence of the act upon the relevant outcome — for example, the cases where a choice of a career indicates (but does not affect) differing probabilities of catching or already having a terrible disease. In my original article I thought it absurd to give such considerations any weight. Yet I knew that the evidential component of the DV formula has had major social consequences in human history, as the literature on Calvinism and the role its view of *signs* (though not causes) of election played in the development of capitalism attests. (It can be a causal consequence of an action that a person believes something that act indicates but does not cause and is made happy by this belief. But someone who introduces this as a reason for doing the action must take care not to countenance such happy consequences as a reason for holding the belief.)[64]

---

[64] For a divergent view of evidentialist considerations, holding that these are appealing only when they match cooperative reasoning in interpersonal situations,

Theorists of rationality have been intent upon formulating the one correct and complete principle to be applied unreservedly in all decision situations. But they have not yet reached this — at any rate we do not have complete confidence that they have. In this situation, won't a prudent and rational individual hedge her bets? I want to say more: namely, that no one of the principles alone is wholly adequate — it's not simply that we haven't yet found the knockdown argument for the one that is correct. I do not say that the framework of decision-value alone will bring theorists to agree. They will continue to differ in the weights they assign to the specific decision principles, even were they to agree about which principles should be included. It is this disagreement about weights that explains the differing choices in Newcomb's Problem, but it is the fact that we do give *weights* (rather than sole allegiance to one principle) that explains the switching of the decision as the amount in the first box is varied. The *DV* structure represents the fact that each of EEU and CEU captures legitimate reasons (of a sort), and we do not want to dismiss completely either sort.[65]

It is somewhat strange that writers on decision theory generally have shown such confidence in their views. For if we formulate the issue about the correct principle of decision as a decision problem, one about which principle of decision should be followed[66] — we might imagine that pills have been developed that can trans-

---

see Susan Hurley, "Newcomb's Problem, Prisoners' Dilemma, and Collective Action," *Synthese*, 86 (1991), 173–96.

[65] "But what explains the disagreement between proponents of CEU and EEU? Is it a factual or a value disagreement?" This questions assumes both proponents share an EU formula and asks whether their disagreement resides within the probability or the utility component. Yet if the *DV* formula is correct, there are *other* things to disagree about, including the weights $Wc$ and $We$, the nature of the formula, and also — to anticipate the next paragraphs — the inclusion of other factors. To ask "fact or value?" — allowing no other alternative — is to assume that what *must* be in common is the simple EU framework and that only *within* it can disagreement arise.

[66] David Gauthier considers the question of what disposition of choice a person should choose to have in *Morals by Agreement* (Oxford: Oxford University Press, 1985), chapter 6, secs. 2–3.

form us into consistent followers of each principle — then it is not obvious what the contending principles of decision will answer, and in particular it is not obvious whether they each will put itself forward as the preferred alternative. That depends upon what the world will be like. If it will offer many situations like Newcomb's Problem itself, with significant payoffs, then taking the EEU-pill can be predicted to have better *causal* consequences, so that the CEU principle will recommend taking the EEU-pill rather than the CEU-pill. If on the other hand the world will offer very many significant situations with the structure of my disease example ("Newcomb's Problem and Two Principles of Choice," p. 125) or the many similar ones (Gibbard and Harper's Solomon example, etc.: see note 58 above), then the person following the EEU principle (without any "tickle" addition) will frequently forgo significant benefits (because of the misfortunes it portends); since this can be predicted, the EEU principle itself will recommend taking the CEU-pill as an act that has higher EEU utility than does taking the EEU-pill. (In this case, the CEU principle also recommends taking the CEU-pill. Is there an example where the EEU of taking the CEU-pill is higher — and so the EEU principle recommends that — although the CEU of taking the pill is not higher, and so the CEU principle does not recommend taking it? Difficulties then would abound.) Just as there is no one particular inductive policy, no one Carnapian c-function, that is best or most effective no matter what the character of the world actually is, so there may be no one best principle of rational decision.[67] And just as we want our inductive procedures to allow for learning, to contain parameters that get specified through some experience of the world, so too we want our principles of rational decision to contain param-

[67] Rudolf Carnap maintained (*Logical Foundations of Probability* [Chicago: University of Chicago Press, 1950]) that sentences asserting that "the degree of confirmation of h on e is n" are, when true, analytic. Yet even he also held that *which* particular confirmation function is to be chosen (c\*, c-dagger, or whatever from among the continuum of inductive methods), and therefore which one will specify this analytic relation, is a matter of pragmatic choice and will depend upon general facts about the universe.

eters that can be specified to fit the discovered character of the world in which decisions are to be made. (In each case, evolution may have accomplished a significant part of the setting of parameters to fit the actual world, but this does not mean we should expect our specific inductive policies or decision principles to be applicable in every imaginable science-fiction situation, or that we should treat them as valid *a priori*.) The framework of decision-values with its incorporated weights that can be altered over time is one way a fitting to the actual world can be accomplished.

The decision-value we specified was based upon the two components CEU and EEU, but any alternative plausible principle of decision, or factor in decision, might be added as a term with its own associated weight. In particular, we could add to the formula the symbolic utility of an action, its SU, which incorporates the utility of the various outcomes and actions *symbolized* by the act, with its own associated weight $W_s$. (It is best not to try to incorporate symbolic utility alongside other utilities, because it may well not obey an expected value formula and because we might want to keep separate track of symbolic utility, since we think it appropriate to give this factor different weight in different kinds of choice situations.) The formula for the decision-value of $A$, $DV(A)$, then would become:

$$DV(A) = W_c \times \text{CEU}(A) + W_e \times \text{EEU}(A) + W_s \times \text{SU}(A).$$

It would be instructive to investigate the formal characteristics of this decision-value structure; it would not be surprising if this principle of weighted combination, like other criteria previously investigated in the literature of decision under uncertainty, sometimes failed to exhibit certain desirable features.[68]

---

[68] See John Milnor, "Games against Nature," in R. M. Thrall, C. H. Coombs, and R. L. Davis, *Decision Processes* (New York: John Wiley, 1954), pp. 49–59, and R. D. Luce and Howard Raiffa, *Games and Decisions* (New York: John Wiley and Sons, 1957), pp. 275–98. Earlier I said that symbolic meaning need not carry over proportionally into probabilistic contexts. Yet the *DV* formula includes symbolic utility as one of the weighted components. We might wonder whether sym-

Symbolic utility is not a different kind of utility, standing to standard utility in something like the way metaphorical meaning stands to literal. Rather, symbolic utility is a different kind of *connection* — symbolic — to the familiar kind of utility. It stands alongside the already familiar connections, the causal and the evidential. The symbolic utility of an action $A$ is determined by $A$'s having symbolic connections to outcomes (and perhaps to other actions) which themselves have the standard kind of utility, just as the CEU of $A$ is determined by $A$'s causal-probabilistic connections to outcomes with the standard utility.[69]

Should we ensure that these types of connection — causal, evidential, and symbolic — are exclusive? The earlier formula for *DV* specified it as a weighted sum of CEU and EEU. However, the EEU of an action includes its causal components, since the conditional probabilities of outcomes given actions, $prob(O/A)$, which the EEU theorist utilizes incorporate causal influences when such exist. In our weighted sum formula, then, should we not interpret the EEU as the expected utility represented by those (portions of) probabilities which are *not* (simply derivative from) causal ones? And similarly, shouldn't the symbolic utility SU of an action be its symbolic utility which is not (simply) derivative from and represented within those very causal and evidential connections?[70]

---

bolic utility will carry over into the weighted *DV* context. However, shifting to a probabilistic situation is a shift to a *different* situation, while shifting to the *DV* formula does not shift the choice situation.

[69] One further condition therefore needs to be imposed on the standard situation for measuring utility discussed in footnote 52. That situation must be one where the actions have no relevant evidential or symbolic connections to utility-outcomes. Utility is to be calibrated in causal contexts, where an expected value principle is followed, and the (sanitized) utilities thus found are to be utilized in situations where actions also stand in evidential and symbolic connections to valued outcomes. However, the value of these latter outcomes is measured in situations that are wholly causal.

[70] The one psychological study I know of that treats both causal and evidential connections, and seeks to disentangle them, is G. A. Quattrone and Amos Tversky, "Causal versus Diagnostic Contingencies: On Self-Deception and the Voter's Illusion," *Journal of Personality and Social Psychology*, 46 (1984), 237–48.

Should we incorporate still further components into the *DV* structure? One suggestion would be explicitly to include a component concerning the way an action fits into a person's image of himself and is self-expressive. However, our three components already cover much of this territory. Although performing an action of the sort that would be done by a certain kind of person may not *cause* the agent to be this kind of person, it may symbolize his being that way, be some evidence that he is, and have the causal consequence of making it easier for him to maintain an *image* of himself as being of that kind. This last is a real causal consequence of an action which may have significant utility. Hence this kind of consequence — how doing a particular action affects the person's self-image — can play a significant explicit role in an explanatory theory of that person's behavior, even though it is a type of consequence which the agent himself cannot easily take into account explicitly — "I am going to do *A* in order to make it easier to maintain my self-image as a person of kind *K*" — without thereby diminishing that very effect.[71] However, we should not interpret expressiveness as exhausted by these other independent categories, narrowly conceived, for, as we said earlier, the categories of the symbolic and the expressive are intertwined.

If we array the category of the linguistic alongside the categories we already have as follows, causal/evidential/linguistic/symbolic, this suggests two questions. How does the symbolic differ in nature from the merely linguistic (the symbolic does lend itself more to utility being imputed back, but this need not happen every

---

[71] Not every mode of action involves a connection to a consequence to be placed within a formula alongside the causal, evidential, and symbolic connections. Consider acting without motive, a mode whose variants are spoken of in the literature of Buddhism, Taoism, and Hinduism. Here, the person does not act so as to become a certain way, or to be a certain way, or to produce results, or to have evidence, or to symbolize anything. Perhaps he acts so as to *align* himself (rightly) with the deepest reality, to be aligned with this deepest reality by letting it act through him. This mode of action needs to be analyzed further, but it does not seem to involve a mode of connection to a consequence.

time; and how might the linguistic arise out of the causal and evidential? When causal and evidential connections (which arise from a branching structure of causal and statistical regularities) are common knowledge, someone might intentionally produce an evidential sign of $p$ in order to get another to believe that $p$. This would be a crucial step beyond a Gricean natural meaning, which is an evidential sign, to an intentional deployment to produce a belief in another, that is, partway to a Gricean non-natural meaning wherein this intention is intended to be recognized.[72] Such an evidential sign might be produced to induce a belief in a true $p$ that the other person cannot independently observe right then. But also — perhaps equally likely — it might first have been produced to deceive the other person into believing $p$, on the basis of planted evidence, when $p$ was false. The first statement that stood for something else might have been a lie, a faked natural sign. If language defined humanity, expressing our rational capacities and distinguishing humans from other animals, then this would give an intriguing twist to the doctrine that we are born in original sin.

*Prisoner's Dilemma*

The Prisoner's Dilemma is a much-discussed situation where each party's selecting a (strongly) dominant action, which appears to be the rational thing to do, leaves each of them worse off than if each had selected the more cooperative dominated action. The combination of (what appears to be) their individual rationalities leads them to forgo an attainable better situation and thus is Pareto-suboptimal.

The general situation is named after one instance of it: a sheriff offers each of two imprisoned persons awaiting trial the following options. (The situation is symmetrical between the prisoners; they cannot communicate to coordinate their actions in response to the sheriff's offer or, if they can, they have no means to enforce any

[72] H. P. Grice, "Meaning," *Philosophical Review*, 67 (1957), 377–88.

agreement they might reach.) If one prisoner confesses and the other does not, the first does not go to jail and the second will receive a twelve-year sentence; if both confess, both receive a ten-year prison sentence; if both do not confess, both receive a two-year sentence. Figure 2 represents the situation they face, where the entries in the matrix represent the number of years to be served in prison: the first number the years for the first prisoner, the second number for the second.

FIGURE 2

|  |  | PRISONER II | |
|---|---|---|---|
|  |  | Don't Confess | Confess |
| PRISONER I | Don't Confess | 2, 2 | 12, 0 |
|  | Confess | 0, 12 | 10, 10 |

Each reasons as follows: "If the other person confesses and I don't I will receive twelve years in prison, whereas if I do I will receive ten years; if the other person doesn't confess and I don't I will receive two years in prison, whereas if I do I will receive no years at all. In either case, whichever thing the other person does, I am better off confessing rather than not. Therefore, I will confess." Each prisoner reasons in the same way: both confess and both receive ten years in prison, whereas if both had not confessed, each would have receive only two years in prison. Individual rationalities combine to produce a joint mess. And the situation is stable in the following sense: neither one has any incentive to perform the other (more cooperative) action, given that the other party is going to confess. Their actions of confessing are in equilibrium.

The Prisoner's Dilemma situation is an instance of a more general structure (see fig. 3) where each party has a choice between two actions — call them $D$ for the dominant one, $C$ for the cooperative — and has the following preferences among the possible outcomes of the combined actions, $a$, $b$, $c$, and $d$. Person I prefers $c$ to $a$ to $d$ to $b$, while person II prefers $b$ to $a$ to $d$ to $c$.

FIGURE 3

|   |   | II |   |
|---|---|---|---|
|   |   | C' | D' |
| I | C | a | b |
|   | D | c | d |

Since person I prefers $c$ to $a$, and $d$ to $b$, action $D$ dominates action $C$ and he chooses to do $D$. Since person II prefers $b$ to $a$, and $d$ to $c$, action $D'$ dominates action $C'$, and she chooses to do $D'$. Together $D$ and $D'$ yield the outcome $d$, while both of them prefer the outcome $a$ (which would result from $C$ and $C'$) to outcome $d$. Therefore, these simple facts about the structure of the $2 \times 2$ matrix and the structure of each person's preference ordering seem sufficient to mark a Prisoner's Dilemma situation.

Some people have argued that a rational person in this situation, knowing the other also is a rational person who knows as much about the situation as he himself does, will realize that any reasoning convincing for himself will be convincing for the other as well, so if he himself concludes the dominant action is best, the other person will as well; if he concludes the cooperative action is best, the other person will as well. In this situation, then, it would be better to conclude the cooperative action is best and realizing all this, he therefore (somehow) does so. This type of argument has had a mixed reception.

The Prisoner's Dilemma parallel's Newcomb's Problem, whether or not the two are (as some have argued) identical in all essential features. Both involve two arguments that lead to differing actions, one argument based upon the dominance principle interpreted in such a way as to be congenial to causal decision theory, the other argument based upon considering what each act would indicate (and what outcome therefore should be bet upon), in a way congenial to evidential decision theory. The argument that in the Prisoner's Dilemma you should expect that the other person will do as you do, even though your action does not causally affect what the other does, fits the principle of maximizing the evidentially expected utility, where the conditional probabilities need not represent any causal influence. Causal decision theory recommends performing the dominant action; evidential decision theory recommends performing the cooperative action when you think the other party is relevantly similar to yourself. It need not be that you are certain you both will act alike; it will be enough if the conditional probabilities of the other party's actions, given your own, vary sufficiently. (Notice too that evidential decision theory might lead to performing the dominant action, if you believe the other party is likely to perform a *different* act than yours, or simply if her act is independent of your own but you ascribe sufficiently pessimistic probabilities to her chances of cooperating.) As was the case with Newcomb's Problem, our confidence in each of these positions may be less than complete, and we may want to give each some legitimate weight.

In the case of Newcomb's Problem, this multiple granting of legitimate weight (or, alternatively, the lack of complete confidence) showed itself in the switching of decisions when the amount of money in the first box was varied. (Yet the structure of the problem was kept constant as judged by the two competing principles of decision which would have maintained their same decision through these changes.) In the case of the Prisoner's Dilemma, the question is what rational agents with common knowledge that they face rational agents should do. Proponents of the two differing arguments find that the abstract structure of figure 3 is sufficient to give their favored argument its compelling grip. All the dominance argument needs is that person I prefers

$c$ to $a$, and $d$ to $b$, while person II prefers $b$ to $a$, and $d$ to $c$. All the evidentially expected utility argument about rational agents seems to need is that each has common knowledge that each is a rational agent and that each prefers $a$ to $d$. If people do lack complete confidence in these arguments, however, we should find that variations in the amounts[73] of the payoffs within the abstract structure of figure 3 (while still maintaining the *order* of the party's preferences) will produce changes in the decision people would make.

Suppose that utility is measured on an interval scale, unique up to a positive linear transformation, with an arbitrary unit and an arbitrary zero point, in conformity to some variant of the standard Von Neumann–Morgenstern axioms.[74] In the situation represented by figure 4, where the matrix entries are such utility numbers, we would think that cooperation is the rational choice.

FIGURE 4

|   |   | II |   |
|---|---|---|---|
|   |   | $C'$ | $D'$ |
| I | $C$ | 1000, 1000 | 0, 1001 |
|   | $D$ | 1001, 0 | 1, 1 |

In general, when the cooperative solution payoffs are very much higher than the dominance ones, and when payoffs for the nonmatching actions offer only slight gains or losses over these two, then we strongly will think that cooperation is rational and

---

[73] More exactly — since utility is measured on an interval scale — in the ratios of differences in amounts. When the discussion to follow ignores this complication in the interests of lucidity, it can be suitably rephrased.

[74] See John Von Neumann and Oscar Morgenstern, *The Theory of Games and Economic Behavior*, 2nd ed. (Princeton: Princeton University Press, 1947), appendix. An examination of philosophical issues about the Von Neumann–Morgenstern and similar sets of conditions is contained in my *The Normative Theory of Individual Choice*.

will find that the dominance argument has little force. Alternatively, in figure 5, the cooperation solution is only slightly better than the dominant one, and the extreme values in the payoffs for the nonmatching actions diverge greatly. When we have no special ties to the other party or particular knowledge of the other party's probabilities of action, then we will think it is rational to perform the dominant action in the figure 5 situation, not running any risk of the other party's performing his dominant action, which he has a large incentive to do. (And if I go through this reasoning, and think he also is very likely to be like me, then I may well settle upon the dominant action in this case, comfortable with the realization that he will also.)

FIGURE 5

|   |   | II |   |
|---|---|---|---|
|   |   | $C'$ | $D'$ |
| I | $C$ | 3, 3 | −200, 500 |
|   | $D$ | 500, −200 | 2, 2 |

These shifts in the decision one would make, which depend upon the (ratios of the differences in the) particular numerical utility entries in the matrix, are in accordance with the earlier principle of maximizing decision-value, for people who give some weight to each of the particular principles CEU and EEU. At what precise point their decision will shift as the utilities are varied will depend upon how confident they are in each of these principles (i.e., what weights they implicitly assign to them) and also upon the probabilities they assign to the other person's action being the same as their own. Notice, however, that even if this last is given a probability of 1, and even if the agent gives greater weight to the EEU principle than to the CEU principle, she will not necessarily perform the cooperative action. If the utility stakes are big enough and fit the situation in figure 5, that fact can combine with the weight that is given to the CEU principle, or with the dominance principle itself (in its causal variant), or with some other principle that gives weight to the security level, to yield a recommendation of the dominant action. Even absolute confidence that the other person will act as you do is not enough to guarantee your performing the cooperative action — in the absence of absolute confidence in, or weight to, the EEU principle.[75] (I have been assuming until now that it is one particular version of the *DV* principle, with its particular weights fixed, that a person applies in all decision situations. However, it might be that for a given set of constituent principles of decision, a person assigns them different weights depending upon the type of decision situation she faces. Still, each type of situation where more than one particular principle received positive weight would be fitted by some *DV* structure or other.)

In the previous section we incorporated the symbolic utility of doing an action, its SU, within the *DV* structure alongside CEU

---

[75] "But wouldn't a correct theory *insist* that when the probability is 1 that the other person will behave as you do, you *should* choose the cooperative action in the Prisoner's Dilemma situation, whatever the magnitude of the utility differences in the matrix? And so isn't this divergence an *objection* to the *DV* structure?" We might wonder, though, whether the person has (one level up) complete confidence in his probability estimate of 1 and whether the lack of complete confidence might affect his action in this high-risk situation (see Daniel Ellsberg, "Risk, Ambiguity, and the Savage Axioms," *Quarterly Journal of Economics*, 75 [1961], 643–69).

Notice too that the argument proceeds too quickly from (1) common rationality, to (2) they will do the same thing, to (3) crossing out the upper-right and lower-left boxes in the matrix, representing divergent actions, to (4) arguing that, given that the choice is between the two remaining boxes, both should choose the one they prefer — each prefers — that is, both should do the cooperative action. Assuming common knowledge of rationality allows us to assume that we will reason in the same way and will end up doing the same thing. But perhaps *that* will result from our each reasoning about all four boxes in the matrix, and our each concluding that in the light of the joint strategic situation persented by the full matrix, including all four boxes, I (and he or she) should do the noncooperative action, and so both end up in the lower-right noncooperative box — *thus* satisfying the condition that we act identically. Our knowing in advance that we will do the same thing means we know we will not end up in the upper-right or lower-left box, but this doesn't mean we can therefore first delete them and then reason about the remaining situation. For perhaps the reasoning whereby we *will* end up performing the same action depends upon our *not* first deleting those divergent corners.

and EEU. It might be thought that if an action *does* have symbolic utility, then this will show itself *completely* in the utility entries in the matrix for that action (e.g., perhaps each of the entries gets raised by a certain fixed amount that stands for the act's symbolic utility), so that there need not be any separate SU factor. However, the symbolic value of an act is not determined solely by *that* act; what the act means or symbolizes can depend upon what other acts are available with what payoffs, and what acts also are available to the other party or parties. What the act symbolizes is something it symbolizes when done in *that* particular situation, in preference to *those* particular alternatives. If an act symbolizes "being a cooperative person," that will not simply be because it has the two possible payoffs it does, but because it occupies a particular position within the two-person matrix — viz., being a dominated action that (when joined with the other person's dominated action) yields a higher payoff to each than does the combination of the dominant actions. Hence, its SU is not a function of those features captured by treating an act in isolation, simply as a mapping of states onto consequences.[76] An act's symbolic value may depend upon the whole decision or game matrix. It is not appropriately represented by some addition to or subtraction from the utilities of consequences *within* the matrix. Many writers assume that *anything* can formally be built into the consequences[77] — how it *feels* to perform the action, the fact that you have done it, or the fact that it falls under particular deontological principles. But if the *reasons* for doing an act $A$ affect its utility, then to build this utility of an action into $A$'s *consequences* would thereby alter the act and change the reasons for doing it; but the utility of *that* altered action will depend upon the reasons for

---

[76] This is how L. J. Savage treats acts within the formalism of his decision theory; cf. his *The Foundations of Statistics* (New York: Wiley, 1954). However, an act cannot be reduced in this way, even apart from issues about its possible symbolic value. See my *The Normative Theory of Individual Choice*, pp. 184–93.

[77] See, for example, Peter Hammond, "Consequentialist Foundations for Expected Utility," *Theory and Decision*, 25 (1988), 25–78.

doing *it*, and to build this into its consequences would alter the reasons for doing the now doubly altered act, and so forth. Moreover, the utilities of an *outcome* can change if the action is done for certain reasons.[78] What we want the utilities of the outcomes to represent, therefore, is the *conditional* utilities of the outcomes given that the action is done for certain reasons.[79] This creates a problem for consequentialism in dealing with dynamic consistency issues; for it might be that the fact of having reached a particular subtree of the decision-tree gives you information which alters the utility of a future outcome. If we attempt to cope with this by insisting that the utilities within the tree always be fully specified conditional utilities, then we cannot have the *same* outcomes at any two different places in the decision-tree — to the detriment of stating general normative principles to govern such trees. (For *each* fact about an act, there might be a description that enables you to list that fact as a consequence of the act, but it does not follow that there is a description such that, for *all* facts about the act, that description incorporates them within the act's consequences. The order of the quantifiers matters.)

These considerations show that in Prisoner's Dilemma situations an action should be conceived as having a utility of its own,

[78] As a result of Newcomb's Problem, cases have been investigated where the *probability* of an outcome alters with the reasons for doing the action, thus giving rise to the literature on "ratifiability."

[79] Or even the conditional utility of the outcome given that the action is done for certain reasons *and leads to the outcome*. In the economic literature on auctions, it is pointed out that a person's estimate of the value of an outcome might change when he discovers that his particular bid was the winning one, when this indicates that other knowledgeable bidders had information, or reached conclusions, that led them to value the outcome less than he did. The ratifiability literature notes that the fact that "I decide to do $A$" can affect the estimate of the probability of a consequence $C$ of $A$, in that prob($C/I$ decide to do $A$) is not equal to prob($C$), while the auction literature notes that "my doing $A$ is successful in bringing about $C$" can affect the utility of $C$, perhaps by altering the probabilities of other information which affects the utility of $C$. Thus, a fully formulated decision theory not only must utilize conditional utility (see my *The Normative Theory of Individual Choice*, pp. 144–58), but the conditional utility it utilizes must be not simply $u$(outcome $O$/the action $A$ is done) but rather $u$(outcome $O$/the action $A$ is done, for reasons $R$, and this $A$ done for $R$ leads to $O$).

not simply as involving a constant utility addition *within* a row of its matrix.[80] But I wish to claim something stronger — namely, that this utility is a *symbolic* utility. This is not simply the usual kind of utility applied to an action rather than an outcome. This utility involves a different kind of connection. In some Prisoner's Dilemma situations, doing the dominated action — what is usually called the "cooperative action" — may have symbolic value for the person. It may stand for his being a cooperative person in interactions with others, a willing and noncarping participant in joint ventures of mutual benefit. Cooperating in this situation then may get grouped with other activities of cooperation that are not embedded in Prisoner's Dilemma situations; not cooperating in this particular Prisoner's Dilemma situation may then come to threaten his cooperating in those other situations — the line between them may not be so salient, and his motivation for cooperation in the others may also be partly symbolic. Giving great utility to being a cooperative person, in a particular Prisoner's Dilemma situation he performs the dominated act that symbolizes this.[81]

This does not mean this person will look only at that act's SU. He also will consider its particular utility entries and how these are evaluated by the CEU and the EEU principles. The decision-value of the act for him will depend upon all three of these things — its SU, CEU, and EEU — and upon the weights he gives to these. Thus, the mere fact that he gives some (positive) symbolic utility to being a cooperative person does not guarantee he will perform the cooperative action in all Prisoner's Dilemma situations.

---

[80] It also is worth mentioning that when the sequencing of the actions is strategically relevant, game theorists do not simply concentrate upon the matrix-representation of a game and its payoffs, but need to consider the game-tree.

[81] Can one build this into the standard decision theory by saying that one constant consequence of his performing the dominant act in the Prisoner's Dilemma situation is that he will think of himself as a noncooperative person, and then representing this in the game matrix by a negative addition, an addition of negative utility, all across the row for that action? Notice that this component of utility would be a function of his attitude toward that act as it stands within the structure of the whole matrix.

I do not claim that the only possible symbolic meaning relevant to the Prisoner's Dilemma situation is "being a cooperative person." Someone might think that performing the *dominant* action in such situations symbolizes "being rational, not being swayed by sentimentality"; thinking this quite important, he gives great symbolic utility (within his *DV* principle) to performing the dominant action, this in addition to the weight he gives to the CEU or dominance principle itself. Some writers on Newcomb's Problem who are proponents of the view that taking what is in both boxes is most rational overcome discomfort at the fact that they and people like themselves do worse on this problem than do maximizers of EEU by saying its "moral" is "if someone is very good at predicting behavior and rewards predicted irrationality richly, then irrationality will be richly rewarded."[82] I take it that such people give very great utility — is that a symbolic utility? — to being rational according to their best current estimate of what precise principles that involves. (It will be a subtle matter to distinguish between someone who gives weight to only *one* particular principle, CEU for example, and someone who gives some weight to CEU and also some lesser weight to EEU yet also attaches great symbolic utility — greatly weighted — to following her best *particular* estimate of what rationality involves.) One would guess that new complications would arise if following a particular decision principle itself has symbolic utility or if engaging in a particular kind of decision process or procedure does.

To say all this about symbolic utility is to say that our responses to the Prisoner's Dilemma are governed, in part, by our view of the kind of person we wish to be and the kinds of ways we wish to relate to others. What we do in a particular Prisoner's Dilemma situation will involve all this and invoke it to different degrees depending upon the precise (ratios of differences among) utility entries in the matrix and also upon the particular factual circum-

[82] Gibbard and Harper, "Counterfactuals and Two Kinds of Expected Utility," 151.

stances that give rise to that matrix, circumstances in which an action may come to have its own symbolic meanings, not simply because of the structure of the matrix.

We knew all this already, of course, at least as a psychological point about why people differ in their responses to Prisoner's Dilemma situations. However, the *DV* principle leaves room for general views about what sort of person to be, as this relates to and groups particular choices, not simply as a possible *psychological* explanation of why (some) people deviate from rationality, but as a legitimate component, symbolic utility, within their *rational* procedure of decision.

In a seminal paper on the repeated Prisoner's Dilemma,[83] Kreps, Milgrom, Roberts, and Wilson showed that your giving a small probability to my performing the cooperative action or your giving this to my believing that you will perform the cooperative action (or your giving a small probability to my believing that you will believe that I will perform the cooperative action) can be sufficient to make it rational for you to begin by performing the cooperative action, in order to encourage me in my cooperative action or consonant beliefs. If you believe I might do the cooperative action (or follow tit-for-tat), and you believe that I will continue to do so only if *you* behave a certain way, then you will have reasons to behave as I think you might, in order to encourage me to do the cooperative action.[84] If the situation is mutual, both will (under certain circumstances) perform the cooperative action. Now the *DV* structure, when it is common knowledge that both follow it, does (promise to) give some probability of each player believing that the other will believe that the first will perform the cooperative action, and hence some probability of each, of both,

---

[83] David P. Kreps, P. Milgrom, J. Roberts, and R. Wilson, "Rational Cooperation in the Finitely Repeated Prisoner's Dilemma," *Journal of Economic Theory*, 27 (1982), 245–52.

[84] As one writer puts it in summary, a player might "take an out of equilibrium action to set in motion the other player's out of equilibrium beliefs and strategies" (Eric Rasmussen, *Games and Information* [Oxford: Basil Blackwell, 1989], p. 111).

performing the cooperative action. (Notice that this point, and the remainder of this paragraph, does *not* depend upon the full *DV* structure which includes a weighting for symbolic utility. The narrower structure first presented, with a weighting only of CEU and EEU, is enough.) And this, not as a perturbation away from full rationality, and not as one's rational adjustment to the other's deviation from rationality (or to the other's belief that you might deviate from rationality), but rather as a part of common knowledge that all participants are *totally* rational. For if the principle of maximizing decision-value is a rational principle, normatively desirable, then if (as it appears to) common knowledge of *DV*-maximization gives some probability of each participant's performing the cooperative action, the argument of Kreps, Milgrom, Roberts, and Wilson applies even under common knowledge of full rationality.[85]

It would be nice to reach a sharper result than that the cooperative action will be performed if the causal, evidential, and symbolic utilities interact so as to lead to this. Under what conditions, for what specifications of weights within a *DV* structure for one (or both) of the participants, will a person choose to perform the cooperative action in the Prisoner's Dilemma situation or follow a tit-for-tat strategy in the repeated Prisoner's Dilemma.[86]

Here we can take only some tentative first steps in listing appropriate assumptions for deriving results. In addition to requir-

---

[85] A side note in passing: in my 1963 doctoral dissertation, I saw the necessity for game-theoretic situations of levels of knowledge infinitely extended, each knowing the structure of the game theoretic situation, each knowing the other knows, each knowing the other knows that he knows, and so on (*The Normative Theory of Individual Choice*, p. 274). But I thought this just was a nit-picking point. Little did I see the far-reaching interest and implications of the condition of common knowledge of rationality. See Robert Aumann, "Correlated Equilibrium as an Expression of Bayesian Rationality," *Econometrica*, 55 (1987), 1–18, and Drew Fudenberg and Jean Tirole, *Game Theory* (Cambridge: MIT Press, 1991), pp. 541–72.

[86] On the tit-for-tat strategy, see Robert Axelrod, "The Emergence of Cooperation among Egoists," reprinted in Campbell and Sowden, *Paradoxes of Rationality and Cooperation*, and *The Evolution of Cooperation* (New York: Basic Books, 1984).

ing that both players follow the *DV* principle, we can add an extremely weak form of the assumption that each should expect the other player to behave as he does, to be fed into the EEU component. The weak predictive principle says that the evidential conditional probability that the other player will do act $C'$, conditional on your doing $C$, is greater than the unconditional evidential probability that she will do $C'$; and similarly for her act $D'$ conditional upon your own. A somewhat stronger principle, but still short of the symmetry assumption that the other rational player will act exactly as you do, would hold that these evidential conditional probabilities, for the first play, are greater than $1/2$. Another principle specifies that the person gives *some* symbolic utility (and some symbolic weight to that) to performing the cooperative act in the Prisoner's Dilemma situation. Moreover, we might assume that performing the dominant act $D$ has a negative symbolic utility of its own, in addition to the absence of the positive symbolic utility of cooperating.[87] Let $S(A/B)$ be the symbolic utility of act $A$ given that the other person does act $B$. If person I assigns positive symbolic utility to performing the cooperative action, then $S(C/C')$ is greater than or equal to $S(C/D')$, and each of these is greater than (the negative quantity) $S(D/D')$, which itself is greater than (the more negative) $S(D/C')$. When the Prisoner's Dilemma structure is repeated many times between the same two persons, the further possibilities of mutually beneficial cooperation affect the utilities within a current play, including the very first one. Moreover, the symbolic utility of an action will change from play to play, depending upon the past actions of the other party. We might see the symbolic utility of performing the cooperative action as declining, the more the other party performs her dominant action, perhaps as declining proportionally to the ratio of the number of times the other party has performed her dominant ac-

---

[87] I speak intuitively here, since on an interval scale of measurement, with an arbitrary zero point, there is no special significance to a measured quantity's being negative.

tion to the number of times she has performed her dominated one. Cooperating with *her* becomes less a symbol of being a cooperative person, the more she has refused to cooperate. On the other hand, the more the other person cooperates, the more symbolic utility your performing the cooperative action will have. And a comparable condition now applies to the negative symbolic utility of performing the dominant act. This disutility also declines in absolute amount the more the other person performs her dominant action and increases in absolute amount the more she performs her cooperative action. The hope is that these conditions, along with other plausible assumptions, will give us sharper results.

*Finer Distinctions: Consequences and Goals*

We have discussed three different modes of connection of action to outcomes — namely, causal, evidential, and symbolic — and have suggested that decision theory needs to utilize and explicitly recognize all three modes. Does decision theory also need finer discriminations *within* these categories? For example, some writers on ethics have claimed that different kinds of causal connections carry different weights in choice situations, even though the resulting probabilities may be identical. There is a significant difference, they claim, between bringing something about and allowing it to happen or abstaining from preventing it. (And we might consider further kinds of causal relation, such as facilitating or aiding its happening.) And some writers have formulated a doctrine of "double-effect," holding that there can be a moral difference (sometimes sufficient to make the difference as to whether an action is permissible) between bringing something about when this results from intending to bring it about as an end or a means to an end and knowingly bringing it about but as a side-effect of one's pursuit of some other goal. Admittedly, these are matters of some controversy,[88] yet it is striking that causal decision theory

---

[88] See Philippa Foot, "The Problem of Abortion and the Doctrine of the Double Effect," in her *Virtues and Vices* (Berkeley: University of California Press,

thus far has taken no notice of these arguably important distinctions; it proceeds instead with an undifferentiated notion of "causal influence." Should normative decision theory make room for such distinctions and give them a role, either in its first-person theory of choice or in its instructions for an adviser? One natural place these distinctions might enter is in the notion of conditional utility. Earlier, in speaking of auction theory, we noted that decision theory should speak of $u$ (outcome $O/A$ is done and $A$ causes or succeeds in bringing about $O$). The precise kind of causal linkage between action and outcome within the last part of this condition might affect the utility of the resulting outcome $O$, that is, yield differing conditional utilities for $O$ and hence sometimes produce different decisions within a principle that utilizes such conditional utilities. Or is the import of these distinctions wholly symbolic, so that by incorporating symbolic utility within our theory we already have made an adequate place for them?[89]

I suggest we see these distinctions, not as dichotomies, but as arrayed along a (not necessarily continuous) dimension. Indeed, we have here not one dimension but two. The first involves the importance of the causal role of the action in relation to the effect or outcome or resulting state of affairs. Here we have (at least) seven relations an action may stand in to a state of affairs. In

---

1978), pp. 19–32; Judith Thompson, "Killing, Letting Die, and the Trolley Problem," and "The Trolley Problem," in her *Rights, Restitution and Risk* (Cambridge, Mass.: Harvard University Press, 1986), pp. 78–116; Warren Quinn, "Actions, Intentions, and Consequences: The Doctrine of Double-Effect," *Philosophy and Public Affairs*, 18 (1989), 334–51; Warren Quinn, "Actions, Intentions and Consequences: The Doctrine of Doing and Allowing," *Philosophical Review* (1989), 287–312; Frances Kamm, "Harming Some to Save Others," *Philosophical Studies*, 57 (1989), 227–60.

[89] Or, instead, are these distinctions framing effects, in the sense of Tversky and Kahneman, which show variance across (descriptions of) situations where there should be invariance? See Amos Tversky and Daniel Kahneman, "Judgment under Uncertainty: Heuristics and Biases," *Science*, 185 (1974), 1124–31; reprinted in Daniel Kahneman, Paul Slovic, and Amos Tversky (eds.), *Judgment under Uncertainty* (Cambridge: Cambridge University Press, 1982). Doesn't the relation of the bringing about/allowing to happen distinction to a baseline seem suspiciously like that of the gain/loss distinction to *its* baseline? This last, of course, is a favored example for framing effects.

decreasing importance, the action may: (1) cause the state of affairs to occur; (2) aid or facilitate its occurrence; (3) remove a barrier to its occurrence; (4) permit or allow its occurrence; (5) not prevent and not avoid its occurrence (when some act available to you would have); (6) not aid or facilitate its nonoccurrence (when some act available to you would have); (7) not aid or facilitate its nonoccurrence (and *no* act available to you would have).

The second dimension also involves the causal role of the action, in relation to the effect or outcome or resulting state of affairs, but this dimension marks not the act's importance but its *robustness*. The idea is that when something is pursued as a goal, certain subjunctives hold true of the person. He would reorganize his behavior in order to reach the goal (or to have a better chance of reaching it); in slightly different circumstances, where *this* action would not reach that goal, he would do something different instead that *would* reach the goal; he would tend to exclude alternative actions that have no possibility of reaching the goal. When something is merely a known side-effect of the action, on the other hand, the person would not alter his behavior if it turned out that his (current or planned) behavior would not produce this side-effect. Of course, if it instead produced another significant effect he wished to avoid, he might do so. It is a question of the *range* of the situations where the behavior would alter. Pursuit of something as a goal involves subjunctives across a wider range of circumstances than acting in the knowledge that something will result as a side-effect of other goal pursuits. Between these two falls aiming at something solely as a means toward the realization of some other goal. In this case, behavior would be reorganized in some situations to realize the means — unlike the side-effect case — but in a narrower range of possible situations than where the effect is an end or goal itself. (Consider, for example, that possible situation where this particular effect no longer serves as a means to the goal.)

Along this dimension of robustness of the causal role, we can distinguish (at least) six connections of a person and an action to an effect or outcome. The action can: (1) aim at the effect as an end; (2) aim at the effect solely as a means. Or it can not aim at the effect at all. And among actions that do not aim at the effect, the person might: (3) know of the effect (which is not aimed at); (4) not know of the effect (which is not aimed at) that she should know of; (5) not know of the effect (which is not aimed at), and it not be the case that she should know of it. Or (6) the state of affairs (which is not aimed at) occurs by accident.

Utilizing these two dimensions, and their categories, we can form a 7 by 6 matrix. (If the two dimensions are not completely independent, some of the boxes may be impossible.) An action and a person's relation to its effect (or to the resulting state) will be specified by its location within the matrix, that is, by its position along the two dimensions.[90] Should decision theory take account of these finer distinctions concerning the mode of causal connection of an action to an outcome, and, if so, how? Are there also finer distinctions *within* the evidential and the symbolic connections that decision theory should mark and take into account? I raise these questions not to answer them here but to place them on the agenda.

The themes discussed in these two lectures about principles and symbolic meaning apply to ethical principles also. By grouping actions together in a class, one action comes to stand for all, and the weight of all is brought to bear upon the one, any one, giving it a coordinate (symbolic) disutility. Deontological constraints might exhibit this same phenomenon. By grouping actions together into a principle forbidding them — "do not murder" — an action

---

[90] For other purposes, we might want to extend such a matrix, adding a third dimension to represent the magnitude of the consequence or effect. (Extending the matrix in this way for legal contexts was suggested to me by Justin Hughes. In legal contexts we might want to know how bad the effect was: how bad was the one aimed at, and how bad was the one which occurred.) But within decision theory, of course, this magnitude is already represented by the utility of the outcome.

is removed from separate utilitarian (or egoist) calculation of *its* costs and benefits. The action comes to stand for the whole group, bearing its weight upon its shoulders. This need not happen in a way that makes the constraint absolute, barring the action no matter what, but it constitutes a far greater barrier to performing it, by throwing its greatly increased (symbolic) disutility into any calculation.[91]

Recall now our discussion in the first lecture of the symbolic meaning of following ethical principles; ethical action can symbolize (and express) being a rational creature that gives itself laws, being a law-making member of a kingdom of ends, being an equal source and recognizer of worth and personality, and so forth. The utility of these grand things, symbolically expressed and instantiated by the action, becomes incorporated into that action's symbolic utility and hence into that action's decision-value. Thus, these symbolic meanings become part of one's reason for acting ethically. A person who maximizes an act's utility broadly conceived, that is, who maximizes its decision-value ($DV$), may be led to perform ethical actions. This person would be pursuing his *own* goals (which need not be *selfish* goals). In terms of the categorization of Amartya Sen,[92] he therefore would be engaged in self-goal pursuit rather than the activity of *not* marginally pursuing *his* own overall individual goal. But note that if falling into this further category of not marginally pursuing his own overall individual goal itself comes to have symbolic utility to him, then it will enter into his $DV$. At that point, when he acts taking account of this symbolic utility, is he once again pursuing his own goal, that is, *his* revised $DV$, so that his attempt (within the $DV$ framework) to enter Sen's other category is doomed to failure? How-

---

[91] Recall also the discussion above of how a meta-principle not to violate any principles might make any violation stand for all, thereby giving every principle heavy deontological weight.

[92] See Amartya Sen, *Ethics and Economics* (Oxford: Basil Blackwell, 1987), pp. 80–88.

ever we decide this, the more general point holds. Being ethical is among our most effective ways of symbolizing (a connection to) what we value most highly, and that is something a *rational* person would not wish to forgo.

We discussed various functions of principles in the first lecture. Accepting and adhering to a particular principle, we saw, could be considered to be a (general) act $A$ and treated within a decision-theoretic framework that was largely instrumental. Now we have presented an alternative framework for decision theory, one that includes evidential and symbolic aspects, not simply causal instrumentality. Within *that* framework, an act of accepting a principle will have a decision-value $DV$, and it will be chosen (from among alternatives) when it has a maximal decision-value. This broader framework opens the way to a revised discussion of why we have principles at all — why if we have that one $DV$ principle we also will have some others — and of why we have some particular ones.

# Modernity and the Rise of the Public Sphere

*CHARLES TAYLOR*

THE TANNER LECTURES ON HUMAN VALUES

Delivered at

Stanford University
February 25, 1992

CHARLES TAYLOR, currently a Professor in the Department of Political Science and the Department of Philosophy at McGill University and Professeur Titulaire at the Université de Montréal, was educated at McGill and at Oxford University, where he received a Ph.D. degree in 1961. He has been a visiting professor or lecturer at Princeton, Queen's, and Hebrew universities, the University of California at Berkeley, and the New School for Social Research, among others, and was a member of the School of Social Science at Princeton's Institute for Advanced Studies. From 1976 to 1981 he was Chichele Professor of Social and Political Theory at Oxford and a Fellow of All Souls College. Professor Taylor's publications include *The Explanation of Behavior* (1964), *Hegel and Modern Society* (1979), *Social Theory as Practice* (1983), and *Source of the Self: The Making of the Modern Identity* (1989). He is a Fellow of the Royal Society of Canada and the British Academy.

I

I want to distinguish — and start a debate — between two kinds of theories of modernity. I shall call them "cultural" and "acultural" respectively. I'm leaning on a use of the word "culture" here which is analogous to the sense it often has in anthropology. I am evoking the picture of a plurality of human cultures, each of which has a language and a set of practices which define specific understandings of personhood, social relations, states of mind/soul, goods and bads, virtues and vices, and the like. These languages are often mutually untranslatable.

With this model in mind, a "cultural" theory of modernity is one that characterizes the transformations which have issued in the modern West mainly in terms of the rise of a new culture. The contemporary Atlantic world is seen as a culture (or group of closely related cultures) among others, with its own specific understandings (e.g., of person, nature, the good), to be contrasted to all others, including its own predecessor civilization (with which it obviously also has a lot in common).

By contrast, an "acultural" theory is one that describes these transformations in terms of some culture-neutral operation. By this I mean an operation which is not defined in terms of the specific cultures it carries us from and to, but is rather seen as of a type which any traditional culture could undergo.

An example of an acultural type of theory, indeed a paradigm case, would be one which conceives of modernity as the growth of reason, defined in various ways (e.g., as the growth of scientific consciousness, or the development of a secular outlook, or the rise of instrumental rationality, or an ever-clearer distinction between fact-finding and evaluation). Or else modernity might be accounted for in terms of social as well as intellectual changes: the transformations, including the intellectual ones, are seen as coming about as a result of increased mobility, concentration of populations, industrialization, or the like. In all these cases, modernity is conceived as a set of transformations which any and every culture can go through—and which all will probably be forced to undergo.

These changes are not defined by their end-point in a specific constellation of understandings of, say, person, society, good; they are rather described as a type of transformation to which any culture could in principle serve as "input." For instance, any culture could suffer the impact of growing scientific consciousness; any religion could undergo "secularization"; any set of ultimate ends could be challenged by a growth of instrumental thinking; any metaphysic could be dislocated by the split between fact and value.

So modernity in this kind of theory is understood as issuing from a rational or social operation which is culture-neutral. This is not to say that the theory cannot acknowledge good historical reasons why this transformation first arose in one civilization rather than another, or why some may undergo it more easily than others. The point rather is that the operation is defined not in terms of its specific point of arrival, but as a general function which can take any specific culture as its input.

To grasp the difference from another angle, the operation is not seen as supposing or reflecting an option for one specific set of human values or understandings among others. In the case of "social" explanations, causal weight is given to historical developments, like industrialization, which have an impact on values but are often not seen as reflecting specific options in this domain. When it comes to explanations in terms of "rationality," this is seen as the exercise of a general capacity, which was only awaiting its proper conditions to unfold. Under certain conditions, human beings will just come to see that scientific thinking is valid, that instrumental rationality pays off, that religious beliefs involve unwarranted leaps, that facts and values are separate. These transformations may be facilitated by our having certain values and understandings, just as they are hampered by the dominance of others; but they aren't *defined* as the espousal of some such constellation. They are defined rather by something we come to see concerning the whole context in which values and understandings are espoused.

It should be evident that the dominant theories of modernity over the last two centuries have been of the acultural sort. Many have explained its development at least partly by our "coming to see" something like the range of supposed "truths" mentioned above. Or else the changes have been explained partly by culture-neutral social developments, such as Durkheim's move from "mechanical" to differentiated, "organic" forms of social cohesion; or Tocqueville's assumption of creeping "democracy" (by which he meant a push toward equality). On one interpretation, "rationalization" was for Weber a steady process, occurring within all cultures over time.

But above all, explanations of modernity in terms of "reason" seem to be the most popular. And even the "social" explanations tend to invoke reason as well, since the social transformations, like mobility and industrialization, are thought to bring about intellectual and spiritual changes because they shake people loose from old habits and beliefs (in, e.g., religion or traditional morality) which then become unsustainable because they have no independent rational grounding, in the way the beliefs of modernity (in, e.g., individualism or instrumental reason) are assumed to have.

But, one might object, how about the widespread and popular *negative* theories of modernity, those that see it not as gain but as loss or decline? Curiously enough, they too have been acultural in their own way. To see this, we have to enlarge somewhat the description above. Instead of seeing the transformations as the unfolding of capacities, negative theories have often interpreted them as falling prey to dangers. But these have often been just as aculturally conceived. Modernity is characterized by the loss of the horizon; by a loss of roots; by the hubris which denies human limits, our dependence on history or God, which places unlimited confidence in the powers of frail human reason; by a trivializing self-indulgence which has no stomach for the heroic dimension of life; and so on.

The overwhelming weight of interpretation in our culture, positive and negative, tends to the acultural. On the other side, the voices are fewer if powerful. Nietzsche, for instance, offers a reading of modern scientific culture which paints it as actuated by a specific constellation of values. And Max Weber, besides offering a theory of rationalization which can at any rate be taken as a steady, culture-independent force, also gave a reading of the Protestant ethic, as defined by a particular set of religio-moral concerns, which in turn helped to bring about modern capitalism.

So acultural theories predominate. Is this bad? I think it is. In order to see why, we have to bring out a bit more clearly what these theories foreground, and what they tend to screen out.

Acultural theories tend to describe the transition in terms of a loss of traditional beliefs and allegiances. This may be seen as coming about as a result of institutional changes: for example, mobility and urbanization erode the beliefs and reference points of static rural society. Or the loss may be supposed to arise from the increasing operation of modern scientific reason. The change may be positively valued — or it may be judged a disaster by those for whom the traditional reference points were valuable, and scientific reason too narrow. But all these theories concur in describing the process: old views and loyalties are eroded. Old horizons are washed away, in Nietzsche's image. The sea of faith recedes, following Arnold. This stanza from his "Dover Beach" captures this perspective:

> The Sea of Faith
> Was once, too, at the full, and round earth's shore
> Lay like the folds of a bright girdle furled.
> But now I only hear
> Its melancholy, long, withdrawing roar,

> Retreating, to the breath
> Of the night-wind, down the vast edges drear
> And naked shingles of the world.[1]

The tone here is one of regret and nostalgia. But the underlying image of eroded faith could serve just as well for an upbeat story of the progress of triumphant scientific reason. From one point of view, humanity has shed a lot of false and harmful myths. From another, it has lost touch with crucial spiritual realities. But in either case, the change is seen as a loss of belief.

What emerges comes about through this loss. The upbeat story cherishes the dominance of an empirical-scientific approach to knowledge claims, of individualism, negative freedom, instrumental rationality. But these come to the fore because they are what we humans "normally" value, once we are no longer impeded or blinded by false or superstitious beliefs and the stultifying modes of life which accompany them. Once myth and error are dissipated, these are the only games in town. The empirical approach is the only valid way of acquiring knowledge, and this becomes evident as soon as we free ourselves from the thralldom of a false metaphysics. Increasing recourse to instrumental rationality allows us to get more and more of what we want, and we were only ever deterred from this by unfounded injunctions to limit ourselves. Individualism is the normal fruit of human self-regard absent the illusory claims of God, the Chain of Being, or the sacred order of society.

In other words, we moderns behave as we do because we have "come to see" that certain claims were false — or on the negative reading, because we have lost from view certain perennial truths. What this view reads out of the picture is the possibility that Western modernity might be powered by its own positive visions of the good, that is, by one constellation of such visions among available others, rather than by the only viable set left after the

---

[1] Matthew Arnold, "Dover Beach," 21–28.

old myths and legends have been exploded. It screens out whatever there might be of a specific moral direction to Western modernity, beyond what is dictated by the general form of human life itself, once old error is shown up (or old truth forgotten). For example, people behave as individuals, because that's what they "naturally" do when no longer held in by the old religions, metaphysics, and customs, though this may be seen as a glorious liberation or a purblind miring in egoism, depending on our perspective. What it cannot be seen as is a novel form of moral self-understanding, not definable simply by the negation of what preceded it.

Otherwise put, what gets screened out is the possibility that Western modernity might be sustained by its own original spiritual vision, that is, not one generated simply and inescapably out of the transition.

Before trying to say how bad or good this is, I want to speculate about the motives for this predominance of the acultural. In one way, it is quite understandable when we reflect that we Westerners have been living the transition to modernity for some centuries out of the civilization we used to call Christendom. It is hard to live through a change of this moment without being partisan, and in this spirit we quite naturally reach for explanations which are immediately evaluative, on one side or the other. Now nothing stamps the change as more unproblematically right than the account that we have "come to see" through certain falsehoods, just as the explanation that we have come to forget important truths brands it as unquestionably wrong. To make such confident judgments on the basis of a cultural account would presuppose our having carried through a complex comparative assessment of modernity's original vision, over against that of the Christendom which preceded it, to a clear unambiguous conclusion — hardly an easy task, if realizable at all.

Indeed, since a cultural theory supposes the point of view in which we see our own culture as one among others, and this at best is a recent acquisition in our civilization, it is not surprising that the first accounts of revolutionary change were acultural. For the most part our ancestors looked on other civilizations as made up of barbarians, or infidels, or savages. It would have been absurd to expect the contemporaries of the French Revolution, on either side of the political divide, to have seen the cultural shift within this political upheaval, when the very idea of cultural pluralism was just dawning in the writings of, say, Herder.

But even when this standpoint becomes more easily available, we are drawn by our partisan attachments to neglect it. This is partly because an immediately evaluative explanation (on the right side) is more satisfying — we tend to want to glorify modernity or vilify it. And it is partly because we fear that a cultural theory might make value judgments impossible. The latter notion is, I believe, a mistake; but mistake or not, it plays a role here.

But another thing which has been going for acultural theories has been the vogue for "materialistic" explanations in social science and history. By this I mean, in this context, explanations which shy away from invoking moral or spiritual factors in favour of (what are thought to be) harder and more down-to-earth causes. And so the developments I adverted to above — the growth of science, individualism, negative freedom, instrumental reason, and the other striking features of the culture of modernity — have often been accounted for as by-products of social change: for instance, as spin-offs from industrialization, or greater mobility, or urbanization. There are certainly important causal relations to be traced here, but the accounts which invoke them frequently skirt altogether the issue whether these changes in culture and outlook owe anything to their own inherent power as moral ideals. The implicit answer is often in the negative.[2]

---

[2] Of course, for a certain vulgar Marxism, the negative answer is quite explicit. Ideas are the product of economic changes. But much non-Marxist social science operates implicitly on similar premises. And this in spite of the orientation of some of the great founders of social science, like Weber, who recognized the crucial role of moral and religious ideas in history.

Of course, the social changes which are supposed to spawn the new outlook must themselves be explained, and this will involve some recourse to human motivations, unless we suppose that industrialization or the growth of cities occurred entirely in a fit of absence of mind. We need some notion of what moved people to push steadily in one direction — for example, toward the greater application of technology to production, or toward greater concentrations of population. But what is invoked here are often motivations which are nonmoral. By that I mean motivations which can actuate people quite without connection to any moral ideal, as I defined this earlier. So we very often find these social changes explained in terms of the desire for greater wealth, or power, or the means of survival, or control over others. Of course, all these things can be woven into moral ideals, but they need not be. And so explanation in terms of them is considered sufficiently "hard" and "scientific."

And even where individual freedom and the enlargement of instrumental reason are seen as ideas whose intrinsic attractions can help explain their rise, this attraction is frequently understood in nonmoral terms. That is, the power of these ideas is often understood not in terms of their moral force, but just because of the advantages they seem to bestow on people regardless of their moral outlook, or even whether they have a moral outlook. Freedom allows you to do what you want; and the greater application of instrumental reason gets you more of what you want, whatever that is.[3]

---

[3] Individualism has in fact been used in two quite different senses. In one it is a moral ideal, one facet of which I have been discussing. In another, it is an amoral phenomenon, something like what we mean by egoism. The rise of individualism in this sense is usually a phenomenon of breakdown, where the loss of a traditional horizon leaves mere anomie in its wake, and individuals fend for themselves — for example, in some demoralized, crime-ridden slums formed by newly urbanized peasants in the Third World (or in nineteenth-century Manchester). It is, of course, catastrophic to confuse these two kinds of individualism, which have utterly different causes and consequences. Which is why Tocqueville carefully distinguishes "individualism" from "egoism" in his well-known discussion in the second volume of *Democracy in America* (part II, chapter 2).

It is obvious that wherever this kind of explanation becomes culturally dominant, the motivation to explore the original spiritual vision of modernity is very weak; indeed, the capacity even to recognize some such thing nears zero. And this effectively takes cultural theories off the agenda.

So what, if anything, is bad about this? Two things.

1. First, I think Western modernity *is* in part based on an original moral outlook. This is not to say that our account of it in terms of our "coming to see" certain things is wholly wrong. On the contrary: post-seventeenth-century natural science has a validity, and the accompanying technology an efficacy, that we have established. And all societies are sooner or later forced to acquire this efficacy or be dominated by others (and hence have it imposed on them anyway).

But it would be quite wrong to think that we can make do with an acultural theory alone. It is not just that other facets of what we identify as modern, such as the tendency to try to split fact from value, or the decline of religious practice, are far from reposing on incontestable truths which have finally been discovered — as one can claim for modern physics, for example. It is also that science itself has grown in the West in close symbiosis with a certain culture in the sense I'm using that term here, as a constellation of understandings of person, nature, society, and the good.

To rely on an acultural theory is to miss all this. One gets a distorted understanding of Western modernity in one of two ways: on one side, we misclassify certain changes, which ultimately reflect the culture peculiar to the modern West, as the product of unproblematic discovery or the ineluctable consequence of some social change, like the introduction of technology. The decline in religious practice has frequently been seen in this light. This is the error of seeing everything modern as belonging to one Enlightenment package.

On the other side, we fail altogether to examine certain facets of the modern constellation, closely interwoven with our understandings of science and religion, which don't strike us as being part of the transformation to modernity. We don't identify them as among the spectacular changes which have produced contemporary civilization, and we often fail to see even that there have been changes, reading these facets falsely as perennial. Such is the usual fate of those, largely implicit, understandings of human agency which I have grouped under the portmanteau term "modern identity,"[4] such as the various forms of modern inwardness or the affirmation of ordinary life. We all too easily imagine that people have always seen themselves as we do, for example, in respect to dichotomies like inward/outward. And we thus utterly miss the role these new understandings have played in the rise of Western modernity. I want to make a claim of this kind below in relation to the rise of the modern public sphere.

And so a purely acultural theory distorts and impoverishes our understanding of ourselves, both through misclassification (the Enlightenment package error) and through too narrow a focus. But its effects on our understanding of other cultures is even more devastating. The belief that modernity comes from one single universally applicable operation imposes a falsely uniform pattern on the multiple encounters of non-Western cultures with the exigencies of science, technology, and industrialization. As long as we are bemused by the Enlightenment package, we shall believe that they all *have* to undergo a range of cultural changes, drawn from our experience — such as "secularization" or the growth of atomistic forms of self-identification. As long as we leave our own notions of identity unexamined, so long shall we fail to see how theirs differ, and how this difference crucially conditions the way in which they integrate the truly universal features of "modernity."

Moreover, the view that modernity arises through the dissipation of certain unsupported religious and metaphysical beliefs seems to imply that the paths of different civilizations are bound

---

[4] See *Sources of the Self: The Making of the Modern Identity* (Cambridge, Mass.: Harvard University Press, 1989).

to converge. As they lose their traditional illusions, they will come together on the "rationally grounded" outlook which has resisted the challenge. The march of modernity will end up making all cultures look the same. This means, of course, that we expect they will end up looking like us.

In short, exclusive reliance on an acultural theory unfits us for what is perhaps the most important task of social sciences in our day: understanding the full gamut of alternative modernities which are in the making in different parts of the world. It locks us into an ethnocentric prison, condemned to project our own forms onto everyone else, and blissfully unaware of what we are doing.

2. So the view from Dover Beach foreshortens our understanding of Western modernity. But it aso gives us a false and distorted perspective on the transition. It makes us read the rise of modernity in terms of the dissipation of certain beliefs, either as its major cause ("rational" explanations) or as inevitable concomitant ("social" expectations). What is beyond the horizon on Dover Beach is the possibility that what mainly differentiates us from our forebears is not so much our explicit beliefs as what I want to call the background understanding against which our beliefs are formulated.

Here I am picking up on an idea which has been treated in the work of Heidegger, Merleau-Ponty, Wittgenstein, and Michael Polanyi, and been further elaborated recently by John Searle and Hubert Dreyfus.[5] The notion is that our explicit beliefs about our world and ourselves are held against a background of unformulated (and perhaps in part unformulable) understandings, in relation to which these beliefs make the sense they do. These understandings take a variety of forms and range over a number of matters. In one dimension, the background incorporates matters

---

[5] Martin Heidegger, *Sein und Zeit* (Tübingen: Niemeyer, 1926); Maurice Merleau-Ponty, *Phénoménologie de la perception* (Paris: Gallimard, 1945); Ludwig Wittgenstein, *Philosophical Investigations* (Oxford: Blackwell, 1953); Michael Polanyi, *Personal Knowledge* (New York: Harper, 1958); John Searle, *Intentionality* (Cambridge: Cambridge University Press, 1983); Hubert Dreyfus, *What Computers Can't Do* (New York: Harper, 1979).

which *could* be formulated as beliefs, but aren't functioning as such in our world (and couldn't *all* function as such because of their unlimited extent). To take Wittgenstein's example from *On Certainty*, I don't normally have a *belief* that the world didn't start only five minutes ago, but the whole way I enquire into things treats the world as being there since time out of mind.[6] Similarly, I don't usually have the belief that a huge pit hasn't been dug in front of my door, but I treat the world that way as I emerge in the morning to go to work. In my ways of dealing with things is incorporated the background understanding that the world is stable and has been there a long time.

In other dimensions, I have this kind of understanding of myself as an agent with certain powers, of myself as an agent among other agents, on certain, only partly explicit footings with them. And I want to add: an agent moving in certain kinds of social spaces, with a sense of how both I and these spaces inhabit time, a sense of how both I and they relate to the cosmos, and to God or whatever I recognize as the source(s) of good.

In my addition here, I have entered controversial territory. While perhaps everyone can easily agree on the kinds of background understandings I cited from Wittgenstein, and it is arguably obvious that I have some sense of myself as agent, the notion that different modes of social belonging, different understandings of time — and even more, of God, the good, or the cosmos — should be part of the background may arouse resistance. That is because we easily can believe that we have background understanding in the inescapable dimensions of our lives as agents, functioning in a physical and social world. But when we come to our supposed relations to God, the good, or the cosmos, surely these things only enter our world through our being inducted into our society's culture, and they must enter in the form of beliefs which have been handed down to us.

[6] Ludwig Wittgenstein, *On Certainty* (Oxford: Blackwell, 1977), paragraphs 260ff.

But this is in fact not how it works. Of course, in any theistic culture there will be *some* beliefs about God, but our sense of him and our relation to him will also be formed by modes of ritual, by the kinds of prayer we have been taught, by what we pick up from the attitudes of pious and impious people, and the like. A similar point can be made about the different kinds of social space. There may be some doctrines formulated about the nature of society and the hierarchical rankings that constitute it which are explicitly proffered for our adherence, but we also come to understand whole "volumes" in the ways we are taught (e.g., to show deference to certain people or at certain times and places). A social understanding is built into what Pierre Bourdieu calls our "habitus," the ways we are taught to behave, which become unreflecting, "second nature" to us.[7]

We know our way around society somewhat the way we know our way around our physical environment, not primarily and principally because we have some map of either in our heads, but because we know how to treat different people and situations appropriately. In this know-how there is, for example, a stance toward the elders which treats them as having a certain dignity. What it is about them which is felt to command this stance may not yet be spelt out: there may be no word for "dignity" in the vocabulary of the tribe. But whatever it is which we shall later want to articulate with this word is already in the world of the youngsters who bow in that particular way, address their elders in low tones and with the proper language, and so forth. "Dignity" is in their world

[7] See *Outline of a Theory of Practice* (Cambridge: Cambridge University Press, 1977) and *Le sens pratique* (Paris: Minuit, 1980). "On pourrait, déformant le mot de Proust, dire que les jambes, les bras sont pleins d'impératifs engourdis. Et l'on n'en finirait pas d'énumérer les valeurs faites corps, par la transsubstantiation qu'opère la persuasion clandestine d'une pédagogic implicite, capable d'inculquer toute une cosmologie, une éthique, une métaphysique, une politique, à travers des injonctions aussi insignifiantes que 'tiens-toi droit' ou 'ne tiens pas ton couteau de la main gauche' et d'inscrire dans les détails en apparence les plus insignifiants de la *tenue*, du *maintien* ou des *manières* corporelles et verbales les principes fondamentaux de l'arbitraire culturel, ainsi placés hors des prises de la conscience et de l'explicitation" (*Le sens pratique*, p. 117).

in the sense that they deal with it, respond to it, perhaps revere it or resent it. It is just not formulated in a description, and hence does not figure in an explicit belief. Its being in their world is part of their background understanding.

It is in similar ways that God or the good can figure in our world. Surrounding express doctrines will be a richer penumbra of embodied understanding. We can imaginatively extend the example of the previous paragraph. Suppose that one of the things which makes the elders worthy of respect is just that they are closer to the gods. Then the divine too, which we revere through these old people, will be in our world in part through our knowing how to treat them. It will be in our world through the appropriate habitus.

We might in fact distinguish three levels of understanding which have been invoked in the above discussion. There is the level of explicit doctrine, about society, the divine, the cosmos; and there is the level of what I called, following Bourdieu, the habitus or embodied understanding. Somewhat between the two is a level which we might call (with some trepidation, because this is a semantically overloaded term) the symbolic. I mean by this whatever understanding is expressed in ritual, in symbols (in the everyday sense), in works of art. What exists on this level is more explicit than mere gesture or appropriate action, because ritual and work can have a mimetic or an evocative dimension, and hence point to something which they imitate or call forth. But it is not explicit in the self-conscious way of doctrinal formulations, which can be submitted to the demands of logic, permit of a metadiscourse in which they are examined in turn, and the like.

We can see why it might be a big mistake to think that what distinguishes us from our premodern forebears is mainly a lot of beliefs of theirs which we have shed. Even if we want, following "Dover Beach," to see their age as one of a faith which we have lost, it might be very misleading to think of this difference in terms simply of *doctrines* to which they subscribe and we do not. Because below the doctrinal level are at least two others: that of embodied background understanding and that which while nourished in embodied habitus is given expression on the symbolic level. As well as the doctrinal understanding of society, there is the one incorporated in habitus, and a level of images as yet unformulated in doctrine, for which we might borrow a term frequently used by contemporary French writers: "l'imaginaire social" — let's call it the "social imaginary."

Why does it matter to see the changeover as more than doctrinal? Because otherwise we may have a very distorted picture of it. When people undergo a change in belief, they shift their views between already formulated possibilities. Formerly, they thought that God exists. But in formulating this belief they were quite aware that there was another option; indeed, usually they were aware that others had already taken the atheist option, that there were arguments for and against it, and so forth. Now when they switch to atheism, they move within positions already in their repertory, between points already within their horizons.

But some of the major changes in embodied understanding and social imaginary alter the very repertory and introduce new possibilities which were not before on the horizon. I hope to show this in a minute in connection with the rise of the public sphere. Modernity involves the coming to be of new kinds of public space, which cannot be accounted for in terms of changes in explicit views, either of factual belief or of normative principle. Rather the transition involves to some extent the definition of new possible spaces hitherto outside the repertory of our forebears, and beyond the limits of their social imaginary.

The consequence of seeing these changes as alterations of (factual or normative) belief is that we unwittingly make our ancestors too much like us. To the extent that we see ourselves as just differing from them in *belief*, we see them as having the same doctrinal repertory as ours, but just opting differently within it. But in order to give them the same repertory we have to align their embodied understanding and social imaginary with ours. We falsely make them in this sense our contemporaries and grievously underestimate the nature and scope of the change that brought our world about.

So an acultural theory tends to make us both miss the original vision of the good implicit in Western modernity and underestimate the nature of the transformation which brought this modernity about. These two drawbacks appear to be linked. Some of the important shifts in culture, in our understandings of personhood, the good, and the like, which have brought about the original vision of Western modernity, can only be seen if we bring into focus the major changes in embodied understanding and social imaginary which the last centuries have brought about. They tend to disappear if we flatten these changes out, read our own background and imaginary into our forebears, and just concentrate on their beliefs which we no longer share. I hope these connections will come clearer in the sequel, as we come closer to grasping just how our understanding of our relations to society, time, the cosmos, the good, and God have been transformed with the coming of our era.

## II

I want now to try to trace some of these transformations by looking at the rise of one facet of modern society, what is often called the "public sphere." What do we mean by a public sphere? It's not easy to say, because, as I shall argue later, we lack a clear, agreed social ontology which would allow us to describe it uncontroversially. I am going to step into the breach and offer my own terminology: I want to describe the public sphere as a common space in which the members of society are deemed to meet through a variety of media: print, electronic, and also face-to-face encounters; to discuss matters of common interest; and thus to be able to form a common mind about these. I say "*a* common space" because although the media are multiple, as well as the exchanges which take place in them, these are deemed to be in principle intercommunicating. The discussion we're having on television now takes account of what was said in the newspaper this morning, which in turn reports on the radio debate yesterday, and so on. That's why we usually speak of the public sphere, in the singular.

The public sphere is a central feature of modern society. So much so that even where it is in fact suppressed or manipulated it has to be faked. Modern despotic societies have generally felt compelled to go through the motions. Editorials appear in the party newspapers, purporting to express the opinions of the writers, offered for the consideration of their fellow citizens; mass demonstrations are organized, purporting to give vent to the felt indignation of large numbers of people. All this takes place as though a genuine process were in train of forming a common mind through exchange, even though the result is carefully controlled from the beginning.

Why this semblance? Because the public sphere is not only a ubiquitous feature of any modern society; it also plays a crucial role in its self-justification as a free self-governing society, that is, as a society in which (a) people form their opinions freely, both as individuals and in coming to a common mind, and (b) these common opinions matter: they in some way take effect on or control government. Just because it has this central role, the public sphere is the object of concern and criticism in liberal societies as well. One question is whether the debate is not being controlled and manipulated here as well, in a fashion less obvious than within despotic regimes, but all the more insidiously, by money, or government, or some collusive combination of the two. Another is whether the nature of certain modern media permits the truly open, multilateral exchange which is supposed to issue in a truly common opinion on public matters.

There is a tendency to consider something which is so important and central to our lives almost as a fact of nature, as though something of the sort had always been there. Modern liberal society would then have innovated in allowing the public sphere its freedom, and in making government in a sense responsible to it instead of the other way around. But something like public opinion would always have existed. This, however, would be an anachronistic error, which obscures what is new, and as yet not fully understood, in this kind of common space. I want to try to cast a little more light on this, and in the process get clearer on the transformations in background understanding and social imaginary which produced modern civilization.

In this discussion, I want to draw in particular on two very interesting books: one by Jürgen Habermas, *The Structural Transformation of the Public Sphere* (published almost thirty years ago but recently translated into English),[8] which deals with the development of public opinion in eighteenth-century Western Europe; the other a very recent publication by Michael Warner, *The Letters of the Republic*,[9] which describes the analogous phenomenon in the British-American colonies.

A central theme of the Habermas book is the emergence in Western Europe in the eighteenth century of a new concept of public opinion. Getting clear what was new in this will help to define what is special about the modern public sphere. Following the anachronistic reading, we might think that what was new in the eighteenth-century appeals to public opinion was the demand that government be responsive to it, but that which government was called on to heed could be deemed to have already been in existence for an indefinite period. But this would be a mistake.

People had, of course, always recognized something like a general opinion, which held in a particular society, or perhaps among humankind as a whole. This might be looked down on, as a source of error, following Plato's low estimation of "doxa." Or it might be seen in other contexts as setting standards for right conduct.[10]

---

[8] Translated by Thomas Burger (Cambridge, Mass.: MIT Press, 1989); German original: *Strukturwandel der Öffentlichkeit* (Neuwied: Luchterhand, 1962).

[9] Cambridge, Mass.: Harvard University Press, 1990.

[10] Habermas (Structural Transformation, p. 91) refers to Locke in this connection.

But in either case, it is different from the new public opinion in three important respects: "the opinion of humankind" is seen as (i) unreflected, (ii) unmediated by discussion and critique, and (iii) passively inculcated in each successive generation. Public opinion, by contrast, is meant (i) to be the product of reflection, (ii) to emerge from discussion, and (iii) to reflect an actively produced consensus.

The difference lies in more than the evaluation, there passive acceptance, here critical thinking. It was not just that the eighteenth century decided to pin Cartesian medals onto the opinion of humankind. The crucial change is that the underlying process is different. Where the opinion of humankind was supposed to have passed down in each case from parents and elders, in a myriad of unlinked, local acts of transmission, public opinion was deemed to have been elaborated by a discussion among those who held it, wherein their different views were somehow confronted, and they were able to come to a common mind. The opinion of humankind is probably held in identical form by you and me, because we are formed by the same socializing process. We share in a common public opinion, if we do, because we have worked it out together. We don't just happen to have identical views; we have elaborated our common convictions in a common act of definition.

But now in each case, whether as opinion of humankind or public opinion, the same views will be held by people who have never met. That's why the two can be confused. But in the later case, something else is supposed: it is understood that the two widely separated people sharing the same view have been linked in a kind of space of discussion, wherein they have been able to exchange ideas together with others and reach this common end-point.

What is this common space? It's a rather strange thing, when one comes to think of it. The two people I'm invoking here have by hypothesis never met. But they are seen as linked in a common space of discussion through media — in the eighteenth century, print media. Book, pamphlets, newspapers circulated among the educated public, as vehicles for theses, analyses, arguments, counterarguments, referring to and refuting each other. These were widely read and often discussed in face-to-face gatherings, in drawing rooms, coffee houses, saloons, and/or in more (authoritatively) "public" places, like Parliament. The sensed general view which resulted from all this, if any, counted as public opinion in this new sense.

I say "counted as" public opinion. And here we get to the heart of the strangeness. Because an essential part of the difference is made by what the process is deemed to amount to. The opinion of humankind spreads through myriad unlinked acts of transmission, as I said above, while public opinion is formed by the participants together. But if one made an exhaustive list of all the face-to-face encounters that occur in each case, the two processes wouldn't look all that different. In both cases, masses of people sharing the same views never meet, but everyone is linked with everyone through some chain of personal or written transmission. Crucial to the difference is that in the formation of public opinion each of these linked physical or print-mediated encounters is understood by the participants as forming part of a single discussion proceeding toward a common resolution. This can't be *all*, of course; that is, the encounters couldn't be the same in all other respects and just differ in how they were understood by the participants. For instance, it is crucial to these linked encounters that they are constantly inter-referring: I attempt to refute in my conversation with you today the *Times* editorial of last week, which took some public figure to task for a speech she made the week before, and so forth. It is also crucial that they be carried on as arguments. If in each case someone just passively accepted what another said — as in the ideal-typical case, of authoritative transmission of tradition from parents to children—these events couldn't be plausibly construed as forming part of a society-wide *discussion*. But without this common understanding of their linkage on the part of the participants, no one even from the outside could take them as constituting a common discussion with a potentially single outcome. A general understanding of what things *count as* is constitutive of the reality here which we call the public sphere.

In a similar fashion, there are clearly infrastructural conditions for the rise of the public sphere. There had to be printed materials, circulating from a plurality of independent sources, for there to be the bases of what could be seen as a common discussion. As is often said, the modern public sphere relied on "print capitalism" to get going. But, as Warner shows, printing itself, and even print capitalism, didn't provide a sufficient condition. They had to be taken up in the right cultural context, where the essential common understandings could arise.[11]

This comes to light if we compare, as Warner does, the uses of circulating print materials to sustain a public sphere with other earlier uses — for instance, to diffuse religious doctrines or modes of piety. Improving devotional books were meant to be read and their contents internalized by each person. Warner quotes Cotton Mather's description of his own practice: "In visits to credible Families, I will bespeak little Studies and Book-shelves for the little Sons that are capable of conversing with such things; and begin to furnish their Libraries and perswade them to the Religion of the Closet."[12] The utility of printing was that it could make possible the wide diffusion of these practices of interiorization. But the "Religion of the Closet" didn't depend for its practice in each individual case on the fact that it was probably being followed simultaneously in hundreds, even thousands of other homes.

By contrast, a pamphlet or editorial, as an intervention in an ongoing public debate, demanded to be read as a speech act addressed to a whole public. It takes on a different meaning for the reader, who "now also incorporates into the meaning of the printed object an awareness of potentially limitless others who may also

---

[11] Michael Warner, *The Letters of the Republic* (Cambridge, Mass.: Harvard University Press, 1990), chapter 1.

[12] Ibid., p. 19.

be reading. For that reason, it becomes possible to imagine oneself, in the act of reading, becoming part of an arena of the national people that cannot be realized except through such mediated imaginings."[13]

Warner's last sentence touches on a crucial point. To see its relevance, let me try to pull together the argument so far. "Public opinion" is different from "the opinion of humankind" because it is supposedly arrived at by critical common discussion. This supposes some kind of common space of discussion, which must be seen as linking people who may never meet. This is what we are calling the public sphere. This public sphere is made possible by the circulation of print materials; but these are not its sufficient condition. It is also partly constituted by common understandings, whose tenour is that these materials count as addressed to a large public, and the various contested readings of them in face-to-face encounters count as parts of a larger, nationwide debate.

But in what form do these common understandings arise? Are they a matter of explicit, generally held beliefs? The example just cited shows that this is not necessarily so and seems not to have been so in the case of the early public sphere. For our understanding of how and to whom a given speech act or text is addressed is usually quite implicit. It is a matter of background understanding and is carried in such things as the mode of address and the tone and language used, which we pick up on without needing to formulate what is going on, as our focal attention is captured by the "content" which is being asserted.

A reader who picked up one of the early broadsheets or newspaper editorials in the mid-eighteenth-century American colonies attacking the corrupt practices of colonial or imperial government could pick up on the common space this speech act supposed in the style and mode of writing. The piece might be signed "Cato," or some other Roman paragon of austere virtue, and was fashioned as an appeal to fellow citizens. It evoked a speech that might have

[13] Ibid., p. xiii.

been made before the people assembled in some virtuous republic. The use of print to evoke a speech before an assembly projects the audience of this bit of writing as a quasi-assembly. In other words, it projects the kind of common space of discussion we call the public sphere, where people who may never meet are nevertheless brought together as discussion partners. It only requires that the social and cultural conditions be right for this move to be taken seriously as against being seen as a bizarre joke, and the public sphere begins to exist.

But a piece of writing does this not by articulating a theoretical description of this sphere or of the nation as a quasi-assembly. It brings it off rather by projecting the sphere as the implicit background of its style, signature, and mode of address. The public sphere has to be supposed as unmentioned context to make sense of this bit of writing. It is projected, as it were, in the background understanding of the text, rather than in its doctrinal content. At the same time, this projection makes use of familiar images, here the highly prestigious reference point of the Roman Republic and its public space, which is projected onto the dispersed colonial population to form the new picture of the people as the subject of a potential common act of decision.[14]

In other words, the understanding which constitutes the public sphere can arise, as in this example, not in the realm of explicit beliefs, but through shifts in background understanding and the social imaginary. This is why we have trouble finding the right concepts to understand it. A social ontology has been widespread which recognizes the acts of individuals, the social structures in which they act (often understood in terms of the rules which define them), and the "ideas" these individuals may have, some of

---

[14] Habermas (*Structural Transformation*, p. 36) also notes how the atmosphere in ancien régime salons was set by the modes of tact which permitted the participants to disregard the great differences of social status among them. Implicitly, the understanding was that, in this company, reason and not social rank should carry the day in discussion, which was to be carried on within the parity of the "simply human" (des bloss Menschlichen).

which concern the nature of society and are formulated by great thinkers from time to time in the masterworks of political theory.

But with the rise of the public sphere we seem to have something which cannot fit into these categories. It doesn't fit into these three pigeonholes, but radically cuts across them. The public sphere is not quite like a social structure, constituted by the rules governing action within it. There are no such definite rules. But more gravely, it is not just a structure, but is also constituted by our understanding of it, and thus seems to fall also into the realm of "ideas." But this understanding is largely not made of "ideas" but of background and the imaginary. Moreover, the action which takes place in this sphere is common action, and not simply that of individuals.

We have a reality here which our "commonsense" social ontology, deeply impregnated by methodological individualism and the bias toward the explicit, cannot cope with. I propose to call this kind of reality a "social" or (in the relevant case) "political form."

We are now in a slightly better position to understand what kind of thing a public sphere is, and why it was new in the eighteenth century. It's a kind of common space, I have been saying, in which people who never meet understand themselves to be engaged in discussion and capable of reaching a common mind. Let me introduce some new terminology. We can speak of "common space" when people come together in a common act of focus for whatever purpose, be it ritual, the enjoyment of a play, conversation, the celebration of a major event, or whatever. Their focus is common, as against merely convergent, because it is part of what is commonly understood that they are attending to the common object, or purpose, together, as against each person just happening, on his or her own, to be concerned with the same thing. In this sense, the "opinion of humankind" offers a merely convergent unity, while public opinion is supposedly generated out of a series of common actions.

Now an intuitively understandable kind of common space is set up when people are assembled for some purpose, be it on an intimate level for conversation or on a larger, more "public" scale for a deliberative assembly, or a ritual, or a celebration, or the enjoyment of a football match or an opera, and the like. Common space arising from assembly in some locale I want to call "topical common space."

But the public sphere, as we have been defining it, is something different. It transcends such topical spaces. We might say that it knits together a plurality of such spaces into one larger space of nonassembly. The same public discussion is deemed to pass through our debate today, and someone else's earnest conversation tomorrow, and the newspaper interview Thursday, and so on. I want to call this larger kind of nonlocal common space "metatopical." The public sphere which emerges in the eighteenth century is a metatopical common space.

What we have been discovering about such spaces is that they are partly constituted by common understandings; that is, they are not reducible to, but cannot exist without such undersandings. New, unprecedented kinds of spaces require new and unprecedented understandings. Such is the case for the public sphere.

What is new is not metatopicality. The church and the state were already existing metatopical spaces. But getting clear about the novelty brings us to the essential features of modernity. We can articulate the new on two levels: what the public sphere *does* and what it *is*.

First, what it does; or rather, what is done in it. The public sphere is the locus of a discussion potentially engaging everyone (although in the eighteenth century the claim was only to involve the educated or "enlightened" minority) in which the society can come to a common mind about important matters. This common mind is a reflective view, emerging from critical debate, and not just a summation of whatever views happen to be held in the population.[15] As a consequence it has a normative status: government

---

[15] This indicates how far the late-eighteenth-century notion of public opinion is from what is the object of poll research today. The phenomenon that "public

ought to listen to it. There were two reasons for this, of which one tended to gain ground and ultimately swallow up the other. The first is that this opinion is likely to be enlightened, and hence government would be well-advised to follow it. This statement by Louis Sébastien Mercier, quoted by Habermas,[16] gives clear expression to this idea:

> Les bons livres dépendent des lumières dans toutes les classes du peuple; ils ornent la vérité. Ce sont eux qui déjà gouvernent l'Europe; ils éclairent le gouvernement sur ses devoirs, sur sa faute, sur son véritable intérêt, sur l'opinion publique qu'il doit écouter et suivre: ces bons livres sont des maîtres patients qui attendent le réveil des administrateurs des États et le calme de leurs passions.

Kant famously had a similar view.

The second reason emerges with the view that the people is sovereign. Government is then not only wise to follow opinion; it is morally bound to do so. Governments ought to legislate and rule in the midst of a reasoning public. Parliament, or the court, in taking its decisions ought to be concentrating together and enacting what has already been emerging out of enlightened debate among the people. From this arises what Warner, following Habermas, calls the "principle of supervision," which insists that

---

opinion research" aims to measure is, in terms of my above distinction, a convergent unity and doesn't need to emerge from discussion. It is analogous to the opinion of humankind. The ideal underlying the eighteenth-century version emerges in this passage from Burke, quoted by Habermas (*Structural Transformation*, pp. 117–18): "In a free country, every man thinks he has a concern in all public matters; that he has a right to form and deliver an opinion on them. They sift, examine and discuss them. They are curious, eager, attentive and jealous; and by making such matters the daily subjects of their thoughts and discoveries, vast numbers contract a very tolerable knowledge of them, and some a very considerable one. . . . Whereas in other countries none but men whose office calls them to it having much care or thought about public affairs, and not daring to try the force of their opinions with one another, ability of this sort is extremely rare in any station of life. In free countries, there is often found more real public wisdom and sagacity in shops and manufactories than in cabinets of princes in countries where none dares to have an opinion until he comes to them."

[16] *Structural Transformation*, p. 119.

the proceedings of governing bodies be public, open to the scrutiny of the discerning public.[17] By going public, legislative deliberation informs public opinion and allows it to be maximally rational, while at the same time exposing itself to its pressure, and thus acknowledging that legislation should ultimately bow to the clear mandates of this opinion.[18]

The public sphere is, then, a locus in which rational views are elaborated which should guide government. This comes to be seen as an essential feature of a free society. As Burke put it, "in a free country, every man thinks he has a concern in all public matters."[19] There is, of course, something very new about this in the eighteenth century, compared to the immediate past of Europe. But one might ask: is this new in history? Isn't this a feature of all free societies?

No; there is a subtle but important difference. Let's compare the modern society with a public sphere with an ancient republic or polis. In this latter, we can imagine that debate on public affairs may be carried on in a host of settings: among friends at a symposium, between those who meet in the agora, and then of course in the ekklesia where the thing is finally decided. The debate swirls around and ultimately reaches its conclusion in the competent decision-making body. Now the difference is that the discussions outside this body prepare for the action ultimately taken by the same people within it. The "unofficial" discussions are not separated off, given a status of their own, and seen to constitute a kind of metatopical space.

---

[17] *Letters*, p. 41.

[18] See Fox's speech, quoted in *Structural Transformation*, pp. 65–66: "It is certainly right and prudent to consult the public opinion. . . . If the public opinion did not happen to square with mine; if, after pointing out to them the danger, they did not see it in the same light with me, or if they conceived that another remedy was preferable to mine, I should consider it as my due to my king, due to my Country, due to my honour to retire, that they might pursue the plan which they thought better, by a fit instrument, that is by a man who thought with them. . . . but one thing is most clear, that I ought to give the public the means of forming an opinion."

[19] Cited in *Structural Transformation*, p. 117.

But that is what happens with the modern public sphere. It is a space of discussion which is self-consciously seen as being outside power. It is supposed to be listened to by power, but it is not itself an exercise of power. It's in this sense extrapolitical status is crucial. As we shall see below, it links the public sphere with other facets of modern society which also are seen as essentially extrapolitical. The extrapolitical status is not just defined negatively, as a lack of power. It is also seen positively: just because public opinion is not an exercise of power, it can be ideally disengaged from partisan spirit and rational.

In other words, with the modern public sphere comes the idea that political power must be supervised and checked by something outside. What was new, of course, was not that there was an outside check, but rather the nature of this instance. It is not defined as the will of God, or the Law of Nature (although it could be thought to articulate these), but as a kind of discourse, emanating from reason and not from power or traditional authority. As Habermas puts it, power was to be tamed by reason. The notion was that "veritas non auctoritas facit legem." [20]

In this way, the public sphere was different from everything preceding it. An "unofficial" discussion, which nevertheless can come to a verdict of great importance, it is defined outside the sphere of power. It borrows some of the images from ancient assemblies, as we saw above from the American case, to project the whole public as one space of discussion. But, as Warner shows, it innovates in relation to this model. Those who intervene are, as it were, like speakers before an assembly. But unlike their models in real ancient assemblies, they strive for a certain impersonality, a certain impartiality, an eschewing of party spirit. They strive to negate their own particularity, and thus to rise above "any private or partial view." This is what Warner calls "the principle of negativity." And we can see it not only as suiting the print, as against spoken, medium, but also as giving expression to this crucial fea-

[20] *Structural Transformation*, p. 82.

ture of the new public sphere as extrapolitical, as a discourse of reason *on* and *to* power, rather than *by* power.[21]

As Warner points out, the rise of the public sphere involves a breach in the old ideal of a social order undivided by conflict and difference. On the contrary, it means that debate breaks out and continues, involving in principle everybody, and this is perfectly legitimate. The old unity will be gone forever. But a new unity is to be substituted. For the ever-continuing controversy is not meant to be an exercise in power, a quasi-civil war carried on by dialectical means. Its potentially divisive and destructive consequences are offset by the fact that it is a debate outside of power, a rational debate, striving without *parti pris* to define the common good. "The language of resistance to controversy articulates a norm for controversy. It silently transforms the ideal of a social order free from conflictual debate into an ideal of debate free from social conflict." [22]

So what the public sphere does is enable the society to come to a common mind, without the mediation of the political sphere, in a discourse of reason outside power, which nevertheless is normative for power. Now let's try to see what, in order to do this, it has to *be*.

We can perhaps best do this by trying to define what is new and unprecedented in it. And I want to get to this in two steps, as it were. First, there is the aspect of its novelty, which has already been touched on. When we compare the public sphere with one of the important sources of its constitutive images (viz., the ancient republic), what springs to our notice is its extrapolitical locus. The "Republic of Letters" was a common term which the members of the international society of savants in interchange

---

[21] See *Letters*, pp. 40–42. Warner also points to the relationship with the impersonal agency of modern capitalism (pp. 62–63), as well as the closeness of fit between the impersonal stance and the battle against impersonal corruption which was so central a theme in the colonies (pp. 65–66), in the framing of this highly overdetermined mode.

[22] *Letters*, p. 46.

gave themselves toward the end of the seventeenth century. This was a precursor phenomenon to the public sphere; indeed, it contributed to shaping it. Here was a "republic" constituted outside of the political. Both the analogy and the difference gave force and point to this image: it was a republic as a unified association, grouping all enlightened participants, across political boundaries; but it was also a republic in being free from subjection; its "citizens" owed no allegiance but to it, as long as they went about the business of Letters.

Something of this is inherited by the eighteenth-century public sphere. Within it, the members of society come together and pursue a common end; they form and understand themselves to form an association, which is nevertheless not constituted by its political structure. This was not true of the ancient polis or republic. Athens was a society (*koinônia*) only as constituted politically. And the same was true of Rome. The ancient society was given its identity by its laws. On the banners of the legions, "SPQR" stood for "Senatus populusque romanus," but the "populus" here was the ensemble of Roman citizens, that is, those defined as such by the laws. The people didn't have an identity, didn't constitute a unity prior to and outside of these laws.

By contrast, in projecting a public sphere, our eighteenth-century forebears were placing themselves in an association, this common space of discussion, which owed nothing to political structures, but was seen as existing independently of them.

This extrapolitical status is one aspect of the newness: that all the members of a political society (or at least all the competent and "enlightened" members) should be seen as also forming a society outside the state. Indeed, this society was wider than any one state; it extended for some purposes to all of civilized Europe. This is an extremely important aspect and corresponds to a crucial feature of our contemporary civilization, which emerges at this time, and which is visible in more than the public sphere. I want to take this up in a minute, but first we have to take the second step.

For it is obvious that an extrapolitical, international society is by itself not new. It is preceded by the Stoic cosmopolis and, more immediately, by the Christian church. Europeans were used to living in a dual society, one organized by two mutually irreducible principles. So the second facet of the newness of the public sphere has to be defined as its radical secularity.

This is not easy to define, and I am taking a risk in using a term which already is thrown around very loosely in attempts to describe modern civilization. If I nevertheless adopt it, it's because I think an awareness of its etymology may help us to understand what is at stake here, which has something to do with the way human society inhabits time. But this way of describing the difference can only be brought in later, after some preliminary exploration.

The notion of secularity I'm using here is radical, because it stands not only in contrast with a divine foundation for society, but with any idea of society as constituted in something which transcends contemporary common action. For instance, some hierarchical societies conceive themselves as bodying forth some part of the Chain of Being. Behind the empirical fillers of the slots of kingship, aristocracy, and so on, lie the Ideas, or the persisting metaphysical Realities that these people are momentarily embodying. The king has two bodies, only one being the particular, perishable one, which is now being fed and clothed and will later be buried.[23] Within this outlook, what constitutes a society as such is the metaphysical order it embodies.[24] People act within a framework which is there prior to and independent of their action.

But secularity contrasts not only with divinely established churches or Great Chains. It is also different from an understanding of our society as constituted by a law which has been ours since

---

[23] See E. Kantorowicz, *The King's Two Bodies* (Princeton: Princeton University Press, 1957).

[24] For an extra-European example of this kind of thing, see Clifford Geertz, *Negara* (Princeton: Princeton University Press, 1980), where the preconquest Balinese state is described.

time out of mind. Because this too places our action within a framework, one which binds us together and makes us a society, and which transcends our common action.

In contradistinction to all this, the public sphere is an association which is constituted by nothing outside of the common action we carry out in it: coming to a common mind, where possible, through the exchange of ideas. Its existence as an association is just our acting together in this way. This common action is not made possible by a framework which needs to be established in some action-transcendent dimension: either by an act of God, or in a Great Chain, or by a law which comes down to us since time out of mind. This is what makes it radically secular. And this, I want to claim, gets us to the heart of what is new and unprecedented in it.

This is baldly stated. Obviously, this notion of secularity still needs to be made clearer. Perhaps the contrast is obvious enough with Mystical Bodies and Great Chains. But I am claiming a difference from traditional tribal society as well, the kind of thing the German peoples had who founded our modern North Atlantic polities, or in another form what constituted the ancient republics and poleis. And this might be challenged.

These societies were defined by a law. But is that so different from the public sphere? After all, whenever we want to act in this sphere, we meet a number of structures already in place: there are certain newspapers, television networks, publishing houses, and the rest. We act within the channels that these provide. Is this not rather analogous to any member of a tribe, who also has to act within established structures, of chieftainships, councils, annual meetings, and the rest? Of course, the institutions of the public sphere change; newspapers go broke, television networks merge, and the like. But no tribe remains absolutely fixed in its forms; these too evolve over time. If one wanted to claim that this preexisting structure is valid for ongoing action, but not for the founding acts which set up the public sphere, the answer might be that these are impossible to identify in the stream of time, any more than they are for the tribe. And if we want to insist that there must be such a moment, then we should remark that many tribes as well hand down legends of a founding act, when a Lycurgus, for instance, laid down their laws. Surely he acted outside of existing structures.

Talking of actions within structures brings out the similarities. But there is an important difference which resides in the respective common understandings. It is true that in a functioning public sphere action at any time is carried out within structures laid down earlier. There is a de facto arrangement of things. But this arrangement doesn't enjoy any privilege over the action carried out within it. The structures were set up during previous acts of communication in common space, on all fours with those we are carrying out now. Our present action may modify these structures, and that is perfectly legitimate, because these are seen as nothing more than precipitates and facilitators of such communicative action.

But the traditional law of a tribe usually enjoys a different status. We may, of course, alter it over time, following the prescription it itself provides. But it is not seen just as precipitate and facilitator of action. The abolition of the law would mean the abolition of the subject of common action, because the law defines the tribe as an entity. Whereas a public sphere could start up again, even where all media had been abolished, simply by founding new ones, a tribe can only resume its life on the understanding that the law, although perhaps interrupted in its efficacy by foreign conquest, is still in force.

That's what I mean when I say that what constitutes the society, what makes the common agency possible, transcends the common actions carried out within it. It is not just that the structures we need for today's common action arose as a consequence of yesterday's, which, however, was no different in nature from today's. Rather the traditional law is a precondition of any common action, at whatever time, because this common agency couldn't exist without it. It is in this sense transcendent. By contrast, in a purely secular association (in my sense), common agency arises simply in and as a precipitate of common action.

The crucial distinction underlying the concept of secularity I'm trying to define here can thus be related to this issue: what constitutes the association? Otherwise put, what makes this group of people as they continue over time a common agent? Where this is something which transcends the realm of those common actions this agency engages in, the association is nonsecular. Where the constituting factor is nothing other than such common action — whether the founding acts have already occurred in the past or are now coming about is immaterial — we have secularity.

Now the claim I want to make is that this kind of secularity is modern; that it comes about very recently in human history. Of course, there have been all sorts of momentary and topical common agents which have arisen just from common action. A crowd gathers, people shout protests, and then the governor's house is stoned, or the chateau is burned down. But prior to the modern day, enduring, metatopical common agency was inconceivable on a purely secular basis. People could only see themselves as constituted into such by something action-transcendent, be it a foundation by God, or a Chain of Being which society bodied forth or some traditional law which defined our people. The eighteenth-century public sphere thus represents an instance of a new kind: a metatopical common space and common agency without an action-transcendent constitution, an agency grounded purely in its own common actions.

But how about the founding moments which traditional societies often "remembered"? What about Lycurgus giving Sparta its laws? Surely these show us examples of the constituting factor (here law) issuing from common action: Lycurgus proposes, the Spartans accept. But it is in the nature of such founding moments that they are not put on the same plane as contemporary common action. The foundation acts are displaced onto a higher plane, into a heroic time, an *illud tempus* which is not seen as qualitatively on a level with what we do today. The founding action is not just like our action, not just an earlier similar act whose precipitate structures ours. It is not just earlier, but in another kind of time, an exemplary time.

And this is why I am tempted to use the term "secular," in spite of all the misunderstandings which may arise. Because it's clear that I don't only mean "not tied to religion." [25] The exclusion is much broader. But the original sense of "secular" was "of the age," that is, pertaining to profane time. It was close to the sense of "temporal" in the opposition temporal/spiritual. The understanding was that this profane time existed in relation to (surrounded by, penetrated by: it is hard to find the right words here) another time, that of God. This could also be conceived as eternity, which was not just endless profane time, but a kind of gathering of time into a unity; hence the expression "hoi aiônes tôn aiônôn" or "saecula saeculorum."

The crucial point is things and events had to be situated in relation to more than one kind of time. This is why events which were far apart in profane time could nevertheless be closely linked. Benedict Anderson, in a penetrating discussion of the same transition I am trying to describe here,[26] quotes Eric Auerbach on the relation prefiguring-fulfilling in which events of the Old Testament were held to stand to those in the New — for instance, the sacrifice of Isaac and the crucifixion of Christ. These two events were linked through their immediate contiguous places in the divine plan. They are drawn close to identity in eternity, even

---

[25] As a matter of fact, excluding the religious dimension is not even a necessary condition of my concept of secular here, let alone a sufficient one. A secular association is one grounded purely on common action, and this excludes any divine grounding *for this association*, but nothing prevents the people so associated from continuing a religious form of life; indeed, this form may even require that, for example, political associations be purely secular. There are for instance *religious* motives for espousing a separation of church and state.

[26] *Imagined Communities* (London: Verso, 1983), pp. 28–31.

though they are centuries (that is, "eons" or "saecula") apart. In God's time there is a sort of simultaneity of sacrifice and crucifixion.

Modern "secularization" can be seen from one angle as the rejection of divine time and the positing of time as purely profane. Events now exist only in this one dimension, in which they stand at greater and lesser temporal distance, and in relations of causality with other events of the same kind. The modern notion of simultaneity comes to be, in which events utterly unrelated in cause or meaning are held together simply by their co-occurrence at the same point in this single profane time-line. Modern literature — as well as news media, seconded by social science — has accustomed us to think of society in terms of vertical time-slices, holding together myriad happenings, related and unrelated. I think Anderson is right that this is a typically modern mode of social imagination, which our mediaeval forebears would have found difficult to understand, for where events in profane time are very differently related to higher time, it seems unnatural just to group them side by side in the modern relation of simultaneity. This carries a presumption of homogeneity which is essentially negated by the dominant time-consciousness.[27]

Now the move to what I am calling "secularity" is obviously related to this radically purged time-consciousness. Premodern understandings of time seem to have always been multidimen-

---

[27] Anderson borrows a term from Walter Benjamin to describe modern profane time. He sees it as a "homogeneous, empty time." "Homogeneity" captures the aspect I am describing here, that all events now fall into the same kind of time; but the "emptiness" of time takes us into another issue: the way in which both space and time come to be seen as "containers" which things and events contingently fill, rather than as constituted by what fills them. This latter step is part of the metaphysical imagination of modern physics, as we can see with Newton. But it is the step to homogeneity which is crucial for secularization, as I am conceiving it.

The step to emptiness is part of the objectification of time which has been so important a part of the outlook of the modern subject of instrumental reason. Time has been in a sense "spatialized." Heidegger has mounted a strong attack on this whole conception in his understanding of temporality; see especially *Sein und Zeit*, division 2. But distinguishing secularity from the objectification of time allows us to situate Heidegger on the modern side of the divide. Heideggerian temporality is also a mode of secular time.

sional. The Christian relating of time and eternity was not the only game in town, even in Christendom. There was also the much more widespread sense of a foundation time, a "time of origins" as Eliade used to call it,[28] which was complexly related to the present moment in ordinary time, in that it frequently could be ritually approached and its force partly reappropriated at certain privileged moments. That's why it could not simply be unambiguously placed in the past( in ordinary time). The Christian liturgical year draws on this kind of time-consciousness, widely shared by other religious outlooks, in reenacting the "founding" events of Christ's life.

It also seems to have been the universal norm to see the important metatopical spaces and agencies as constituted in some mode of higher time. States, churches, were seen to exist almost necessarily in more than one time-dimension, as though it were inconceivable that they have their being purely in the profane or ordinary time. A state which bodied forth the Great Chain was connected to the eternal realm of the Ideas; a people defined by its law communicated with the founding time where this was laid down; and so on.

The move to what I am calling secularity comes when associations are placed firmly and wholly in homogeneous, profane time, whether or not the higher time is negated altogether or other associations are still admitted to exist in it. Such I want to argue is the case with the public sphere, and therein lies its new and unprecedented nature.

I can now perhaps draw this discussion together and try to state what the public sphere *was*. It was a new metatopical space, in which members of society could exchange ideas and come to a common mind. As such it constituted a metatopical agency, but one which was understood to exist independent of the political constitution of society and completely in profane time.

[28] Mircea Eliade, *The Sacred and the Profane* (New York: Harper, 1959), pp. 80ff.

An extrapolitical, secular, metatopical space: this is what the public sphere was and is. And the importance of understanding this lies partly in the fact that it was not the only such, that it was part of a development which transformed our whole understanding of time and society, so that we have trouble recalling what it was like before. I just want to mention here two other such extrapolitical, secular spaces which have played a crucial role in the development of society: first, society considered as extrapolitically organized in a (market) economy; and, second, society as a "people," that is, as a metatopical agency which is thought to preexist and found the politically organized society. Both of these deserve much fuller exploration. But I shall not be able to do that here. I want only to draw some of the lessons for our understanding of the transition to modernity that emerge out of this discussion of the rise of the public sphere.

### III

Earlier I was saying that metatopical spaces are partly constituted in common understandings and that these are often carried in the social imaginary and the background, rather than in explicit ideas about society. A new kind of metatopical space requires new kinds of common understandings. We have now seen a little more what this involves in the case of the public sphere. It required that people be able to conceive an extrapolitical and purely secular space and agency. What is involved in this coming about?

My hypothesis is that premodern metatopical spaces were constituted in higher time. But this was not the case because people had conceived the possibility of a solely profane time and opted for multidimensionality. Rather my suggestion is that multidimensional time was the englobing horizon of their world. It took a revolution to purge time-consciousness and allow only the profane and homogeneous. So in terms of the alternatives discussed in the first section, the transition shouldn't be seen as a change in ideas, but as one which comes about through transformations in background understanding and the social imaginary. This kind of transition comes about, in the main, not through people conceiving new ideas and then acting on them, but through the coming to be of new social forms which are partly constituted by, and hence help to spread, new background understandings and a new social imaginary.

Of course, ideas play some role. And just because of this, it is easy to fall into the error of believing that the change is primarily one of ideas. For instance, in this rise of the extrapolitical and secular modes of metatopical space in the eighteenth century, the seventeenth-century theories of the state of nature and social contract probably had a part. These are images of the political as constituted out of the prepolitical, and by common action.

But the ideas are very different from the practices, and the second doesn't simply spring from the first. The social contract was, at the outset, something of a foundation myth invented for purposes of normative justification. It could ground certain norms of legitimacy, but it couldn't animate a new social practice or open a new kind of metatopical space. This happened with the rise of the public sphere, which was far from being the mere application of a preexisting theory.

In general, building a new metatopical space has to be something more than just the application of a theory, because people have to come to be able to act in concert with others, which means they have to develop common background understandings and cultivate a common imaginary around recognized symbols and rhetoric. Even where the theory is widely known, and realizing it seems to be aspired to, peoples can fail to enact it, because the modes of common action it requires are still too foreign to them to bring off. For instance, where democratic life has an important place for mass peaceful demonstrations, it is utterly disrupted by mob intimidation and violence. But mass nonviolent action is not easily in the repertory of every people at any time in their history. These forms of action have to be developed before the "theory" can be "applied."[29] The experience of Paris in 1792–94 is echoed in Bucharest 1989–91.

The social contract theory may have had a role in the rise of the public sphere. It may have helped feed the new social imaginary that this sphere required. But it ought to be clear that modern secular society didn't arise primarily through the framing of ideas which were later "applied." Indeed, if the considerations of the preceding paragraph are true, this *couldn't* have been the case. In order to change the social world the ideas have to come to animate real metatopical spaces, and this can never be just a matter of "application," the way one puts a blueprint into effect in constructing a building. Or rather, this can only happen when the ideas are so familiar to the common understandings and practices of a people that they can be unproblematically carried out. Only ideas which are not very novel can be effected in this way. For changes of the scale we are describing, it is virtually certain that they will have to be effected first in the semiblind process by which new spaces are constructed out of mutations in practice which transform the background understanding and imaginary in unplanned ways.

There has, of course, been an illusion of plan-application in modern revolutionary action, with what disastrous unintended consequences modern history is an eloquent witness. This has been powered by the modern model of agency as ideally animated by instrumental reason. This has risen along with secularization, for complex reasons which I can't go into here, but it is not necessarily connected to it.

In any case, it seems characteristic of the kind of transition we're dealing with here that, unlike a change powered by new ideas, its important innovations are nowhere clearly formulated. It is therefore hard to understand, even for those who make it, perhaps especially for them.

---

[29] I have discussed this in "Comprendre la culture politique," in Raymond Hudon and Réjean Pelletier, *L'engagement intellectuel: Mélanges en l'honneur de Léon Dion* (Québec: Les Presses de l'Université Laval, 1991).

This emerges clearly in the way our social imaginary can remain muddled and divided. The revolutionaries who planned to remake the world in secular fashion after destroying the sacral monarchy of France drew on an older notion of higher time in order to mark their age as a new dawn. They introduced a new calendar. The enterprise didn't, indeed couldn't, last very long. But it shows how much the new is still shot through with the old.

And generally, we still draw on the old images of higher time in our political life. We think of our founders as giants, living in a heroic age. This is especially clear in the rhetoric of the American republic, but lots of us go in for it in less spectacular ways. These incoherences are harmless; maybe they aren't even incoherent — any more than Christian artists in the Renaissance when they used the images of classical paganism, which had ceased to be objects of serious belief.

But there are moments when we want to have the solidity of living in political entities grounded in something more than ordinary common action. We can see this in particular in nationalist politics. The modern nation is a community which is conceived as ideally taking its own destiny in hand by common action, in the face of all the old structures of higher time, grounded as it is on a purely natural principle of unity (anyway, in theory). But nations cannot resist projecting their genesis backward in time and hiding the artifice involved in gathering them into one political entity. The unity of French or Ukrainians is projected back into a past where most presumed compatriots didn't speak French or what we now recognize as Ukrainian. It is placed there *an sich* as a seed just waiting to grow, a common will which somehow preceded its empirical manifestations. This is the fictitious, bogus side of modern nationalism, much talked about, and it forms one facet of the reality captured in Anderson's well-crafted title, *Imagined Communities*.[30]

---

[30] The other side is, of course, that the communities have to repose to some degree on common understandings. These are constitutive and don't have to be fictitious.

But perhaps the most important cost of this half-understanding is that we tend to denature the process in our retrospective undersanding. Because what has shifted is and has always been largely in the background, we tend to miss it. It's hard to get clear on the shifts in time-consciousness. We too easily tend to think that people always had our secular understandings of events in homogeneous, profane time and then just added some rather bizarre beliefs about God, eternity, and so on. That's why it seems just like dropping a number of rather tenuous illusions when they come to take on our contemporary view.

In the process, we gravely misidentify both where our ancestors were and where we are. We don't understand their beliefs, because we no longer grasp the background in which they were held. Eternity, for someone firmly in an understanding of time as exclusively secular, is just the damn thing going on without end. Sacral kingship is just a lot of ghostly stuff somehow trailing around power. It's hard for us to understand the shape of the good for them, why they valued what they valued.

But failing to see how they differed is also failing to get clear on what's peculiar to us. We only get a clear view on homogeneous, profane time when we've got the contrast formulated. So by projecting it on them we fail to get a very firm grip on our own background. And this hampers our understanding of ourselves.

That means we miss some of the connections or put them in the wrong places. So that we can easily think that secularity must be incompatible with religious belief (because it must have arisen through a change in belief), but it isn't at all. It is a change in time-consciousness, which massively reorders the relations of God (and not only God) to society, but it isn't by itself a denial of God. At the same time, some of the connections which do hold escape us, such as that between secularity and individualism. We have a wrong view of where our real choices lie. Commitment to certain goods, which seems to us optional, may be deeply embedded in our current manner of being. So that we not only wrongly believe that we are in a position to repudiate them, but have a rather distorted view of them.

An undistorted understanding of the transition to modernity will show it to be not just a shift of belief, but a massive reordering of what is taken for granted, of the relations among society, agency, time, and thus also God and the cosmos. We have moved from one constellation to the other. Once we see how massive a change has come about here, we shall no longer be tempted to see it as a change in beliefs within a single culture. We shall be induced to adopt a cultural theory of modernity. And this, in turn, will enable us to get clearer on what our modern culture is really about. As always, identifying the other undistortively will allow us better to understand ourselves, as well as seeing better what distinguishes Western modernity from the alternative modes which are springing up in the extra-European world.

The necessity of a cultural theory has perhaps not yet been demonstrated, but I hope that the considerations above on the rise of the public sphere have helped to show that we have to enlarge our usual categories to understand the whole transition. An examination of some other modern social forms should complete the process and clinch the case for a cultural theory.

## IV

How does something like the public sphere arise? I said earlier that it only needed the right cultural and social conditions for an editorial addressing the "public" as though they were together at a meeting to be treated not as an odd joke, but as a move in a new, seriously intended game. What are these conditions?

It would be great to be able to explain this. We would be at the very heart of the enterprise of explaining the rise of modernity. I have no such ambition here. But it is clear that an important preliminary to any explanation is getting clear on the scope of the phenomenon to be explained. A little reflection suggests that it is not the public sphere alone, that this is part of a wider reality which emerges at this time.

The public sphere is an extrapolitical and secular metatopical space. The suggestion is not farfetched that it should be understood against the background of other developments which accentuated the significance of the extrapolitical secular.

One such development was the revolution in natural science. The "mechanization of the world picture" took the natural universe decisively out of the Great Chain of Being and placed it very firmly in homogeneous, profane time. This undoubtedly played a role. But it did so more as a conception of the world than as a new social space or practice — even though on this latter plane the exchange of the small fraternity of scientific thinkers anticipated the later development of the public sphere. But what we should also be attentive to is the emergence of new kinds of social spaces beyond the narrow purview of the scientific elite, which could have provided a context for the rise of the public sphere.

Habermas places its emergence in this kind of context, noting that the new public sphere brought together people who had already carved out a "private" space as economic agents and owners of property, as well as an "intimate" sphere which was the locus of their family life. The agents constituting this new public sphere were thus both "bourgeois" and "homme." [31]

I think there is a very important link here. The importance of these new kinds of "private" space — that is, the heightened sense of their significance in human life — and the growing consensus in favour of entrenching their independence in the face of state and church bestowed in fact exceptional importance on an extrapolitical and secular domain of life. It is hard not to believe that this in some way facilitated the rise of the public sphere.

I would like to place these forms of privacy in a further historical context. This is what I have called the "affirmation of ordi-

---

[31] *Structural Transformation*, chapter 2, sections 6 and 7.

nary life." [32] By this I mean the broad movement in European culture, which seems to have been carried first by the Protestant Reformation, which steadily enhances the significance of production and family life. Whereas the dominant ethics which descend from the ancient world tended to treat these as infrastructural to the "good life" (defined in terms of supposedly "higher" activities, like contemplation or citizen participation), and whereas mediaeval Catholicism leaned to a view which made the life of dedicated celibacy the highest form of Christian practice, the Reformers stressed that we follow God first of all in our callings and in our families. The ordinary is sanctified or, put in other terms, the claims to special sanctity of certain types of life (the monastic), or special places (churches), or special acts (the Mass) were rejected as part of false and impious belief that humans could in some way control the action of grace.

But to say that all claims to special sanctity were rejected is to say that the nodal points where profane time especially connected with divine time were repudiated. We live our ordinary lives, work in our callings, sustain our families, in profane time. In the new perspective, this is what God demands of us, and not any attempts on our part to connect with eternity. That connection is purely God's affair. Thus the issue whether we live good or bad lives was henceforth situated firmly in ordinary life and within profane time.

Transposed out of a theological and into a purely human dimension, this gave rise to the constellation of modern beliefs and sensibility which makes the central questions of the good life turn on how we live our ordinary lives and turns its back on supposedly "higher" or more heroic modes of life. It underlies the "bourgeois" ethic of peaceful rational productivity in its polemic against the aristocratic ethic of honour and heroism. It can even appropriate its own forms of heroism, as in the Promethean picture of

[32] See *Sources of the Self* (Cambridge, Mass.: Harvard University Press, 1989), chapter 13.

humans as producers, transforming the face of the earth, which we find with Marx. Or it can issue in the more recent ethic of self-fulfillment in relationships, which is very much part of our contemporary world.

This is the background against which we can understand the two developments Habermas picks out. First, the saliency given to the "private" economic agent reflects the significance of the life of production in the ethic of ordinary life. This agent is private, over against the "public" realm of state and other authority. The "private" world of production now has a new dignity and importance. The enhancing of the private in effect gives the charter to a certain kind of individualism. The agent of production acts on his or her own, operates in a sphere of exchange with others which doesn't need to be constituted by authority. As these acts of production and exchange come to be seen as forming an ideally self-regulating system, the notion emerges of a new kind of extrapolitical and secular sphere, an "economy" in the modern sense. Where the word originally applied to the management of a household, and therefore to a domain which could never be seen as self-regulating, in the eighteenth century the notion arises of an economic system, with the Physiocrats and Adam Smith, and that is the way we understand it today.

The (market) economy comes to constitute a sphere, that is, a way in which people are linked together to form an interconnecting society, not only objectively but in their self-understanding. This sphere is extrapolitical and secularly constituted. But it is in an important sense not public. The time has come perhaps to distinguish some of the senses of this overworked term.

There seem to be two main semantic axes along which this term is used. The first connects "public" to what affects the whole community ("public affairs") or the management of these affairs ("public authority"). The second makes publicity a matter of access ("this park is open to the public") or appearance ("the news has been made public"). The new "private" sphere of economic agents contrasts with "public" in the first sense. But these agents also came to constitute what we have been calling a public sphere in the second sense, because this sphere is precisely a metatopical common space, a space in which people come together and contact each other. It is a space, we might say, of mutual appearance and in that sense a "public" space.

But the economic sphere proper is not public even in that second sense. The whole set of economic transactions is linked in a series of causal relations, which can be traced, and by which we can understand how they influence each other, but this is neither a matter of common decision (by "public authority"), nor do these linked transactions lie in some public domain of common appearance. And yet I want to speak of a "sphere" because the agents in an economy are seen as being linked in a single society, in which their actions reciprocally affect each other in some systematic way.

The economy is the first mode of society of the new sort which I defined above, a society constituted purely extrapolitically and in profane time. It forms part of the background to the rise of the public sphere. It seems very plausible that the explanation of each is interlinked with that of the other.

The second background Habermas picks out is the intimate sphere. Here we see a development of the second main constituent of ordinary life, the world of the family and its affections. As the eighteenth century develops, this becomes the locus of another demand for "privacy," this time defined in relation to the second kind of "publicness," that concerned with access. Family life retreats more and more into an intimate sphere, shielded from the outside world, and even from the other members of a large household. Houses are more and more constructed to allow for the "privacy" of family members, in relation to servants as well as outsiders.

The enhanced value placed on family life, in the context of another long-term development, toward greater concentration on subjectivity and inwardness, has as one of its fruits the eighteenth-century cherishing of sentiment. Another shift occurs, as it were, in the centre of gravity of the good life, within the broad development which affirms ordinary life, and a new importance comes to repose in our experiencing fine, noble, or exalted sentiments. This new ethic both defines and propagates itself through literature. Perhaps its central vehicle was the epistolary novel. Rousseau's *Julie* was a paradigm case.

This literature helped define a new understanding of an intimate sphere of close relations, the home at its finest of noble sentiments and exalted experience. This understanding of experience was further enriched by a new conception of art in the category of the "aesthetic." This is another fruit of subjectification, of course, because art understood in this category is being defined in terms of our reaction to it. It is in this century that music becomes more and more detached from public and liturgical function and comes to join the other arts as objects of aesthetic enjoyment, enriching the intimate sphere.

This intimate realm was also part of the background against which the public sphere emerged. And not only because it constituted part of the domain of the (extrapolitical and secular) "private," but also because the intimate domain had to be defined through public interchange, both of literary works and of criticism. This is only superficially a paradox, as we shall see below. A new definition of human identity, however "private," can only become generally accepted through being defined and affirmed in public space. And this critical exchange itself came to constitute a public sphere. We might say that it came to constitute an axis of the public sphere, along with, even slightly ahead of, the principal axis which concerned us above: exchange around matters of public (in the first sense) policy. People who never met came to a mutually recognized common mind about the moving power of Rousseau's *Julie*, even as they came to do in the early revolutionary period about the insights of his *Contrat social*.

It is against this whole economic and intimate-sentimental background that we have to understand the rise of the public sphere in Europe. And this means that we should understand it as part of a family of extrapolitical and secular constitutions of "society." On one side, it relates to the economy, even further removed from the political realm in that it is not a domain of publicity in any sense. On the other side, it helped to nourish the new images of popular sovereignty, which gave rise to new and sometimes frightening forms of political action in this century. These three forms need to be treated together, if we are to understand them adequately. I cannot undertake this here.

## V

In conclusion, I want to link this discussion with the issue I raised in the first section: cultural and acultural theories of modernity. I spoke there about the popularity of acultural accounts, that is, explanations of Western modernity which see it not as one culture among others, but rather as what emerges when any "traditional" culture is put through certain (rational or social) changes. On this view, modernity is not specifically Western, even though it may have started in the West. It is rather that form of life toward which all cultures converge, as they go through, one after another, substantially the same changes. These may be seen primarily in "intellectual" terms, as the growth of rationality and science; or primarily in "social" terms, as the development of certain institutions and practices: a market economy, or rationalized forms of administration. But in either case the changes are partly understood in terms of the loss of traditional beliefs, either because they are undermined by the growth of reason or because they are marginalized by institutional change.

Even the social explanations assume that these beliefs suffer from a lack of rational justification, since the solvent effect of social change is held to lie in the fact that it disturbs old patterns which made it possible to hold onto these earlier beliefs in spite of their lack of rational grounding. For instance, the continuance of a static, agricultural way of life, largely at the mercy of the vagaries of climate, supposedly makes certain religious beliefs look plausible, which lose their hold once humans see what it is to take their fate in their own hands through industrial development. Or a largely immobile society leads individuals to see their fate as bound up closely with that of their neighbours and inhibits the growth of an individualism which naturally flourishes once these constricting limits are lifted.

The acultural theory tends to see the process of modernity as involving among other things the shucking off of beliefs and ways which don't have much rational justification, leaving us with an outlook many of whose elements can be seen more as hard, residual facts: that we are invidiuals (i.e., beings whose behaviour is ultimately to be explained as individuals), living in profane time, who have to extract what we need to live from nature, and whom it behooves therefore to be maximally instrumentally rational, without allowing ourselves to be diverted from this goal by the metaphysical and religious beliefs which held our forebears back.[33] Instrumental rationality commands a scientific attitude to nature and human life.

At the heart of the acultural approach is the view that modernity involves our "coming to see" certain kernel truths about the human condition, those I have just adverted to. There is some justification for talking of our "coming to see" the truth when we consider the revolution of natural science which begins in the

---

[33] This development of instrumental rationality is what is frequently described as "secularization." See, for instance, Gabriel Almond and G. Bingham Powell, *Comparative Politics: A Developmental Approach* (Boston: Little Brown, 1966), pp. 24–25: "A village chief in a tribal society operates largely with a given set of goals and a given set of means of attaining these goals which have grown up and been hallowed by custom. The secularization of culture is the processes whereby traditional orientations and attitudes give way to more dynamic decision-making processes involving the gathering of information, the evaluation of information, the laying out of alternative courses of action, the selection of a given action from among those possible courses, and the means whereby one tests whether or not a given course of action is producing the consequences which were intended." And later: "The emergence of a pragmatic, empirical orientation is one component of the secularization process" (p. 58).

seventeenth century. But the mistake of the acultural approach is to lump all the supposed kernel truths about human life into the same package, as though they were all endorsed equally by "science," on a par, say, with particle physics.[34]

I have been arguing that this is a crucial mistake. It misrepresents our forebears, and it distorts the process of transition from them to us. In particular, seeing the change as the decline of certain *beliefs* covers up the great differences in background understanding and in the social imaginary of different ages. More, it involves a sort of ethnocentrism of the present. Since human beings always do hold their explicit beliefs against a background and in the context of an imaginary, failure to notice the difference amounts to the unwitting attribution to them of ours. This is the classic ethnocentric projection.

This projection gives support to the implicit Whiggism of the acultural theory, whereby moderns have "come to see" the kernel truths. If you think of premoderns as operating with the same background understanding of human beings as moderns (i.e., as instrumental individuals) and you code their understandings of God, cosmos, and multidimensional time as "beliefs" held against this background, then these beliefs do, indeed, appear to be arbitrary and lacking in justification, and it is not surprising that the social changes dislodged them.

But our examination of the rise of the social sphere suggests that this is not what happened. It is not that we sloughed off a whole lot of unjustified beliefs, leaving an implicit self-understanding which had always been there, to operate at last

[34] Even Ernest Gellner, who is light years of sophistication away from the crudities of Almond and Powell, puts himself in the acultural camp, for all his interesting insights into modernity as a new constellation. He does this by linking what I am calling the supposed "kernel truths" with what he calls "cognitive advance," in a single package. The modern constellation unchained science, and that in his view seems to confer the same epistemic status on the whole package. "Specialization, atomization, instrumental rationality, independence of fact and value, growth and provisionality of knowledge are all linked with each other" (*Plough, Sword and Book* [Chicago: University of Chicago Press, 1988], p. 122).

untrammeled. Rather, a constellation of implicit understandings of our relation to God, the cosmos, other humans, and time was replaced by another in a multifaceted mutation. Seeing things this way not only gives us a better handle on what happened. It also allows us to understand ourselves better. As long as we think that our implicit self-understanding is the universal human one, as long as we fail to note its contrast with others, so long shall we have an incomplete and distorted understanding of it. This is always a price of ethnocentrism.

From a standpoint immured within any culture other cultures look weird. No doubt we would look strange — as well as blasphemous and licentious — to our mediaeval ancestors. But there is a particularly high cost in self-misunderstanding which attaches to the ethnocentrism of the modern. The kernel truths of the acultural theory incorporate an — often unreflective — methodological individualism and a belief in the omnicompetence of natural science. Impelled by the latter, its protagonists are frequently tempted to cast our "coming to see" the kernel truths as sort of "discovery" in science. But the discoveries of natural science are of "neutral" facts, that is, truths which are "value-free," on which value may be subsequently placed by human beings, but which themselves are devoid of moral significance. It belongs to the range of such "natural" facts that we are individuals, impelled to operate by instrumental reason, maximizing our advantage when we are not deterred from doing so by unfounded belief.[35]

Now, this hides from view two important connections. First, the way in which our implicit understanding of ourselves as agents always places us in certain relations to others. Because of the very nature of the human condition — that we can only define ourselves in exchange with others, those who bring us up, and those whose society we come to see as constitutive of our identity — our self-understanding always places us among others. The place-

---

[35] Thus Gellner includes "independence of fact and value" in his package, along with "growth and provisionality of knowledge" (*Plough, Sword and Book*, p. 122).

ments differ greatly, and understanding these differences and their change is the stuff of history. We have already come across one very important such difference, admittedly in a conjectural mode, when I spoke earlier of our ancestors' sense that a metatopical agency required a constitution beyond profane time. We have broken with them because we have found a way of understanding our placement in relation to others, even metatopically, entirely in profane time. This was the shift which helped bring about modern individualism. But this mustn't be misunderstood as the birth of a human identity which only subsequently discovers a need for, or determines its relations to, others. The human of the "state of nature" was, indeed, an important constituent of the early modern imaginary, but we mustn't make the mistake of understanding the people who imagined it in its light. Modern "individualism" is co-terminous with — indeed, is defined by — a new understanding of our situation among others, one which gives an important place to common action in profane time, and hence to the idea of consensually founded unions, which receives influential formulation in the myth of an original state of nature and a social contract. Individualism is not just a withdrawal from society, but a reconception of what human society can be. To think of it as pure withdrawal is to confuse individualism, which is always a moral ideal, with the anomie of breakdown.

Similarly, our understanding of ourselves always incorporates some understanding of the good and our relation to it. Here too there are radical differences. The good may be conceived theistically, or as in the cosmos (as with Plato's Idea of the Good). But it may also be understood as residing in us, in the inherent dignity of the human person as a reasoning being, for instance, as we find with Immanuel Kant. However understood, the notion of a human identity without such a sense brings us close to the unimaginable limit of total breakdown.[36]

[36] I have tried to argue this point at greater length in *Sources of the Self*, chapters 1–4.

All this is occluded, indeed doubly. Seeing the evolution of instrumental individualism as the discovery of a "natural" fact not only involves projecting our background onto our ancestors. In addition, the naturalist, scientistic outlook which generates this error has been heavily intricated with the representational, foundationalist epistemology which descends from Descartes and Locke. This epistemology has suppressed all recognition of the background. It conceives our knowledge of the world as consisting of particulate, explicit representations. This means that we not only project our own background backward, but also render this error invisible by repressing all awareness of backgrounds as such.[37] The ethnocentric colonization of the past cannot be brought to light, because the very terms in which it might appear have been abolished.

The very idea of individuals who might become aware of themselves and then only subsequently, or at least independently, determine what importance others have for them and what they will accept as good belongs to post-Cartesian, foundationalist fantasy. Once we recognize that our explicit thoughts can only be entertained against a background sense of who and where we are in the world and among others and in moral space, we can see that we can never be without some relation to the crucial reference points I enumerated above: world, others, time, the good. This relation can, indeed, be transformed as we move from one culture or age to another, but it cannot just fall away. We cannot be without *some* sense of our moral situation, *some* sense of our connectedness to others.

The naturalistic account of the discovery of the kernel truths, implicit in the acultural theory, misses all these connections. When the old metaphysical and religious beliefs crumble, we find as a

---

[37] I have discussed the nature of this modern epistemology and its suppression of the background at greater length in "Overcoming Epistemology," in Kenneth Baynes, Jomes Bohman, and Thomas McCarthy (eds.), *After Philosophy: End or Transformation* (Cambridge, Mass.: MIT Press, 1987), and "Lichtung oder Lebensform," in *"Der Löwe spricht . . . und wir können ihn nicht verstehen"* (Frankfurt: Suhrkamp, 1991).

matter of neutral fact that we are instrumental individuals, and we need to draw from elsewhere our values and acceptable grounds for association with others. In contrast, I want to describe the change as moving us from one dense constellation of background understanding and imaginary to another, both of which place us in relation to others and the good. There is never atomistic and neutral self-understanding; there is only a constellation (ours) which tends to throw up the myth of this self-understanding as part of its imaginary. This is of the essence of a cultural theory of modernity.

Our stand on two important issues rides on which line we adopt. (1) We understand the transition differently. If we take the acultural view, we shall tend to see modern culture emerging out of the discovery of the kernel truths as "natural" facts, either directly by the growth of reason or through the effect of social change in dislodging the old, unjustified beliefs. On the cultural view, this culture comes from a mutation in our understanding of how we are placed in relation to God, good, cosmos, time, and others. The change can't be explained by the discovery of natural fact, for although some of the genuine discoveries of science are relevant here, they vastly underdetermine the changes which actually took place. Rather, we have to see the changes as in part powered by the moral and spiritual force of certain self-understandings. Less tersely, we have to see changes as coming about through the interlacing of such spiritual idées-forces and the evolution of institutions and practices which they enable and which enable them, without our being able to make either of them primary, "base" to the other's "superstructure."

So, on one view, individualism arises when the kernel truth of our being individuals is allowed to emerge from the rubble of crumbling metaphysical and religious belief and stand forth as a natural fact. On the other, individualism breaks through as a spiritual ideal, connected, among other things, to the new significance of the profane; and it triumphs through the development of those social forms whose timid beginnings initially may have facilitated it, and to which it imparts in return great power: the market economy, the public sphere, "rationalized" bureaucracy (in Weber's sense), consensual politics, among others.

(2) Our understanding of the moral issues, struggles, and tensions of modern society will also greatly differ. On one view, modernity means the receding of moral horizons, the ever-greater tendency of individuals to withdraw from modes of social solidarity. This is the view from Dover Beach, whether coded positively or negatively. On the other approach, the tensions and struggles of modernity are to be understood in relation to its own inherent moral horizon and favoured social forms. The strains are to be explained partly by the tensions implicit in these and partly by the ways in which the social developments they facilitated have rendered them problematic — the way the development of the market economy and rationalized bureaucracy are at present endangering individualism, consensual politics, and the public sphere, for instance.

On line (1), I believe that the short discussion above of the rise of the public sphere may already have begun to suggest the superiority of the cultural approach. It remains, of course, to continue this argument by looking at the connected development of other modern social forms: popular sovereignty, revolution, and nationalism.

On line (2), the forward agenda involves examining some of the malaises of modernity, cultural and political, to see what light can be cast on them from each perspective. I believe that here too the superiority of the cultural theory cannot but shine forth, as we look at, for example, the place of the politics of recognition in our contemporary society, or the way in which our typically modern sense of connectedness to the cosmos impacts on modern politics. But I can only hope to redeem this claim quite a bit further down the road.[38]

---

[38] I have begun to raise these issues, in *The Malaise of Modernity* (Cambridge, Mass.: Harvard University Press, 1992), and *The Politics of Recognition* (Princeton: Princeton University Press, 1992).

# On Doing Science in the Modern World

DAVID BALTIMORE

THE TANNER LECTURES ON HUMAN VALUES

Delivered at

Clare Hall, Cambridge University
March 9 and 10, 1992

DAVID BALTIMORE was educated at Swarthmore College, and the Massachusetts Institute of Technology, and received a Ph.D. degree in Biology from the Rockefeller University in 1964. That same year he became a research associate at the Salk Institute, and in 1972, a professor of biology at MIT. He was appointed American Cancer Society Research Professor in 1973, the following year joined the staff of the MIT Center for Cancer Research, and in 1982 was named the first director of the Whitehead Institute. He served as President of Rockefeller University from 1990 to 1991, and is currently a member of the faculty of that institution. In 1975 he was awarded the Nobel Prize in Physiology or Medicine, an honor he shared with Howard Temin and Renato Dulbecco for work on the enzyme reverse transcriptase, an enzyme that enables cancer-inducing RNA viruses to replicate within the host organism. Knowledge of this enzyme was also essential to early research on AIDS. He has continued to conduct research on the polio virus and the human immunodeficiency virus (HIV), and was cochairman of a major study of AIDS sponsored by the National Academy of Sciences and the Institute of Medicine. He is a member of the National Academy of Sciences, the American Academy of Arts and Sciences, the Institute of Medicine, the Pontifical Academy of Sciences, and is a Fellow of the Royal Society.

I

I have entitled these talks "On Doing Science in the Modern World" because I have the feeling that the societal framework in which science is being done today is different from even that of the recent past. Science is a victim of its own success. It has gone from being the province of gentlemen to being a central force of society; from a financially marginal part of governmental outlays to a significant one; from a minimal part of the academic enterprise to a dominant one. The pivotal role of science has brought it into the political spotlight, which is fundamentally changing the internal workings of the enterprise. In these two lectures I hope to highlight the increasing power of the political dimension in the process and evaluation of science.

Let me start, however, by putting my opportunity to comment on these issues in perspective. First, I am a biomedical scientist and at best a voyeur when it comes to the other sciences. Therefore, my comments will mainly focus on issues of biomedical science. In fact, biomedical science has borne a large share of the politicization of modern science, I believe, because it is the science of life and therefore is of deepest concern to the general population.

Second, I am an American and only know well the political process in America. Therefore, of necessity, my remarks will be placed in an American context. Much of what I will say, however, is, I believe, more widely relevant if for no other reason than that the diseases of America seem to spread quickly to the rest of the world. I assume that what I have to say will be especially relevant to Great Britain, because your political course in recent years has been so parallel to ours.

Finally, although I myself have been caught up in political turmoil during the last few years, I will make only a few comments on my own experience in favor of consideration of events that have not involved me. However, you can assume that all of my attitudes have been colored by my experiences.

Although my personal experiences have led me to think about the changing perception of science in the contemporary world, there are many events on the international scene that might lead one to think along these lines. For instance, there has been a remarkable movement of biomedical research activities out of Switzerland and Germany in the last few years, driven, it would seem, by the unfriendly political environments in those countries. Interestingly, America has been a great beneficiary, with research laboratories of the major pharmaceutical manufacturers of those countries coming to ours. Then we have the incredible charade of adjudicating the discovery of the AIDS virus through investigative reporting, congressional hearings, international lawsuits, and debates over patent rights. Or we might remember how the annual International AIDS Conference has become a political circus. In fact, the AIDS problem has been a focus of political concern from the moment of its appearance, and the spillover into other areas of biomedical research will be with us forever. Finally, I can point to an issue in which I have been centrally involved, the debates over recombinant DNA technology that took place in the middle 1970s and 1980s and involved legislatures around the world. The power of this technology and of all of modern life science is so great, and it touches deep moral and ethical concerns so closely, that this alone is sufficient reason for the politicization of science.

## SCIENCE IN A POLITICAL SETTING

Science done under government auspices must be seen as part of the political process because anything done by governments is by definition political. Science as it is done today, however, really dates back only to the end of World War II, when the U.S. government committed itself to the massive funding of basic scientific investigation. Before then, science was largely a European affair and was done in the context of the particular organization of the individual countries.

At the end of World War II, President Roosevelt's closest scientific adviser, Dr. Vannevar Bush, wrote a report that established a blueprint for the development of postwar science in the United States. Wartime development work had been very effective, but Bush worried that we had drained the bank of basic knowledge and that it needed to be replenished. In particular, the 1945 report, called "Science — The Endless Frontier," set the future course for funding of scientific research.

Bush had a very pure view of science that fit the idealistic aftermath of the war very well. His plan was to set up the National Science Foundation as the funding agency for science, and he consciously separated it from the other, goal-oriented agencies of the government. Bush also tried to make the NSF as independent as possible from political interference but of course recognized that Congress and the president must have the final say over any governmental agency. The plan worked moderately well in that NSF has been the major source of funds for pure, non-health-related science. Its isolation from political realities, however, has hamstrung its growth, and the National Institutes of Health, which is a goal-oriented agency, now funds much more basic research than NFS.

In today's political world, there is not as much room for pure science as there was in 1945 and what support there is has tended to be strongest for megaprojects like the super-conducting super-collider. The previous director of the NSF was able to get a hefty increase for its budget, but at the expense of turning it toward being an arm of U.S. industrial policy. But let me turn to NIH, because I know more about health-related research and because the most ominous events involve that agency.

NIH developed rapidly and effectively with very little political interference until the late 1960s. Under the supportive eyes of a few key members of Congress, its budget grew while the scientific community largely controlled its policies. In the early 1970s, the War on Cancer was born and the perspective changed. It was Senator Edward Kennedy who initiated the idea of a focused and well-funded attack on the cancer problem, but President Nixon stepped in and took the idea as his own, announcing a Presidential War on Cancer. The bill that provided the funds also gave the president and Congress new powers to appoint the directors of the National Cancer Institute and NIH. The consequence, among others, was that appointments have been much more difficult to make, leading recently to a two-year hiatus in filling the job of NIH director. Nixon did much more to inject politics into scientific decision making. His most egregious act was the abolition of the independent group of scientific advisers that had brought rational considerations on scientific matters to the White House all through the 1960s, an organization known as the President's Science Advisory Committee. This was a clear statement that politics, not rational analysis, should reign in the area of science policy.

Since 1970 there has been an acceleration in the involvement of political considerations in scientific affairs. Probably the most dramatic case was that of the Star Wars missile defense program, which was derided by most knowledgeable scientists and yet became a major drain on resources because of its political support in the Reagan White House.

In 1990 the NSF republished Vannevar Bush's 1945 report and Daniel Kevles wrote a very thoughtful appraisal of the influence of the report as a preface to the new edition. He documented the rise of the political involvement in the conduct of science and eloquently warned that, although it is exactly the danger foreseen by Bush, it is now an unalterable part of the scene. Let me quote from this preface:

> The world — and the structure of R&D — have changed a great deal since Bush wrote his report, but major principles he advanced in it merit reaffirmation. The long-term national in-

terest still calls for investment in the human and intellectual capital that are essential, ultimately, to national power in the modern world. Science still operates best in an environment of freedom, including freedom from security restrictions. However, Bush's principle of an apolitical science — a system of federally supported research kept comparatively free of the policy controls of democratic government — is no longer viable. . . . Science and technology are so pervasively important in American life as to be irreversibly involved in all parts of the nation's political system. Policy for them is no longer something special but is the product of the normal political interaction among the White House, the bureaucracy, and the Congress. If major principles of *Science — The Endless Frontier*, originally advanced in response to political circumstances, are to prevail, they must be fought for — not least by the basic-research community — in the ordinary rough-and-tumble processes of American governance.

Professor Kevles rightly points to the two sides of the issue. On the one hand, politicization is a tribute to the important role that science plays in the modern world. But basic research flourishes best in the absence of political interference so that politicization can be self-defeating. From the point of view of the public, there should be strong support for leaving scientists to make their own decisions, but the political process dictates that politicians make the decisions and they find it hard, even if they believe the arguments, to allow any entity that they fund — particularly one that absorbs as many resources as are poured into science — to handle its own affairs.

We in the United States have recently had a number of highly publicized cases in which the dominance of the political agenda over science has been writ large. Let me focus on the one that has done the most damage, the hounding of Stanford University over the issue of indirect costs that led to the resignation of its president, Donald Kennedy. Kennedy was the chief spokesman for science in academia, being both articulate and an accomplished biologist. There is no question that both the accounting practices at Stanford and governmental oversight of its procedures had been lax, but the response was wholly out of proportion to the offense. The clear villain here is a U.S. congressman who, in the tradition of Senator Joseph McCarthy, uses his investigative right as a weapon of fear and self-aggrandizement. In the Stanford case, he smelled blood and struck with a vengeance. The hunting metaphor here is appropriate because he is an animal hunter whose greatest pleasure is apparently to shoot ducks and other wild game.

Congress's treatment of Stanford is a classic case of unprincipled exploitation of the political process. Certainly Congress had the right to investigate — the question is how should it respond? If it was sympathetic to the goals and importance of higher education, it could have worked with the university to tighten up procedures. After all, Stanford is a national resource both for education and for research.

At a time when global competitiveness is a phrase on every lip, one would imagine that the Congress would recognize that the universities are the generators of the scientific base on which industry is founded and are therefore critical institutions for economic growth, never mind their important educational and cultural roles. Universities in the United States, and I know this is true in Britain too, are institutions under great financial stress because of lack of government support for so many years. The Congress is now trying to take hundreds of millions of dollars from Stanford, enough to seriously erode its strength, with no evident appreciation for its national importance. It is also trying to extend this sledgehammer approach to other universities, notably MIT.

This is the clearest present case of the government using its funding of research as a tool to gain political advantage by harassment of the recipients of the funding. The Congress argues that it has the right to uncover misuses of government funds and there is no doubt that it does have this right. The problem is that, in classic demagogic tradition, it is using its right to ridicule and undermine the universities with no regard for their importance and fragility. The hearings held by Congress could have been an occasion at which sympathetic members of Congress might have acknowledged the importance of Stanford and the superb job done by Donald Kennedy in running the university for the last ten years, while of course also underlining the need for fiscal responsibility. Rather, our game-hunting congressman took the occasion to demean Dr. Kennedy and to excoriate the university. American higher education took a blow from which it will be a long time recovering. In fact, the relationship between the government and the great research universities of America will never be the same because the level of mutual suspicion and disrespect has risen so high.

It is ironic that one of the few parts of the American economy that is working well, the universities, should be under attack. To some extent, I suppose, they are convenient scapegoats for a deep concern over the declining fortunes of America on the world economic scene. But the fault lies in our inability to translate the fruits of research into competitive products. Our present-day economic system, which has poured money into the pockets of the already-wealthy while the middle and lower socioeconomic groups fall further and further behind, rewards financial manipulation, not effective manufacture or industrial innovation. As people's salaries have declined, they have turned away from progressive forces hoping that conservative approaches will return prosperity. This misreading of the solution explains why the country has turned in the last decade to leadership that has simply stolen their labor and turned it into profits for the rich. I am not exaggerating: a recent report showed that in the booming 1980s 60% of the economic growth went to the richest 1% of American families and all but 6% went to the top 20%. At the same time, the bottom 40% of families had an actual decline in income (*NY Times*, March 5, 1992, p. 1). In such economic circumstances it is easy for unscrupulous politicians to manufacture scapegoats. The shame is that when the research institutions become the scapegoats, future opportunities for building out of the hole become increasingly limited.

For all the discussion in America of the need to upgrade education, the parts of our system that work best, the research universities, are not being publicly supported and, worse, are being hounded. There is no doubt that the present climate is going to bring increasing regulation of science and educational institutions. We will end up spending more on administration and less on matters of substance. We will find students turned off by a more regimented life in science. Scientists will be driven to companies because of the unpleasantness of academic life. While that might actually be beneficial in the short run, it will bring back Vannevar Bush's greatest fear — that we drain the pipeline of ideas and end up falling behind because we have not supported the long-term perspective which can only be taken in universities and research institutes.

## CHANGING POLITICS

I have argued that the political dimension of science has widened considerably and that part of the changed circumstance is due to the pivotal role that science plays in the modern world. But it is important to realize that changes in politics also have played a critical role. In the United States, at least, our politics has become much more populist in the last decades. By this I mean that we are a truer democracy, with more power in the hands of the voters and less in the hands of powerful individuals. Many influences have brought about this change and it is still coming to equilibrium. One has been increasing access to the ballot box — there is universal suffrage and the impediments to registration and voting have been limited. Another is the increased power and speed of the media. Here the growth of television, bringing Washington into the homes of every American each night, has had a big effect. A particular influence has been the post-Watergate press, which increasingly emphasizes investigative reporting. Politicians are having to answer for every vote they make, every aspect of their private lives. Another influence is the growth of special interest group politics, forcing politicians to pay attention to minority opinions because of the force of their political organizing and the tenacity of their concern. This has had a special importance for biomedical research because of the power of the antiabortion and animal rights groups.

The growth of populism has been so great that the traditional forms of political influence are much less effective today. It used to be that political influence was focused on Washington, but today influence must be exerted through grass-roots education because politicians are paying more attention to the voters and less to the lobbyists who speak to members of Congress directly. In many ways, of course, this is a salutary trend but it has its downside for science, the arts, and higher education because these are aspects of society that have little direct impact on the average voter and are often viewed with suspicion. In fact, in the United States we have a new biomedical support group called Research!America that has as its goal the education of the public about the importance of biomedical research to the health of the nation. In a country of 250 million people spread over the 3,000 miles that separate the Atlantic from the Pacific, sending such a message is difficult and expensive.

ASILOMAR AS AN EXAMPLE OF COOPERATION

Although President Nixon was particularly responsible for increasing the political involvement in science, it was actually the biomedical research community itself that precipitated the most intense political concern. In the mid-1970s, when the ability to exchange genetic material between organisms was first developed, research scientists raised the question of whether this capability might pose hazards for the general population. We call this new form of experimentation recombinant DNA technology. From the initial questioning there evolved an exemplary process, run largely by the scientific community, that satisfied the political concerns which had been generated by the initial call for caution. The key event was a meeting organized by a group of scientists, of which I was one, in Asilomar, California, in 1975.

The Asilomar meeting was organized to consider whether the recombinant DNA technology was potentially dangerous as a form of biological experimentation. It was the first time in history that the scientific community itself raised in public an issue about the safety of its own activities. The result was a proposed set of guidelines under which many benign forms of the new technology could go forward. There were, however, experiments for which it was recommended that they should only be done with great care and others that at least temporarily should not be done at all. Most importantly, an ongoing mechanism of evaluation was established under the auspices of the government that could monitor the situation as it unfolded and recommend changes in the guidelines that would reflect the changing evaluation of potential hazards.

The process worked very smoothly. In open meetings, covered by the press and attended by critics and supporters, recommendations were made to the director of the National Institutes of Health as to what modifications were appropriate in the guidelines. As it turned out, the feared consequences of the new technology did not materialize and over about ten years the guidelines were systematically liberalized, so that now there is but a vestige of the process left, which is focused solely on the issue of human genetic engineering. One of the experimental protocols that was initially virtually forbidden involved making cloned DNA representations of viruses. I can remember when, at the end of the 1970s, the guidelines were sufficiently liberalized so that such experiments could be performed in ordinary laboratory circumstances. The study of viruses was then my major activity; as much as I supported the guidelines, having been one of their architects, my frustration level was high and the changed regulations allowed me to realize an experimental dream. I mention that because it is important to realize that the biomedical research community had voluntarily put a moratorium on experiments that it very much wanted to do and that individual scientists were prevented from using a technology that could have greatly increased their investigative power.

The regulation of recombinant DNA technology was a model of responsible, effective regulation largely because it was left in the hands of the scientific community. This was not for lack of interest on the part of politicians. They held hearings, carried out investigations, and kept the process very much in view. But they were convinced that the community was handling the problem responsibly. A large number of bills were proposed in Congress to make the guidelines into law, but none was ever enacted because we were able to convince the members of Congress that the situation required flexibility and that laws would be counterproductive. To avoid legislation required that many of us spend long days in the halls of Congress, allaying the fears of the representatives. An important circumstance was that no untoward incident occurred, so that politicians could consider the situation coolly, without the pressure of a highly publicized event. This is somewhat miraculous because although the technology is benign, there are so many practitioners that one might expect someone to charge that he or she had been harmed by a laboratory procedure. To this day, I know of no such charge.

The era of good feelings between the research community and the politicians has not lasted. It seems to me that this is more because of changes on the political side than on the scientific side. But political swings do not occur on their own; they are usually driven by public discontent. It is important to ask where this discontent arose. I want first to argue that failings of the scientific community are at least partly responsible. To make the argument, I am going to go back to the early 1960s, when I was a graduate student tasting the pleasures of experimental science for the first time.

A LIFE OF SCIENCE

I grew up in science with a belief that being selfish was what was expected. Science graduate students of the post-*Sputnik* 1960s thought ourselves to be particularly lucky because we could do only what we enjoyed and still be considered socially useful. We would congratulate ourselves on our good fortune. Entering a life of science is always a joy. Before that one had spent some twenty years growing up, learning facts, developing skills like spelling and mathematics, playing sports, discovering the opposite sex, if you were lucky maybe doing a little traveling and learning a foreign language and doing some rote laboratory work. But nothing had prepared me, at least, for what came next. I can remember when I studied science in college wondering what it meant to do research. It was impossible to formulate a clear idea of where the frontier of knowledge lay. I can remember an inchoate perplexity about what research really was. Now I can diagnose my difficulty — I had no idea how to formulate a problem that could be investigated. Having not had any experience in a research lab, I could not imagine how a problem was posed in research terms. But, of course, not having the experience, I also could not even formulate my concern — it was no more than a vague hole at the center of my being waiting for definition. I suspect it is that way for all young scientists who have not been in a lab. Actually, I'd been lucky in that I'd had a little taste of research in high school. It stayed with me as a memory but, by the end of college, was so disconnected from the book-learning I had absorbed that it stayed as a motivation but not an understanding. Then, in graduate school, the light dawned when I finally had the opportunity to do real experiments. First, the little questions were posed for me, then I saw how to pose them myself, then bigger questions made sense, and within about a year I saw open to me the world of the unknown but the knowable. I began to see how one formulates an answerable question. I assume that such a moment comes for all experimental scientists. Even theoreticians must need to formulate what is studiable so that the frontier becomes evident.

That epiphanal time was to me a realization of what I was meant to do. Not being religious, I do not mean that I was meant by God to do research, but I do suspect that I was meant by my genetic inheritance to do research. Coming to that realization was like putting on a calfskin glove that fit perfectly: it was a warm, enveloping experience. But both my parents had grown up in the depression and my father was from a very poor family. They had worked hard in their lives to earn a living and the idea of a profession being an enjoyment was foreign to my father and something my mother had only found in later life. Did I have a right to indulge my new-found passion? The only way to do research was on government money: could I really make a life spending the government's money to indulge my habit? As I looked to the feedback coming from the outside world in the early 1960s, the answer was a resounding yes. It was clear that the nation had committed itself to greatness in science and that my private passion was a public good. What a relief to me and to a whole generation of scientists who grew up after, but in the shadow of, the Great Depression and World War II: sanctioned self-indulgence.

### A Mature Science

But not now. First of all the whole issue of whether scientific investigation is an unconditional good is debated widely. Many people argue that what scientists find is not necessarily good for society. The physicists in the post–atomic bomb era first raised these doubts and now, with Chernobyl and the ozone hole and industrial pollution, the doubts have become a widespread strain of concern. Research has become so much more expensive and so many more resources are going to research that the questions and doubts are multiplying and coming from more places.

But I see another problem. When I entered molecular biology it was in its infancy. We knew so little and, perhaps as importantly, we did not know how we were ever going to decipher the complex problems of human biology. All of that has changed. We now have a powerful, mature science that has a clear idea of how it will answer the problems ahead of it. We have an optimism that any problem is solvable, that the techniques and concepts we have today are sufficient to carry us to the deepest conceivable knowledge of ourselves, and that it is going to get easier as the technologies mature further. It is a heady feeling and those who enter the field feel it and are making themselves into experimental miracle workers.

But with power comes responsibility and that is where the change lies. Because total self-indulgence is not now a stance that all can take. With such power the scientific community has the responsibility to choose the problems it studies with an eye to how it can contribute to the welfare of the world. Does a scientist who can help to learn about AIDS, whose skills provide the ability to contribute to the conquest of this modern plague, have the right to continue investigating an arcane problem of bacterial transposons? I hear the answer from my colleagues as soon as I pose the question: "Maybe," they will say, "the answer will come from work on transposons." Quoting back to me things I might have said once, they will go on, "Head-on research is often the least effective way to get an answer. When we deal with the unknown, answers often come from unexpected quarters."

True, true — because I've made such arguments myself they come easily to my mind and I deeply believe them. But they are not always the right arguments and are not always applicable. Let's remember the Manhattan Project, the American crash program to design an atomic bomb. It was a great success because a group of physicists gave up the self-indulgence of unfettered research and dedicated themselves to making a bomb. The basic underpinnings were there, years of unfettered research had provided the basic understanding — what was needed and provided was research that never lost sight of its goals. It is crucial that the problem was an appropriate one: the basic research knowledge was there. Had the nation chosen in 1970, for instance, to solve the cancer problem that way, no good would have come of it. The basic knowledge of cancer in 1970 was simply not there to build upon. A problem must be ripe for a head-on approach to succeed.

## Dedicated Science

But today I fear that too many in the scientific community are unwilling to ask what problems are ripe for a dedicated attack. We are living by the myth that nothing is ripe, that all problems are basic ones. In the infancy of molecular biology, even in 1975, that was certainly the case. There was virtually no human disease that could be seriously attacked by the methods and concepts of molecular biology. It was an infant science, although one with a rapidly increasing sophistication of concept. The last fifteen years have seen a sea change in that perspective. Molecular biology is now a mature science, one with great power to ameliorate human disease.

The best example of the new status of molecular biology is the biotechnology industry. It dates from the late 1970s and saw spectacular growth in the 1980s. It marks the maturity of molecular biology in two ways. One is methodological: there is now a significant segment of the science being done with a direct goal-orientation and it is being successful. The second difference wrought by industrial development is that it is the vehicle for direct contribution to society. Real drugs are on the market as a result of the efforts of the last fifteen years. My favorite example is erythropoietin. Here is a protein made by our bodies in vanishingly small quantities that was a laboratory curiosity fifteen years ago. It is, however, a protein that allows the body to make more red blood cells. For individuals who need more red blood cells, like people on kidney dialysis, this protein can be a literal lifesaver. Today, thanks solely to the efforts of the biotechnology industry, it is available in the local pharmacy. People who need more red blood cells can have them. What better proof can there be of the maturity of molecular biology?

Let me return to the methodological aspect of the biotechnology industry. A scientist in a company can sometimes work in as unfettered a way as he or she can in a university or research institute. But that is very rare. More characteristically, work in a company setting is directed to certain goals. They may be long-term goals or they may be vague goals, but efforts directed outside of their framework is discouraged. The management sets the goals (in the best circumstances with strong input from the scientists) and then those goals establish the pattern of research unless corporate targets change. The willingness of large numbers of molecular biologists to work within the framework of such goals and their success as measured by new products now available, and many more to come soon, shows what can be done by a Manhattan Project mentality allied to the contemporary power of molecular biology.

## AIDS, THE GENOME PROJECT, AND CANCER

The question I want to raise here is whether the sophistication of molecular biology, as measured by its ability to produce the goods, should not change the expectations of scientists in the field. We might ask whether applied biological science should not have a higher status in universities than it presently enjoys. Should we not be educating young scientists to think about their newly acquired powers of investigation both as a way to discover new principles and phenomena and as a way to solve societal problems? In a sense, the question is whether genetic engineering, a shorthand phrase that subsumes recombinant DNA technology and other technologies, isn't becoming a real form of engineering. We have chemical engineers alongside chemists and electrical engineers alongside physicists, so why not biological engineers alongside biologists?

There is another opportunity for a more targeted approach to biological research. The pharmaceutical and biotechnology industries mount programs designed to produce defined products that can be sold. Thus, we get agents that can ameliorate heart disease, stimulate red and white blood cell production, fight viral diseases. Sometimes companies even discover the basis of mysterious diseases, like the Chiron Corporation's discovery of the virus that causes hepatitis C. But there is another form of research that companies rarely engage in effectively: research on diseases where the pathology and even the etiology is obscure. My favorite example here is AIDS and I want to discuss it at some length. I'll also comment on cancer research. I could take rheumatoid arthritis or a variety of autoimmune diseases just as well.

My thesis about AIDS is that it is a disease that we should be attacking using an industrial paradigm but that we are attacking it using a basic research paradigm and are therefore wasting time and resources. This position has evolved from my co-chairmanship in 1986 of a committee to advise the country on a response to the AIDS problem appointed by the Institute of Medicine and National Academy of Science in the United States. It seemed to me five years ago and it still does that AIDS is the type of problem one approaches head-on. It is, after all, caused by a small virus and it attacks one of the most accessible systems in the body, the immune system. There are certainly aspects of the AIDS problem we do not understand, and nondirected basic research has to be a part of an attack on the problem, but an organized, preferably worldwide approach could, I believe, accumulate the relevant information much more rapidly than leaving the problem to the whims of the research community. Here, in fact, Great Britain, although devoting only a small fraction of the resources of the United States, has what seems to be a better-coordinated and better-led program that has brought in a very impressive cadre of scientists to study the problem. We seem to be afraid to say that we have identified a national need and we are going to make sure that the best minds put their attention to it. Why not conscript scientists when their skills could avert a disaster? To say that outright would be a drastic change in the relationship of biomedical scientists to their country and one that should only be contemplated in an emergency, but AIDS certainly represents that emergency.

The issue of targeted research versus investigator-initiated research comes up in another context, the genome project. This is a project to map at high resolution the genes of humans and other key species. It has been controversial because it involves diverting resources from the usual intensive, small-science research efforts to one that will require an enormous input of coordinated, repetitive labor and massive data analysis problems. It will give us invaluable information, but acquiring that information might involve new forms of research organization. I have for a long time harbored the hope that the project can be done without giving up the small-science approach, but this is becoming increasingly unlikely. It may be that the only way to actually get the work done is to give the problem to industry because few universities have been willing to undertake anything but minimal aspects. This notion has scared the research community both because it does not want to see large resources going to industry and because of the fear that work done by industry will not be freely available. The issues here go beyond the scope of this discussion.

One other area where targeted research may soon become an issue is cancer research. The progress in understanding cancer over the last fifteen years has been nothing short of miraculous and yet the mortality statistics show only marginal improvements. We hear accusations that cancer scientists are just wasting money and are not really focusing on the problem. It is not a fair charge but it is a reasonable question to ask if the time is not coming for a reassessment of our strategies and a more targeted approach. I am not sure what is the right answer, but it does seem to me that the question should be asked. Patient-advocates are a major force in setting research priorities in AIDS research and I suspect that cancer is soon going to see the same advocacy.

What I am saying is that the discontent of the political world with the activities of the scientific community is partly our own fault. We have not been willing to undertake critical evaluations of our own activities and therefore left ourselves open to the charge of insensitivity, of self-indulgence. While that was not a problem twenty-five years ago — when our science was nascent and the public hungered for achievements in pure science as a way of demonstrating American superiority over the Russians in the post-*Sputnik* era — in the contemporary world, when America is living through a time of diminishing financial expectations, this won't wash. The biomedical research community has to ask itself: how can we contribute best to the alleviation of suffering? How can we demonstrate most directly our importance for the future health and well-being of the people of this earth? If the general population truly believed that we were devoting ourselves to those questions, perhaps our political stock would rise and we would not find ourselves under such political pressure.

I mentioned in passing the notion that America and perhaps other parts of the developed world are living through a period of diminishing expectations. That perception derives from a fascinating book written last year by Paul Krugman, an MIT economist. The book was called *The Age of Diminished Expectations* (MIT Press, 1990) and argues persuasively that the American public has simply given up hoping that things will get better economically and is lowering its sights for the future. To quote Krugman:

> One might have expected that America's economic problems would have come to a head . . . through the political process. Relative to what almost everyone expected twenty years ago, our economy has done terribly; surely one should have expected a drastic political reaction. I find the lack of protest over our basically dreary economic record the most remarkable fact about America today. . . . it is astonishing how readily Americans have scaled down their expectations.

With real wages having fallen for 40% of the population and the middle class dissolving away, one might think that people would hunger for politicians who could face up to the problems and offer solutions, but Krugman argues, rather, that people are expecting less and are willing to settle for politicians who offer illusory goals like reduced taxes. This may go a long way toward explaining why the political world is so peevish in relation to the arts and sciences. Maybe it is a redirection of frustrations that must be there in a generation undergoing such a radical transformation from the expectations of its parents.

## Reprise

I have covered a lot of territory in this talk so maybe a reprise is in order before we break until tomorrow. I started by asserting that the public has become more skeptical of science leading the political world to take an increasing interest in the activities of scientists. Events on the international scene indicate this as well as events in America. Science that is funded by the government is inevitably under some political scrutiny, but in the post–World War II era, when Vannevar Bush wrote his seminal report, science was relatively independent of political control. Nixon changed the situation dramatically with the War on Cancer and other acts. The situation has escalated recently, with the Stanford situation being the most dangerous because a great institution is in jeopardy. With education and research as the bedrocks of progress, the attack on higher education threatens to undermine the opportunity of the United States to grow out of its present economic problems. It seems that the research universities have become scapegoats for the failures of American economic life.

The increased politicization of science is partly a result of the changing nature of politics. With grass-roots influence high, populism has set in, making it particularly difficult to sell the notion of the importance of science.

The political world's attention was drawn to modern biology by the Asilomar meeting in 1975, which was an example of an effective relationship between politicians and scientists. Relationships deteriorated afterward.

Looking back to my beginnings in science, I can see the change partly as a lack of understanding of the responsibility of a mature science to take societal challenges head-on, as was done so effectively in the Manhattan Project. Molecular biology today is such a mature science, as seen by the power of the biotechnology industry. One problem I believe should be taken on by the molecular biology community in an organized, structured research effort is AIDS. The one project that has been taken on is the genome project. The cancer problem may be ready for such an attack. We could do pure research without being concerned about such problems when the science was nascent and the country was rich, but not now. Today America has so lost its way that even its expectations of improvement have seriously diminished and it is likely that part of the attack on science and education comes from frustration.

Tomorrow I will consider how the issue of political involvement in science forces us to think about the difficult question of what constitutes truth in science. I will also consider whether science doesn't have a natural protection from political interference. Finally, I will discuss some practical remedies that the scientific community can employ to minimize political interference in its activities.

## II

Science is a search for provisional truths that provide unitary understanding of disparate observations. Being provisional, and very much a function of just what observations have been made, science is a very personal undertaking. When external political forces begin to impinge on science, the result can be a chilling of the creative force as the scientist tries to satisfy the needs of a political master. Science today still enjoys relative freedom from political dictation. We can compare our situation to that of geneticists in the Soviet Union under Lysenko to understand what political repression can become. But neither is science in the United

States free of political second-guessing, as it was in the period after World War II.

For the last six years I have personally been involved in a controversy that would have been a minor event were it not for the involvement of the political world. You probably know that data gathered in the laboratory of a then-MIT professor, named Theresa Imanishi-Kari, with whom I was collaborating, were challenged and ultimately she was accused of falsification of data. The issue is in the courts and will not be resolved for some time yet, but the discussion of the issue has raised some very fundamental questions about the proper conduct of science and it is these questions on which I want to comment.

## VERIFICATION IN SCIENCE

The issue is: how is science verified? How do we know what's right, what's wrong? For the nonscientists in the audience, let me spend a moment on the question before considering the answer. Some outside of science but, I dare say, few within science may think that science progresses from truth to truth. In fact, it might better be said that science progresses from misconception to misconception, from error to error. When a paper is published, the authors generally believe they have made an honest stab at the truth of the situation, but most would agree that putting something into the literature is akin to entering into a ongoing discussion in which the later contributions will alter, refine, and ultimately could invalidate today's contribution. From this process emerge provisional truths, statements that would get wide agreement in the community of scientists and therefore are the truth of their time. They get into textbooks and get taught to students, but rarely with a sufficient warning that this knowledge is provisional, subject to change, may even be invalidated. Thus, in asking how science is verified, we are really asking about the procedures in the scientific community that maintain and underlie the ongoing debate about truth.

## Repetition

A common belief about the process of scientific verification is that truth emerges from repetition, that if others can repeat an experiment that will show the experiment to be a correct one. Repetition is an important form of verification within a laboratory; it is particularly important as a way for a scientist to check on his or her own experiments. But repetition is not really how the ongoing debate in science is maintained. Certain types of experiments, like the isolation of a particular stretch of DNA, are easily repeated; but for complicated experiments, repetition is not commonly attempted by one laboratory to check on another. In a deep sense, there really is no way to repeat an experiment exactly. To appreciate this point, one need only reflect on the fact that time is a variable that can never be repeated — at a more mundane level, a laboratory that undertakes a repetition of an experiment in the literature will have different water from the original laboratory, as well as reagents and supplies from a different manufacturer. In fact, given the many variables that differentiate one laboratory environment from another, the inability to repeat a result is not particularly surprising.

In my laboratory, we sometimes want to repeat a published experiment because the methodology would be a valuable one for our own experimental program. Not infrequently, an attempt at repetition fails and a tenacious scientist may call the originating laboratory to see if there are any tricks that might not be obvious in the publication. A long period can ensue in which the experiment may work in one laboratory and not another. I have even sent students to the originating laboratory to watch the experiment firsthand. Finally, some subtle difference may emerge as the culprit. No, for complicated experiments, repetition is not a significant form of verification — it is rather a difficult achievement, rarely undertaken.

Repetition is not frequent for another reason: there are too many interesting questions abroad for many scientists to be willing to repeat an observation with any exactitude. Repetition is just not as exciting as finding something new. In biology, the problem is compounded by an aspect of biological research known as "the system." Each biologist has a system he or she employs; some have a few systems. The system encompasses the organism under study, the level at which it is studied — biochemical or cellular or organismal — and the types of experimental approaches used. Different immunologists, for instance, have favorite organisms and favorite antigenic responses they study. This is not a matter of aesthetics; it takes years to build up the reagents and expertise necessary to study one system and to change involves a major investment. Also, someone who has spent years honing his or her skill at the performance of some set of complicated techniques is going to continue using those techniques rather than change approaches and require new training. There is a built-in technical conservatism that is inevitable in science and is enshrined in the notion of a system. But you see the problem: if each scientist has his or her private range of action, who will repeat the experiments of another when the original experiment came from an individual perspective that may be shared in its details by no one else?

Thus, because of the virtual impossibility of performing a true repetition and because of the desire of scientists to move on to the next question and because of experimental conservatism, verification is rarely accomplished by repetition. What actually happens is, epistemologically speaking, better. A new paper that, let us say, has introduced a new concept causes people working in other systems to try to incorporate the concept into their own work and to test its applicability. Rather than repeating the work of another, they test it by building upon it. If in their systems this concept works, it receives the very strongest form of verification. If it fails, we have a classic problem — is the concept wrong or is it limited to only a range of systems and not universal? As a verifier, I do not care, because if it is inapplicable to my system, I'll go on to things that are applicable and leave the new concept aside. Note that I will not prove it right or wrong, only limit its applicability. If it is an important new idea, others will do the same and ultimately its range of applicability will become evident.

Let us say that no one finds a new concept applicable: how is this information conveyed to the rest of the scientific community? Few people publish negative results, partially because few journals will accept papers that have no positive news. The news does travel, however, mainly through two routes: the grapevine and the literature. The grapevine is quite effective: scientists see each other frequently at meetings and visits. Often the inability to utilize a new idea or method is transmitted in these encounters and experiences are compared. Even though the literature may not include negative results, it carries the message very effectively when no papers appear that carry the concept forward. Lacking any new news, the community comes to the view that the concept was probably of limited value and people go on to think about other things.

### Resurrection

Meanwhile, what is the epistemological status of the concept enunciated in one paper and not supported further? Is it considered wrong, or just of limited applicability? Could it be that the data on which it was formulated were wrong either for reasons of experimental imperfection or because of conscious misrepresentation? Ordinarily, none of that is ever sorted out. The paper stays in the literature, available to all who wish to peruse it. In fact, the literature has millions of such papers in it, ones that made no positive contribution to the ongoing process of accumulation of knowledge. And one day, maybe a few years after the initial publication, some unsuspecting young student, dutifully examining all of the antecedents to his project, may come across this paper and bring it to his professor and say: Is this right? Should I incorporate this idea into my thinking? What the professor responds depends on many factors. Let us assume that pettiness does not enter into the picture. She is most likely to say that this idea was not productive and therefore has been discarded in most people's thinking. Times may be different however, and she may see that the idea dovetails well with other current ideas and may suggest that it be given a second chance. Or maybe the systems in her laboratory are very close to the original one and she says that it would be foolish to ignore the possibility that this idea is applicable, at least here. Thus, the concept may have a new life. In the real world of science my hypothetical situation comes up all of the time: there is a constant dialogue with history. And it could well happen that this resurrected notion turns out to be applicable and may suddenly gain currency. Other experimental systems may have emerged that now behave in accordance with the notion, showing that it was of general significance but that the systems being studied were just not in a position to incorporate the idea at the time it was first enunciated.

### FABRICATION

I glancingly noted one possibility in my analysis: that the original work that provided new data for the literature might have been fabricated. Let us further consider this possibility.

The pertinent issues are what damage is done by conscious data fabrication and how is it detected? The damage is real. Others can be misled and time, money, and careers can be wasted by following up ideas that are false. Fabricated data will not, however, always generate false ideas; in some well-known cases the perpetrator probably had preliminary data that indicated the existence of a new phenomenon and the fabricated data were an approximately correct representation of the truth. This is not to excuse data fabrication — whether it is done in the name of truth or of sheer fantasy, it is anathema to science because it erodes the confidence that science is disinterestedly searching for elusive truths. But fabricated data are actually part of a continuum because nature never speaks to us directly; data are a representation of physical reality, not reality itself. As an example, consider that every time a graph is prepared from numerical data, subtle decisions about the scales and choice of axes can shape the data so that they appear to support a particular interpretation; thus ideas are always shaping the presentation of data, which is perhaps one definition of the word "fabrication." But, from the previous discussion of the power of a new idea to shape research directions, it should be evident that any new idea must be based on honestly accumulated data, if for no other reason than because an idea will shape the activities of others. For the very reason that most science is not verified by repetition, it is imperative that a scientist be able to trust his or her peers. "Trust" is the key word here and it is trust that is undermined by conscious fabrication.

The other question I raised is how data fabrication is detected. One possibility is that it may not be detected, but the power of the ideas it generates to control the work of others will be rapidly diminished as they find it impossible to build upon those ideas. Thus, the normal processes of science will root out ineffective ideas, however they were generated. There is in molecular biology a famous case of many years ago of Mark Spector, who managed to fabricate data on a grand and cynical scale that were relevant to some of the major issues of the day about how growth is controlled in cells. The doubts about him started almost immediately because his data did not fit in with any previous work, but even with doubts about, it was hard to ignore the possibility that he had found a uniquely effective way into a difficult problem, a problem with which we are still wrestling. It took a short time, a few months, for the community to cool on Spector's work and to develop doubts about his veracity. The major reason was that no one could find anything that fit with his data. Also, attempts to get key reagents from him were of no avail. Thus, when a co-worker caught him at his fabrication and he was unmasked, his influence had already waned. But many hours were spent in many laboratories in a fruitless attempt to develop his notions in new directions. I myself was part of the attempt to develop Spector's leads because they related to the field in which I was working and you can be sure that I was furious about his deception.

## DEALING WITH FABRICATION

In summary, the publication of false data is morally wrong, disruptive, and eroding of one of the key currencies of science, trust. But its effects are transient and easily absorbed within the ordinary activities of science and, I dare say, most fabrication is probably not unmasked but has little long-term result because the processes of science handle the problem. Thus, what should be done to detect and root out fabrication? Should we unmask it ruthlessly and unrelentingly or should we simply not condone it and shun those who knowingly perpetrate it? The latter approach approximates the behavior of the scientific community up to a few years ago. The ethic was clear and strong — falsity is wrong particularly because of its erosive effect on trust. But because the ethic was so clear, and the shunning of those who participated in fraud was so absolute, the processes for handling fraud were fairly informal and the punishments were meted out in an unobtrusive way.

Now that is changing, at least in the United States. The issue which has brought fraud to a prominent place is money — the U.S. Congress appropriates the money for most American science and it is now insisting that the wasted money due to fraudulent activities be unmasked. Never mind that the cost of discovering fraud is clearly more than the price tag of the fraudulent work, never mind that the process of discovery is erosive of trust and disruptive of the effective course of science. The mind set here is that of the investigator of any governmental activity and seems to have its roots in the notion of prevention by example — if one fraud is detected and punished, it is believed that this will inhibit further frauds.

With the Congress focusing attention on fraud, if I am right and it is not a big problem, why is the scientific community not protesting that the focus is misguided? Why are the institutions of science falling all over themselves to set up commissions and studies, to write reports, and to devise procedures for handling misconduct? To my knowledge, it is not because the elders of science have become convinced that misconduct is more widespread; all of the written documents seem to emphasize that the problem remains rare. Rather, I believe, it is out of fear — fear that funds will be cut unless the whims of Congress are appeased. Long ago Vannevar Bush warned that deep governmental involvement in science could lead to governmental control of the activities of scientists. There is every indication that such a trend is on the rise.

If it is not clear enough, let me state explicitly that I believe that science is best served, and therefore the public is best served, if the doing and evaluation of science is left to the scientists. The criteria that laypeople, especially politicians, might apply to science are likely to be wrongly focused because they will be evaluating science by myths rather than realities. I can illustrate this from another point of view.

It is often said that one crime in science is data selection: that when one selects from a mass of data just those which are supportive of a given notion, and ignores contradictory data, one is misrepresenting reality and is guilty of scientific misconduct. True, one needs in scientific publication to reflect the data honestly. But in saying that one must realize that data are always selectively presented and when data selection becomes fraud science comes to an end. The issue is intent to deceive and it must be distinguished from intent to convince.

I'll give you a recent example from my own laboratory. The other day one of my postdoctoral fellows described an unexpected finding during a meeting of our group. Another of my fellows got excited by this and indicated that it explained an experience of his a few months ago when he had slightly changed the materials he used for an experiment he had done numerous times and suddenly the experiment had not worked in the usual way. He had assumed that something had gone wrong but now saw that the alteration of procedure had been responsible in a way he had not then imagined possible. He had never mentioned what he thought was a failed experiment and had we written up his data for publication the aberrant experiment would not have been part of it. Would that have been misconduct? It was the conscious elimination of an experiment from the record. It would certainly not have been misconduct by any reasonable criterion because, until it was explained, it had no meaning.

One can only publish that which one believes is meaningful. Furthermore, every anomaly that appears in the laboratory cannot be followed up or we would spend our time spinning wheels. Judging what is reliable science is a personal decision made on the basis of experience and on whether the results fit a pattern. Random observations are not science. The reporting of every activity of a laboratory might serve history well but it would not serve science.

### SCIENCE AND THE FIRST AMENDMENT

Having considered some of the detrimental aspects of political interference in science that come from my own experiences in research, let me turn to a more general and more speculative point of view. Here I will get into legal issues that are clearly beyond my own areas of direct knowledge and I may get out on a limb and have it sawed off behind me. Nonetheless, after conversations with legal experts, and after reading a number of articles on the subject, I am convinced that there is a deep truth here, even if I can only represent it in imprecise terms. I might say that the writing of Natasha Lisman, a Boston lawyer, has been particularly instructive to me (*Boston Bar Journal*, Nov./Dec. 1991, pp. 4–7).

In American law, the fundamentals of protection of human rights are found in the first ten amendments to the Constitution. They were written by the founding fathers of America in an effort to ensure that government would never become an unduly oppressive force and are known as the Bill of Rights. A key contributor to their formulation was Thomas Jefferson, a man of science. Let us examine whether the First Amendment to the Constitution might be applicable to the issue of what limits there are on the federal government's right to control science.

The First Amendment states that no law shall be made that abrogates free speech. This has been interpreted in a very strong way by the U.S. Supreme Court; it has only allowed the government to make laws that restrict the right to free speech in situations where there is a compelling need. An illustrative restriction is one against shouting "fire" in a crowded room.

## Is Science Speech?

Is science speech and therefore does science fall under the First Amendment umbrella? Commentators for many years have argued that science is speech and is protected. Mainly they have seen that science is embodied in publications, considered nonverbal speech, and therefore fits squarely into the First Amendment. In a more general form, we can see science as an ongoing argument in which the literature of science is a public debate. Just as in political speech or in the gropings of humanists or social scientists, the debate is meant to elicit the truth.

To the public, it may seem odd to argue that the literature of science is a debate because the general view is that science is an amalgam of facts, that it proceeds from discovery to discovery. It would be salutary for nonscientists to sit in on a laboratory discussion where a newly published paper is being analyzed. The first thing you might hear is a hearty judgment of the quality of the research summed up in the classic epithet "bullshit." As tempers cooled, elements of believable data would be sifted out from those that seem inconceivable. The grounds of skepticism could be many: the methods might not be reliable; the data might show only marginal effects; the investigators may have been wrong so often that they are considered a priori unreliable; there may be other data in the literature that are contradictory but accorded more belief because of how the experiment was done or even because of who did it; the implications may be at such variance with accepted theory that the burden of proof is set very high. In any case, these are all issues of judgment, no different from the judgments made in the political or social arena where the arguments are also about logic, personalities, history, and methodology.

One might think that in nonscientific discussions ideology plays a larger role than it does in science, but it is remarkable how much ideological baggage is carried around by the average scientist. As you might guess, this is more characteristic of older scientists and is probably the basis of the often-noted decrease in creativity as scientists age. The ideologies may not fit on the liberal-conservative axis by which political ideologies are gauged, but they are nonetheless fiercely held and can color a scientist's view so completely that no data can sway his or her belief. I know of one investigator who held a particular view of a problem for years in the face of very strong counterevidence, some of it accumulated in his own laboratory, and who therefore played no role in elucidating an important area of study because his ideological preconceptions completely blinded him to the weight of the evidence. But there are many other stories of scientists who held to unpopular beliefs and were vindicated. The work for which I was awarded the Nobel Prize is a good example — the heretical notions were not mine but those of my co-recipient, Howard Temin, but many scientists had to adjust strongly held preconceptions because of the work. As an aside, I have always thought that the speed with which our new perspective was accepted — within days of the first report, confirmation came and new supportive data started flowing — was because not one but two of us simultaneously came across the same phenomenon. This provides a very strong argument for the salutary role played by redundancy in science.

All of this is meant to point out that science is not a cut-and-dried activity. It depends on debate, judgment, hunch, and preconceptions as much as any intellectual activity. It therefore fits within the framework of the most widely accepted theory of the First Amendment: that in a democracy, truth emerges from the marketplace of ideas and that any hindrance to the free flow of ideas is antithetical to democratic process. The notion that the First Amendment protects scientific activity would not be foreign to those who wrote the amendments. As I noted earlier, Thomas Jefferson was himself a scientist and clearly had science in mind in supporting the doctrine. It seems clear that for him governmental control of science would be as wrong as governmental control over any form of expression in the arts or in political life. On a different plane, Jefferson would have realized that science is an important engine moving society forward and that any interference in the progress of science would be counter to the long-range interests of the country.

The notion that there are two cultures, one of science and one of the humanities, is generally accepted and was, as I remember, the basis for C. P. Snow's treatise on "Two Cultures and the Scientific Revolution." For years, the "two cultures" thesis has seemed flawed to me, however plausible it was on the surface, but I was unable to articulate a counterargument. It is certainly evident that in some sense the culture of the laboratory and the culture of the humanist are different, with one emphasizing the agreement with outside reality and the other focused on the purer products of the mind. The First Amendment argument, however, has helped me see that there are clear identities in the searches involved in the two types of enterprises and that the search for truth is a process of successive approximation and vigorous debate, no matter what type of truth is desired.

### Experimentation as Speech

It is easily seen that the debates of science and the publications of science are protected activities under the First Amendment. What is less certain to many commentators is that experimentation itself is protected. Some believe it is not, but the more liberal analysts of the Constitution believe that it is. To me it seems clear that it has to be an artificial distinction to separate publication from experimentation. Many have argued that experimentation is an extension of the discussion of science, but it seems to me that it is meaningless to conceive of science without it. Experimentation is so integral to the process of science that to protect publication and not protect experimentation is meaningless. Actually, the discussions of science are a prelude to experiments so that to regulate experimentation limits discussion and therefore is a direct abridgment of freedom of speech.

It may seem odd to argue that laboratory manipulations are a form of speech but the Supreme Court, in other situations, has agreed that actions can form an integral part of speech. As Lisman has said, "the Supreme Court's recent decisions. . . . make clear that. . . . When conduct serves as an important vehicle for a protected activity, or constitutes a form of such activity itself, it falls within the scope of the First Amendment." She continues, "For scientists, freedom of inquiry that does not include the right to engage in experimentation is like freedom to drive without either vehicle or fuel."

This whole issue may seem very theoretical but it has quite practical aspects. In the United States, there are limitations on the use of animals and on the use of fetal tissue that have a clear impact on what experiments can be performed. I know that similar problems exist in Britain. In the early days of recombinant DNA experimentation, when some were afraid of its power, it was argued that such experiments should be banned because humans cannot cope with the consequences. As Lisman has noted, "A bedrock principle of First Amendment law is that speech, whether verbal or in the form of symbolic conduct, cannot be suppressed either because society finds its content offensive or disagreeable or because it fears its potential misuse."

No one has attacked restrictions on scientific activities on First Amendment grounds but I know that such suits are under consideration. If it can be demonstrated that the regulations are a result of particular religious beliefs, they could be easily found in violation of the separation of church and state as well as being in violation of the First Amendment. If they are found to result from moral beliefs, the Supreme Court would have to balance one right against another. In previous times, one could have some hope that the Court would find in favor of the right to research freedom as a form of speech; with the Court having become so conservative, we can be less sure what would happen. Another approach might be to argue that the government, by funding research, does not gain the authority to regulate it in contravention of a constitutionally protected right of freedom of speech. Historically, the doctrine has been accepted that the federal government may not establish such regulations, but that argument was considerably weakened recently by a Court decision upholding the prohibition of abortion counseling as part of federally funded programs. In general, in America, the Court has become so conservative that we fear that many previous precedents extending rights enunciated in the Bill of Rights may fall with new decisions. But the assertion of rights requires many years of litigation and setting the stage through cases brought now may prove important in the future.

IMPROVING SCIENCE'S IMAGE

These lectures have been quite negative in tone because I have emphasized the threats to scientific freedom. It is important to recognize that these comments are made against a background of great successes and that biomedical science, whatever its problems and long-range prospects, is today a vibrant, exciting, and productive science. In the United States, you cannot pick up the daily paper without reading about the elucidation of a new genetic disease or the discovery of a new element of the cancer problem or some other advance in biomedical research. One feels privileged to be in the life sciences today to witness and be part of one of the great revolutions in human knowledge. My comments here are meant to help understand the dangers that come from these successes and to suggest ways to ameliorate the problems before they become too severe.

Science is suffering from something of an image problem and for an enterprise so dependent on public support that could mean trouble ahead. The ambivalence of the public toward science is at least partly because of the recent nuclear and chemical disasters: certainly the fewer Chernobyls and Bhopals we have, the better will be the image of science. The problem is not immense: polls still find that the image of scientists in the general population is quite positive, especially compared to that of politicians. But what can be done to improve the image of science?

I have suggested that part of the problem derives from a general frustration in the population deriving from its inability to see a way to improve its deteriorating economic fortunes. We are seeing today attacks on the freedom of artists, scientists, and institutions of higher learning. It cannot be coincidence alone that has brought these together; it suggests rather that the politicians are seeking to blame the intellectuals for their own failings. It is a resurgence of the anti-intellectualism that often accompanies straitened economic circumstances and there is little the scientific community can do about it except to work, as citizens, for more enlightened government policies that can help return a sense of optimism about the future.

### ACTIONS OF THE SCIENTIFIC COMMUNITY

A critical feature of improving science's image is the recognition that some of the problem lies in the scientific community. While the activities of scientists may be apart from the ordinary activities of the general population, we are funded from their labors and we must show ourselves to be responsive to the needs of the population if we are to maintain a healthy relationship. At this juncture of history, it seems to me that we need to carefully assess where our science can help to solve societal problems and to make a conscious effort to organize our efforts so as to have an impact. As I indicated yesterday, this will require us to work in a more coordinated fashion than we are used to, but that is the only way to solve a multifarious problem like that of AIDS.

At the same time, and I cannot overemphasize this distinction, we must insist that there are problems not ripe for solution, where the only hope is maintaining a strong, investigator-initiated, basic research effort. A problem like aging, where the underlying biology is totally obscure — where we still have no idea how the clock works and how it controls the biological phenomena — is a problem whose solution can only be hindered by a head-on attack. Similarly, the nervous system is still obscure enough that it needs the efforts of the whole scientific community — chemists, physicists, mathematicians, and biologists — to uncover its secrets.

In a similar vein, it is important that we be honest in our assessments and not over-promise. I can remember U.S. government officials promising that a vaccine against the AIDS virus would be available soon, at a time when the scientific community knew how unlikely that was. But we heard few voices insisting that a vaccine was far off, if it could be made at all. Now, eight years after the promise was made, we are still a long way from even knowing if a vaccine is possible. Another area where honesty is needed is cancer research. Phenomenal advances in that field have taken place over the last fifteen years, but they have not brought us any closer to finding a magic bullet that would solve the problem. In fact, the discovery of the multiplicity of oncogenes, the realization of how close the genes of cancer are to the normal genes that run our bodies, and the understanding of how easy it is for a cancer cell to develop new oncogenes has made the whole notion of a single or lasting control of cancer cells quite unlikely. There is still debate here, with some asserting that there may be one underlying pathway in the cell that can be controlled, but it is crucial that we not promise what we cannot deliver and that the uncertainty be honestly presented.

## SETTING PRIORITIES

As part of the problem of honesty there is one element of science policy that has always eluded the community but which we need to face: the setting of priorities. Today particularly, when high energy physicists, astronomers, space scientists, and biologists all have extraordinary plans that are exceedingly costly, some choices may have to be made among the various opportunities. The scientific community has generally felt that it deserved more funding and that, rather than setting priorities, it should be possible to do everything. There is certainly a point where that is no longer a conceivable argument and that time may be now. Our fear is that if we try to set priorities then we can doom some important projects and that it is best never to say that a given project is of lower priority than another. The difficulty is that we then leave priority-setting up to the politicians. That gets us the space station, which most scientists seem to feel is a waste of precious resources. Sometimes, of course, the politicians have their way no matter what we say, the obvious example being the star wars program.

Along the same lines, the scientific community's approach to politicians is fairly uniformly to approach tin can in hand. We know well how to ask for new money. But I believe that we also have a responsibility to examine closely how the money we have is being spent. Biomedical research in the United States will receive $9 billion next year. That is a phenomenal amount of money and yet the research community will tell you that it is strapped for funds. There is no doubt that the difficulty of acquiring the funds for research is driving good people out of research. It is hurting the image of science and causing young people to make other career choices. This may be reaching crisis proportions. It is easiest to say that the answer lies in more funds, but that is not a politically feasible answer at a time of deep deficits and a shrinking tax base. Even with reduced international tensions, it seems unlikely that there will be a large peace dividend going to the research community. Therefore, for our own direct good as well as that of our image we must look closely at whether savings could be made in existing programs. I must say that in the United States, at least, the bureaucrats often make it difficult for scientists to examine questions of priority and types of expenditures, but we must insist on the need to assess the effectiveness of programs.

## Peer Review

There is one area in which there have been calls for reforms where I believe the scientific community should not compromise: peer review. In making decisions about quality or strategy, the scientific community must have autonomy. Because of the very technical and specialized nature of individual scientific disciplines, there is a very small group of people who can understand what represents the highest-quality science. It is particularly hard for politicians to understand this reality because it sounds to them like an irreconcilable conflict of interest. Peer review often does look like all the worst aspects of decision making wrapped together — insider trading, the fox guarding the chicken coop, a license to steal ideas, a total lack of accountability. It is actually so civilized a mode of decision making that politicians have a hard time believing that it can work fairly. Sometimes it breaks down, and it is under particular stress at a time of very limited resources, but it is a necessary form of self-governance.

## Scientific Literacy

One problem of which I believe we are all aware is the need for greater scientific literacy in our populations. Both because of the need to function in an increasingly technical world and because those who vote on scientific issues need to understand them, it is of paramount importance that the scientific community devote time to education of nonspecialists. In doing this, we must be aware of the need to meet people at their own level, rather than treating everyone as a neophyte specialist in one's own discipline.

That involves changing one's style from a professional one to a pedagogic one, something that is difficult for scientists and requires conscious effort. Many of the people we must reach are not in school anymore, making the media our only outlet. We need particularly to figure out how to get better science integrated into commercial television, both on news broadcasts and in entertainment shows.

While we are discussing the media, there is another side to our relationship to the press. The press is notably unscientific in its presentation of issues. At the same time, science has become increasingly pervasive in the lives of the public — more drugs are available and used, more synthetic chemicals are in products, computers are increasingly important in all professions and even in the home, prediction of genetic defects is becoming available, bone marrow transplants are becoming a standard part of medical practice, and on and on. But every innovation brings with it decisions about how to employ the new capability, whether and how to regulate it, how to evaluate its strengths and dangers.

It is through the press that the public hears about issues. Newspapers for the decision-makers but television for most of the populace, and magazines to a lesser extent, are the routes through which issues become evident and in which debates take place. For instance, there was recently a long editorial in the *Wall Street Journal* about silicone breast implants (Feb. 8, 1992, p. A24). One issue it raised was whether the silicone causes an autoimmune disease called scleroderma. In the editorial we find the statement that "some incidence of scleroderma would be natural in any group of a million women." This vague assertion is used to raise doubts about the significance of the reported cases of scleroderma among women with breast implants. For anyone with the slightest scientific training it is evident that this is hyperbole, not rational argument. The relevant question is: how does the rate of disease compare in a control group and in a group with implants? A newspaper designed for reading by a literate public should be ashamed to use such an unscientific argument. The *New England Journal of Medicine*, by contrast, has on its staff a group of statistical consultants. The editors know that what appears in the *Journal* affects medical practice and they take this responsibility seriously. Why can't the supposedly responsible segment of the daily press be as careful? It would not have been hard for the *Wall Street Journal* to have found the background rate of scleroderma and it should have a scientific ombudsman who raises such issues. And this is not an isolated case — if you read the papers with an eye to the problem, it is evident that scientists could make a significant contribution to the debates that rage daily about issues of science, medicine, and technology. At the end of the horoscope column in many newspapers it says, "The horoscope is intended for entertainment only. The predictions have no proven scientific basis." I often think that the whole newspaper ought to be read with such a disclaimer in mind.

The process of decision making is one at which scientists are especially adept because they spend their lives evaluating data and drawing conclusions. I'm not arguing that scientists should be *deciding* the issues posed by science — such decisions ultimately must rest with the public. But I am suggesting that scientists should have more input, that the public world should want more rationality in the consideration of public policy issues.

A particular area of concern here is issues of environmental safety where arguments are made with surprisingly little scientific input. In this area, an almost religious reverence for Nature, for the notion of a world without human intervention, seems to control the debate. But the whole world is already altered by human life and the problem is choosing among alternatives, one that is poorly handled by religious absolutism.

An appropriate counterargument here is that many public policy issues have a large moral dimension and that scientists are not better than anyone else at moral judgments. I would go further and say that scientists are often the worst judges of moral issues because they are too ready to believe in their own rationality and generally out of touch with the thinking of the community. But that does not mean that we must entirely give up rationality when we come to difficult choices. A productive dialogue can highlight the moral dimension to a problem and allow for rational discussion of those elements that need such illumination. In particular, scientists can often see where a moral argument is really a question of lack of information and where either some research or a good approximation can keep the discussion moving.

Finally, I want to make a suggestion that is very much in tune with the times — that we privatize science a bit. Here I do not mean that we make science the province of industry — with the present short-range thinking in industry that would be a disaster. Rather, I am suggesting that if we can get more nongovernmental funds into science, we can greatly improve the flexibility of the scientific community to make its own decisions. For instance, in the United States we are prevented from using public funds for certain types of human reproductive and fetal research. The charities and private donors should be encouraged to use their funds for these areas. Private funds can be used more flexibly than public for the purchase of equipment and the support of personnel. In the end, the government controls all parts of society so it can prevent just about anything unless there is constitutional protection, but often the political realities require that the government be stricter about its own funds than about funds from elsewhere.

### Concluding Remarks

This is all I wanted to say. To summarize it would take too long and probably not be useful. So I wish to end with thanks. I have greatly appreciated the opportunity to put together my thoughts on these issues in a pair of lectures and I am most grateful to all of you who sat through these two days with not a slide or an overhead. To participate in the remarkable tradition of the Tanner Lectures is a singular honor and an enormous pleasure. I look forward to discussing these issues in the seminar tomorrow and hope that the questions I have raised may engender debate and, might I hope, action in the future on both sides of the Atlantic.

Thank you.

# Science and Revolutions

R. Z. SAGDEEV

THE TANNER LECTURES ON HUMAN VALUES

Delivered at

Brasenose College, Oxford University
March 9–16, 1992

ROALD Z. SAGDEEV is a graduate of Moscow State University. He worked for five years at the Institute of Atomic Energy, served as the head of the Plasma Theory Laboratory of the Institute of Nuclear Physics in Novosibirsk from 1961 to 1970, and later was head of the Institute of High Temperature Physics, Moscow. He was Director of Moscow's Institute for Space Research for fifteen years, where he oversaw the satellite encounter with Comet Halley and served as a science adviser to Mikhail Gorbachev. He is currently a Distinguished Professor in the Department of Physics at the University of Maryland, College Park, and Director of the East-West Science and Technology Center. Professor Sagdeev is a member of Russia's Academy of Sciences and a foreign member of the United States' National Academy of Sciences. He is known for his pioneering work in nonlinear physics and plasmas, especially on such physical phenomena as collisionless shocks and weak and strong plasma turbulence.

I. The Second Russian Revolution —
   Is This the Last?

I spent quite a number of years doing space research so I would like to start with the reference to *Sputnik I*, and its launch thirty-five years ago. For many of us, it signified the beginning of a new era of scientific discoveries. We compared the forthcoming future with the epoch of the great geographical discoveries. We thought: so this is what is going to happen on the scale of the solar system and the universe!

However, thirty-five years later, during the year called "International Space Year" by the United Nations, we have to confess that we were bad prophets. Instead of living in the epoch of great geographic discoveries, we, former Soviets, now realize that we are living in the epoch of great *historical* discoveries: those of our own past. The old paradigm we had for many years is best expressed in a joke. We used to say: "The past unpredictable, the future is bright." Now that is obsolete.

I would like to invite you to make a brief historic excursion to that period, then proclaimed "the grand historic experiment," which was launched in October 1917. At the time of the "Great October Revolution," the Bolsheviks in Russia were only a minority. The first multiparty elections in Russian history, held two weeks after the October Revolution, brought the Bolshevik party only 25% of the votes. But it didn't stop them from implementing their rule. Lenin declared that this 25% of the populace represented the most conscious avant-garde of the working class, mostly in St. Petersburg, in Moscow, and in industrialized central Russia.

This grand historic experiment followed the wisdom suggested by Marx and Engels that theory and practice must be unified — the theory based on what Bolsheviks thought to be the ultimate science: Marxism. At that particular junction of history, there were people who predicted that the experiment would fail, that in order to be successful it had to satisfy necessary preconditions. Those people who were quite skeptical were called "social traitors" by Lenin and the Bolsheviks. In fact they were followers of Marx and Engels and the leaders of contemporary European social democracy. They had quite a few followers inside Soviet Russia too.

The principal Marxist prerequisite for the success of the socialist revolution was the proper external environment, in which the developed capitalist Western nations would be ready to embark on the socialist experiment. In other words, they suggested that the Russian experiment could succeed only if this external environment was already on its way to socialism.

Although Lenin rejected this argument, he too feared his revolution could not succeed alone. All of his hopes were for a worldwide proletarian revolution. Nevertheless, this revolution did not come about, even though there were some very brief sparks in Germany and in a few other countries. In fact the only place where the Bolshevik revolution was able to establish itself, at least for a few months, was in Hungary.

On Stalin's accession to power he soon changed Lenin's formula. With no "worldwide revolution" forthcoming he developed a modification of the Marxist theory. For many years — from early childhood — we were taught Stalin's theory about the possibility of the construction of socialism in a single isolated country, surrounded by the capitalist environment. External conditions, or prerequisites, according to Stalin, could be replaced by a state of utmost mobilization or readiness to fight. That was how we lived for seventy years — in a state of alert.

In 1940, the Soviet Union added to its empire the Baltic states. The final composition of the USSR, at that time, totaled sixteen republics. Despite the hardships and losses in World War II, that heroic period created a lot of illusions inside the country. There was a feeling, based on the international solidarity of the allies and on the revival of genuine national patriotism, that the regime would change the conditions of its experiment. But it was only delusion. Very quickly, beginning with the end of World War II, Stalin again came back to his original posture, his totalitarian behavior.

During 1944 and 1945, based on the results of World War II, Bolsheviks were capable of taking over Eastern Europe, which led to the formation of what we called for several decades the socialist camp. In an ironic way, Marx's warning against a premature attempt to build socialism was right.

The first recognition that the experiment was not doing well came in 1956, with the famous pronouncement from Khrushchev at the Twentieth Party Congress. At that time, the failure of the Communist experiment was attributed to the specifics of Stalin's personality and to the fashion in which the country was run — the idea of a "personality cult." Khrushchev attempted to implement small changes and modifications in the rigid Stalinist model. However, the next few decades indicated that a simple mending of the wrong systemic concept could not be successful. The last attempt to modernize, to revise the ongoing experiment, was launched by Gorbachev, after several decades of the stagnation of the regime.

Gorbachev developed a scenario that now probably would be regarded as a new utopia. It was based on the assumption that the Communist system could provide "friendly, nice governments" with a "human face," with a big Gorbachev ruling from the Kremlin, loved by everyone, and small "Gorbachevs" everywhere from Berlin to Prague. Perhaps he thought that this was the way the system could repair itself. It is not accidental that at that very same time he was talking about "new thinking" and universal human values.

Those most important values proclaimed by the great French Revolution — *liberté, égalité,* and *fraternité* — were implanted in Soviet reality in a very peculiar way. I don't think we, at that time, were familiar with the notion of democratic "freedom" at all. The notion of *égalité* was transformed into a kind of egalitarianism, which is now backfiring, in our attempt to move to a market economy. The only achievement of which we all were indeed proud, even those who were critical of the socialist experiment, was the *fraternité* among the different nationalities and ethnic groups, united in one Soviet Union. But what is happening now in this respect has revealed that we were living with the wrong notion of *fraternité* — one that had to be imposed from above. With liberalization of control it immediately exploded in a multitude of interethnic conflicts and even bloodshed, as we see now.

However, in one particular aspect, Gorbachev succeeded tremendously. It was in the implementation of *glasnost'* and openness in our country. In 1989, the Soviet Union had competitive political elections for the first time. If not completely multiparty, they were at least based on a competitive electoral process. When the nation elected the Congress of People's Deputies I had my own chance too, for a brief period — before this congress was eliminated — to enjoy being a part of this distinguished group of people, together with the late academician Andrei Sakharov.

In 1990, this very congress ended the one-party monopoly of the Bolsheviks. It was a very important event, the advent of a multiparty system. I remember how slowly we approached this moment. In 1987 and 1988, I myself was quite skeptical about the possibility of a quick implementation of a multiparty system. Of course, to some extent, we shared the wisdom of "Radio Yerevan," the legendary and inexhaustible source of political anecdotes. Once it joked: "A multiparty system is utopia for the Soviet Union. The poor country is barely capable of feeding even one party!"

In August 1991, we witnessed an abortive coup, which essentially formally ended the CPSU. From that very moment the CPSU became only an illegal underground party, just as it was in tsarist Russia. But this time it happened with the support of the majority of the population. The next outstanding step, which came at the end of 1991, was the abolition of the Soviet Union and the formation of fifteen independent states. (I still have difficulty calling it the Commonwealth of Independent States. I am waiting for someone to suggest a better formula. My only satisfaction comes from the fact that Sovietologists themselves have to look for a new name.)

This profound political transformation was intertwined with economic evolution and changes in the country. In historic retrospect, going back to the beginning of the "grand historic experiment," the economic dimension of the whole picture started with a "war communism economy," from 1917 to 1922. This is a period when the economy of the country was ruined, when all normal incentives and interregional and industrial ties were broken. It was a time when the functioning of the economy was implemented only with terror or, as the Communists would say, "with iron discipline." The economy of war communism, after some period of temporary stability, eventually gave rise to an economic experiment which Lenin called "the New Economic Policy" — from 1923 to approximately 1929. In 1929, Stalin decided to abolish this particular subprogram and launched massive collectivization of land use, accompanied with what he called the "Great Socialist Industrialization of the Country." In such a framework, after surviving the bloody conflict of World War II, the country reached the Cold War in 1945–46, which led to the creation and buildup of a tremendous military machine. We now finally admit that it was a period when we were building our own military-industrial complex, comparable only to the Americans'. This of course was an unbearable burden for the national economy. Some analysts consider that the military-industrial development, which led to an unduly high fraction of military expenditures of the national budget, was probably one of the principal reasons for the failure of the "grand experiment."

The first signs of failure were detected in 1962. In order to feed people, Khrushchev launched the import of grain. For a moment we thought it was a brief retreat, but bringing grain from abroad revealed a very well defined illness of the system. After 1962, there was only a continuous escalation of grain imports. These massive imports of grain were done on the basis of oil exports, generating Soviet-style petro-dollars to pay for the grain imports. And not only that: they also paid for the prolongation of the "grand historic experiment." Some of my colleagues, among contemporary members of the Congress of People's Deputies, were calling these grain imports the giant conspiracy with the United States of America — as the biggest exporter of grain. Although the grain sales may have benefited both governments, the result was to continue the agony of the Bolshevik regime, and a system that couldn't feed its people.

By late 1970, it was very clear that oil exports alone were unable to support a decent standard of living. In the atmosphere of political and economic stagnation the leaders of the country — not for general consumption, but at least for internal consumption inside the politburo — launched another slogan. Marshall Ustinov, the minister of defense in the 1970s and 1980s (he was the second man in the state and many people thought that since Brezhnev was almost completely debilitated Ustinov was number 1 in the hierarchy), even suggested: "The Soviet people are very patient. They need only two things. Bread and defense."

By 1985, when Gorbachev took power in the Kremlin, the direct military expenses in the Soviet Union contributed up to 20–25% of the total budget. In many ways Gorbachev's revolution, as the first part or the beginning of the Second Russian Revolution, was driven by an understanding of the ridiculousness of such overinflated military expenditures. Probably the very first move he made with extreme boldness was an attempt to bring this budget down. He did not want to do it on unilateral basis versus the United States, the main rival. Probably if he had tried to do it unilaterally, he would have encountered fervent resistance from the Soviet military-industrial complex. So this is why he entered into far-reaching arms control and eventually arms reduction dialogue with the Western world, first of all with the United States.

The very first signs of success in arms control allowed Gorbachev to launch economic reforms, which he thought would completely change but assure the framework of the "grand historic experiment" of communism. He launched the first cooperatives, the first laws on economic independence of enterprises, even if they were still state-owned, and so on. But instead of the expected success, *perestroika*'s dividends, these reforms very quickly led to the complete collapse of the national economy.

There are different explanations for such an unexpected outcome for the economy, which deteriorated in only two years. One particular explanation, which I would consider farfetched, came from the political proponents of SDI. They say that it was SDI that finally ruined the Soviet economy. Even some of the current Soviet politicians and analysts share that view.

I was, from the very beginning, very close to the focal point in the debates over SDI. And I think it was one of the most important and impressive achievements of Gorbachev that he did not accept the challenge posed by Reagan's SDI program. Instead he eventually adopted what was then called an "asymmetric response." In fact the "asymmetric response," even as vaguely as it was formulated, prevented huge Soviet expenditures in the area of antiballistic missile defense. If the race with SDI had developed further, Gorbachev and his advisers had in mind a cheaper approach based on a different technique to counter SDI developed by the American side. But in historic retrospect, in the evolution of relations between superpowers, the SDI dialogue played a very important role. I cannot resist mentioning an interesting historic parallel.

In 1945, Niels Bohr paid an unsuccessful visit to Winston Churchill. He made his own home analysis and came to the conclusion that the nuclear arms race could only lead to the abyss. He wanted to convey it to Western leaders — and he started with Churchill — the wisest man of the epoch. He tried to explain that the best way to avoid a nuclear arms race would be to share, to some degree, the secrets of the nuclear weapons with the Soviets. And when he left Churchill's office, the prime minister asked only one question: "Why is this man not in prison?"

When Reagan suggested sharing SDI technology with the Soviets in 1983, no one asked such a question anymore about the proponents of openness. So it was tremendous progress, at least in that psychological aspect. However, traditional SDI, even if the technology was shared, would not have led to strategic stability. It would rather have undermined it, at least in the old framework of the superpower relations.

Now Yeltsin, during his February 1992 meeting with President Bush at Camp David, suggested that indeed superpowers could cooperate, if not in SDI, at least in a kind of limited joint defense. Most probably it is quite different from the so-called GPALS (Global Protection against Limited Strikes). However, it is very difficult to predict how things will develop in this particular sphere. Many of the former warriors of battles over SDI do not share the view that even limited SDI should be developed.

Coming back to the evolution of the national economy of the former Soviet Union, the actual reason for the economic bankruptcy of Soviet power is, of course, much deeper than simple budget allocations. As far back as 1917, at the very dawn of the Bolshevik era, Lenin came to the recognition that in the final account the outcome of the grand historic experiment of Soviet Russia would be determined in face-to-face competition with the capitalist world: the achievement of the best economic efficiency. History and nuclear deterrence have provided a unique time span over the last forty years — without major hot wars — to resolve the disputes by direct economic confrontation. The failure of the socialist economy (at least in its Soviet-imposed version) revealed a fundamental, perhaps even "genetically" inherent, deficiency of the system: its inability to create sufficient incentive and motivation to work and to produce economic wealth.

To compensate for the absence of a genuine economic algorithm, like the marketplace, Soviet rulers capitalized largely on the vast natural resources of the country — in combination with the cheap labor force. That rapacious exploitation of national treasures — rich reserves of oil and gas, for instance — accelerated industrialization, but led to another national catastrophe: environmental degradation beyond any measure known in the developed world.

The legacy of such a predatory policy will be felt for generations to come. And not only in the ecological dimension, but in the strong disproportions in the national economy, oriented toward delivering raw materials as the main source of income.

For decades an embarrassed leadership of the country tried to attribute one economic crisis after another to different mishaps, like droughts or technical shortcomings in industrial planning. But no matter what they did, there was no cardinal improvement of the situation. Before the final curtain fell, rejecting, at last, the obsolete Communist system on the basis of its hopeless performance, in a last desperate attempt, some orthodox architects of the socialist economy argued that the situation was the fault of science. They blamed the scientific and technological community for its failure to build a master supercomputer, capable of centrally running the national economy.

The greatest economic catastrophe was in 1991. Industrial production fell more than 15% in only one year. Similarly bleak forecasts are floating among economists. The same 15%, maybe even a higher drop, is expected in only the first few months of 1992, before some stabilization occurs. In that particular situation the sole hope is associated with the forthcoming privatization, with moving the country toward a market economy. But this transition is assessed now in the framework of a different historic experiment, the one representing a different systemic transformation — a phase "transition," as physicists would say — in this case, from socialism to capitalism. How can we implement such a transition quickly?

In some of the economic strategies that are suggested in Moscow, and in almost every other corner of the former Soviet Union, a great deal of attention is paid to the formula of forthcoming massive privatization. There is one particular psychological difficulty that is associated with the very history of our system. For seventy years the Soviet people were told that all the things they have — all the assets of the national economy — are common assets, collective property belonging to all of us. The simple traditional formula for privatization, established in international practice on a smaller scale, and still used in the United Kingdom, is when state property could be sold directly to individuals or to groups of people. It wouldn't work in the former Soviet Union because no one could explain to people why they should now have to buy the property that they already co-own. This is why some economists suggested a more sophisticated formula. Instead of selling simply for worthless rubles, populists are prepared now to distribute special bonds or coupons. Each of the bonds is for use in privatization on an equal basis with money. While this interesting economic experiment is still in the state of debate, we could probably compare the beginning of this process with the launching of a massive *Monopoly* game on the scale of the country. The Baltic states, for instance, have already implemented such an experiment. Most of the privatization was on the basis of such bonds.

What are the chances that this experiment, these strategies, would succeed? People are not patient anymore. They want more than the old formula of "bread and defense." After all, the defense budget is going down tremendously. And this is accompanied by the shortage of bread. What are the chances of success of this reverse "phase transition"? We can only speculate about the models which are on the table. Most of these models are based on the recognition of the intrinsic coupling of political and socio-economic dimensions. This is what essentially makes the whole transition a "Catch-22." It causes complications and even keeps several options in this transition open to failure.

One could get a great deal of insight, as most of the analysts are doing now, by comparing the Second Russian Revolution of 1985–91 with the great French Revolution.

The French Revolution, like most revolutions in history, was preceded by tremendous economic and political changes in society, with the rise of the future dominant social layer, the new class. In the French case it was the "third estate" — the bourgeoisie. And eventually this social layer took over. It wanted to create a completely different political and legal framework for itself. Could we find a similar analogy in the Second Russian Revolution, if this is essentially a revolution intended to establish a market economy, based on a capitalist approach?

Who are this "third estate"? This social layer, the class of entrepreneurs, was effectively nonexistent in 1985. If we scanned through the former Soviet Union we would discover very scattered though energetic groups of people, trying to become entrepreneurs. However, clearly it was not yet the class that drove the Second Russian Revolution.

The second candidate for the leadership in such a systemic phase transition could be the class of peasants. However, those who are familiar with the state of affairs in Soviet agriculture tell us that as a politically and socially conscious class the peasants in the Soviet Union have ceased to exist. What we now call "kolkhozniks," the collectivized farmers, throughout Soviet history were among the most oppressed social groups in the country. In this period of reform, instead of actively moving to privatization, they have proven themselves to be a passive, indifferent, and declassified social layer. Using Marxist terminology, one could call them "lumpenized." They have neither the will nor the stamina for privatization and hard work on the land. This is why Yeltsin's reform of land use is not progressing quickly enough.

Such an analysis immediately casts doubts on two potential components of the "third estate" which might have driven the Second Russian Revolution. But then who could have brought about this revolution? I think this is a genuine historic anomaly in many ways. This revolution was driven not by the emerging economically dominant class, but by the class of employees: white-collar and blue-collar. They simply revolted against their employer, the state. They wanted to have another employer. In many ways such a drive was inspired by the example of the prospering West, perceived as the kingdom of freedom, as well as a consumer paradise. Why not try another experiment?

The very nature of such an anomaly can create serious obstacles that might be fatal for the current Russian Revolution, and perhaps for Yeltsin's government. The expectation that a new employer would be much better than the previous one requires, in the eyes of the people, a visible change in conditions of material life, as "dividends" of the new freedom. During the last couple of years material life has deteriorated enormously. For many of those who were expecting instant gratification, this is a terrible period of disillusionment. While this disenchantment has not resulted in public riots (which political analysts consider a miracle), this has to be explained. However, there are already signs that against the background of interethnic clashes economic disillusionment is capable of creating strong resistance to Yeltsin's reforms.

One particular form of this economic disillusionment, leading to resistance and riots, might be the breakup of the infrastructure of the regime. This infrastructure is still based on the remnants of the old command economy and the state-owned railway network and oil, gas, and coal producing industries. They are the most valuable parts of the economic and social system, as vital strategic components of the infrastructure.

From time to time we hear that the coal miners of Donbass or Kuzbass are on the verge of new strikes. It immediately brings us to the recognition that the strikes of these very coal miners in the Soviet Union, two or three years ago, led to the collapse of Soviet rule or at least contributed significantly.

And as ironic as it might sound, an additional complication is created by the overabundance of pluralism in the country. So long awaited during the Communist monopoly, it is flourishing now in the multitude of political parties and economic scenarios for a transition to a market economy. The uncompromising hot debates between the adherents of different approaches are evolving into a principal obstacle on the way to political, social, and economic reforms. There is only one consolation — practically no political party or movement denies the implementation of the market system. That is how deeply the former centralized socialist economy discredited itself.

However, the particular scenarios to implement the market are different. There are many models: one is similar to the Polish-style "shock therapy"; another a more smooth transition similar to the one in Hungary; and there is even the forced introduction of the market economy, under autocratic rule, or the "Pinochet model." The real danger is that while the discussions continue precious time is running out. The potential for economic breakup, political chaos, and anarchy (even if it probably looks slim) may give rise to political demagogues, capitalizing on national chauvinistic feelings and nostalgia for a firm hand.

It is very difficult to give a final assessment or specific numerical quantitative predictions in the very complicated system which has been created now as a result of a great anomaly in the social and political revolution in the Soviet Union. All attempts to make any predictions should be discarded. After all, no one was able to predict such a quick and explosive collapse of the Soviet Union and demolition of Communist rule, despite the widely accepted arguments about the robustness and stability of the regime.

In 1989, after the demolition of the Berlin Wall, which led to the reunification of Germany, all of Europe was in a state of motion. In my circle of physicists we joked that something was going wrong with entropy and the second law of thermodynamics on a worldwide scale. Unification of Germany and the creation of the United Europe clearly were decreasing the entropy. Adding here an important parallel development in modern physics — the grand unification in the theory of elementary particles — would even more enhance the great loss of entropy, in complete violation of the second law of thermodynamics. The only chance to save thermodynamics was in the disintegration of the Soviet Union. The impenetrable closed system, a black hole, exploded like a "Big Bang" with its debris flying in every direction.

Future historians will probably try to explain the process which was launched with the Second Russian Revolution, the process which replaced the collapse inside the black hole with a Big Bang. It is a great historic event.

II. THE INTELLECTUAL COMMUNITY AND REVOLUTIONS

The intellectual community rarely has been the direct beneficiary of revolutions. History gives us many examples of this type. In some respects the intellectual community has played a dual role during revolutionary times: as a patient, the victim of change; and as a doctor, preparing and implementing the revolutionary processes.

It was precisely in this way that the great French Revolution was built on intellectual grounds, on the ideas of enlightenment and reason. And it even provided the principal revolutionary slogans, the ideas of French intellectuals. The logic of such intrinsic interaction between the intellectual community and the revolutionary processes stems from the very fact that there is scientific rational thinking and an eternal quest for objectivity. This essentially drives intellectuals to search for the truth, not only when they are dealing with phenomena in the natural world, but also when they have another object under study: human society. Sometimes we can trace, in history, the examples where this process of intellectual thinking and approach to social political phenomena first was motivated by a deep and often even subconscious desire to introduce the same type of reasoning one would apply in physics and mathematics to any kind of natural phenomena.

This is why scientists are quite prominent among the first revolutionaries, and often the first prisoners after the success or failure of revolutions. Maybe the very folly of such attempts by intellectuals was and still is in mistaking reason for order, harmony, and determinism. After all, if political thinkers have to borrow a recipe from natural sciences for the resolution of eternal conflict— order versus chaos — they should learn from a great debate among the best physicists of the twentieth century on how much chaos should be allowed in the natural world.

I would like to quote Albert Einstein in one of his letters to Niels Bohr, arguing against quantum mechanics and the uncertainty principle. He said, "God doesn't play dice." In a very funny though painful way, Soviet Bolshevik philosophers in the twenties and the thirties used arguments similar to that of Einstein. They pressed physicists, demanding that they "liberate" quantum mechanics from the "bourgeois" principle of uncertainty. And Einstein himself finally fell victim to the attacks of Soviet philosophers. They demanded that the theory of relativity be "liberated" from the dubious role played by imaginary observers.

The lack of conceptual understanding that chaos is an essential part of universal harmony was the reason for the failure of many attempts to interpret social and political phenomena. All the utopian models suggested for rearranging human societies have proven to be hopeless. One can go back and find one of the first models in the speeches of Socrates or during the medieval epoch in Francis Bacon's model in *The New Atlantis*. As a matter of fact, despite all the criticism, these models were invented and suggested by our fellow scientists. I should add: not for self-promotion — not one of them had pretensions of being promoted as an important political leader.

However, the rational thinking of intellectuals was irrepressible. This is how the first science of dissent was born — as the denial of the simple obvious wisdoms, which had essentially proven to be fragile — in relation to new experimental evidence or new ideas. Maybe Socrates was one of the first of this type of dissidents. And his departure from the contemporary point of view seems indeed quite peculiar. It consisted in the fact that he denied ancient Greek democracy. He thought that the most harmonious and rational way of ruling would be rule by a single person, by someone who is wise. This is how Socrates became one of the first victims, among intellectuals, who tried to intervene in the political arena.

Negative utopias, which painted apocalyptic outcomes of great social experiments, had much better luck. All of us are still under the spell of the allegoric parallels with the totalitarian regimes of the twentieth century drawn by George Orwell in *1984*, by Aldous Huxley in *Brave New World*, or (less familiar to Western audiences) by Russian political satirist Evgeny Zamyatin, who wrote his principal novel *We* as early as 1923.

However, probably the earliest prophet of negative utopia was Fëdor Dostoyevsky with his novel *The Possessed*. He essentially predicted the cataclysmic bloody outcome of the attempt to establish large-scale social experiments based on Marxist ideas and their implementation by force. His concerns were the historic cataclysm which my generation in the Soviet Union lived through.

No one knows better than the Soviet intelligentsia how things developed, since this social group was the successor, and in many ways the heir, to the old Russian intelligentsia of the nineteenth century. Even the very word "intelligentsia" is of Russian origin. And I haven't heard any direct attempt to apply this word to the European or American environment. At my last session of the Congress of People's Deputies in Moscow in September 1991, I had an interesting conversation with one of the most prominent contemporary Russian writers and a man who was promoting "new thinking" for the Second Russian Revolution, Daniel Granin.

He was serious when he asked me, "Did you find an intelligentsia in the United States?"

The founders of the Soviet State thought they were establishing a social order based on supreme science — scientific communism. What we would usually call science, by definition, was given the role of servant. While "supreme wisdom," the basics of communism given in the form of pronouncements by classics of Marxism, was to be largely untouched by the armies of the Soviet breed of Marxist philosophers, the rules for functioning of science were not introduced in the holy scriptures of communism as final and rigid. That left real leverage in the hands of those who had to interpret the heritage of scientific communism for the early Soviet state. In many ways it predetermined the role of hostage played by science and the scientific community throughout the major part of Soviet history.

As a serf to the party, science had to contribute in several dimensions of internal development. One of them was to help in indoctrinating the nation, in shaping the future *Homo sovieticus* by the technique of soul engineering. A second role was anticipated by Vladimir Lenin: science had to equip society with the best possible technical knowledge and expertise, so the country eventually could enter into competition with the capitalist world by running a cost-efficient economy. That goal required the pragmatic approach to the cadre of old Russian intelligentsia, the carriers of the knowledge accumulated by humankind. The fear of political and ideological disloyalty of this layer of the social strata, in the early Soviet state, always kept the government and Communist party in a state of paranoia.

Stalin developed further Lenin's concept of the role of the intelligentsia, in trying to create a new breed of Soviet white-collar workers faithfully loyal to the regime. In addition to party loyalty they also had to be capable of producing knowledge and applying that knowledge for the benefit of the Soviet economy, national defense, and the party's "historic mission" of social engineering — to create a "new Soviet man."

The history of the complicated interplay between science and the regime, when fully analyzed, will help us understand better the hidden dynamics of Soviet society. If the Soviet intelligentsia was the successor to the old Russian one, in a certain ironic sense the oppressive Bolshevik regime could be considered no less a genuine successor to the autocracy of the tsarist regime. The repression and, to some extent, terror were not completely invented by the Bolsheviks from the very beginning. We can trace some elements of the oppressive policies to the old prerevolutionary Russia. Alexander Herzen, one of the best brains among the Russian intelligentsia in the nineteenth century, who spent the last part of his life in exile in London, quoted an interesting example of the "ingeniousness" of the tsarist police. His friend and colleague in revolutionary thinking and activities, the Russian poet Nikolai Ogarev, once was subjected to a sophisticated search by the police inspectors. Unable to suppress their triumph, after discovery of eight volumes of *The History of the French Revolution*, they exclaimed: "Ah ha, these are revolutionary books." Then they attributed to the same category the last discovery: the book which was called *Sur la révolution du globe terrestre* by Georges Cuvier. It was more than enough for poor Ogarev to be "liberated" from his library and sent to prison for a number of years.

Lenin developed his suspicions about the intelligentsia to a much more sophisticated level. In a number of his articles, beginning with prerevolutionary times, he depicted the Russian intellectuals as a political layer subservient to the bourgeoisie. He even said the attempt to fight for political or individual freedoms and liberty, of which the intelligentsia is extremely fond, was a special hidden invention of the bourgeoisie, to strengthen its domination over the "proletarian" working class.

One explanation of why Lenin was so much against the intellectual social layer, from which he himself emerged, might come from the fact that his closest former colleagues in the Russian social democratic movement, the most intellectual part of Russian social democracy, slowly drifted toward Menshevism, a milder form of Marxism. Often they criticized Lenin for political extremism and adventurism.

However, there was a deeper reason for hating the intelligentsia. Lenin knew that intellectuals would use rational thinking and reasoning to argue against any kind of adventurist slogans which would be put forward by the Bolsheviks.

Lenin was the first who came forward with the appeal to create a new Soviet intelligentsia which would be faithful to the working class, an intelligentsia that originated from the proletarians. This slogan, if not completely implemented, eventually resulted in a kind of a painful joke, popular during the peak of Stalin's domination: "We intelligentsia are indeed proletarians of intellectual labor."

The call for a new intelligentsia, subservient to the regime, was taken by Joseph Stalin as part of his attempt to implement the whole procedure, based almost on genetic engineering to create a "new Soviet man." The typical approach to produce this new breed was based on what Soviet ideologists in the 1930s used to call "soul engineering." The army of writers, "soul engineers," was mobilized by the Bolsheviks to indoctrinate people.

However, such simple soul engineering was not enough. It was complemented by Stalin with the great terror, a drive which eventually exterminated many of those who were unable or who refused to undergo the process of soul engineering. It was within the context of the great terror that Stalin and others invented unprecedented technical innovations to reeducate the old breed of the intelligentsia. They established a system of intellectual serfdom. The regime built special camps in the gulag where the best scientists and engineers were brought to work on defense projects, demanded by the government. They lived in conditions similar to those of prisoners. Intellectual serfdom clearly had no counterpart even during the tsarist autocratic regime.

Many of those who were quite prominent and who are famous now were intellectual serfs, in these places called sharagas. Among them were such bright engineers as Sergei Korolev, the father of the first *Sputnik*, or Andrei Tupolev, known for a series of passenger jets and bombers, still used by the armies of the Commonwealth of Independent States.

The best description of such sharagas was given by Alexander Solzhenitsyn in his novel *The First Circle*. He himself had experienced a few years of "reeducation" in a similar type of sharaga, where he worked as a technician in radio electronics.

Ironically enough, people who were kept in such special installations to develop a "new Soviet man" were mostly supporters of the regime. Those who, from the very beginning, demonstrated their unwillingness to collaborate with the regime had to emigrate. Others, less lucky, were exterminated. These were people who stayed on the other side of the barricade. Among those who emigrated, we can recall a number of the brightest names in engineering and technology, such as Igor Sikorsky, who brought prominence to helicopters. And many more were on the cultural side of this list: Bunin, Nabokov, Rachmaninoff, Stravinsky.

The displacement of the "brains" by revolutions does not necessarily suppress individual productivity. An interesting historic example of this type of emigration producing a positive creative impact could be found in the late eighteenth and early nineteenth century in the United Kingdom. I have in mind the physicist Benjamin Thompson, who had to flee from the revolutionary United States because he was considered a royalist, a supporter of the British crown. So, as a young teacher of physics, he left the United States. It was here, in the United Kingdom, that he first established his name in science. He had a dramatic scientific and political career. At the peak of his political activity, during the Napoleonic Wars, he was prime minister of Bavaria, earning the title of Count Rumford. But his name belongs to science as a discoverer of the mechanical equivalent of thermal energy.

At a certain moment, Stalin thought he had succeeded in rebuilding the mentality and psychology of the Soviet intelligentsia. He found the "new man" who could be promoted as an example for generations — a model of loyalty to the Communist party and an example of the brightest scientific achievements, which could be paralleled only by the achievement of Stakhanov in industrial heroism. Just as Stakhanov was the beginner of a huge line of "heroes of socialist labor," Stalin thought that Otto Schmidt, mathematician and polar explorer, eventually could become a role model for the new scientists. However, Otto Schmidt, even if he could have developed into a leader of Soviet socialist science, clearly did not fit the model. After the Germans launched the war, Stalin quickly dismissed him, because he was of German origin. But Stalin had another scientist he selected as an exemplary man. He was brought up in a family of farmers. His conduct of agricultural sciences in the perception of the Bolshevik regime promised the delivery of magic technology, capable of producing agricultural miracles. His name was Trofim Lysenko.

In many ways the ideological battle that Lysenko waged first against the president of the Soviet Agricultural Academy, Nikolai Vavilov — and then against the whole discipline of genetics as a science — had another painful, even bloody historic parallel. It reminds one of the ideological debate over the nature of chemistry which took place in France at the time of the Jacobins. As the result of this debate, Antoine Lavoisier was beheaded. Lavoisier had a very powerful and dangerous ideological opponent, the leader of the attacks against the foundations of chemistry — Jean-Paul Marat himself. Marat demanded that science, and chemistry in particular, be completely different, a "people-friendly science," in his terms.

With Lysenko playing a similar role, the bright Soviet geneticist Nikolai Vavilov was dismissed as the president of the Agricultural Academy. This post was taken by Lysenko's followers. Then Vavilov died in prison during World War II.

What did the Soviet intelligentsia do within the framework of such a repressive regime? The absolute majority of intellectuals preferred their own way to survive decently. They called it "internal emigration" or "internal exile": staying inside a narrow circle of a few close friends to be able to talk openly and freely about events in the political world, events outside their small kitchens, where most people gathered to talk. So internal exile in the kitchen was the principal mode of survival for the Soviet intelligentsia for many decades. However, even that was quite risky and dangerous. The regime wanted the intellectuals to become its accomplices. Everyone was under tremendous pressure.

Nikolai Vavilov, in one of his confidential exchanges, which one of his contemporaries later recalled, suggested silently on a piece of paper, in English, "If you your lips will keep from slip / five things you must beware / of whom you speak / to whom you speak / and how and when and where." However, this wisdom did not help Vavilov himself.

One particular example of how the authorities demanded that everyone give an oath of loyalty and accept the role of accomplices could be provided by the story of Boris Pasternak. In the late thirties, the epoch of the great terror, the regime introduced a humiliating procedure. Every employee of the factory, enterprise, or institution, from time to time, was called to a huge meeting. These were special gatherings convened to condemn the "enemies of the people" and unanimously adopt a resolution calling for capital punishment for the "enemies." Boris Pasternak was present at one of these meetings of fellow writers when someone demanded capital punishment for a group of Soviet military commanders and marshals accused of being traitors — German spies. Pasternak was the only one in the huge crowd who abstained from the ballot. Later, during the night, he wrote a personal letter to Comrade Stalin, explaining his abstention: he said that he came from a family of intellectuals, with a very strong Tolstovian urge toward nonviolence.

In such a condition of internal emigration, internal exile, I think the Soviet intelligentsia developed a tremendous inferiority complex — a kind of personality split — which later was reflected in the behavior of different people.

The victory in World War II was greeted by many as a chance for the reconciliation of society, based on patriotic feelings. However, Stalin and the regime were not ready for this: many Soviet physicists were put to work first on nuclear and then on hydrogen bombs. Among them were such people as Igor Tamm and his then young pupil, Andrei Sakharov. Igor Tamm could not have been accused of being a blind collaborator with the regime. He himself had a stormy revolutionary youth. In 1917, during a brief period of democracy after the February Revolution which followed the resignation of Tsar Nicholas II and preceded the Bolshevik October Revolution, young Igor Tamm returned from vacation from his classes at the University of Edinburgh. During this time he joined the social democratic movement and became one of the prominent younger leaders of the Mensheviks. And at the first Congress of all Russian Soviets, in June 1917, as one of the very few Mensheviks, he voted to stop the war. He was part of the group known as "internationalists" at that time.

However, he quickly understood during the next few months that there was no ecological niche for the Menshevik type of social democracy during the Bolshevik regime. He left politics and never returned. No one could accuse Tamm of trying to collaborate with Stalin after all his political experience with the regime. It was the feeling of patriotism that followed the end of World War II and very naive strategic thinking that drove the Soviet physicists to "restore" the nuclear balance and stability in the world. They made the hydrogen bomb and delivered it into the hands of Stalin and Lavrenti Beria.

Two scientists were a true driving force behind the Soviet efforts in the nuclear bomb program: Igor Kurchatov and Yuly Khariton. While Kurchatov achieved prominence and official recognition during the Khrushchev era (he even accompanied Nikita Khrushchev during a famous visit to England in 1956), Khariton was long kept in a shadow of secrecy. He was the scientific head of the classified installation from the very beginning and his involvement in the bomb program was most natural. He co-authored the very first Soviet scientific paper in the still open prewar scientific literature on nuclear physics — the paper on how to achieve the nuclear chain reaction.

Kurchatov and Khariton formed an extremely powerful tandem. But there were many more outstanding people who contributed to the success of the Soviet nuclear bomb project. The heroes of that program were, in many ways, able to parallel the efforts of the Manhattan program. One could identify even the specific counterparts, playing similar roles on both sides of the ocean.

However, I think there was no Soviet counterpart to Robert Oppenheimer. There was no one in the USSR who experienced or voiced even the slightest doubts about delivering the ultimate superbomb into the hands of Stalin and Beria. It is true, of course, that the famous Peter Kapitsa, one of the greatest Russian physicists of the twentieth century, left the nuclear program almost at the very beginning in 1946. But he did so as a result of a personal conflict with Beria. Nobel prize–winning theoretical physicist Lev Landau tried to stay as far as possible from the actual designs. He had a deep internal conflict with their production — not surprising in a man who suffered in the purges of 1937.

There were reasons why there was no Russian Oppenheimer, the open adversary of the hydrogen bomb — or why there was no one who would doubt the need for the Soviet Union to develop its own nuclear weapons. The bleeding wounds left by World War II were still fresh and painful. Everyone remembered that, even according to official assessments, the country lost more than 20 million of its citizens. If, among the scientific community, there were individuals who did not share the ideology of the regime they were patriots. Also, it would have been extremely risky to oppose the ideological dogmas promoted by Stalin in the presence of Beria as supervisor of the atomic program. Many of these people believed the Soviet Union needed its own strategic weapons to restore parity with potential enemies. They were also optimists that the postwar period in the USSR might be quite different than in 1937. Many hoped the wartime grand unification of Soviet society against the principal enemy, the Nazis, would change the repressive character of a Communist regime and that the Soviet Union could even join the international community of free nations.

The team of Kurchatov and Khariton was driven by genuine motivation, by enthusiasm. Both men provided the utmost examples of tireless, unselfish effort. They also proved themselves to be not only moral leaders, but also physical protectors. A few years after the war, the government boldly launched a new wave of repression and ideological pogroms, under the slogan "struggle against cosmopolitanism."

Stalin needed the nuclear bomb desperately; he was already a few years behind the Americans. In fact, the first test explosion took place four years after the Americans had already achieved a breakthrough. The international race — initially to build the nuclear bomb — was lost irreversibly to the United States. Despite that, however, there was an equally important race: an internal competition. The ruthless government had another group of scientists and engineers who were given the task to ready themselves to play the role of a "shadow nuclear team." The very presence of such shadow competitors introduced a kind of sword of Damocles over the heads of the Kurchatov-Khariton team members. The forthcoming test in 1949 was awaited with a mixture of great hope and desperation by both teams, the actual creators of the nuclear weapons and the shadow team — among which there were candidates to become the "Lysenkos of physics." The success of the test liberated the actual weapons designers from direct threat and finally led to the dissolution of the shadow team. But it in no way liberated the Soviet scientific community from the role of intellectual serfs of the system still instilling genuine fear. The real awakening came with the Twentieth Party Congress, which was an eye-opener for most of the people. It unlocked, though only for a few moments, the gates for internal exiles too and inspired people to rethink the past history.

With the advent of the Brezhnev regime, the intelligentsia was split into two large groups. One was still subservient to the regime. Many, among intellectuals, were yet unable to reconcile their behavior and conscience and were not ready to burn the bridges of dependence on the regime. Clearly "being precedes consciousness," as the Marxist dictum says. The other group was much smaller: only a few among the intellectuals were ready to break with the establishment: people like Andrei Sakharov, Yury Orlov, and others. The regime, substantially weakened, was unable to undertake any kind of massive repression as in the past, replacing it with episodical imprisonment of open and active dissidents and implementing, in place of soul engineering, a special kind of psychiatric treatment against some of them.

Looking at this particular practice with what we know nowadays, we can only ridicule the typical diagnosis of the "illnesses" of these dissidents: for example, "delirium of social reformism." I guess in 1985, with the advent of Gorbachev as general secretary of the Communist party, this particular formula of diagnosis had to be immediately abandoned. Otherwise the first patient who would have had to be treated for such an illness would have been Mikhail Gorbachev himself.

The *perestroika* period launched the massive escape for internal exiles. I was part of that particular group of the Soviet intelligentsia which promoted *glasnost'*, new thinking, and political reforms. We were all extremely excited. We realized that we were living in unusual revolutionary times. Valery Bryusov, a Russian poet of the early twentieth century, once said: "One is blessed who has visited this world in its crucial moments." We felt that we were indeed living these crucial moments.

Slogans of the Second Russian Revolution came from the Soviet intelligentsia, from Soviet scientists, writers, intellectuals, and thinkers — and not only slogans.

In fact, quite a few prominent leaders of the Pugwash movement came from inside the Soviet scientific community too, with its drive for international ties and cooperation: Peter Kapitsa, Lev Artsimovich, and others. The best scientific brains on both sides of the ocean applied their minds to the thermonuclear deadlock. Through the most difficult periods of confrontation during the Cold War, the Pugwash meetings remained the only reliable channel for important arms control discussions between the Soviets and Americans.

Among interlocutors on the American side were Georg Kistiakowsky and Jerome Wiesner, presidential science advisers in different administrations of that epoch. Even Henry Kissinger, when he was still a professor of political science at Harvard, was a participant in Pugwash brainstormings. Several important initiatives in international arms control found their way through quiet diplomacy at Pugwash-style meetings of scientists. Such was the case with the first, most important treaty banning nuclear tests in the atmosphere, in the sea, and in space. The scientists tried very hard at that time, in the early sixties, to extend the ban on underground testing, to make it comprehensive. It is only now with the Cold War left behind that there is a historic chance to eliminate all types of nuclear explosions forever.

The early ideas of Pugwashites were precursors of the new thinking and the global breakthrough of the late 1980s. There were even more important documents of the epoch, coming from the scientists, those who were brave enough to raise their voice of dissent, as Andrei Sakharov did. The very first draft of the Soviet constitution, the constitution that had a chance to be the first democratic one, was written by Sakharov in 1989. I remember the days when he was writing this draft. He was able to finish this draft only a few hours before the extraordinary session of the Congress of People's Deputies in mid-December 1989. And the very first chapter of this constitution called for the end of the monopoly of the Bolshevik party and the introduction of the multiparty system.

I was only a few meters from Gorbachev's chair at the Presidium when Sakharov, made desperate by denial of the opportunity to speak from the podium, approached Gorbachev asking for a few seconds to speak. Gorbachev switched off the microphone he controlled so that only a few people could hear the subsequent conversation. Because I was close enough, I can quote, as a witness, what Sakharov said: "I have to speak against the Communist party monopoly. I've got a huge bag of letters from my constituency, demanding the abolition of the party monopoly."

In response Gorbachev said, "So what? I've got three bags from my constituency demanding to keep it."[1]

That was how Sakharov was denied the last chance to speak. The stenographic records of the Congress report dryly on Sakharov's last appearance at the podium with the microphone switched off: "Sakharov on the podium. He opens his mouth. Nothing can be heard."

But we all *heard* what he wanted to say. The draft of the constitution was published by the newspapers a few days later, after Sakharov had already died. However, the revolution was continuing.

### III. SCIENCE AND THE "SOVIET UNION"

Future analysts will ask: what happened to the supreme ideas of Marxist scientific communism? Why did such an experiment planned in historic dimensions fail, destroying under its collapsing ruins one of the largest scientific and technological communities of the modern world?

---

[1] Indeed, better late than never: Gorbachev has by now clearly undergone his own personal *perestroika*, at least on that issue. In December 1991, a few days before stepping down from power, in a newspaper interview he said, "The goal is to accelerate the shaping of genuine political pluralism. Democracy cannot live without it."

The past leaders of the country clearly overinflated the size of the academic and engineering communities. It was even an object of pride for them to claim that every third scientist in the world was Soviet. Even if the official statistics were right, the actual budget was not large enough to support the productive research of such an army of scientists.

A still bigger exaggeration was the social myth of the Bolshevik epoch that half of the engineers in the world were in the Soviet Union. How does one reconcile that assertion with the general technological backwardness of the USSR as compared with the Western world? The massive decline in professional standards of the engineering community reveals the profound failure of the social system in preparing and using the cadre of engineers. However, it would be wrong to consider that the scientific and engineering technological communities were uniformly mediocre and backward in the Soviet Union. Rocketry has consistently been one of the exclusions. The space program, from the very beginning in the early fifties, was surrounded with special care by the government. One explanation of the success of the Soviet *Sputnik*, and its descendants, is that the system, for several decades, was using space achievements as proof of the superiority of socialism over capitalism.

However, the whole area of the space industry was originated by the military's need for rocketry. Early successes in the nuclear program were associated with the needs for nuclear deterrence. Later, the atomic sciences became a kind of cult for many years, before the Chernobyl accident destroyed the nuclear spell. Here too the spectacular rise and failures of science were unrelated to any real interest the Bolsheviks might have had. They cared nothing for science per se.

In talking about the impact of revolutions on scientific life, I could not avoid reflecting that revolutions rarely try to spare their brains. Even if no one was beheaded on the guillotine — as was the founder of chemistry, Antoine Lavoisier, at the peak of the

French Revolution — there were many other tests that the scientific community had to survive.

In 1917–20, at the peak of economic chaos and civil war in Russia, a very thin layer of the scientific intelligentsia was indeed an endangered species, not only because of the blood being spilled everywhere in the country, but also because of the unavoidable economic disaster. At that historic moment, Maxim Gorky, who played a role as a moderator between the intellectuals and the regime in the early Bolshevik rule, talked to Lenin about launching extraordinary measures to rescue a very small group of intellectuals — scientists, writers, and artists. As a result of this pressure, Lenin agreed to initiate special food rations for this endangered intelligentsia. This gesture played a very important role in establishing an uneasy relationship between the Bolshevik government and the scientific community. On the one hand, scientists clearly were given a minimal living for survival. On the other hand, if they did not know it at the time, they were doomed to be converted into intellectual serfs by the future Bolshevik regime. Only a very few scientists at this juncture in history understood that the system would not be kind to or supportive of creative work. Among them was the famous physiologist and Nobel prize winner Ivan Pavlov. For a brief moment in 1920, he tried to leave Russia, unable to work in the atmosphere of the "war communism economy." He approached the Soviet government with a petition for an exit visa. His colleagues in Scandinavia had created a special chair for the renowned academician. The scientific community has only recently learned what Lenin's reaction was to this application. On the petition written by Pavlov, Lenin wrote: "Ivan Pavlov is known as an outspoken opponent of the Communist party and Soviet power. This is why it is highly undesirable that Pavlov should go abroad. He would use this opportunity to denounce us. I suggest that we not give him an exit visa but instead double his food ration."

We can only smile at this episode. In a certain sense it tells us that Lenin was probably quite familiar with the technique Pavlov used to study and develop *conditioned reflexes*.

In many ways, "Soviet" science is facing a similar risk of losing its brains in these extremely difficult economic conditions of this transitional period. Using an earlier notion from the early Soviet years, I would say we are entering a period of "war capitalism."

What kind of intellectual and legal legacy is this scientific community in the Commonwealth of Independent States trying to preserve now? The past offers us an insight. The Russian Imperial Academy was established in 1725. It was originated exclusively due to the tremendous energy and determination which Peter the Great brought to this issue. In the process of thinking and preparing the draft and the charter of the future Russian Academy, he visited most of the Western European countries. He spent a substantial period in England, learning about the Royal Society. There are no official records of that particular period which could indicate whether he had a chance to talk to Sir Isaac Newton, who was at that time the president of the Royal Society. However, there are records, and even letters, in which Peter the Great and Edmund Halley talked about potential ways of developing science, especially applied science related to sea navigation, in the young Russian Empire. In a very funny way, Peter the Great was much more exposed to the archenemy of Newton, his great German contemporary Leibnitz, who developed his own proposals. He suggested that Russia, which had to overcome sheer illiteracy, should not start with establishing an Academy of Science. He strongly advised that Russia should start with colleges, universities, and educational institutions. However, Leibnitz did not impress Peter the Great.

Despite his advice, Peter decided to open the Russian Academy, although he died a few months prior to its inauguration. Nevertheless, the Academy was built and the first few decades of its activities brought outstanding scientific discoveries, through the work of such scientists as Leonard Euler, Daniel Bernoulli, and others.

The Soviet Academy in many ways was the heir to this great Russian Academy, famous not only for the names of its foreign guest researchers, but also for the names of its genuine Russian geniuses, like Mikhail Lomonosov and Dmitry Mendeleyev. However, the Soviet Academy was immediately put under the strict control of the Soviet government and the Communist party — and, as such, became a product of the social conditions of its epoch.

Fortunately, two completely different factors played an important role in saving Russian science through the Soviet Academy. One of them was the combination of the deep and strong traditions established by the great Russian scientists of the eighteenth and nineteenth centuries and their pupils, the "keepers of the flame," who survived the period of indoctrination and pressure. They were able to pass on the flame of real science to the next generation, despite every attempt by the government to change the heredity of this intelligentsia.

There was a second factor which played a very important role, though it was not intended to keep science alive, at least in the form that was established by Lomonosov and Mendeleyev — the militarization of Soviet science. As painful and sad as it was, it provided the flux of almost limitless material resources to support not only applied sciences associated with the design and production of weapons and rockets, but also basic sciences, such as physics and chemistry. Unfortunately, due to the ideological intervention and internal misfortune of Soviet biology brought on by Lysenko, Soviet biology was unable to take advantage of similar support, even if designed with completely different motivations.

There were two forms of militarization of science, established and very well known in international science. The first explicit form is associated with direct involvement of the scientific community in deliberate invention and design of weapons or armaments. This form of militarization was most important throughout the Soviet period. Stalin and Bolshevik leaders needed a magic wand to rescue them from confrontation with the capitalist world. So, in that sense, the Russians followed the case of Alfred Nobel, who designed dynamite, or F. Haber, who during World War II suggested the use of poisonous gases as chemical weapons. In the area of chemical weaponry alone, which for many years was the principal source of support for Soviet chemistry, we have as a legacy of this period almost a hundred thousand tons of obsolete chemical weapons. Their very presence represents a dangerous challenge, not only to the scientific community, but to society as a whole. Destruction of the arsenals of chemical weapons — thanks to a banning treaty — will require serious and expensive measures.

The second form of militarization was indirect: involvement of almost every individual scientist in the Soviet Union in support work on contracts or grants given by the Ministry of Defense or military industry. This was the most dangerous development. In an often hidden way, the military-industrial complex established its domination over the Soviet intellectual community, whereas in most other societies the survival and development of basic science was always based on the relationship between science and society.

There are two schools of argument in this debate. How can one justify immediate support of basic research which is not going to produce valuable practical results within the next five years or maybe even within the next generation of scientists? Some of the thinking stresses that eventually, after several generations of scientists, the results of today's basic science would be used by industries everywhere, and the final revenues today cover all the money spent by the government and taxpayers in the past.

The second view is much more radical: the support for contemporary basic research has already been paid for by the priceless achievements of the past generations of scientists, such as Faraday, Maxwell, and Mendeleyev. Their scientific discoveries are so widely used now that the revenues that people get from these past discoveries more than pay for basic research for the centuries ahead.

However, this point of view alone would not save science, in the current atmosphere in the Commonwealth of Independent States, which is in a condition of political and economic deterioration. The scientific community nowadays is losing not only the budget and economic support — it has found itself in a rather hostile psychological climate.

The implementation of scientific discoveries and technologies throughout the Soviet period was accompanied by negative side effects. This has caused a rise of antiintellectual sentiments in the former Soviet Union that we are experiencing now. The negative indirect impacts attributed to science, such as the Chernobyl disaster, essentially wiped out nuclear energy science from Soviet technological and scientific life. There were several other environmental consequences of Bolshevik rule, such as air and water pollution, loss of valuable soils through erosion due to the building of exemplary Stakhanovite enterprises of socialist industry, as well as the monstrous dams across great Russian rivers — even attempts to change the climate in vast areas of the Soviet Union by redirecting the flow of the northern rivers. This particular project, which was conceived during the last thirty years of Soviet power, was supported by the official government and was almost ready for implementation. The rivers of Siberia had to be redirected to bring waters to arid areas of former Soviet Central Asia, such as the deserts of Uzbekistan and Turkmenistan. The project created concerns about the irreversible damage to the environment. Throughout this period, the official Soviet Academy of Science did not contribute much to the protection of environmental interests or the balance between humans and nature, as evidenced by the most criminal documents, legislating the beginning of construction works at such places as Lake Baikal, as well as the "Leningrad Dam," which has essentially spoiled a huge area of the Finnish Bay. Many of these projects were implemented with the approval of — I would rather say the rubber stamp of — the Soviet Academy. This explains the tremendous idiosyncrasies among the taxpayers and the "man on the street" against science.

The ongoing political chaos only reinforces such feelings. Take one particular example of how this antiintellectualism has been expressed recently. In 1989, a public opinion poll was taken in Moscow, perhaps the largest intellectual center of the country. Participants were offered a list of the most important national institutes like the Council of Ministers, the national health system, the Supreme Soviet, the Communist party, the Academy of Science, the KGB, and so on. The question was which of these institutions played the most negative role throughout the Soviet period. I was myself amazed to discover that the Academy of Science appeared as one of the top enemies of the public in that list, well ahead of the KGB. It created a hot internal debate. My own explanation of such an anomaly is that in the first few years of *perestroika* and *glasnost'* the KGB tried to stay low key. The scientific community, in contrast, was in the first rank of those engaged in the political struggle against the former regime. It was within Academy of Science and the intellectual community that the real dissent was originated in Soviet life during the last several decades. The general public took self-criticism, initiated by the academics and scientists in the mass media, as a signal that something was deeply wrong in the Academy of Science, even compared to the KGB.

However, what was happening at that time was a very positive phenomenon. The scientists were bringing up all the issues of *perestroika*. In some sense I could compare that period of the very active politicization of scientific and intellectual community, from 1985 until the current period, with the self-sophistication of the Enlightenment in Western Europe in the end of the eighteenth century.

The Academy of Science and the scientific community provided the early nucleus of condensation for political rethinking. It was inside the Moscow academic community that a first political club

(Moscow Tribune) was organized. Brainstorming of different political issues was led by Andrei Sakharov and a few other outstanding scientists, writers, historians, philosophers. I too took part in many of these brainstormings. Eventually, this political club played an important role in sending the first deputies and first delegates from the scientific community to the first popularly elected parliament in the country: the Congress of People's Deputies of the Soviet Union, Congress of People's Deputies of the Russian Federation, and so on.

This club gave rise to another very active political organization inside the Academy of Science which was called the Club of Voters of the Academy of Science. It still exists and helps to elect deputies from academic institutes to represent the scientific community in the Parliament of the Russian Federation.

However, what we have now is a situation in which the whole Soviet scientific community could be declared an "endangered species." There are different dangers in the current political and economic chaos accompanying transition to a market-economy system. One particular problem, which is discussed worldwide, is the "brain drain." I would separate the brain drain as a component of the problem which, in my view, is not a danger at all. First, I would dismiss the potential negative impact of the external brain drain — that is, the risk that former Soviet scientists would emigrate or would be invited to different foreign countries. After all, the very notion of a "brain drain" on an Academy-wide scale is purely a Russian invention. It was conceived and implemented by Peter the Great and played a tremendous role in establishing the scientific culture in this originally almost illiterate country. Isn't it time that Russian science shoud repay the international scientific community?

Seriously, however, I don't believe that the scale of the external brain drain could be considered as dangerous as the scale of the problem *inside* the former Soviet Union. The number of people who could securely find jobs outside the former Soviet Union, for instance, would be fairly limited due to different (mostly economic) considerations. The internal brain drain is a much more serious problem. The economic situation in Russia, and in other republics, has forced scientists to struggle for sheer economic survival, to avoid hunger and starvation. The current salaries of typical Soviet scientists are miserable compared to a decent living standard. A recent decree of the Russian Academy issued only a few days ago established a ceiling for the salaries of directors of institutes of the Academy. So the salaries for the leading scientists and administrators are now measured at slightly more than 3,000 current rubles. If we convert this into dollars, that is only about 30 to 40 dollars a month.

The most dangerous situation we can find now affects the younger generation of scientists, who are paid the equivalent of 10, 15, or 20 dollars per month and are clearly unable to support their families. It is from this particular stratum that the internal brain drain is stealing scientists. They are seeking sheer survival — and this survival could be found in newly created commercial enterprises, cooperatives, and joint ventures. While in principle this might be a healthy development in moving to a market economy, unfortunately, at the moment, the work in these sectors is still unsophisticated. The brains of scientists are used for rather routine applied software or simple biotechnology projects at best, but not for further development of basic science.

This economic disaster in many ways is bringing with it a bitter revenge. The long dependence of Soviet science on the military-industrial complex is having a strong impact. The very first step taken by the military-industrial complex after Gorbachev declared the first reduction of the military budget a few years ago was an immediate drastic cut in R&D money, while all the weapons and armaments were kept intact. This led to the termination of grants and contracts in almost every area in physics, chemistry, and even biology — not to mention applied engineering. At the peak of the military cuts, the "Soviets" are in danger of losing their most important assets, truly international treasures, the cadre of high energy physicists, molecular biologists, biotechnologists, and experts in space technology and space research.

Having spent so many years in the space area, I can give you a few examples of what is at risk now in space assets accumulated by the Soviet Union. In many areas of space technology, the Soviets are unchallenged even by the American space community. There are several categories of launchers in the arsenal of the Soviet space community which are completely absent from the current spectrum of American space activity, such as the super-launcher *Energia*, which could be successfully applied to enhance the much-publicized American space program based on lunar/Mars exploration to build a manned space station in terrestrial orbit. I am not going to debate the issue of whether the emphasis on manned exploration or on the very expensive manned installations in space is meaningful, at least in the current fiscal climate. However, since the United States has expressed, and reiterated, determination to develop such a program, it could get numerous benefits from interacting with existing Soviet space assets.

In many ways, all of us recall that the principal driving force in space exploration, and in building space technology, was precisely the competition between two space programs launched by *Sputnik I* — what we can call the "Space Race," which drove the space programs on both sides of the ocean. With the risk that Soviet space assets could simply sink or disappear, our American friends very soon could face another syndrome which could inhibit their space program. I would call it "the loneliness of the long distance runner." At the same time, we should recall how much international cross-fertilization helped the American space program and the Soviet space program too. One can go back to the history of the last years of World War II. Werner von Braun, designer of the ill-fated V-2, was essentially the man who brought the rocket culture to the United States. Who knows: there may be dozens of such brains like Werner von Braun who could perish in the current economic decline of the Soviet Union.

I remember vividly that a few years ago, at the peak of Gorbachev's popularity, as well as his international initiatives, he himself promoted many grand international ventures, including international projects in space. One particular project he was very fond of related to flight to Mars. Among the space scenarios of launching sophisticated telescopes, unveiling secrets of the universe, or launching orbital labs which would enhance our knowledge of global change and in particular of ozone layer depletion and global warming, there was always a special interest in flying to Mars. This interest one could find not only in the former American administration; it was also entertained by the Bolshevik government long before Gorbachev came to power. The Brezhnev government supported the project to send a mission to Mars and to bring back a sample of Martian soil.

In some way, such an interest in flying a mission to Mars, unmanned or manned, was considered by Soviet authorities the type of "ultimate science" after which there would be no need to support any petty scientific projects. Everything would be received at once: soil from Mars would answer all the questions of the secrets of solar system formation, and so on. Bolsheviks entertained this ultimate science, as they promoted Marxist scientific communism, which was going to answer *all* the questions.

In the last attempt I witnessed, Gorbachev suggested a joint U.S./Soviet mission to Mars. I think he saw Mars as an alternative to funding SDI, for the military-industrial complex. I was waiting in the line to be introduced to President Reagan at a state dinner in the Kremlin when Mikhail Sergeevich seized my hand and said, "Mr. President, this is the scientist I was talking about. He is inciting both of us to fly to Mars." I confess it was at least a slight exaggeration. I had always supported unmanned exploration. For a brief moment President Reagan was indeed interested. I saw sparks in his eyes. I could see that Gorbachev wanted, immediately, to capitalize on the first psychological impact. He said, "You know, Professor Sagdeev has very close friends in the United

States who are equally energetic in promoting flight to Mars." At this very moment Gorbachev made an unforgivable mistake. Instead of giving the name of General Abrahamson, he gave the name of Carl Sagan.[2] So the project died.

No one is talking anymore about a flight to Mars in the former Soviet Union. In the eyes of our taxpayers, the space program as a whole is criminal, an accomplice of the former Bolshevik regime. It was precisely in the interests of Bolshevik propaganda that many of the launches were undertaken and, after every launch, the Soviet government and the TASS news agency would issue a brief triumphant communiqué. "Another victory of socialism! Another proof of the superiority of the system!" Taxpayers have come to the conclusion that we probably don't need any more proof.

However, the issue of rescuing the assets of our science is still with us. This problem, the issue of survival, of possibly rescuing the best parts of the Soviet scientific community, is coming from two different lines of thinking. It is undeniable that due to its shortcomings, such as indoctrination and overbureaucratization, Soviet science achieved much less than it could have with the resources it spent. But at the same time, it had a large number of really bright young scientists. It had leaders of internationally known scientific schools, in almost every field of contemporary science. What remains of the science of the former Soviet Union should be considered an international treasure.

Second, and not least important of the arguments, is that to support the Russian scientific community would symbolize political support for the forces of democracy, because it was the scientific community that prepared and launched the fight against the totalitarian regime. It now needs help. It needs help against extermination by economic chaos and it needs help against the potential risk of the resurgence of reactionary forces. In many ways, I think we are living now, emotionally and psychologically, through

---

[2] At the time General Abrahamson was director of the SDI program. Carl Sagan was an outspoken critic of the SDI program and of the Reagan administration.

times similar to those when the Soviets very impatiently waited for the opening of the second front. It was a great victory and a joy for all of us when the second front was launched from this very country, the United Kingdom, across the English Channel.

The same type of second front, not military, but the hand of friendship and support, should now be given to the Soviet scientific community. This second front would help assure that the political changes in the former Soviet Union are irreversible.

*The Broadest Pattern of Human History*

JARED DIAMOND

THE TANNER LECTURES ON HUMAN VALUES

Delivered at

University of Utah
May 6, 1992

JARED M. DIAMOND earned a Ph.D. degree in Physiology from Cambridge University in 1961. A Professor of Physiology at UCLA Medical School, he is also a Research Associate with the American Museum of Natural History and the Los Angeles County Museum of Natural History. He is a contributing editor to *Discover* and writes a regular column, "Nature's Infinite Book," for *Natural History* on the subject of human biology, including human evolution, genetics, distribution, and language. A MacArthur Foundation Fellow from 1985 to 1990, he is a Fellow of the American Academy of Arts and Sciences and the American Ornithologists Union, and a member of the National Academy of Sciences and the American Philosophical Society. He has led a number of National Geographic Society expeditions to the Solomon Islands and New Guinea.

INTRODUCTION

As world travel developed in recent centuries from 1492 onward, it quickly became obvious that peoples with very different economies, technologies, and political organizations coexisted in the modern world. At one extreme were the large Iron Age states occupying much of Europe, Asia (except Siberia), and North Africa, plus the smaller Iron Age states of West Africa. Comparable in political organization, but lacking in iron technology, were the Inca Empire of the Andes and the Aztec state of Mexico. The range of societies continued through the Neolithic settled chiefdoms of other parts of the Americas and Polynesia, with some of those societies (such as Polynesian Hawaii and the Mississippian civilization of Indian North America) verging on the level of states. The list went on to the Neolithic tribal farming societies of New Guinea and the remainder of the New World and concluded with the hunter-gatherers of the Arctic, Australia, and scattered areas of the Americas, Africa, and Asia.

This snapshot of the diverse world as of 1492 was subsequently illuminated by archaeologists, who obtained in effect a series of snapshots at earlier times. It then became clear that the geographic differences among human societies as of 1492 resulted from differences, extending back over at least 10,000 years, in the dates of first appearance of developments such as stone tool grinding, metallurgy, pottery, and plant and animal domestication. For example, mass production of copper tools, which was beginning to be widespread in the Andes in the centuries before 1492, was already spreading in parts of Eurasia 5,000 years before that. The stone technology of the Tasmanians, when first encountered by literate observers in 1642, was simpler than that of Upper Paleolithic Europe tens of thousands of years earlier.

The collisions among these disparate peoples shaped the modern world through conquest, epidemics, and genocide. These collisions set up reverberations that have still not died down after many centuries and that are being played out in some of the most troubled areas of the world today (such as South Africa and the former Soviet Union).

In the present essay, I shall explore the hypothesis that these differences between human societies resulted not from differences between the peoples themselves, but from effects of environment and geography — that is, from contrasts between the real estate that different peoples inherited. Two caveats are necessary at the outset, since many people may initially consider this topic an unfit one for polite discussion. First, this whole subject stinks of racism, because nineteenth-century Europeans explained the observed geographic differences in complexity of human societies in terms of supposed parallel differences among peoples in their mental abilities. Despite much effort to document these supposed differences, no sound supporting evidence has been forthcoming. Available evidence even supports the reverse conclusion. For example, Alaskan Inuit (Eskimo) children have been reported to score considerably higher on standard "intelligence" tests, such as the Stanford-Binet test, than white Americans, even though the latter might be supposed to have had a big advantage on such tests because of the tests' relationship to formal schooling. Again, my own impression of the many New Guinea peoples with whom I have worked during the past thirty years is that they appear on the average considerably more intelligent than white Americans, though I have no idea whether this impression (if correct) reflects superior human genetics or else effects of more social stimulation in New Guinea societies. Nonetheless, the lingering, even if tacit, assumption that mental differences contribute to the worldwide differences among human societies remains widespread. The persistence of this pernicious wrong assumption would alone be sufficient reason to seek to replace it by a correct and convincing explanation.

I should also make one other point clear at the outset. Although it may be convenient to use the conventional phrase "rise of civilizations" to refer to these global patterns, I am not thereby assuming that Iron Age states are "better" than hunter-gatherer tribes, nor that the abandonment of the hunter-gatherer life-style for iron-based statehood represents "progress," nor that the transition has led to an increase in human happiness. Even if one did attempt to decide which condition was "better," one would have to evaluate a very mixed picture. For example, compared to hunter-gatherers, citizens of modern Westernized states enjoy a longer life-span and lower risk of death by homicide, and also suffer from much less social support from friendships and extended family. Instead, my motivation for investigating these geographic differences in human societies is simply that they cry for explanation, as the broadest pattern of human history.

The differences between the histories of Eurasia, the Americas, sub-Saharan Africa, and Australia are too great to be dismissed as accidents resulting from contributions of individual geniuses or individual societies. When we are dealing with these spatial scales of whole continents and these time scales of tens of thousands of years, there must have been environmental factors, rather than accidents, to account for these differences. Thus, when I talk about "the broadest pattern of human history," I do not expect to contribute anything to answering such questions as why Napoleon rather than his enemies lost the Battle of Waterloo. Instead, I would like to explain questions such as why copper tool manufacture emerged much earlier in the Old World than in the New World and never emerged in Australia.

I shall begin with a brief discussion of human societal variation within Polynesia, to illustrate how large differences among human societies descended from a common ancestral society can be clearly attributed to environmental differences. I shall then turn to one of the most dramatic collisions in recent human history, that between the Inca emperor Atahuallpa and the Spanish conquistador Pizarro at the Peruvian town of Cajamarca in 1532, as a starting point for understanding the more general problem of the differences between human development in the Americas and in Eurasia. Next, I shall examine whether the insights derived from that American/Eurasian collision prove useful in understanding the history of sub-Saharan Africa. Finally, I shall turn to the histories of Native Australia and Tasmania, where the insights derived from the American/Eurasian/African comparisons prove irrelevant, and where additional factors emerge that may also have been significant elsewhere in the world.

## POLYNESIA: A MODEL FOR THE INFLUENCE OF GEOGRAPHY ON SOCIETY

Polynesia provides particularly clear evidence of differences between human societies conditioned by differences in geography. All Polynesian islands, plus some Pacific islands that belong geographically to Melanesia and Micronesia, were settled by descendants of a single ancestral people. They are known archaeologically as the Lapita people, named after the archaeological site on New Caledonia where their pottery was first excavated and described. The Lapita people spread directly from the tropical Bismarck and Solomon Archipelagoes near New Guinea, and ultimately from Indonesia and Southeast Asia. Thus, the recent populations of all Polynesian islands were derived from founding groups bearing essentially the same culture, language, technology (based on stone rather than metal), and kit of domesticated plants and animals. Polynesia offers to the historian the further advantage of a modest time depth: human colonization of Polynesia began around 1600 B.C. and was largely completed by around A.D. 500, except for a few islands (such as New Zealand, the Chathams, and Henderson) settled perhaps as late as A.D. 1000.

To these rather uniform human colonizing stocks, Polynesia presented huge differences in the environment. Polynesian islands range from sub-Antarctic to tropical, and from tiny islets to virtual continents. Correspondingly, there were huge differences among recent Polynesian societies, before they began to be modified by European influence. These differences among societies are clearly correlated with the geographic differences among Polynesian islands. Thus, Polynesia illustrates how, within a time span much shorter than the span of human occupation on any continent except Antarctica, and with a history devoid of the complications inevitable in multiple human colonization waves bringing varying cultural and social inheritances, geography can cause one people to diversify.

The areas of difference among Polynesian societies include their sources of food, their economic specialization, their social organization, their political organization, and their elaboration of cultural products. As regards food, Polynesians included hunter-gatherers on the Chatham Islands and on New Zealand's South Island, but most Polynesians were farmers. However, Polynesian agriculture varied in intensity, in whether it utilized no or up to three species of domestic animals, in whether it depended on (New Zealand's North Island) or dispensed with (Hawaii) food storage, in the development of irrigation systems, and in the development of aquaculture (unique to Hawaii). Economic organization ranged from societies where each household produced what it needed (societies of small isolated islands), to societies such as those of Tonga, the Societies, and Hawaii, with hereditary craft specialists including canoe builders, navigators, stonemasons, bird-catchers, toolmakers, and tattooers. Polynesian social organization ranged from nearly egalitarian on the atolls and Chathams, to the highly stratified societies of Tonga, the Societies, and especially Hawaii. The society of the latter archipelago was based on about ten hereditary, nearly endogamous castes, maintained in the highest classes by brother-sister marriage reminiscent of the Inca Empire.

Polynesian political organization ranged from local units of a few hundred people on small isolated islands, to self-contained communities of one or two thousand people, each occupying a valley of the Marquesan Islands, to Tonga and Hawaii, whose political organizations approached the state level. These incipient states imposed taxation in the form of labor, carried out large public works projects, and maintained ownership of land in the hands of the chiefs. As for Polynesian culture, people of the Chathams manufactured only small, individually owned objects, but monumental architecture was produced on numerous islands (including Easter, Hawaii, Mangareva, the Marquesas, Societies, and Tonga), Hawaii had luxury goods produced for the chiefs by craft specialists, and Easter may even have developed writing.

To a considerable degree, these enormous differences among Polynesian societies can be related to differences in the environments that they inhabited. Roles of at least six relevant variables can be recognized: suitability for agriculture, isolation, area, island type, productivity, and geographic effects on the size of the largest political unit.

First, although most Polynesian islands were suitable for growing the Asian domesticated plants that the Polynesians brought with them and/or the native Pacific plants that they domesticated, two islands at high, nearly sub-Antarctic latitudes did not permit Polynesian agriculture: the Chathams and most of New Zealand's South Island. On these islands, the founding farmers inevitably became hunter-gatherers.

A second variable obviously critical to the size of the largest political unit that could be maintained is island isolation. Some Polynesian islands are so remote (Easter, the Chathams) that there is no evidence of any further Polynesians arriving after the first settlement, and there was correspondingly no known place to which the descendants of those first settlers could emigrate if their home island became overcrowded. The size of the largest political unit could obviously be no greater than Easter or the Chathams themselves. Other islands lie in archipelagoes where many islands are visible from each other, although the whole archipelago itself is isolated (e.g., Hawaii). The Tongan archipelago consists not only of islands close enough for regular voyaging, but close enough to other archipelagoes (Fiji and Samoa) for regular trade. Thus, the whole Tongan archipelago eventually became cemented into a single political unit with trade relations and extensions of power to Fiji and Samoa.

Third, island size ranges from tiny atolls of a few acres, through giant Hawaii (6,400 square miles), to the miniature continent of New Zealand (100,000 square miles).

Fourth, island type varies from low flat atolls with thin soil and lacking permanent fresh water, to high volcanic islands with rich soil and permanent streams (e.g., the Societies and Marquesas). The larger islands variously have (most islands) or lack (Easter and the Marquesas) reefs and shallow water productive of fish and shellfish.

Correlated with these differences in island type and latitude were differences in human population density, dependent on plant growing conditions and access to seafood. Human densities ranged from about 1 person per 20 square miles on New Zealand's cold South Island, to 250 people per square mile on Hawaii, Tonga, the Societies, and Samoa, to 1,000 people per square mile on Anuta.

Finally, the size of the largest political unit reflected not only an island's total area or population, but also whether the island was fragmented by topography and accessible to other islands. For example, not only was the Marquesas Archipelago not unified politically, but neither were its individual islands, because populations on each island were confined to narrow, deep, steep-walled valleys separated by high ridges and communicated with populations of other valleys mainly by sea. In contrast, Easter Island is gently rolling, with no such barriers to human movements.

These differences in island geographic properties lead straightforwardly to the above-mentioned differences in population density and in number of people encompassed within a single political unit. Size of political unit is in turn correlated with economic diversification, social stratification, political organization, and range of cultural products. These relations have been explored at length by archaeologist Patrick Kirch in his books *The Evolution of the Polynesian Chiefdoms* and *Feathered Gods and Fishhooks*.

Thus, Polynesia illustrates clearly how differences in geography can cause a single people to diversify quickly and greatly in their food supply, economy, social and political organization, and cultural products. Let us now consider whether differences in geography, operating for much longer times and on a much grander spatial scale, have similarly caused the observed diversity of peoples among the major continents themselves.

## ATAHUALLPA AND PIZARRO: THE COLLISION OF THE OLD AND NEW WORLDS

The largest population shifts of modern times have been the colonization of the New World by Europeans and the reduction or disappearance of most groups of Amerindians (Native Americans). Discounting the few visits of small numbers of Norse to sites on the east coast of Canada, leaving no discernible impact or legacy, the collision of the Old and New Worlds began abruptly in 1492, after 10,000 years without demonstrated contact between the emerging complex societies of the two hemispheres. (This is not to deny continued contact across Bering Straits.) One of the most dramatic single moments in that collision was the first encounter of the Inca emperor Atahuallpa with the Spanish conquistador Francisco Pizarro at the Peruvian highland town of Cajamarca on November 16, 1532. Since that first meeting immediately resulted in the capture of Atahuallpa, and thereby led to the Spanish conquest of the Inca Empire, it provides a good starting point for analysis. We shall see that the reasons why Pizarro captured and killed Atahuallpa, rather than Atahuallpa doing the same to Pizarro's sovereign, are diagnostic for the collision of the two hemispheres, and for many other major collisions in recent world history.

The events that day at Cajamarca are well known, because they were recorded in writing by several of the Spanish participants. To get a flavor of those events, let us begin with excerpts from those eyewitness accounts:[1]

> The Indians' camp looked like a very beautiful city. So many tents were visible that we were truly filled with great apprehension. We never thought that Indians could maintain such a proud estate, nor have so many tents in such good order. Nothing like this had been seen in the Indies up to then. It filled all us Spaniards with fear and confusion. But it was not appropriate to show any fear, far less to turn back. For had they sensed any weakness in us, the very Indians we were bringing with us would have killed us. So, with a show of good spirits, and after having thoroughly observed the town and tents, we descended into the valley and into the town of Cajamarca.
>
> We took many views and opinions among ourselves about what should be done. All were full of fear, because we were so few and were so deep in the land where we could not be reinforced. All assembled in the Governor's [Francisco Pizarro's] quarters to debate what should be done the following day. Few slept, and we kept watch in the square, from which the camp fires of the Indian army could be seen. It was a fearful sight. Most of them were on a hillside and close to one another: it looked like a brilliantly star-studded sky. There was no distinction between great and small or between foot-soldiers and horsemen. Every one performed sentry rounds fully armed that night. So also did the good old Governor, who went about encouraging the men. On that day all were knights. I saw many Spaniards urinate without noticing it out of pure terror.
>
> [Pizarro] signalled the artillery man to fire the cannons into their [the Indians'] midst. They [the Spaniards] all placed rattles on their horses to terrify the Indians. With the booming of the shots and the trumpets and the troop of horses

---

[1] The following translation of the original Spanish texts is based on that by John Hemming in his book *The Conquest of the Incas* (San Diego: Harcourt Brace Jovanovich, 1970).

with their rattles, the Indians were thrown into confusion and panicked. The Spaniards fell upon them and began to kill them. They [the Indians] were so filled with fear that they climbed on top of one another — to such an extent that they formed mounds and suffocated one another. The horsemen rode out on top of them, wounding and killing and pressing home the attack.

The Governor armed himself with a quilted cotton coat of armor, took his sword and dagger and entered the thick of the Indians with the Spaniards who were with him. With great bravery he reached Atahuallpa's litter. He fearlessly grabbed [Atahuallpa's] left arm and shouted, "Santiago!" but he could not pull him out of his litter, which was on high. All those [Indians] who were carrying Atahuallpa's litter appeared to be important men, and they all died, as did those who were travelling in the litters and hammocks. Many Indians had their hands cut off but continued to support their ruler's litter with their shoulders. But their efforts were of little avail for they were all killed. Although [the Spaniards] killed the Indians who were carrying [the litter], other replacements immediately went to support it. They continued in this way for a long while, overpowering and killing the Indians. Seven or eight Spaniards spurred up and grabbed the edge of the litter, heaved on it, and turned it onto its side. Atahuallpa was captured in this way, and the Governor took him to his lodging. Those who were carrying the litter and those who escorted [Atahuallpa] never abandoned him: all died around him.

They [the Indians] were so terrified at seeing the Governor in their midst, at the unexpected firing of the artillery and the eruption of the horses in a troop — which was something they had never seen — that, panic-stricken, they were more concerned to flee and save their lives than to make war. The footsoldiers set about those who remained in the square with such speed that in a short time most of them were put to the sword. All the other fighting men whom the Inca had brought were a mile from Cajamarca and ready for battle, but not an Indian made a move. When the squadrons of men who remained in the plain outside the town saw the others fleeing and shouting, most of them broke and took to flight. It was an extraordinary sight, for the entire valley of 15 or 20 miles was completely filled with men. It was a level plain with fields of crops. Many Indians were killed. Night had already fallen and the horsemen were continuing to lance Indians in the fields, when they sounded a trumpet for us to reassemble outside the camp. On arrival we went to congratulate the Governor on the victory.

In the space of two hours — all that remained of daylight — all those troops were annihilated. That day, six or seven thousand Indians lay dead on the plain and many more had their arms cut off and other wounds. Atahuallpa himself admitted that we had killed seven thousand of his Indians in that battle. The man killed in one of the litters was his steward (the Lord of Chincha), of whom he was very fond. The others were also lords over many people and were his councillors. The cacique lord of Cajamarca died. Other commanders died, but there were so many of them that they go unrecorded. For all those who came in Atahuallpa's bodyguard were great lords. It was an extraordinary thing to see so great a ruler captured in so short a time, when he had come with such might.

Truly, it was not accomplished with our own forces, for there were so few of us. It was by the grace of God, which is great.

Let us now trace out the chain of causation in this extraordinary confrontation. We begin with the most proximate question: Why was it that Pizarro captured Atahuallpa at Cajamarca and killed his followers, instead of Atahuallpa capturing Pizarro and killing Pizarro's followers? After all, Pizarro had only 62 soldiers mounted on horses plus 106 foot-soldiers, while Atahuallpa commanded an army of about 40,000. We shall then consider the next most proximate question: how Atahuallpa came to be at Cajamarca at all; how Pizarro came to be there; and why Atahuallpa walked into what seems to us, with the gift of hindsight, to have been such an obvious trap.

For each of these questions, we shall ask whether the responsible factors identified in the confrontation between Atahuallpa and Pizarro also played a broader role in the collision of the Old and New Worlds, and in other collisions. Finally, we shall explore the ultimate factors responsible for the proximate factors that we have identified.

*Why did Pizarro capture Atahuallpa?* Pizarro's military advantages lay in steel swords and guns (Pizarro had both muskets and artillery), to which the Incas could oppose only stone and wooden weapons. In other similar confrontations throughout the New World and on other continents, steel weapons and guns proved similarly decisive in conquests of people lacking those weapons. This advantage of weaponry is too obvious to require further elaboration.

One other advantage enjoyed by Pizarro does, however, warrant examination. The tremendous advantage that the Spaniards gained from their horses leaps out of the eyewitness accounts. The shock of a horse's charge, the speed of attack that it permitted, and the raised fighting platform that it provided left foot-soldiers nearly helpless in the open. Similarly, Cortes's conquest of the Aztec Empire was carried out by a tiny force of 500 soldiers and 16 horsemen, armed with steel swords, muskets, and crossbows.

The military advantage of horses was not only due to the terror that they inspired in soldiers fighting against them for the first time. By the time of the Great Inca Rebellion of 1536, the Incas had learned how best to defend themselves against cavalry, by ambushing and annihilating Spanish horsemen in narrow passes. But the Incas, like all other foot-soldiers, were never able to resist cavalry in the open. When Quizo Yupanqui, the best general of the Inca emperor who succeeded Atahuallpa, besieged the Spaniards in Lima in 1536 and tried to storm the city, two squadrons of Spanish cavalry charged a much larger Indian force on flat ground, killed Quizo and all his commanders in the first charge, and routed Quizo's army. A similar cavalry charge of 26 horsemen routed the best troops of the Inca emperor Manco, as he was besieging the Spaniards in Cuzco.

The transformation of warfare by horses began around 4000 B.C., when the domestication of horses in the Russian steppes north of the Black Sea empowered the first speakers of Indo-European languages to launch the spread of those languages over almost all of Europe and much of Asia. Horses permitted people possessing them to cover far greater distances than was possible on foot, to attack by surprise, and to flee before a superior defending force could be gathered. Horses proceeded to revolutionize warfare in the Near East and Mediterranean, especially following the invention of the horse-drawn battle chariot around 1800 B.C. In 1786 B.C., horses enabled the Hyksos to conquer then-horseless Egypt, and later enabled the Huns and Mongols to invade and terrorize Europe. Horse-drawn chariots transformed warfare in China, and also in the kingdoms emerging in West Africa around A.D. 1000. While our first image of North American Indians is often of mounted warriors on the Great Plains, we forget that horses arrived there only in the seventeenth and eighteenth centuries and proceeded to transform not only Plains warfare but also the Plains economy, by making it feasible to follow migrating herds of buffalo. As all of these examples illustrate, the role of horses at Cajamarca exemplifies their military value that lasted for 6,000 years and became applied on all the inhabited continents. Not until the First World War was the military dominance of cavalry finally superseded.

*How did Atahuallpa come to be at Cajamarca?* While the Incas would probably have succumbed eventually to the Spanish invaders, as did the Aztecs, even if Atahuallpa had not been captured at Cajamarca, his capture there on the second day of his contact with Spaniards simplified matters enormously for Pizarro. Atahuallpa and his army came to be at Cajamarca because they had just won decisive battles in a civil war that left the Incas divided and vulnerable. Pizarro quickly appreciated those divisions and exploited them to his advantage. The reason for the civil war was that an epidemic of smallpox or measles, spreading among South American Indians after its arrival with Spanish settlers on the coast, had killed the Inca emperor Huayna Capac in

1525 and then immediately killed his heir Ninan Cuyuchi, precipitating the civil war between Atahuallpa and his half-brother Huascar. If it had not been for the epidemic, the Spaniards would have been facing a united empire.

Atahuallpa's presence at Cajamarca is thus symbolic for one of the most important factors in the course of world history: diseases transmitted by invading peoples to settled peoples lacking immunity. Smallpox, measles, influenza, typhus, bubonic plague, and other infectious diseases endemic in Europe decimated many peoples on other continents and was a decisive factor in European conquests. For example, a smallpox epidemic devastated the Aztecs after the failure of the first Spanish attack in 1520 and killed Cuitlahuac, the Aztec emperor who briefly succeeded Montezuma. Throughout the Americas, diseases introduced with Europeans spread from tribe to tribe far in advance of the advancing Europeans themselves, killing an estimated 90 or 95% of the pre-Columbian Indian population. For instance, the most populous and highly organized Indian society of North America, the Mississippian civilization, disappeared between 1492 and the late 1600s, when Europeans themselves made their first beginnings of settlement on the Mississippi. Soon after the British settlement of Sydney in 1788, the first of the epidemics that decimated Aboriginal Australians began. A well-documented example from Pacific islands is the epidemic that swept over Fiji in 1806, when a few European survivors from the wreck of the ship *Argo* struggled ashore. Similar epidemics characterize the histories of Tonga, Hawaii, and other Pacific islands.

I should not leave the impression, however, that the role of disease in history was confined to paving the way for European expansion. Diseases of tropical Africa, India, Southeast Asia, and New Guinea greatly retarded European conquest and furnished the most important obstacle to European colonization of those areas.

*How did Pizarro come to be at Cajamarca?* Pizarro came to Cajamarca through European maritime technology, which built the ships that took him across the Atlantic from Spain to Panama, and then in the Pacific from Panama to Peru. In addition to the ships themselves, his presence also depended on the political organization that enabled Spain to finance, build, staff, and equip the ships. Another related factor was the role of writing, in making possible the quick spread of much more detailed and accurate information than could be transmitted by mouth. That information coming back from earlier voyages motivated later European explorers and settlers to embark and provided them with detailed sailing directions. Maritime technology coupled with political organization was similarly essential for European spread to other continents, and for expansions of some other peoples (e.g., of Arabs along the coast of East Africa around 2,000 years ago).

*Why did Atahuallpa walk into the trap?* Armed with hindsight, we find it astonishing that Atahuallpa marched into such an obvious trap at Cajamarca. The Spaniards who captured him were equally surprised at their success.

The immediate explanation is that Atahuallpa had very little information about the Spaniards and their power and intent. He derived that little information by word of mouth, following Pizarro's landing on the Peruvian coast in 1527 and again in 1531. It simply did not occur to Atahuallpa that the Spaniards would attack him without provocation and that they were formidable.

Equally surprising to us today is Atahuallpa's behavior following his capture. He offered his famous ransom in the belief that, once paid off, the Spaniards would release him and then depart. He failed to understand that Pizarro's force was the spearhead of an invasion of permanent conquest, rather than an isolated raid.

Atahuallpa was not alone in these fatal miscalculations. After Atahuallpa had been captured, Francisco Pizarro's brother Hernando Pizarro persuaded Atahuallpa's leading general Chalcuchima, in command of a large army, to deliver himself into the Spaniards' power. The Aztec emperor Montezuma made an even grosser miscalculation when he took Cortes for a returning god and admitted Cortes and his little army into the Aztec capital of Tenochtitlan.

On a mundane level, the miscalculations by Atahuallpa, Chalcuchima, Montezuma, and countless other native leaders deceived by Europeans were due to the fact that no living inhabitant of the New World had been to the Old World, so of course there could be no specific information available about the Spaniards. Even so, we find it hard to avoid the conclusion that Atahuallpa "should" have been more suspicious, had his society had experience of a broader range of human behavior. Pizarro too arrived at Cajamarca with no information about the Incas other than what he had learned by interrogating the Inca subjects he encountered in 1527 and 1531. However, while Pizarro himself happened to be illiterate, he belonged to a literate tradition. From written records, the Spaniards knew of many contemporary civilizations remote from Europe and knew several thousand years of European history. Pizarro explicitly modeled his ambush of Atahuallpa on the success of Cortes, who had advanced his conquest of the Aztec Empire by capturing the emperor Montezuma. In short, literacy made the Spaniards heirs to a huge range of knowledge of human behavior and history unavailable to the Incas and Aztecs. That knowledge encouraged Pizarro to set his trap, and Atahuallpa to walk into it.

## ULTIMATE FACTORS DETERMINING THE OUTCOME OF THE COLLISION OF OLD AND NEW WORLDS

We have so far identified proximate factors in European colonization of the New World: military technology employing guns, swords, and horses; infectious diseases endemic in Eurasia; European maritime technology; the political organization of large and wealthy European states; and writing. Let us now enquire why these proximate advantages came to characterize Europe rather than the New World. Theoretically, the Incas might have been the ones to develop Iron Age weapons and firearms, to be mounted on animals more formidable than horses, to bear diseases to which Europeans lacked resistance, to have oceangoing ships and advanced political organization, and to be able to draw on the experience of thousands of years of written history. Why did these advantages go to the Old World, rather than the New World?

One convenient starting point for tracing the chain of causation (see figure) is to appreciate why Eurasia had evolved many more infectious diseases endemic in crowded populations than had the Americas. The infectious diseases of Eurasia owe their evolution to the domestic animals of Eurasia, for two reasons. First, many infectious diseases require large human populations in order to be able to maintain themselves. In a small population, an infectious disease may quickly infect the whole population, kill some people, and immunize the survivors, leaving the disease to die out because there are no more people left to infect. The size of the human population required to sustain an infectious disease depends on factors such as the duration of infection of each patient and the number of new victims infected per patient. Many of our familiar modern infectious diseases could have sustained themselves only in the large, dense human populations that appeared with the rise of agriculture and of human concentration into villages and cities. For example, measles requires a population of over 100,000 people in order to maintain itself.

Second, most human infectious diseases evolved from similar diseases of domestic animals with which humans came into close association. For instance, measles, smallpox, influenza, and falciparum malaria evolved from corresponding diseases of dogs, cattle, pigs, and birds (possibly chickens), respectively. It is striking that, whereas Europeans transmitted many diseases that caused devastating epidemics in Amerindians, the latter gave no diseases in return to Europeans — with the possible exception of syphilis (it remains uncertain whether syphilis arose in the Old or New World).

The paucity of crowd infectious diseases in the Americas partly reflects the fact that densely populated farming communities and

## Factors Underlying the Broadest Pattern of History

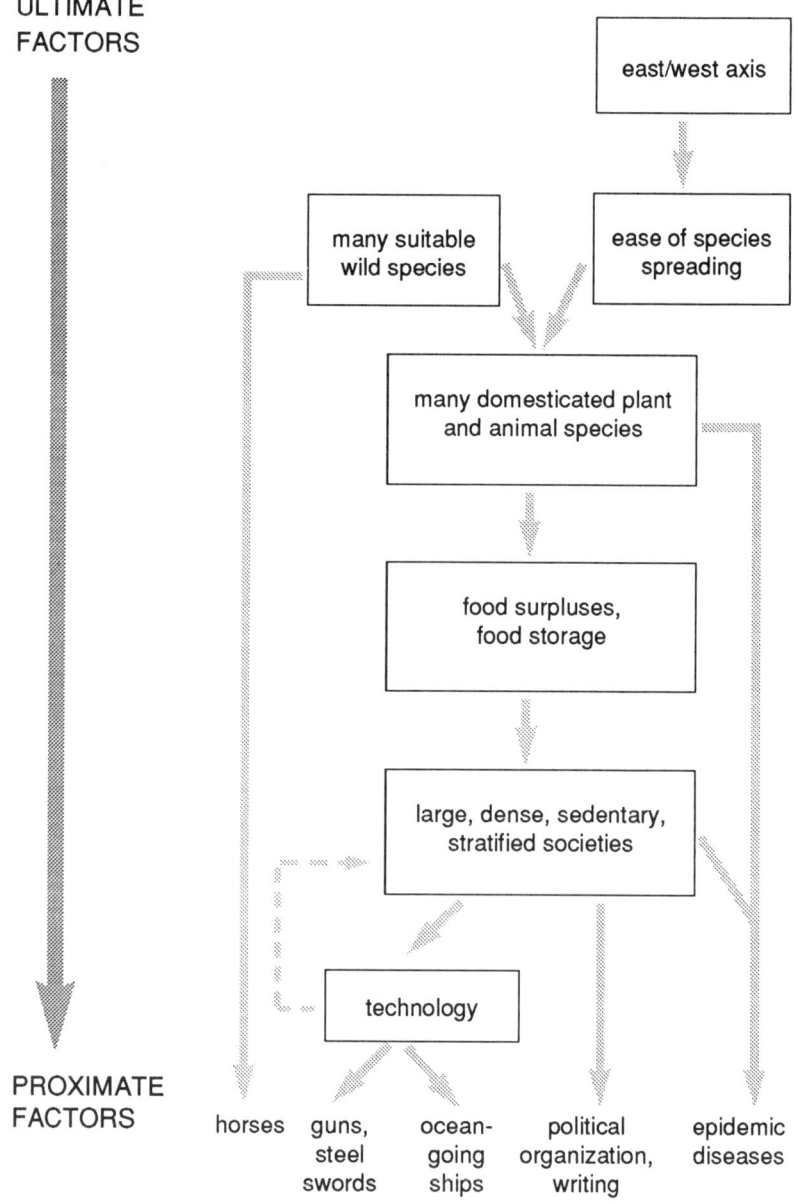

cities arose later in the New World than in the Old World. Even more importantly, it reflects the extreme paucity of domesticated animal species in the New World. New World domesticates consisted solely of the dog throughout the Americas, the llama and alpaca and guinea pig in the Andes, the turkey in North America and Mexico, and the Muscovy duck in lowland tropical South America. Contrast those few species with the wide range of domesticated animals in Eurasia: the horse, cow, sheep, goat, pig, and dog distributed widely throughout Eurasia; many local domesticates, such as reindeer and water buffalo; domesticated small mammals, notably rabbits and cats; and domesticated birds, including the chicken, mallard duck, and goose.

Why were far more animal species domesticated in Eurasia than in the Americas? Since the Americas harbor several thousand wild bird species and a thousand or more wild mammal species, one might suppose that the Americas offered plenty of starting material for domestication. In fact, of wild mammal and bird species over the whole world only a tiny fraction has been successfully domesticated. Domestication requires that an animal be bred in captivity and genetically modified to make it more useful to humans. To be suitable for domestication, wild species must possess a suite of characteristics shared by only a few: willingness to breed in captivity, with mates selected by humans rather than by the individual animal itself; submissive behavior within groups or herds of its own species, a behavior that can be transferred to humans; and a diet that can be readily supplied by humans. Dozens of potentially valuable wild species, including Asian and Indian elephants and cheetahs, have been tamed but not domesticated. Thousands of years ago, humans domesticated almost all possible worthwhile wild mammal species, with the result that there have been no significant additions to our suite of domesticated large wild mammals in modern times, despite much effort put into attempts to domesticate species such as eland and American bison.

Eurasia ended up with the most domesticated species partly because, as the world's largest land mass, it offered the most wild species to begin with. That preexisting difference was magnified by the extinction, around 11,000 years ago at the end of the last Ice Age, of about 80% of the large mammal species of North and South America. Those extinctions included several species that might have been expected to furnish useful domesticates had they survived, such as North American horses and camels. As a result, Amerindians inherited far fewer species of large wild mammals than did Eurasians, leaving them only the llama and alpaca (possibly variants of the same wild species) as domesticates. We shall similarly see that sub-Saharan Africa, New Guinea, and Australia have yielded no large domesticated mammals at all, although Africa and New Guinea did yield domesticated plants.

Old World/New World differences in domesticated plants are qualitatively similar to these differences in domesticated mammals, though much less marked. The Americans did yield many valuable plants, of which maize, potatoes, tomatoes, and others have now spread worldwide. However, in contrast to the numerous productive domesticated grains of the Old World (wheat, barley, oats, millets, and others), the Americas yielded only one productive grain (corn), and the complexities of its reproductive system meant that the development of maize's wild ancestor (teosinte) to yield a productive crop required thousands more years of effort on the part of Amerindians than did the development of Old World grains.

Thus, Eurasia's advantage over the Americas in domesticated animal and plant species was initially due to the greater pool of candidate wild species in Eurasia, especially after the extinction of most large mammals of the Americas. A further advantage of Eurasia derives from the fact that its major axis is oriented east/west, whereas the major axis of the Americas is north/south. Eurasia's east/west axis means that its latitudinal bands and climate zones are 9,000 miles broad. Within these broad bands, wild species adapted to that climate replace each other longitudinally as a result of local evolution. In contrast, the latitudinal bands of the Americas range from at most only 4,000 miles broad down to only a few hundred miles in parts of Central America and Patagonia.

As a result, species that were domesticated in particular parts of Eurasia were able to spread long distances within the climate band to which they were already adapted. For example, chickens and ducks domesticated in Southeast Asia quickly reached Europe; horses domesticated in European Russia reached China and Western Europe; and the sheep, goats, and cattle of the Mideast spread in all directions. The Romans already enjoyed Asian peaches and citrus fruit, Indian sesame and cucumbers, and Central Asian onions and hemp, in addition to the wheat and barley that they inherited from the Near East.

In the Americas, however, the llama, alpaca, guinea pig, and potato of the Andes were never able to spread through the tropical lowlands of northern South America and southern Central America to reach Mexico, with the result that Mesoamerican civilization remained entirely without pack animals. Correspondingly, the turkey, domesticated in Mexico and/or North America, was never able to reach the Andes. Maize did spread to South America and North America from its origins in Mexico, but it took thousands of years to transform the maize that evolved in Mexico's climate into a maize adapted to the shorter growing season and seasonally changing day lengths of North America, and thus to feed the rise of North America's Mississippian civilization beginning only around A.D. 1000. Various domesticated plant species, such as beans and cotton and tobacco, were grown in both North America and South America, suggesting at first sight that they did succeed in spreading through unfavorable climate zones. In fact, though, many of these seemingly shared species were actually domesticated independently in North and South America.

Domesticated plants and animals were important in many ways to the rise in human population densities and social and political organization. Domestication allows people to become sedentary, whereas most hunter-gatherers move seasonally or more often in order to follow food sources. Domestication favors the storage of surplus food, thereby making some time available for purposes other than obtaining food. Domesticated plants and animals yield far more edible calories per acre than do wild habitats, in which most species are inedible to humans. As a result, population densities of farmers and herders are typically 10 to 100 times greater than those of hunter-gatherers. As already mentioned, those higher population densities favored the evolution of specialized infectious diseases of humans.

Domesticated mammals have been significant for reasons other than as a ready source of meat. Horses, cattle, and donkeys revolutionized land transport, permitting people to travel faster and further, carrying much heavier loads, than possible for people on foot. Several domesticated mammals yielded milk, as well as other useful products such as hides and wool. Livestock made it possible for an individual farmer to plough land faster, to plough soils that would otherwise have been uneconomical to plough, and thus to raise more food.

Those dense, sedentary populations made possible by plant and animal domestication were important in the development of human society and political organization for several reasons. First, a more numerous people has the advantage in wars of conquest and can extend its territory at the expense of a less numerous people. Before the European invasion of the Americas, some of the largest population shifts in the last 10,000 years of human history had involved expansions of farmers over the former territories of hunter-gatherers living at much lower population densities: the replacement of hunter-gatherers related to pygmies and modern Khoisan peoples (so-called Bushmen and Hottentots) over much of sub-equatorial Africa by Bantu farmers and herders; and the replacement of populations related to modern Papuans and Aboriginal Australians throughout Indonesia, the Philippines, and parts of Southeast Asia by the expansion of Austronesian farmers. Second, hunter-gatherer societies tend to be relatively egalitarian (without inherited chiefs) and to have small-scale political organization, at the level of the band or tribe, whereas moderate-sized agricultural societies are often organized in chiefdoms, and empires are confined to large agricultural societies.

Finally, in a large, dense society of settled farmers, a political upper class can free itself of the need to feed itself, and can thereby devote itself entirely to political activities, by obtaining surplus food from the primary producers through taxation. Taxation or barter of stored food surpluses also supports professional specialists who can devote themselves to the development of metallurgy, writing, and other technology. Food surpluses can also be used to support professional standing armies. This last consideration was the decisive factor in the eventual success of the British colonists of New Zealand at defeating New Zealand's well-armed indigenous Maori population. While the Maori were able to win stunning temporary victories, they could not maintain a professional army constantly in the field and were eventually worn down by the full-time soldiers of the colonists.

Thus, the Old World's greater number of domesticatable plants and especially animals, and the greater ease with which such species could spread through suitable climate zones in the Old World, contributed directly to most or all of the proximate advantages resulting in Old World colonization of the New World. The chain of causation is most straightforward in the case of the Old World's possession of horses; its suite of infectious diseases deadly to nonexposed peoples, its higher human population densities, and its earlier emergence of centralized states. The same factors contributed indirectly to the more rapid development of Old World technology, among whose achievements metal tools and weapons, firearms, and writing proved especially important.

## African Collisions

As in Eurasia and the New World, agriculture did arise independently in certain parts of Africa — the Sahara and the zone immediately south of the Sahara. Best known of the native African domesticated plants is coffee, which was indigenous to Ethiopia and has now spread around the world. Other indigenous Ethiopian cultigens include the cereals known as teff and finger millet, the banana-like ensete, and the oil-yielding noog. The grains sorghum and bulrush millet were indigenous to (and domesticated in) the Sahara, while domesticates of tropical West Africa included African rice, African yams, groundnuts, and the oil palm.

However, sub-equatorial Africa has yielded no native plant cultigens. In addition, writing, herding, and possibly metallurgy did not arise independently in the Sahara and sub-Saharan Africa but entered from the outside. Most of sub-equatorial Africa was occupied by pygmy and Khoisan hunter-gatherers, until domestic livestock reached the latter around A.D. 0, just ahead of the invading farmers. Agriculture and metallurgy entered sub-equatorial Africa with the invaders themselves: the Bantu peoples, whose history constitutes one of the major population expansions and replacements of recent history. Originating from the area of tropical West Africa now within the borders of eastern Nigeria and southern Cameroon, the Bantu spread several thousand years ago to East Africa, whence around 2,000 years ago they suddenly expanded over almost the whole of southern Africa. That latter expansion carried them over a thousand miles in 200 years, from the East African lakes south to the shores of Natal. That Bantu expansion over southern Africa was powered by the advantages they derived from agriculture, herding, and metal.

Thus, African history has been molded by the local availability (or lack thereof) of domesticatable plant and animal species and by the long north-south axis of Africa that greatly slowed the spread of such species from north to south. Specifically, the Bantus' suite of domesticatable plants halted their invasion of southern Africa before they could occupy the Cape of Good Hope, with heavy political consequences for the Republic of South Africa today.

With this brief introduction to African history, let us now consider Africa's domesticated animals in more detail. Almost all of those adopted south of the Sahara entered from the north, ultimately from Eurasia. The sole indigenous sub-Saharan domesticate is a bird, the guinea fowl. All of the mammalian domesticates — cattle, sheep, goats, horses, even dogs — entered sub-Saharan Africa from the north.

The lack of indigenous domesticated animals in sub-Saharan Africa may at first seem surprising, since we think of Africa as *the* continent of big wild mammals. In fact, none of Africa's famous big wild mammals proved domesticatable; even today, modern breeders have had no significant successes, except for some ongoing efforts with the eland, a large antelope. Consider how closely related some wild African mammals are to Eurasian species that did prove domesticatable. African zebras and rhinoceroses were never domesticated, though the Eurasian horse, a member of the same mammalian order (Perissodactyla, the odd-toed hoofed mammals), and a member of the same genus as the zebra, was domesticated with the momentous military results already discussed. All of Africa's famous antelope species, plus its buffalo and hippopotamus, could not be domesticated, although Eurasian cattle, sheep, and goats (members of the same mammalian order, Artiodactyla, or even-toed hoofed mammals) did prove suitable for domestication. Among the world's pigs, only the Eurasian pig has been domesticated — not Africa's indigenous bush pigs, giant forest pig, and warthog, nor the peccaries of the New World. African jackals were not domesticated, though the related Eurasian wolf (a member of the same genus) was.

Imagine what the course of African history might have been, had zebras, rhinoceroses, and hippopotamuses lent themselves to domestication! We have seen that cavalry mounted on Eurasian horses proved invincible to peoples without horses. What would have happened if rhinoceroses or hippopotamuses had been domesticated south of the Sahara, and if sub-Saharan Africans mounted on those animals had then invaded North Africa and Europe? But that did not happen — because of Africa's suite of wild mammal species and their unsuitability for domestication.

Instead, as mentioned, the livestock adopted in Africa were Eurasian species that spread from north to south in Africa and thereby contributed to Africa's population buildup. That spread from north to south was much slower than the east/west spread of the same livestock species within Eurasia, because of difficulties in adapting to the different climate zones encountered along Africa's north/south axis, and because of problems of susceptibility to diseases of indigenous African mammals, such as trypanosomes transmitted by tsetse flies.

As one example of these difficulties of spread of domesticated mammal species along Africa's north/south axis, horses did not power the rise of West African kingdoms until the first millennium A.D., although horses had already reached Egypt around 1800 B.C. and transformed North African warfare soon thereafter. As a second example, cattle, sheep, and goats already reached Egypt, North Africa west of Egypt, and Sudan, and the Sahara at various times in the sixth and fifth millennium B.C. Those livestock reached the northern edge of the Serengeti in the third millennium B.C., where their spread halted. It took more than 2,000 years more for livestock to cross the Serengeti and reach southern Africa. Sheep reached South Africa around A.D. 0, cattle and goats and dogs a few centuries later — just ahead of the invading Bantu. As a final example, humped Zebu cattle originating from India have thrived better than humpless cattle in many parts of sub-Saharan Africa, but Zebu cattle did not reach East Africa until around A.D. 1500, even though they had reached Egypt by around 2,000 B.C. All of these examples illustrate the difficulties with which domesticated animals entering Africa from the north adapted themselves to the climates and diseases that they encountered in their spread southward in Africa.

The rise of agriculture in southern Africa, where no indigenous domesticatable plant species occurred, was similarly delayed by difficulties in adapting along Africa's north/south axis. Agriculture is of considerable antiquity in Africa north of the equator: farming reached Egypt and the rest of North Africa, the Sahara, and Sudan already in the sixth and fifth millennia B.C., Ethiopia by 4000 B.C., and Nigeria around 3000 B.C. But it was not until around A.D. 0 that farming spread over most of sub-equatorial Africa. Four examples will illustrate the role of climate barriers along Africa's north/south long axis to that spread.

First, Mideastern and Mediterranean crops, such as the Egyptian staples of wheat and barley, require winter rains and seasonal variation in day length for their germination. Those crops were not able to spread south of the Sudan, beyond which they encountered summer rains and little or no seasonal variation in day length. Instead, the development of agriculture in the Sahara and sub-Sahara had to await the domestication of native plant species adapted to Central Africa's summer rains and relatively constant day length, such as sorghum and millet.

Second, and ironically, those same crops of Central Africa were unable to spread all the way south into the Mediterranean zone of South Africa, where once again winter rains and large seasonal variations in day length prevail! Instead, South Africa's Cape region required crops adapted to winter rains and seasonally varying day length, like the crops of the Mideast and Mediterranean. But those crops could not survive conditions in Central Africa and hence could not be transmitted overland through chains of farmers from the Mediterranean to the Cape. Instead, wheat and barley, oats and rye, and grapes reached the Cape only with European settlers in the seventeenth century. The Bantu advance southward halted in Natal, beyond which the zone of winter rainfall began. (That halt had notorious consequences for modern South African politics, because the Bantu were not occupying the Cape when Europeans arrived. The indigenous population of the Cape consisted of Khoisan peoples, otherwise known as Hottentots and Bushmen, who were wiped out by European infectious diseases and murder.) The Cape was not the only part of Africa where the native African crops of sorghum and millet proved unsuitable: they also did not thrive in wet tropical West Africa, where the staples instead became yams and other crops domesticated from native West African plants.

Third, tropical Asia was the source of many tropical crops highly suitable for tropical Africa. Some of those Asian crops, such as bananas and plantains, lacked African counterparts. Others, such as Asian yams and taro, did have African counterparts, but the Asian species were more productive or else thrived better in Africa's wet climate zones than did native African species. Tropical America also yielded crops suitable for tropical Africa, notably maize and cassava. Those tropical Asian and American crops now provide the staple foods of most of sub-equatorial and tropical West Africa, rather than African native crops themselves. But the Asian crops did not reach Africa until around or after A.D. 0, presumably with Arab and Indonesian seagoing traders across the Indian Ocean. The tropical American crops did not reach Africa until after the arrival of Europeans in the New World. Had the Indian Ocean and Atlantic Ocean been bridged by land similar to the broad expanse of Eurasia, these productive and suitable crops would have reached Africa thousands of years earlier, just as Asian crops and chickens reached Europe early.

A final example involves the expansion of the eastern Bantu from East Africa southward. That expansion awaited the Bantus' acquiring sorghum and finger millet and cattle in East Africa; their kit of wet tropical West African domesticates was insufficient to enable them to spread throughout drier southern Africa.

Just as in Eurasia and the Americas, the spread of domesticated plants and animals through Africa and the resulting buildup of human population densities and social and political organization were significant for the spread of technology. This fact is evident from the histories of writing, pottery, and metallurgy in sub-Saharan Africa. Although writing developed in Egypt by 3000 B.C. and had already reached Nubia by 850 B.C., it did not arise independently in the rest of Africa; it was brought in from the outside much later, by Arabs and Europeans. Second, pottery, like crops and domesticated animals, spread quickly through the northern half of Africa but then very slowly through sub-equatorial Africa. Pottery was recorded in the Sudan and Sahara around 6000 or 7000 B.C., from Ethiopia in the middle of the fifth millennium B.C., and from the fourth millennium B.C., in Ghana, but did not reach the Cape until around A.D. 0.

The history of metal in sub-Saharan Africa is more complex. It is clear that metallurgy was brought into most of sub-equatorial Africa from the outside, by the Bantu expansion around A.D. 0. However, it remains unclear whether metallurgy also reached sub-Saharan Africa solely from the outside or whether some developments were indigenous. In sub-equatorial Africa the first exploited metal was iron, which arrived very soon after iron was brought to Egypt and the rest of North Africa by the Phoenicians early in the first millennium B.C. Within a few centuries, iron technology is recorded in West Africa (Niger and Nigeria), very soon thereafter in the Lakes area of East Africa, and just after A.D. 0 throughout most of sub-equatorial Africa with the invading Bantu. Iron might similarly have reached tropical West Africa from the outside, spreading either from the Nile or across the Sahara from North Africa. However, bellows-driven furnaces to melt native copper were in use in Niger as early as 2000 B.C. It is therefore possible that that local technology evolved independently into copper smelting and then into iron smelting just before the arrival of iron from the north.

In short, domesticated plants and animals, which played a decisive role in the collision of the Americas and Eurasia, were doubly decisive in African history. Sub-equatorial Africa lacked domesticatable plants and animals; Africa just south of the Sahara had numerous domesticatable plants, but no such animals except for the guinea fowl. The north/south long axis made the spread of useful plant and animal species throughout Africa slow and difficult.

Those facts had two major consequences. The first result was that the indigenous Khoisan people of most of sub-equatorial Africa never developed or adopted agriculture, and they acquired livestock from the north late, just before most of them were overwhelmed by the far more numerous, better-armed Iron Age Bantus. We do not know whether diseases carried by the Bantus played a role in their replacement of Khoisan peoples over most of southern Africa, but we do know that European diseases contributed heavily to Khoisan decimation in South Africa. The second result was that the Bantus, though their ancestors domesticated some plants locally in tropical West Africa, acquired other valuable domestic plants and animals only later from the north. The resulting advantages of Europeans in maritime technology, weapons, tools, and writing permitted Europeans to colonize Africa, rather than Africans colonizing Europe. A consequence of that European colonization is the geographically and socioeconomically crazy boundaries of modern African states, which inherited those boundaries from colonial regimes and which now find those boundaries undermining their economies and political stability.

### Australia

As of 1492, Australia remained the sole continent inhabited only by hunter-gatherers. There were no farmers or herders, no political organization beyond the level of the tribe or band, no writing, and no manufacture of metal tools. This outcome of Australian history has clearly been conditioned by three features of Australian geography.

First, to this day, no native Australian plant or animal species has proved suitable for domestication, except that some plant species domesticated in New Guinea also occur (but were not domesticated) in a small area of tropical northeast Australia. Second, Australia had room for only a small population of hunter-gatherers. The continent's total area is about 3,000,000 square miles, compared to 9,400,000 for North America, and most of Australia's area is notoriously low in rainfall and productivity and can support only small human populations. As far as its ability to support hunter-gatherers is concerned, Australia is not a continent but only a medium-sized island, smaller even than New Guinea. The estimated total population of Aboriginal Australians at the time of European discovery was about 300,000.

Finally, Australia is not only small but effectively isolated, both by water barriers and by the contrasting habitats facing each other across those water barriers. Contact between Aboriginal Australia and outside humans, following Australia's sundering from New Guinea (formerly joined to the Australian continent) by rising sea level about 12,000 years ago, appears to have been confined to two areas in recent times. First, across Torres Straits from Australia's tropical Cape York Peninsula lies New Guinea, which developed or acquired the bow and arrow, agriculture, chickens, pigs, and pottery. None of those New Guinea features entered Australia. Although there was some trade along the island chain in Torres Straits, the influence of New Guineans on Australians was tenuous and did not diffuse beyond Cape York. Second, Indonesian fishermen seasonally visited northern and northwestern Australia, and some of their metal objects and other products have been found among coastal Australian peoples of those areas. However, that connection too was tenuous, may have begun only recently, and brought Indonesians to an arid and ecologically inhospitable part of Australia, unsuitable for developing agriculture even if the visiting Indonesians did carry domesticated plants and animals with them.

The resulting hunter-gatherer economy prevailing throughout Australia at the time of European discovery determined the outcome of the European/Australian confrontation. European colonists sent out on oceangoing ships by centralized political states, carrying firearms, infectious diseases to which Australians lacked resistance, metal tools, and crops and livestock, decimated Aboriginal Australians unintentionally and intentionally.

Can we, however, attribute the differences between Australian and Eurorasian history solely to Australia's inability to support the independent development of native agriculture and herding? If this were true, one might expect human development in Australia to have kept pace with the pace in Eurasia, until plant and animal domestication beginning around 10,000 years ago finally made more complex social and political organization and technological development possible in Eurasia. However, in some respects the technology and development of Native Australia as of 1492 was less advanced than that of Late Pleistocene Europe, long before crops and livestock reached Europe. For example, Late Pleistocene Europe possessed the bow and arrow, a much more diverse kit of specialized stone tools, and apparently more extensive and diverse jewelry and art than did Australia. This suggests the possibility that factors already operating on hunter-gatherers slowed the pace of development in Australia compared to Eurasia. For further evidence of this speculation, let us now turn to the contrast within the Australian region, between mainland Australia and the nearby island of Tasmania.

## Tasmania

Tasmania is an island of about 27,000 square miles, lying 130 miles south of the Australian mainland, in the temperate zone at the latitude of Chicago or Vladivostok. When discovered by Europeans in 1642, Tasmania was occupied by 4,000 people physically rather similar to mainland Australians, but with the simplest technology of any recent peoples on earth. Tasmanian technology was considerably simpler than that of the Aboriginal Australians on the opposite mainland of Australia, with which Tasmania had been connected at Late Pleistocene times of low sea level until the land bridge was severed around 12,000 years ago.

Features of mainland Australian culture absent in Aboriginal Tasmania include the following. Tasmanians were unable to light a fire *de novo*; if a family's fire went out, they had to rekindle it from the fire of another family. Tasmanian weapons were restricted to a hand-held spear and club; lacking were the spear-thrower, boomerang, and shields of mainland Australia. Tasmanian tools were made solely of stone and wood, without the bone tools of mainland Australia. Those stone tools were very simple and consisted just of scrapers without ground edges, in contrast to the much more diverse and specialized stone tools of the opposite Australian mainland. With only those scrapers, Tasmanians were unable to fell a tree or hollow out a canoe. Those Tasmanian scrapers were one-piece unhafted tools, unlike the compound or hafted axes and adzes of mainland Australia. Since the Tasmanians lacked sewing, they were unable to sew bark canoes or compound clothing, and their clothing consisted only of single-piece capes thrown over the shoulder. The Tasmanian lacked nets, traps, and ropes. Instead of canoes, which they could not hollow out or sew, their watercraft consisted solely of rafts capable of remaining afloat for only about ten miles, thereby preventing Tasmanians from exploiting the resources of islands lying further offshore. Despite living mostly on the seacoast, the Tasmanians did not catch fish.

One cannot reasonably argue that all of those cultural inventions would have been unhelpful and that the Tasmanians had a material culture perfectly adequate to their needs. For humans anywhere in the world, it is convenient to be able to light a fire oneself, and a bow or spear-thrower can discharge a projectile further and with greater force than can a hand-held spear. Nets and traps are useful to any hunter of small game. Despite Tasmania's cold wet winters, the Tasmanians lacked warm clothes, techniques of food storage, and substantial winter houses that would have increased their comfort and protected them against respiratory diseases. Fish have been found a useful source of protein by practically all other peoples living on the seacoast. How did these extraordinary deficits in Tasmanian material culture arise?

We know that Tasmania was occupied by people long before the land bridge connecting Tasmania to southern Australia was severed 12,000 years ago. That is, although Tasmania is now an island, people walked to Tasmania tens of thousands of years ago. Once that land bridge was severed, however, there was absolutely no further contact between the peoples of Tasmania and mainland Australia for 12,000 years, because both peoples lacked watercraft capable of crossing the intervening water barrier of 130 miles and because the islands in those straits were uninhabited. The Tasmanians thus lived in their own isolated universe for 12,000 years, until Europeans began to settle their island around 1800 and exterminated them within a few decades. Tasmanian history is a story of human isolation unprecedented — except in science fiction.

From Tasmania's lack of many material objects present on the opposite Australian mainland, we can surely conclude that Tasmanians did not independently invent those objects if they were invented in Australia. (Perhaps some of those objects entered mainland Australia from New Guinea or Indonesia following the isolation of Australia and were not invented by either Tasmanians or Australians.) Astonishingly, the archaeological record reveals that Tasmanians also *abandoned* some cultural practices that they brought with them from Australia and that persisted on the Australian mainland. Those losses include bone tools and the practice of fishing, both of which disappeared from Tasmania around 1500 B.C. Bone tools were initially present in Tasmania as spatulas, awls, and needles, which might have been used to sew warmer clothes than those used by Tasmanians as of 1642. Fish had formerly constituted about 20% of the meat intake of Tasmanians and could have been smoked to provide a winter food supply.

Nevertheless, fishing was abandoned, even though the same fish species that Tasmanians used to catch still occur and are easily caught in Tasmanian coastal waters.

What sense can we make of these losses? Just as some anthropologists have tried to argue that Tasmania's very simple material culture in other respects was adequate, they have also tried to argue that bone tools and fishing were not useful to Tasmanians, or even that Tasmanians were better off not fishing. These rationalizations seem to me to defy common sense. Instead, the question should be phrased why Tasmania lost these practices *despite* their obvious utility.

An interpretation developed by Australian archaeologist Rhys Jones goes as follows. All human societies experience fads, in which they temporarily either adopt practices of little use or else abandon useful practices. For example, peoples on various Pacific islands have temporarily decided to taboo or dispense with pigs, even though pigs were their sole edible land mammal other than dogs and rats! There are several instances of people killing off all the pigs on their island, only eventually to realize that pigs were useful after all and to import a new breeding stock of pigs from other islands. Similarly, ancestral Polynesians made pottery, but derived Polynesian society abandoned the making of pottery, a loss or taboo for which no one has been able to suggest a reasonable economic motive.

Whenever such senseless taboos or losses arise in an area with many competing human societies, only some societies will adopt the taboo at a given time. Other societies will retain the useful practice and will either outcompete the societies that lost it or else will be there as a model or source for the societies with the taboos to repent their error and reacquire the practice. Had Tasmanians remained in contact with mainland Australians, they could have relearned the skill of fishing or making bone tools, or alternatively they might have been outcompeted and replaced by tribes retaining these useful arts. But that could not happen in Tasmania, with only 4,000 people divided among nine tribes. Under those circumstances, the cultural losses were more likely to be irreversible.

Such cultural losses in isolation were not unique to Tasmania. The Chatham Islands, lying in sub-Antarctic waters several hundred miles east of New Zealand, were settled about a thousand years ago by New Zealand Maori who had to abandon farming, became hunter-gatherers, and gave rise to an isolated society of 2,000 people. Over the eight centuries between founding and European discovery, the Chatham Islanders also underwent a simplification of material culture and restricted their useful variety of fishhooks, bird spears, polished adzes, and ornaments. A possible second example is that the rising seas that isolated Tasmania from Australia simultaneously isolated two other islands or island groups lying between Tasmania and Australia, Flinders and King. Each of these islands was large enough to hold only a few hundred hunter-gatherers. Stone tools discovered by archaeologists show that both Flinders and King formerly supported human populations, but it is unknown how long these populations survived the rising sea levels that isolated them. Perhaps a few hundred hunter-gatherers are too few to maintain human society indefinitely in total isolation, with the result that these populations of Flinders and King died out. Finally, there are about a dozen cases of former Polynesian populations disappearing on very small, isolated Polynesian islands, of which Pitcairn is best known because of its rediscovery by the *Bounty* mutineers many centuries after the disappearance of Pitcairn's former population. Again, the populations of these so-called mystery islands of Polynesia may just have been too small to survive indefinitely in isolation.

Thus, the most likely message of the differences between Tasmania and mainland Australia is that, all other things being equal, the rate of human development is faster, and the rate of loss slower, in areas occupied by many competing societies with many individuals. If it is valid to draw this conclusion for the comparison of 4,000 Tasmanians with 300,000 mainland Australians, perhaps the same principle also contributed to the differences between Australia's hunter-gatherers and those of much larger Eurasia, or between the farmers of sub-Saharan Africa, the much larger Americas, and the still larger Eurasia.

## Conclusion

As for the overall meaning of this whirlwind tour through human history, it is that our history has been molded by our environment. The broadest pattern of human history — namely, the differences between human societies on different continents — seems to me to be explicable in terms of differences in continental environments. In particular, the availability of wild plant and animal species suitable for domestication and the ease with which those species could spread without encountering unsuitable climates have contributed decisively to the varying rates of rise of agriculture and herding. Agriculture and herding in turn have contributed decisively to human population numbers, population densities, and food surpluses, and hence to development of human society and politics. In addition, the story of Tasmania and other isolated societies gives us a hint that the number of competing societies itself may have been a factor in human development.

As a biologist usually at home in laboratory experimental science, I am acutely aware that these interpretations can be dismissed as unprovable speculation. The same objection can be raised against any historical interpretation. That is the reason why we are uncomfortable about considering history a science — it is classified as a social science, which is not considered quite scientific.

Nevertheless, remember that the word "science" is not derived from the Latin word for "experiment" but from the Latin word for "knowledge." In science, we seek knowledge and understanding by whatever means are available. There are many fields which no one hesitates to consider sciences, even though we cannot do experiments — fields such as astronomy, paleontology, and much of geology and evolutionary biology. We cannot manipulate stars, start and stop ice ages, or play with evolving dinosaurs, but we can still gain considerable insight into these basically historical fields by other means. We surely ought, then, to be able to understand human history, since introspection gives us more insight into the ways of past humans than of dinosaurs. For that reason I am optimistic that we really can eventually arrive at convincing explanations for the broadest pattern of human history.

# THE TANNER LECTURERS

## 1976-77

| | |
|---|---|
| OXFORD | Bernard Williams, Cambridge University |
| MICHIGAN | Joel Feinberg, University of Arizona<br>*"Voluntary Euthanasia and the Inalienable Right to Life"* |
| STANFORD | Joel Feinberg, University of Arizona<br>*"Voluntary Euthanasia and the Inalienable Right to Life"* |

## 1977-78

| | |
|---|---|
| OXFORD | John Rawls, Harvard University |
| MICHIGAN | Sir Karl Popper, University of London<br>*"Three Worlds"* |
| STANFORD | Thomas Nagel, Princeton University |

## 1978-79

| | |
|---|---|
| OXFORD | Thomas Nagel, Princeton University<br>*"The Limits of Objectivity"* |
| CAMBRIDGE | C. C. O'Brien, London |
| MICHIGAN | Edward O. Wilson, Harvard University<br>*"Comparative Social Theory"* |
| STANFORD | Amartya Sen, Oxford University<br>*"Equality of What?"* |
| UTAH | Lord Ashby, Cambridge University<br>*"The Search for an Environmental Ethic"* |
| UTAH STATE | R. M. Hare, Oxford University<br>*"Moral Conflicts"* |

## 1979-80

| | |
|---|---|
| OXFORD | Jonathan Bennett, University of British Columbia<br>*"Morality and Consequences"* |
| CAMBRIDGE | Raymond Aron, Collège de France<br>*"Arms Control and Peace Research"* |
| HARVARD | George Stigler, University of Chicago<br>*"Economics or Ethics?"* |

| | |
|---|---|
| MICHIGAN | Robert Coles, Harvard University<br>*"Children as Moral Observers"* |
| STANFORD | Michel Foucault, Collège de France<br>*"Omnes et Singulatim: Towards a Criticism of 'Political Reason' "* |
| UTAH | Wallace Stegner, Los Altos Hills, California<br>*"The Twilight of Self-Reliance: Frontier Values and Contemporary America"* |

## 1980–81

| | |
|---|---|
| OXFORD | Saul Bellow, University of Chicago<br>*"A Writer from Chicago"* |
| CAMBRIDGE | John Passmore, Australian National University<br>*"The Representative Arts as a Source of Truth"* |
| HARVARD | Brian M. Barry, University of Chicago<br>*"Do Countries Have Moral Obligations? The Case of World Poverty"* |
| MICHIGAN | John Rawls, Harvard University<br>*"The Basic Liberties and Their Priority"* |
| STANFORD | Charles Fried, Harvard University<br>*"Is Liberty Possible?"* |
| UTAH | Joan Robinson, Cambridge University<br>*"The Arms Race"* |
| HEBREW UNIV. | Solomon H. Snyder, Johns Hopkins University<br>*"Drugs and the Brain and Society"* |

## 1981–82

| | |
|---|---|
| OXFORD | Freeman Dyson, Princeton University<br>*"Bombs and Poetry"* |
| CAMBRIDGE | Kingman Brewster, President Emeritus, Yale University<br>*"The Voluntary Society"* |
| HARVARD | Murray Gell-Mann, California Institute of Technology<br>*"The Head and the Heart in Policy Studies"* |
| MICHIGAN | Thomas C. Schelling, Harvard University<br>*"Ethics, Law, and the Exercise of Self-Command"* |
| STANFORD | Alan A. Stone, Harvard University<br>*"Psychiatry and Morality"* |

| | |
|---|---|
| UTAH | R. C. Lewontin, Harvard University<br>*"Biological Determinism"* |
| AUSTRALIAN<br>NATL. UNIV. | Leszek Kolakowski, Oxford University<br>*"The Death of Utopia Reconsidered"* |

## 1982–83

| | |
|---|---|
| OXFORD | Kenneth J. Arrow, Stanford University<br>*"The Welfare-Relevant Boundaries of the Individual"* |
| CAMBRIDGE | H. C. Robbins Landon, University College, Cardiff<br>*"Haydn and Eighteenth-Century Patronage<br>in Austria and Hungary"* |
| HARVARD | Bernard Williams, Cambridge University<br>*"Morality and Social Justice"* |
| STANFORD | David Gauthier, University of Pittsburgh<br>*"The Incompleat Egoist"* |
| UTAH | Carlos Fuentes, Princeton University<br>*"A Writer from Mexico"* |
| JAWAHARLAL<br>NEHRU UNIV. | Ilya Prigogine, Université Libre de Bruxelles<br>*"Only an Illusion"* |

## 1983–84

| | |
|---|---|
| OXFORD | Donald D. Brown, Johns Hopkins University<br>*"The Impact of Modern Genetics"* |
| CAMBRIDGE | Stephen J. Gould, Harvard University<br>*"Evolutionary Hopes and Realities"* |
| MICHIGAN | Herbert A. Simon, Carnegie-Mellon University<br>*"Scientific Literacy as a Goal in a High-Technology<br>Society"* |
| STANFORD | Leonard B. Meyer, University of Pennsylvania<br>*"Music and Ideology in the Nineteenth Century"* |
| UTAH | Helmut Schmidt, former Chancellor, West Germany<br>*"The Future of the Atlantic Alliance"* |
| HELSINKI | Georg Henrik von Wright, Helsinki<br>*"Of Human Freedom"* |

## 1984-85

| | |
|---|---|
| OXFORD | Barrington Moore, Jr., Harvard University<br>*"Authority and Inequality under Capitalism and Socialism"* |
| CAMBRIDGE | Amartya Sen, Oxford University<br>*"The Standard of Living"* |
| HARVARD | Quentin Skinner, Cambridge University<br>*"The Paradoxes of Political Liberty"* |
| | Kenneth J. Arrow, Stanford University<br>*"The Unknown Other"* |
| MICHIGAN | Nadine Gordimer, South Africa<br>*"The Essential Gesture: Writers and Responsibility"* |
| STANFORD | Michael Slote, University of Maryland<br>*"Moderation, Rationality, and Virtue"* |

## 1985-86

| | |
|---|---|
| OXFORD | Thomas M. Scanlon, Jr., Harvard University<br>*"The Significance of Choice"* |
| CAMBRIDGE | Aldo Van Eyck, The Netherlands<br>*"Architecture and Human Values"* |
| HARVARD | Michael Walzer, Institute for Advanced Study<br>*"Interpretation and Social Criticism"* |
| MICHIGAN | Clifford Geertz, Institute for Advanced Study<br>*"The Uses of Diversity"* |
| STANFORD | Stanley Cavell, Harvard University<br>*"The Uncanniness of the Ordinary"* |
| UTAH | Arnold S. Relman, Editor, *New England Journal of Medicine*<br>*"Medicine as a Profession and a Business"* |

## 1986-87

| | |
|---|---|
| OXFORD | Jon Elster, Oslo University and the University of Chicago<br>*"Taming Chance: Randomization in Individual and Social Decisions"* |

| | |
|---|---|
| CAMBRIDGE | Roger Bulger, University of Texas Health Sciences Center, Houston<br>"*On Hippocrates, Thomas Jefferson, and Max Weber: The Bureaucratic, Technologic Imperatives and the Future of the Healing Tradition in a Voluntary Society*" |
| HARVARD | Jürgen Habermas, University of Frankfurt<br>"*Law and Morality*" |
| MICHIGAN | Daniel C. Dennett, Tufts University<br>"*The Moral First Aid Manual*" |
| STANFORD | Gisela Striker, Columbia University<br>"*Greek Ethics and Moral Theory*" |
| UTAH | Laurence H. Tribe, Harvard University<br>"*On Reading the Constitution*" |

## 1987–88

| | |
|---|---|
| OXFORD | F. Van Zyl Slabbert, University of the Witwatersrand, South Africa<br>"*The Dynamics of Reform and Revolt in Current South Africa*" |
| CAMBRIDGE | Louis Blom-Cooper, Q.C., London<br>"*The Penalty of Imprisonment*" |
| HARVARD | Robert A. Dahl, Yale University<br>"*The Pseudodemocratization of the American Presidency*" |
| MICHIGAN | Albert O. Hirschman, Institute for Advanced Study<br>"*Two Hundred Years of Reactionary Rhetoric: The Case of the Perverse Effect*" |
| STANFORD | Ronald Dworkin, New York University and University College, Oxford<br>"*Foundations of Liberal Equality*" |
| UTAH | Joseph Brodsky, Russian poet, Mount Holyoke College<br>"*A Place as Good as Any*" |
| CALIFORNIA | Wm. Theodore de Bary, Columbia University<br>"*The Trouble with Confucianism*" |
| BUENOS AIRES | Barry Stroud, University of California, Berkeley<br>"*The Study of Human Nature and the Subjectivity of Value*" |

| | |
|---|---|
| MADRID | Javier Muguerza, Universidad Nacional de Educación a Distancia, Madrid<br>*"The Alternative of Dissent"* |
| WARSAW | Anthony Quinton, British Library, London<br>*"The Varieties of Value"* |

## 1988-89

| | |
|---|---|
| OXFORD | Michael Walzer, Institute for Advanced Study<br>*"Nation and Universe"* |
| CAMBRIDGE | Albert Hourani, Emeritus Fellow, St. Antony's College, and Magdalen College, Oxford<br>*"Islam in European Thought"* |
| MICHIGAN | Toni Morrison, State University of New York at Albany<br>*"Unspeakable Things Unspoken: The Afro-American Presence in American Literature"* |
| STANFORD | Stephen Jay Gould, Harvard University<br>*"Unpredictability in the History of Life"*<br>*"The Quest for Human Nature: Fortuitous Side, Consequences, and Contingent History"* |
| UTAH | Judith Shklar, Harvard University<br>*"American Citizenship: The Quest for Inclusion"* |
| CALIFORNIA | S. N. Eisenstadt, The Hebrew University of Jerusalem<br>*"Cultural Tradition, Historical Experience, and Social Change: The Limits of Convergence"* |
| YALE | J. G. A. Pocock, Johns Hopkins University<br>*"Edward Gibbon in History: Aspects of the Text in The History of the Decline and Fall of the Roman Empire"* |
| CHINESE UNIVERSITY OF HONG KONG | Fei Xiaotong, Peking University<br>*"Plurality and Unity in the Configuration of the Chinese People"* |

## 1989-90

| | |
|---|---|
| OXFORD | Bernard Lewis, Princeton University<br>*"Europe and Islam"* |

| | |
|---|---|
| CAMBRIDGE | Umberto Eco, University of Bologna<br>*"Interpretation and Overinterpretation:<br>World, History, Texts"* |
| HARVARD | Ernest Gellner, Kings College, Cambridge<br>*"The Civil and the Sacred"* |
| MICHIGAN | Carol Gilligan, Harvard University<br>*"Joining the Resistance: Psychology, Politics, Girls, and Women"* |
| UTAH | Octavio Paz, Mexico City<br>*"Poetry and Modernity"* |
| YALE | Edward N. Luttwak, Center for Strategic and International Studies<br>*"Strategy: A New Era?"* |
| PRINCETON | Irving Howe, writer and critic<br>*"The Self and the State"* |

## 1990–91

| | |
|---|---|
| OXFORD | David Montgomery, Yale University<br>*"Citizenship and Justice in the Lives and Thoughts of Nineteenth-Century American Workers"* |
| CAMBRIDGE | Gro Harlem Brundtland, Prime Minister of Norway<br>*"Environmental Challenges of the 1990s:<br>Our Responsibility toward Future Generations"* |
| HARVARD | William Gass, Washington University<br>*"Eye and Idea"* |
| MICHIGAN | Richard Rorty, University of Virginia<br>*"Feminism and Pragmatism"* |
| STANFORD | G. A. Cohen, All Souls College, Oxford<br>*"Incentives, Inequality, and Community"*<br>János Kornai, University of Budapest and Harvard University<br>*"Market Socialism Revisited"* |
| UTAH | Marcel Ophuls, international film maker<br>*"Resistance and Collaboration in Peacetime"* |

| | |
|---|---|
| YALE | Robertson Davies, novelist<br>*"Reading and Writing"* |
| PRINCETON | Annette C. Baier, Pittsburgh University<br>*"Trust"* |
| LENINGRAD | János Kornai, University of Budapest and Harvard University<br>*"Transition from Marxism to a Free Economy"* |

## 1991–92

| | |
|---|---|
| OXFORD | R. Z. Sagdeev, University of Maryland<br>*"Science and Revolutions"* |
| CALIFORNIA | |
| LOS ANGELES | Václav Havel, former President, Republic of Czechoslovakia<br>(Untitled lecture) |
| BERKELEY | Helmut Kohl, Chancellor of Germany<br>(Untitled lecture) |
| CAMBRIDGE | David Baltimore, former President of Rockefeller University<br>*"On Doing Science in the Modern World"* |
| MICHIGAN | Christopher Hill, seventeenth-century historian, Oxford<br>*"The Bible in Seventeenth-Century English Politics"* |
| STANFORD | Charles Taylor, Professor of Philosophy and Political Science, McGill University<br>*"Modernity and the Rise of the Public Sphere"* |
| UTAH | Jared Diamond, University of California, Los Angeles<br>*"The Broadest Pattern of Human History"* |
| PRINCETON | Robert Nozick, Professor of Philosophy, Harvard University<br>*"Decisions of Principle, Principles of Decision"* |

# INDEX TO VOLUME 14, 1993

## THE TANNER LECTURES ON HUMAN VALUES

Abel, 97, 98

Aborigines, Australian, 374–75; conquest of, 383–84; decimation of, by epidemics, 366; isolation of, 383; population size of, 383

abortion counseling, as protected speech, 297

*Absalom and Achitophel* (Dryden), 102

acquired immune deficiency syndrome. *See* AIDS

acultural theory of modernity: defects of, 208–10, 213–20; definition of, 205; dominance of, 208, 210–13; emphasis of, on growth of reason, 205, 206–7, 253; emphasis on social change, 205–6, 207, 211, 213, 253–54; ethnocentrism of, 255–56, 258; negative theories of modernity and, 207–8; on process of "coming to see" the truth, 254–55, 256, 258–59; on tensions of modernity, 260

Adam (first man), 87, 97, 104

Adenauer, Konrad, 71, 75

aesthetic, the, recognition of, 252

affections, binding of behavior by, 126

Africa: colonization of, 366, 367, 377–78, 379–80, 382; disease in, 366; extent of animal and plant domestication in, 372, 376; patterns of conquest within, 376–77, 379, 380, 381, 382; revolutionizing of warfare in, 365; spread of agriculture in, 374, 376, 379–80; spread of domesticated animals in, 377–79; spread of technology in, 381; variety of human societies in, 353, 355, 356

*The Age of Diminished Expectations* (Krugman), 281

aging, basic knowledge of, 299

agriculture: abandonment of, 388; and development of infectious diseases, 369, 371; displacement of hunter-gatherers by, 374–75, 376; and environmental destruction, 111; geographic factors affecting, 358; impact of plant and animal domestication on, 374; indifference of peasants to reform of, 319; Polynesian, variations in, 357; science of, 329; and sociopolitical organization, 375

AIDS: discovery of, 264; intellectual honesty about, 299; as political issue, 264; research on, 276; targeted research on, 279–80, 283, 299

Ainslie, George, 133, 135, 137, 144

Albania, 74

alehouses, biblical motifs in, 89–90

Algiers, 93

Allais paradox, 162

Almond, Gabriel, 254n, 255n

American Indians, 91, 104; disappearance of, 360; diseases of, 369; domesticated animals and plants of, 372; technology of warfare of, 365

American Revolution, 328

Americas, the: European colonization of, 360–68, 375; extent of animal and plant domestication in, 371–73; revolutionizing of warfare in, 365; scarcity of infectious diseases in, 369, 371; as source of African domesticated plants, 380; variety of human societies in, 353, 355, 356

*Anarchy, State, and Utopia* (Nozick), 159, 162n

Anderson, Benedict, 239, 240, 245

Andes region, 353, 373

[ 399 ]

animal domestication, 353, 356, 357; and development of infectious diseases, 369, 371; extent of, in New World vs. Old World, 371–73; and patterns of conquest, 376, 377–78, 381–82; and population density, 374, 380–81; preconditions for, 371; scarcity of, as factor in persistence of hunter-gatherers, 374, 382–83, 384; and sociopolitical organization, 374–75, 380–81, 384; spread of, in Africa, 377–79; taboos against, 387; transformation of warfare by, 364–65

animal rights movement, 271

animals, scientific research with, 296

*Annus Mirabilis* (Dryden), 93

Antarctica, 357

antiabortion movement, 271

Antichrist, overthrow of, 91–93

*Anti-Equilibrium* (Kornai), 29

anti-intellectualism, 298, 342–43

Anuta, 359

Apple computers, 31

Arabs, and Africa, 367, 380, 381

archaeology, snapshots of human societies, 353

Arctic, the, 353

*Areopagitica* (Milton), 100

*Argo* (ship), 366

arms control, 314–16, 335

Arnold, Matthew, 208–9

Artsimovich, Lev, 335

Asia: revolutionizing of warfare in, 365; as source of African domesticated plants, 380; variety of human societies in, 353. *See also* Eurasia

Asilomar conference (1975), 272, 282

Astell, Mary, 104, 106, 107

asymmetrical response doctrine, 315

Atahuallpa (Incan emperor), 355–56, 360, 362, 363–64, 365, 366, 367, 368

atheism, intolerance for, 105

Athens, ancient, 234

Atlantic Alliance, 76, 77

atomic bomb, 275, 276–77, 331–34

auctions, value of outcomes in, 191n.79, 198

audits, credibility of, 129n

Auerbach, Eric, 239

Australia: comparisons in material culture of, with Tasmania, 384–85, 386, 388–89; contact of Tasmania with, 386, 387–88; epidemics in, 366; European colonization of, 366, 383–84; extent of plant and animal domestication in, 372, 382–83; and human social variation, 353, 355, 356; isolation of, 383; persistence of hunter-gatherers in, 382–84

Austrian economics, 27n, 28

Authorized Version of the Bible, 88–89

*Azariah and Hushai* (Pordage), 102

Aztec Empire, 353, 364, 365, 367–68

Bacon, Francis, 323

Bale, John, 101

Baltic states: emancipation of, 78–79; and German reconstruction, 74; incorporation of, into Soviet Union, 310; privatization in, 318

Bantu, the, 374, 376–77, 378, 379–80, 381, 382

Barone, E., 4

Battle of Waterloo, 355

behavior: binding by contract, 127; binding by principles, 126–30; binding by prospect of punishment, 128–29; motiveless, 182n; observability of principles, 129; symbolic, 150–63

belief: misattribution of cultural changes to, 219–20; modernity as loss of, 208–10, 214–15, 253–54, 255; relationship of, to secularity, 246–47; unformulated understandings behind, 215–20, 255

Benjamin, Walter, 240n

Beria, Levrenti, 331, 332, 333

Bering Straits, 360

Bernoulli, Daniel, 340

Bhopal chemical disaster, 298

Bible, the: authorized interpretation of, 88–89; Chosen People of, 91; end of authority of, 105–7; English translations of, 87–89; and household religion, 89; infallibility of, questioned,

99–101; as inspiration for radicals, 87, 94–95, 106; and liberation of the uneducated, 96, 97; literary importance of, 101–3; millennialism of, 91–95; omnipresence of, 89–90; popular lectures on, 89; prohibition on translation of, 87; reinforcement of status quo by, 103–5; reinterpretation of myths of, 97–99; as source of political wisdom, 90; struggle against idolatry in, 95; temporal sense of, 239–40; view of monarchy in, 90–91, 94–95

Big Bang, 322

Bill of Rights, 292–93, 297

biology, molecular: contributions of, to medicine, 277–78; expectations of researchers in, 278; fabrication of data in, 289–90; infancy of, 275–76; maturity of, 276, 277

biomedical science: areas in, for basic research, 299; control of policy in, 265–66; dedication to goals in, 276–77, 278; education of public about, 271; and freedom of speech, 296; government funding of, 265–66; as political issue, 264; private funding of research in, 304; projects for targeted research in, 278–80; promises of, 299; public discontent with, 273, 280–81, 282; regulation of research in, by scientific community, 271–73; relocation of research efforts in, 264; repetition of experiments in, 286; responsiveness of, to social needs, 298–99; selection of research problems in, 275–77; setting research priorities in, 300–301

biotechnical industry: contributions to medicine, 277–78; development of products for market, 278–79

Bismarck Archipelago, 356

Blake, Adm. Robert, 93

Boadicea, 103

Bohr, Niels, 315–16, 323

Bolshevik Revolution: conditions for success of, 309–10; seizure of power by, 309; as successor to tsarism, 326. *See also* Communist (part(y)(ies) (Soviet and Eastern European)

bone tool technology, 385, 386, 387

Book of Homilies, 95

*Book of Martyrs* (Foxe), 88

Book of Psalms, 102

*Bounty* (ship), 388

Bourdieu, Pierre, 217, 218

bourgeoisie, the: the revolutionary class, 319; subservience of intelligentsia to, 326

*Brave New World* (Huxley), 324

breast implants, 302–3

Brezhnev, Leonid, 44, 314, 334, 347

Brute, Lady (Vanbrugh's character), 106

Bryusov, Valery, 334

Bucharest, Romania, 244

Buddhism, 182n

budget constraints: hard, 20, 21, 22–23; soft, 20, 21n, 23, 46–47

budget deficit: elimination of, 55–56; of market-socialist economies, 10, 11, 47

buffalo, hunting of, 365

Bulgaria, 74

Bunin, Ivan, 328

Bunyan, John, 89, 97

bureaucracy: capitalist, 30, 31; limitations on, 16–17

Burke, Edmund, 230n.15, 231

Bush, George, 71, 72, 316

Bush, Vannevar, 265, 266–67, 270, 282, 291

Bushmen, 374, 380

Cade, Jack (Shakespeare's character), 87

Cain, 97

Cajamarca, Peru, siege of, 355–56, 360–68

California, 72–73

Calvinism, 177

Cameroon, 376

Canada, 77, 360

cancer: basic knowledge of, 277, 299; control over research into, 266; intellectual honesty about, 299; targeted research on, 280, 283

Cape of Good Hope, 377, 379–80, 381

Cape York Peninsula, 383
capitalism: as alternative of socialism, 50; assignment of property rights under, 19–20; bureaucracy vs. entrepreneurship in, 30–31; combining of, with socialism, 26–27, 45; competition of socialism with, 316–17, 325; entry-exit rules of, 22–23; evolution of, 49; Marxist view of, 25–26; relations of market-socialist economies with, 8; selection of, through democratic elections, 34–35; separation of ownership and control under, 17–18; social discipline under, 21; trade imbalance with, for market-socialist economies, 10. *See also* free economy, transition from socialism to
Carnap, Rudolf, 179&n
caste system, Hawaiian, 357
Catholic Church: concept of good life by, 249; identification of, with idolatry, 95; intolerance for, 105; overthrow of, as Antichrist, 91–93
causal decision theory, 172n.58, 173; on choice between dominant and cooperative actions, 186–87, 188–89, 193–94, 195; differentiation of relations in, 197–200; evidential, symbolic, and linguistic categories of utility and, 181, 182–83; maximization of conditionally expected utility under, 175–80, 181
causation, connection of actions to outcomes by, 151–52
Ceausescu, Nicolae, 44
certainty effect, 162
c-function (decision theory), 179
Chain of Being, 209, 235, 236, 238, 241, 248
Chalcuchima (Incan general), 367, 368
*Challenger* space shuttle, 112
chaos, vs. order, 323
chariot, transformation of warfare by, 365
Charles I (king of England), 92–95
Charles II (king of England), 95, 101
Charter of Paris, 80
Chatham Islands, 356, 357, 358, 388

chemical weapons, 341
chemistry, ideological debate over, 329
Chernobyl nuclear accident, 275, 298, 337, 342
China, 3, 37, 373; appearance of market socialism in, 5; performance of market socialism in, 10; revolutionizing of warfare in, 365
Chiron Corporation, 279
choice. *See* decision making
Chosen People: campaign of, against Antichrist, 92–93; conquests of, 91; disappointment of millennialist hopes of, 93–94; economic interests of, 93; idolatry of, 95
Christendom: temporal sense of, 239–40, 241; transition to modernity from, 210. *See also* Bible, the; Catholic Church; church, the; Protestant Reformation; Puritanism
Chrysler Corp., 18
church, the: concept of good life by, 249; diffusion of doctrine by, 225; extrapolitical status of, 235; recognition of private realm as distinct from, 250; time dimension of, 241; as type of common space, 229. *See also* Bible, the; Catholic Church; Christendom; Protestant Reformation; Puritanism
Church of England, 88–89, 106
Churchill, Winston, 50, 75, 315–16
Clarkson, Thomas, 97
Claudius (Shakespeare's character), 103
climate: adaptation of domesticated animals to, 378–79; and development of wild animal and plant species, 372–73; engineering of, 342; and spread of domesticated plants, 379–80
clothing, and technological primitivism, 385
Club of Voters of the Academy of Science, 344
Cold War, 313, 335
colonialism. *See* conquest
Columbus, Christopher, 104
commitment, personal, 144–46
Commonwealth of Independent States, 312–13, 328, 339, 342

Communism: arrogance toward environment, 111–12, 113–14; bribing of society, 113; legacy in Germany, 71–72, 74. See also Marxism; socialism; socialism, classical

Communist part(y)(ies) (Soviet and Eastern European): banning of, 78, 312; end of monopoly of, 312; loyalty of intelligentsia to, 325, 329; objectives of leadership of, 14–15; political monopoly of, 6–7, 13, 15, 24, 26, 321, 336; political reform of, 311, 312, 334–36; public opinion about, 343; replacement of, with multiparty system, 336; science as servant of, 325; and space exploration, 347, 348

community: nation as, 245; romantic visions of, 48

competition: in development of human societies, 387–88, 388–89; entry-exit rules and, 22–23

compromise, resolution of conflict through, 165

conflict: methods of resolving, 165; and social order, 233; symbolic meanings in, 157–58. See also conquest

Congress, U.S.: attention of, to scientific fraud, 290–91; control in, over biomedical research, 266; exertion of political influence on, 271; scientific funding by, 265–69; and self-regulation of scientific community, 273

Congress of all Russian Soviets, 331

Congress of People's Deputies, 312, 314, 324, 335–36, 344

conquest: availability of domesticatable plant and animal species as factor in, 376–77, 377–78, 379–80, 381–82; as biblical theme, 91, 99; development of metallurgy as factor in, 375, 376, 381; of hunter-gatherers, 383–84; political organization behind, 367; population density as factor in, 374–75; role of disease in, 365–66, 380, 382; and social specialization, 375; and strategic miscalculations of the defeated, 367–68; superiority of information in, 367, 368; technology of, 364–65, 366–67

Constitution, Soviet (1989), 335–36

consumption, contraction under market socialism, 10

contracts: binding of behavior by, 127; between firm managers and state, 13–14, 15, 16, 17–19, 23. See also social contract

*Contrat social* (Rousseau), 252

cooperation, choice of, over dominant action, 183–97

coordination games theory, 149n

Cope, David, 173n.61

Coppe, Abiezer, 100

copper tool technology, 353, 355, 381

Cortes, Hernando, 364, 367–68

Council of Ministers, Soviet, 343

credit: controls on, 56; stimulation of private sector through, 63. See also budget constraints

Cromwell, Oliver, 93, 94, 95

Cuitlahuac (Aztec emperor), 366

cultural exchange, 77

cultural theory of modernity: definition of, 205; perspective offered by, 247; pluralism of, 210–11; on tensions of modernity, 260; understanding of transition in, 259

culture(s): convergence of, 214–15, 253; inevitability of changes in, 213, 214; Polynesian, variations in, 358; recognition of changes in, 213–14; scientific, vs. humanistic, 295; secularization of, 254n; transformation of (*see* acultural theory of modernity; cultural theory of modernity); variety of, 214, 215. See also human societies

currency: convertibility of, 57–58; devaluation of, 56–57

Cuvier, Georges, 326

Cuzco, Peru, 364

czarism. See tsarism

Czechoslovakia: association of, with European Community, 76; environmental destruction in, 111, 113–14; and German reconstruction, 74; postsocialist transition in, 11; privatization in, 64

*Das Kapital* (Marx), 25

data, experimental: fabrication of, 288–90; problems in selection of, 291–92; professional judgment of, 293–94

David, King, 98

debt, principles in assumption of, 127n.13. See also budget deficit; trade deficit

decentralization: in economic decision making, 7–8; private ownership as precondition for, 19

decision making: causal probabilities in, 173; choice between dominant and cooperative actions in, 183–97; conditional probabilities in, 170–81, 186, 188–89, 194–95, 196; differentiation of causal influences in, 197–200; domains of utility in, 181–83; economic, under market socialism, 7–8; principled (see principles); scientific argument in, 303–4; sunk costs as influence on, 144–50; symbolism as determinant of, 150–63, 180–81, 200–202

deficit: budget, 10, 11, 47, 55–56; trade, 10, 11

Defoe, Daniel, 103

Dell, William, 97

democracy: dissent against, 324; enlargement of, in U.S., 270–71; modes of common actions of, 243; selection of economic system through, 34–35

democratic consensus: and economic stabilization, 56, 58–59; importance of social welfare to, 66; as precondition for economic transformation, 52–54; and transformation of property relations, 62

Deng Xiaoping, 7, 44

Descartes, René, 258

desires, symbolic meaning of, 155–57

despotism, control of debate by, 221

deterrence, 127n.12, 128–29

Diggers, 97–98, 106

diminishing expectations, 281–82

discussion, public. See public opinion; public sphere

diseases(s): adaptation of domesticated animals to, 378–79; development of, in Eurasia, 369; role of, in conquest, 365–66, 380, 382; scarcity of, in the Americas, 369, 371; treatment of (see biomedical science)

DNA, recombinant. See recombinant DNA technology

doctrine: diffusion of, 225; relationship of, to understanding, 218–19

dominance principle, maximizing conditional expected utility and, 171, 173–74, 175

dominant action, choice of, over cooperation, 183–97

Donbass coal mines, 320

Donne, John, 102

Dostoyevsky, Fëdor, 324

"Dover Beach" (Arnold), 208–9, 215, 218, 260

Drake, Sir Francis, 92

drama, biblical influence on, 101–2

Dreyfus, Hubert, 215

drugs, as outcome of biological research, 277–78

Dryden, John, 93

Dunkirk, 93

Durkheim, Émile, 207

dystopias, 324

Easter Island, 358, 359

economic organization: Polynesian, variations in, 357; variation of human societies in, 353

economics, research strategy of, 28–29

economy: diminishing expectations about, 281–82; as extrapolitical secular sphere, 250–51, 253

economy, free. See free economy

Edward VI (king of England), 87, 88

égalité, 311–12

egoism, distinction of individualism from, 212n

Egypt, 365, 378, 379, 381

Einstein, Albert, 323

election (being favored), signs of, 177

Eliade, Mircea, 241

Elizabeth I (queen of England), 88, 92, 99

enclosure movement, 99

*Energia* (rocket launcher), 346
Engels, Frederick, 309-10
English Civil Wars, 90, 91, 92, 93-94
English Revolution, 94-95, 105, 106-7
Enlightenment, the, 213, 214, 343
entrepreneurs: in development of free economy, 65; as revolutionary class, 319
entrepreneurship: evolution of, in economic transition, 61; innovative function of, 30-31
entropy, loss of, 321-22
entry, market: guaranteeing right of, 52; market-socialist vs. capitalist rules of, 22, 23
environment: consequences of Soviet science for, 342-43; destruction of, 111, 113; exploitation of, by socialist production, 317; human arrogance toward, 111-12, 113-14; as name for nature, 112; protection of, by international community, 81-82; public debate about, 303. *See also* geography
Erbery, William, 98
erythropoietin, 277-78
Esau, 97
Eskimos (Inuit), 354
Estonia, 79
eternity: humanity's place in, 112-13; secular understanding of, 246; temporal relationships within, 239-40, 241
Ethiopia, 376, 379, 381
ethnic violence, 312, 320, 354
ethnocentrism, 255-56, 258
Euler, Leonard, 340
Eurasia: development of infectious diseases in, 369; extent of animal and plant domestication in, 371-73, 384; as source of African domesticated animals, 377, 378; variety of human societies in, 353, 355, 356
Europe: colonization of Africa by, 366, 377-78, 379-80, 382; colonization of Australia by, 366, 383-84; colonization of New World by, 360-68, 375; colonization of Tasmania by, 386; introduction of African technology from, 381; partnership of, with North America, 73, 76-77; political and economic restructuring in, 73, 79-80; revolutionizing of warfare in, 365; united, 73, 75-76, 82-83, 322; variety of human societies in, 353

———, Eastern, 3; Bolshevik takeover of, 311; ideological transformation in, 24-25; imposition of market system in, 34; Marxist tradition of, 25; performance of market socialism in, 32, 37, 38; political reform of, 311; privatization in, 63, 64; social welfare in, 66; Walrasian economics in, 27
European Political Union, 76
Eve (first woman), 87, 101, 104
evidential decision theory, 172; causal, symbolic, and linguistic categories of utility and, 181, 182-83; on choice between dominant and cooperative actions, 186-87, 188-89, 193-94, 195, 196-97; maximization of conditionally expected utility under, 175-80, 181
evolution. *See* natural selection
*The Evolution of the Polynesian Chiefdoms* (Kirch), 360
exchange rates, 56-57, 58
exit, market, market-socialist vs. capitalist rules of, 22-23
expected utility principle, 171-72, 174-81
experiments, scientific: fabrication of data in, 288-90; problems of data selection in, 291-92; professional judgment of, 293-94; as protected speech, 295-97; repetition of, 285-87; resurrection of, 287-88
expressiveness, symbolic actions as form of, 152-54
extermination, as biblical theme, 91, 99

faith. *See* belief
family: ethical significance of, 249; as sphere of privacy, 248, 251-52
Family of Love, 99
Faraday, Michael, 341
*Faustus* (Marlowe), 100
*Feathered Gods and Fish Hooks* (Kirch), 360

February Revolution, 331
fetal tissue, scientific research with, 296
Fiji, 359, 366
financial sector, in development of free economy, 64–65
Finnish Bay, 342
fire, 385
First Amendment, U.S. Constitution, and government control of science, 293–97
*The First Circle* (Solzhenitsyn), 328
Fisher, Samuel, 100–101
fishing: abandonment of, 386–87; as food source, 386; and technological deficits, 385
Flinders Island, 388
Ford, Henry, II, 18
Ford Motor Co., 18
foreign aid, in restructuring of socialist economies, 59, 79–80
foreign exchange: conversion of, 57–58; legalizing trade in, 57; reserves of, 59
foreign policy, of united Europe, 76, 77
Fox, George, 94, 97
Foxe, John, 87, 88
France, 92, 245
*fraternité*, 311, 312
fraud, scientific: damage caused by, 288–89, 290; detection of, 289–90; policing of, 290–91; and selection of experimental data, 291–92
free economy, definition of, 51–52
free economy, transition from socialism to: cushioning of, through social welfare, 65–67; difficulty of, 42; implementation of, 317–21; motive force of, 319–20; political requirements for, 52–54; stabilization program for, 55–60; transformation of property relations in, 60–65; Western assistance to, 59, 79–80
free society, public debate in, 230n.15, 231
free speech, and government control of science, 292–97
French Revolution, 211, 244, 245; class forces in, 319; intellectual foundations of, 322; legacy of, in Soviet Union, 311–12; scientific philosophy of, 329, 337–38
Freud, Sigmund, 150, 158

GATT (General Agreement on Tariffs and Trade) Uruguay Round negotiations, 81
Gellner, Ernest, 255n, 256n
generalizations, accidental, derivation of scientific laws from, 119–20, 121
General Motors, 18
genetics: as form of engineering, 278; ideological conformity of, 329; political repression against, 283; regulation of research in, by scientific community, 271–73
Geneva Bible, 88, 89
genome project, 280, 283
geography, as factor in human diversification, 354, 355, 357, 358–60
German Bible, 87
Germany: assistance of, to European restructuring, 79–80; choice of economic system in, 34–35; partnership of, with North America, 72, 76–77; postsocialist transition in, 11; privatization in, 64; reconstruction in, 71–72, 74–75, 82; reunification of, 71, 73, 78, 82–83, 321–22; role of, in Europe, 73, 75–76; scientific research in, 264; socialist revolutionary activity in, 310; tribal societies of, 236; worldwide responsibilities of, 73–74, 80–82
Ghana, 381
Gibbard, Alan, 172n.58, 179
Gideon, 98
*glasnost*, 6, 312, 334, 343
Global Protection against Limited Strikes (GPALS), 316
goals: causal role of actions in pursuit of, 199–200; definition of identity by, 131, 132; guidance of scientific research by, 276–77, 278; principles as means to, 143–44
God: background understandings of our relations to, 216, 217, 218, 220, 246, 247, 259; changes of belief about, 219; duty to, in ordinary life, 249; as

foundation for society, 236, 238; temporal sense of, 239–40
good, the: association of, with ordinary life, 249–50, 251–52; background understandings of our relations to, 216, 218, 220, 246–47, 258, 259; modernity's vision of, 209–10, 220; relation of self-understanding to our concept of, 257, 258
Goodman, Nelson, 160–61
Gorbachev, Mikhail, 7, 44, 71; arms control agreements of, 314–15; and Communist party monopoly, 336; economic reforms of, 9n.10, 26n.21, 314–15, 345; and German reunification, 78; political reforms of, 311, 312, 334–36; and space exploration, 347–48
Gorky, Maxim, 338
government. *See* state, the
grain, Soviet import of, 313–14
Granin, Daniel, 324–25
Great Britain: AIDS research in, 279; and colonization of Ireland, 91, 99, 104; privatization in, 318; and settlement of antipodes, 366, 375; in WWII, 349
Great Chain of Being, 235, 236, 241, 248
Great Depression, 275
Great Inca Rebellion, 364
"Great Socialist Industrialization of the Country," 313
Greece, ancient, democracy in, 324
Grice, H. P., 183
guilt, symbolic removal of, 153–54
gulags, 327–28
Gulf war, 76
guns, transformation of warfare by, 364

Haber, F., 341
Habermas, Jürgen, 250, 251; on atmosphere of public sphere, 227n; on emergence of public opinion, 222; on nature of public discussion, 232; on participants in public sphere, 248; on public scrutiny of government, 230–31
habitus, 217, 218, 219
Halley, Edmund, 339

Ham, 104
*Hamlet* (Shakespeare), 87, 103
happiness, and human social organization, 355
hard budget constraint, 20, 21, 22–23
Hariot, Thomas, 99
harmony, vs. chaos, 323
Harper, William, 172n.58, 179
Harrington, James, 105–6
Harvard University, 43
Hawaii, 353, 357, 358, 359, 366
Hayek, F. A., 5n.8, 24, 27n, 28, 33, 36, 37
Hegel, Georg Wilhelm Friedrich, 51
Heidegger, Martin, 215, 340n
Heidelberg University, 72
Henderson Island, 356
Henrietta Maria, Queen, 92, 95
*Henry VI* (Shakespeare), 87
Henry VIII (king of England), 88, 106
hepatitis C, 279
Herder, Johann Gottfried, 211
Herzen, Alexander, 326
Hinduism, 182n
history: connection of cultural transformation with, 206; materialistic explanations of, 211; scientific explanations of, 389–90
*The History of the French Revolution*, 326
Hitler, Adolf, 79
Hobbes, Thomas, 90, 105
homogeneous time, 240&n, 241, 242, 246
Honecker, Erich, 44
horses, transformation of warfare by, 364–65, 377–78
Hottentots, the, 374, 380
household religion, 89
housing, and technological primitivism, 385–86
How, Cobbler, 96
Huascar (Incan prince), 366
Huayna Capac (Incan emperor), 365–66

human societies: accounting for differences between, 354–55; collisions between, 354–56, 360, 364–68; comparative levels of "civilization," 355; geography as factor in diversification of, 354, 355, 357, 358–60; variations in, 353, 355. *See also* culture(s); society

humanity: obligation toward nature, 114; place in eternity, 112–13; place in nature, 112

Hungarian Academy of Sciences, 43

Hungary: appearance of market socialism in, 5; association of, with European Community, 76; choice of economic system in, 34–35; economic reform in, 321; and German reconstruction, 74; history of reforms in, 43; postsocialist transition in, 11; privatization in, 64; socialist revolutionary activity in, 310; system of economic incentives in, 33

Huns, the, 365

hunter-gatherer tribes, 353, 355; contact of, with Europeans, 383–84; displacement of, by agriculture, 374–75, 376; geographic factors affecting, 358; isolation of, 383, 388; persistence of, 374, 382–83, 384; Polynesian, 357

Hurley, Susan, 134n.19, 148n.32

Husák, Gustav, 44

Huxley, Aldous, 324

hydrogen bomb, 331–34

Hyksos, the, 365

Iacocca, Lee, 18

IBM, 31

Ice Age, extinction of mammal populations by, 372

ideas, and background understandings, 243–44

identity: definition of, by commitments, 145; definition of, by principles, 131–32, 150; human, definition of, through public exchange, 252; modern understanding of, 214

idolatry, campaign against, 95

imagination, social. *See* social imaginary

*Imagined Communities* (Anderson), 245

Imanishi-Kari, Theresa, 284

implants, silicone breast, 302–3

Inca Empire, 353, 357; civil war in, 365–66; disadvantages of, relative to Europe, 368–69; military technology of, 364; Spanish conquest of, 355–56, 360–68

income: distribution of, 269; property rights to, 19

India, 366, 373, 378

Indians. *See* American Indians

individualism: definition of, in relation to others, 257; as fruit of scientific reason, 209; and loss of superstition, 210, 258–59; nonmoral explanations for rise of, 212; and recognition of realm of the private, 250; spiritual breakthrough of, 259–60

Indo-European languages, spread of, 365

Indonesia, 356, 374–75, 380, 383, 386

induction, fit to experience of world, 179–80

industrial policy: importance of research universities to, 268; science as instrument of, 265

industry: allocation of research resources to, 280; use of basic research by, 341

inferences, drawing from general principles, 118–21

inflation: appearance of, under market socialism, 10, 11; double-digit, symbolic meaning of, 162n; public expectations concerning, 58–59

information, as instrument of conquest, 367, 368

injustice, comparative, 125–26

Institute of Medicine, 279

intellectual functions of principles of action, 117–26, 167–68

intelligence, cross-cultural comparisons of, 354

intelligentsia, 324–25; divisions in, 334; economic hardships of, 338–39; emigration of, 328; and political reforms, 334–36, 343–44; pressures for ideological conformity among, 329–31; proletarian-based, 327; rebuilding of, 327, 329; response of, to repression, 330; role of, in Soviet society, 325–

26; service of, to the state, 331–34; suspicion of Soviet rulers toward, 326–27; terror against, 327–28
internal exile, 330, 331, 334
International AIDS Conference, 264
"International Space Year," 309
interpersonal functions of principles of action, 121, 126–30, 131
intimacy, recognition of sphere of, 248, 251–52
intolerance, biblical sanction for, 104–5
intrapersonal functions of principles of action, 126, 132, 133–44
Inuit, the (Eskimos), 354
Ireland, English colonization of, 91, 99, 104
Iron Age states, 353, 355
iron technology, 381
irrationality: fighting irrationality with, 146, 148; of symbolic utility, 154
Isaac, 239–40
island type, effect on human societies, 359
isolation: effect of, on political organization, 358–59; and persistence of hunter-gatherers, 383; and technological primitivism, 384–89

Jacob, 97, 98
Jacobins, 329
James I (king of England), 88, 90–91, 92
Japan, 72, 74
Jefferson, Thomas, 293, 295
Jesus Christ, 239–40, 241; Second Coming of, 91, 94, 98; skepticism of, 99
Jones, Rhys, 387–88
Joseph, 98
judiciary: constraining personal preference in decisions, 122, 123–24; deciding particular cases from general principles, 117–18, 121–26; drawing distinctions between cases, 119n; state-firm contracts, 16
*Julie* (Rousseau), 252
justice: comparative, 125–26; observability of principles in, 129

Kádár, Janos, 7, 44
Kant, Immanuel, 132, 142, 154–55, 168, 230, 257
Kapitsa, Peter, 332, 335
Kennedy, Donald, 267–68, 269
Kennedy, Edward, 266
Kevles, Daniel, 266–67
KGB, 18, 343
Khariton, Yuly, 331–32, 333
Khosian peoples, 374, 376, 380, 382
Khrushchev, Nikita, 311, 313–14, 332
King Island, 388
King James Version of the Bible, 88–89
Kirch, Patrick, 360
Kissinger, Henry, 335
Kistiakowsky, Georg, 335
knowledge, empirical approach to, 209
Koran, the, 100
Korolev, Sergei, 328
Kreps, David P., 129n, 194–95
Krugman, Paul, 281–82
Kurchatov, Igor, 331–32, 333
Kuzbass coal mines, 320

Lake Baikal, 342
land area, effect on human societies, 359
Landau, Lev, 332
Lange, Oscar, model of market socialism, 4, 5n.8, 8–9, 12–13, 17, 27, 28, 30, 31
Lapita people, migrations of, 356
Late Pleistocene Europe, 384
Latin America, 87. *See also* Americas, the; Aztec Empire; Inca Empire; Mesoamerican civilization
Latvia, 79
Laud, Archbishop William, 89, 92
Lavoisier, Antoine, 329, 337–38
law, the: concept of, in tribal society, 236–38; as foundation of society, 235–36. *See also* judiciary
lecturers, dissemination of popular theology by, 89
Leibnitz, Gottfried Wilhelm, 339
Leicester, Earl of, 92

Lenin, V. I., 26n.20, 78, 309; on conditions for revolution, 310; economic policy of, 313, 316; and financial support of scientists, 338–39; scientific philosophy of, 325; suspicions of, about intelligentsia, 326–27
Leningrad Dam, 342
Lerner, A., 4
*Le sens pratique* (Bourdieu), 217n
*The Letters of the Republic* (Warner), 222
Levellers, the, 94–95, 96–97, 97–98, 106
*Leviathan* (Hobbes), 105
liberalism, reputed innovations in public sphere, 221–22
liberation theology, 87
*liberté*, 311
Lilburne, John, 96
*Light Shining in Buckinghamshire* (pamphlet), 90
Lima, Peru, 364
linguistic utility, distinction of, 182–83
Lisman, Natasha, 292, 296
literacy: as instrument of conquest, 367, 368; scientific, 301–3
literature, intimacy in, 252
Lithuania, 79
Locke, John, 258
Lollards, the, 87
Lomonosov, Mikhail, 340
London economic summit (1991), 79
Lord of Cajamarca, 363
Lord of Chincha, 363
lunar exploration, 346
Luther, Martin, 87
Lycurgus, 237, 238
Lysenko, Trofim Denisovich, 283, 329, 333, 340

McCarthy, Joseph, 268
Manchester, England, 212n
Manco (Incan emperor), 364
Mangareva Island, 358
Manhattan Project, 276–77, 278, 283, 332
Maori, the, 375, 388

Mao Zedong, 44
Marat, Jean-Paul, 329
Marian Martyrs, 88
maritime technology: and conquest, 366–67; and technological primitivism, 385, 386
market economy, as extrapolitical common space, 242, 250. *See also* capitalism; free economy, transition from socialism to market entry, 22, 23, 52
market exit, 22–23
market socialism: accomplishments of, 45–46; adoption of, as reform ideology, 25; application of, 5–6; as artificial construct, 32–33; assignment of property rights under, 19–20; budget constraints under, 20, 46–47; combining capitalism and socialism through, 26–27, 45; complementarity of market and planning in, 31–32; defense of, 37–38; differences between blueprint and theory of, 8–9; disillusionment with, 36; economic decision making in, 7–8; economic incentives under, 8, 33; economic performance of, 9–12; entry-exit rules of, 22, 23; failure of, 11–12, 24, 31, 46–47, 48; imposition by ruling elite, 34; influence of Walrasian theory on, 27, 28; learning from experience of, 37; path from theory to realization, 4–5; political power under, 6–7; predominance of state ownership under, 7; replacement of bureaucratic capitalism by, 30; replacement of classical socialism with, 3–4; role of state in, 12–17; selection of, through democratic elections, 34–35; social discipline under, 21–22
Marlowe, Christopher, 99–100
Marquesan Islands, 358, 359
Mars exploration, 346, 347–48
Marshall Plan, 72
Marsin (Mercin), M. (M.M.), 101, 106
Marvell, Andrew, 93
Marx, Karl, 28, 78; criticism of markets, 25; revolutionary theory, 309–10, 311; romanticization of production, 249–50
Marxism: bias against markets, 25–26; intellectual tradition, 25; materialistic

view of cultural change, 211n; preconditions for revolution, 310; scientific basis, 325. *See also* Communism; Communist part(y)(ies) (Soviet and Eastern European); socialism; socialism, classical
Mary I (queen of England), 88
Massachusetts Institute of Technology (MIT), 268
mass media: and democratization of U.S. politics, 270–71; presentation of scientific issues by, 302–3; public exchanges through, 220–21 (*see also* public opinion; public sphere)
materialism, in explanations of cultural change, 211
Mather, Cotton, 225
Maxwell, James Clerk, 341
measles epidemics, role in conquest, 365–66
medicine. *See* biomedical science
Mediterranean region, 365
Mediterranean Sea, 93
Melanesia, 356
Mendeleyev, Dmitry, 340, 341
Menshevism, 327, 331
Mercier, Louis Sébastien, 230
Merleau-Ponty, Maurice, 215
Mesoamerican civilization, 373
metallurgy, 353; development of, in Africa, 381; and patterns of conquest, 375, 376, 381
metatopical common agency, 238, 241, 242, 257
metatopical common space, 238, 241–42; definition of, 229; evolution of, 242–45
Mexico, 353, 373
Micronesia, 356
Microsoft Corp., 31
middle class, in development of free economy, 65
Midianites, the, 91
Milgrom, P., 194–95
military-industrial complex, Soviet, 313–15, 316, 340–41, 345–46, 347

millennium: advent of, 91; and mercantilism, 93; and overthrow of Antichrist, 91–93; revolutionary upheaval and, 93–95
Milton, John, 89, 91, 98, 99, 100, 102
mind, common, formation of, 220, 221, 223, 228, 229, 233, 236, 241
mining, and environmental destruction, 113
Ministry of Defense, Soviet, 341
Mises, Ludwig von, 19, 24, 27n, 36, 37
Mississippian civilization, 353, 366, 373
MIT, 268
modernity: and association of the good with ordinary life, 249–50; background understandings behind, 246–47; as change in our unformulated understandings, 215–20, 255; cultural vs. acultural theories of, 205–20 (*see also* acultural theory of modernity; cultural theory of modernity); inspiration by positive visions, 209–10, 213, 220; negative theories of, 207–8; public sphere as feature of, 221–22
molecular biology. *See* biology, molecular
monarchy: biblical view of, 90–91, 94–95; destruction of, 94–95, 245; metaphysical idea of, 235; secular understanding of, 246
Mongols, the, 365
Montezuma (Aztec emperor), 366, 367–68
moral behavior: symbolism of, 154–55, 158–59, 200–202; understanding through principles, 167–68
morality, and scientific argument, 303–4
moral judgments, attunement to situations, 130
moral law: drawing inferences from, 120–21; selection criteria in determining, 123
moral theory, causal relations in, 197
Morgenstern, Oscar, 163n.52, 187
Moscow, Russia, 309, 343
Moscow Tribune, 343–44
Moses, 91, 104
music, aesthetic value of, 252

myth(s): biblical, reinterpretation of, 97–99; modernity as loss of, 209–10

Nabokov, Vladimir, 328
Napoleon (emperor of France), 355
Napoleonic Wars, 328
Natal, 376, 379
National Academy of Science, 279
National Cancer Institute, 266
National Institutes of Health (NIH), 265–66, 272
National Science Foundation (NSF), 265
nationalism, temporal sense of, 245
Native Americans. *See* American Indians
NATO, 76, 78
natural meaning, 183
natural selection: of capacity for symbolization, 156–57; economic, 22–23; reinforcement of desires by, 156–57; of social institutions, 32–33; time preference as mechanism of, 133–34
nature: human obligation toward, 114; humanity's place in, 112; order vs. chaos in, 323. *See also* environment
Nayler, James, 97
Nazis, 82, 166, 333
Near East, revolutionizing of warfare in, 365
Neolithic settled chiefdoms, 353
Neolithic tribal farming societies, 353
nervous system, basic knowledge of, 299
Netherlands, the (Holland), 93
neurosis, 150–51
*The New Atlantis* (Bacon), 323
New Caledonia, 356
Newcomb, William, 170n
Newcomb's Problem, 170–83, 185–86, 191n.78, 193
"Newcomb's Problem and Two Principles of Choice" (Nozick), 179
New Economic Policy, 313
New England, English colonization of, 99
*New England Journal of Medicine*, 303
New Guinea, 353, 354, 366, 372, 382–83, 386

Newton, Sir Isaac, 240n, 339
New Zealand, 356, 357, 358, 359, 375, 388
Nicholas II (tsar of Russia), 331
Nietzsche, Friedrich Wilhelm, 208
Niger, 381
Nigeria, 376, 379, 381
NIH, 265–66, 272
Nile River, 381
Nimrod, 91
Ninan Cuyuchi (Incan emperor), 366
*1984* (Orwell), 324
Nixon, Richard, 266, 271, 282
Nobel, Alfred, 341
*nomenklatura*, 19
nominal anchor for currency revaluation, 57, 58
non-natural meaning, 183
*The Normative Theory of Individual Choice* (Nozick), 172n.59, 195n.85
Norse exploration, 360
North Atlantic Treaty Organization (NATO), 76, 78
North Island (NZ), 357
novels, exaltation of intimacy in, 252
NSF, 265
Nubia, 381
nuclear test ban treaty, 335

*Oceana* (Harrington), 105–6
Odysseus, 137
Ogarev, Nikolai, 326
oil, Soviet export of, 314
*On Certainty* (Wittgenstein), 216
oncogenes, 299
opinions, changing of, 24–25, 35–37. *See also* public opinion
Oppenheimer, Robert, 332
order, vs. chaos, 323
Orlov, Yury, 334
Orwell, George, 324
ownership, communal, 48
ownership, private. *See* private ownership
ownership, state. *See* state ownership

ownership, worker, 48

Paleolithic, Upper, European society in, 353
Panama, 367
Papuans, the, 374–75
*Paradise Lost* (Milton), 97, 102
*Paradise Regained* (Milton), 102
Parliamentarian Army, 94, 95
Parliament of the Russian Federation, 344
*A Passionate Pamphlet in the Cause of Economic Transition* (Kornai), 43
Pasternak, Boris, 330
Patagonia, 373
patriarchy, biblical, 103–4
Paul, St., 101, 104
Pavlov, Ivan, 338–39
peasants, as revolutionary class, 319
Peasant's Revolt (1381), 87
peer review, 301
people, the: emergence of political society from, 242; sovereignty of, 230–31, 253
*perestroika*, 47, 51, 315, 334, 343
personal functions of principles of action, 131–33
Peru, 367
Peter the Great (tsar of Russia), 339, 344
pharmaceutical industry, development of products for market, 278–79
Philippines, the, 374–75
philosophy of life, collapse of, 36
Phoenicians, the, 381
physics: debate over order and chaos, 323; nuclear, 332, 333; theory of elementary particles, 322
Physiocrats, 250
Pinochet model, 321
piracy, 93
Pitcairn Island, 388
Pizarro, Francisco, 355–56, 360–68
Pizarro, Hernando, 367
Plains Indians, 365

plant domestication, 353, 356, 358; extent of, in New World vs. Old World, 372–73; and patterns of conquest, 376–77, 379–80, 381–82; and population density, 374, 380–81; scarcity of, as factor in persistence of hunter-gatherers, 374, 382–83, 384; and sociopolitical organization, 374–75, 380–81, 384; spread of, in Africa, 379–80
Plato, 222, 257
Pleistocene, Late, in Europe, 384
poetry, biblical influence on, 102
Poland: appearance of market socialism in, 5; association with European Community, 76; choice of economic system in, 34–35; economic reform in, 321; economic stabilization in, 54n; failure of market socialism in, 47; and German reconstruction, 74; postsocialist transition in, 11, 47; privatization in, 64
Polanyi, Michael, 215
Polish syndrome, 47
political clubs, 343–44
political organization: as foundation for successful conquests, 367; geographic factors affecting, 358–60; plant and animal domestication as factor in, 374–75, 380–81, 384; Polynesian, variations in, 357–58; variation of human societies in, 353
polls, public opinion, 229n
Polynesia, 353, 355; cultural taboos in, 387; cultural variation in, 358; disappearance of populations of, 388; economic organization of, 357; epidemics in, 366; food sources of, 357; geographic factors affecting societies of, 358–60; geographic setting of, 356–57; human settlement of, 356; political organization of, 357–58; social organization of, 357
population density: and development of infectious diseases, 369; effect of, on human societies, 359; as factor in conquest, 374–75; plant and animal domestication as factor in, 374, 380–81
populism, 270–71
Pordage, Samuel, 102

positive reinforcement, and repetition of actions, 140–41

*The Possessed* (Dostoyevsky), 324

pottery, 353; development of, in Africa, 381; taboos against, 387

poverty, biblical sanction for, 104

Powell, G. Bingham, 254n, 255n

precedent, legal, constraining power of, 122

President's Science Advisory Committee, 266

prices: and currency revaluation, 57; deregulation of, 56; influence of foreign trade on, 58; setting of, under market socialism, 8

primogeniture, attack on, 97–98

principal-agent model of contract theory, 13–14, 17–19, 23

principles: announcement of, 127; applicability of, vs. confidence in, 129–30; assessment of, from actual consequences, 166–67; as barrier to temptation, 126, 133, 137–44, 147–48; binding of behavior by, 126–30; connection of actions to symbols by, 138, 139–43, 150, 160, 200–201; and connection with rationality, 168–69, 201; as constraint on personal preferences, 122–24; definition of identity by, 131–32, 150; effects on behavior of violating, 140–42, 146–48; facilitation of temptation by, 139; filtering of choices by, 132–33; functions of, 117, 131–33; 163–65; furthering of understanding by, 167–68; general, true particular judgments as consequence of, 117–26; grouping of actions by, 137–38, 147, 200–201; impartiality in, 149; justification of, 164; marking of boundaries with, 149–50; observability of, 129; optimal choice of, 142–43, 202; personal investment in, 147–48; persuasive power of, 121; predictive power of, 118–21, 122–23; reliance of others on, 126, 127, 128–29, 130, 131, 148n.32; reliance of the self on, 132; as safeguard against comparative injustice, 125–26; satisfaction of expectations by, 122; sincerity of, 127–29; suitability of, to particular goals,

164–66; symbolic utility of, 168–69; as transmitters of probability, 119–21, 163; as transmitters of utility, 163

prison camps, for intellectuals, 327–28

Prisoner's Dilemma, 183–97

privacy: emergence of realm of, 248–50; manifestation of, in economic sphere, 250–51; manifestation of, in family life, 248, 251–52

private ownership: legal foundation for, 62–63; predominance of, in free economy, 52; replacement of state ownership with, 63–64, 318; stimulation of, 63; transferring social production to, 60–62

private sector: development of, under market socialism, 7; role of, in economic stabilization, 59

privatization. *See* free economy, transition from socialism to; private ownership; private sector

probabilit(y)(ies): causal, in decision making, 173; conditional, in decision making, 170–81, 186, 188–89, 194–95, 196; principles as transmitters of, 119–21, 163

production: contraction of, under market socialism, 10; decline of, in Soviet Union, 317; ethical significance of, 249–50; politicization of, 14–15; privatization of, 60–62

profit: as indicator of success, 8, 20; manipulation of, by state incentives, 33; maximization of, 8, 23; redistribution of, 23

property rights: guarantee of, 52, 62–63; market-socialist vs. capitalist assignment of, 19–20; in state firms, 63–64

Protestant Reformation, 87, 249

Providence Island Company, 93

*The Provoked Wife* (Vanbrugh), 106

psychiatry, political uses of, 334

public, definition of, 250–51

public opinion: common space of discussion of, 223–24; contrast with unreflected general opinion, 222–23, 228; deliberative process of, 223, 224–25; emergence of, 222; rationality of, 230–

31, 232; and transformation of property relations, 62
public opinion polls, 229n
public ownership. *See* state ownership
public sphere: background understandings behind, 226–28, 229, 242–45, 255–56; as central feature of modernity, 221–22; control of debate within, 221; definition of, 220–21; deliberative process of, 229; developments concurrent with rise of, 248–53; disregarding social rank in, 227n; evolution of common space of, 242–45; extrapolitical status of, 231–34, 241–42; infrastructure of, 225; nature of common space of, 228–29, 241–42; radical secularity of, 235–42; responsibility of government to, 229–31; significance of acts of communication in, 225–26; and social order, 233
publishing, explosion of, 95–96
Pugwash movement, 335
punishment, as deterrent to misbehavior, 128–29
Puritanism: household religion of, 89; Old Testament emphasis of, 99
pygmies, 374, 376
Pym, John, 93

Quakers, 97
quantum mechanics, 323
Quine, W. V., 123
Quizo Yupanqui (Incan general), 364

Rachmaninoff, Sergey, 328
racism: biblical sanction for, 104; in explanation of human social variations, 354
"Radio Yerevan," 312
Ralegh, Walter, 92, 99
Ranters, 97, 100, 106
rationality: combination of individual rationalities and, 183, 184, 185, 186–88, 189n, 193, 194–95, 196; connection of principles with, 168–69, 201; and experience of world, 179–80; and loss of traditional belief, 208, 209, 215, 253, 254; modernity as growth of, 205, 206–7, 253; of moral behavior, 201–2; nonmoral explanations for rise of, 212; and political sloganeering, 327; of public opinion, 230–31, 232; in public policy debate, 303–4; in revolutionary processes, 322–23; and secularization process, 254n; and universal principle of decision making, 178; and utopian thought, 323–24

Reagan, Ronald, 71, 266, 315, 316, 347–48

reason. *See* rationality

reasons: actions as consequences of, 169; effect of, on utility of action, 190–91; testing, against general principles, 124

recombinant DNA technology: banning of research on, 296; as form of engineering, 278; political debate over, 264; regulation of research in, by scientific community, 271–73

reform, definition of, 50–51
reform socialism. *See* market socialism
regicide, 94–95
regret, in estimating utility of rewards, 137n.23
relativity theory, 323
Renaissance, the, 245
repetition of experiments, 285–87
"Republic of Letters," 233–34
republics, ancient: nature of public discussion in, 231–32; political identity of, 234
reputation, and announcement of principles, 127
research, strategy of, 28–29. *See also* relevant subentries under biomedical science; science
Research!America, 271
reserves, as requirement for economic stabilization, 59
resurrection of experiments, 287–88
revolution: application of theory in, 244; class forces in, 319–20; definition of, 50–51; emigration of intellectuals from, 328; millennarian atmosphere of, 93–95; rational foundations of, 322–23; as road to free economy, 51; social imagery of, 245. *See also* Bol-

shevik Revolution; February Revolution; French Revolution; Second Russian Revolution

rewards: distancing oneself from, 149; effect of sunk costs on utility of, 145–46; reducing delay of, as principle, 139; time preference in utility of, 133–37, 135 (fig.)

rivers, redirection of, 342

*The Road to a Free Economy* (Kornai), 43–44

Roberts, J., 194–95

rocketry, 337, 346

Romania, 11, 74, 244

Rome, ancient, 87, 226, 227, 234, 373

Roosevelt, Franklin D., 265

Rousseau, Jean-Jacques, 252

Royal Society, 339

Russia, domestication of horses in, 364–65, 373

Russian Academy of Science, 345

Russian Imperial Academy of Science, 339–40

Russian Revolution. *See* Bolshevik Revolution; February Revolution; Second Russian Revolution

*The Rusticks Alarm to the Rabbies* (Fisher), 100

Sagan, Carl, 348

Sahara Desert, 376, 378, 379, 381

St. Petersburg, Russia, 309

Sakharov, Andrei, 312, 331, 334, 335–36, 344

Salmon, Joseph, 97, 100

Samoa, 359

Samson, 98

*Samson Agonistes* (Milton), 98, 102

Samuel (prophet), 90–91

Savage, Leonard J., 162

Schelling, Thomas, 149n

Schmidt, Otto, 329

Schumpeter, Joseph A., 22, 23, 30–31

science: advances of, 254–55; appropriation of, in revolutionary thought, 322–23; and arms control initiatives, 335; blaming, for failures of socialism, 317; brain drain on, 344–45; contributions of, to political reforms, 335–36, 343–44; cultural foundation of, 213; debate over order and chaos in, 323; dedication to goals in, 276–77, 278; derivation of laws of, 119–20, 121; discovery of truth by, 256, 258–59; of dissent, 323–24; and economic hardships, 338–39, 342, 344–49; emergence as social force, 263; fabrication of data in, 288–90; framing of research questions in, 274–75; and freedom of speech, 292–97; funding of research in, 264–65, 304; and historical explanations, 389–90; improving public image of, 297–304; intellectual freedom in, 266–67; limitations of, 111–12; literacy about, 301–3; loss of assets of, 345–49; and mechanistic worldview, 248; militarization of, 340–41, 345–46; negative side effects of, 342–43; participation of, in public policy debates, 303–4; peer review in, 301; pleasure of, 274, 275; policing of fraud in, 290–91; political repression against, 283, 328; political supervision of, 267–69; problems in, of data selection, 291–92; proficiency and size of cadre of, 336–37, public discontent with, 273, 280–81, 282, 298, 342–43, 348; as public good, 275; regulatory environment in, 270; search for truth in, 283, 284–88, 293, 295; selection criteria for laws of, 122–23; selection of research problems in, 275–77; as servant of socialism, 325, 329–34; setting research priorities in, 300–301; subservience of, to political agenda, 266–67; support of tsarism for, 339–40; survival of basic research in, 341–42; utopian models of, 323, 324; verification in, 284–88. *See also* biomedical science

"Science — The Endless Frontier" (V. Bush), 265, 266–67

scientific consciousness. *See* rationality

scleroderma, 302–3

Searle, John, 215

Second Coming, 91, 94, 98

Second Russian Revolution: beginning of, 314–15; driving force behind, 319–

20; new thinking of, 334–36, 343–44; privatization of economy by, 317–21
secularity: background understandings behind, 246–47; contrast of, with legality, 235–36; contrast of, with metaphysicality, 235, 236, 238; contrast of, with tribal society, 236–38; relationship of common agency to common action in, 237–38; relationship to belief, 246–47; rise of, 244; temporal sense of, 239–42
secularization, process of, 254n
security policy, of united Europe, 76, 77
Sedgwick, William, 98
*Sein und Zeit* (Heidegger), 240n
self-creation, 132
self-image, as factor in behavior, 182
self-interest, adherence to principles and, 117
self-legislation, 132
self-understanding: background of, 216–18, 259; ethnocentric, 255–56; realization of, in relationship to others, 256–57, 258; relation of, to concept of the good, 257, 258
Sen, Amartya, 201
sentiment, exaltation of, 251–52
Serengeti Plain, 378
Sergeevich, Mikhail, 347
Shakespeare, William, 87, 103
sharagas, 327–28
Sibbes, Richard, 95
Siberia, 342, 353
Sidney, Sir Philip, 92
Sikorsky, Igor, 328
silicone breast implants, 302–3
simultaneity, 240
Singapore, 72
slavery, biblical sanction for, 104
smallpox epidemics, role in conquest, 365–66
Smith, Adam, 250
Snow, C. P., 295
Sobel, J. Howard, 173nn.61, 62
social change: human motivation in, 212; modernity as result of, 205–6, 207, 211, 213, 253–54; variety of cultural responses to, 214, 215
social contract, 243, 244, 252, 257
social democracy, 310, 327, 331
social discipline, 21–22, 49
social imaginary, 219–20, 242, 255, 257; ambiguities in, 245; changes in, 259; and rise of public sphere, 227, 228, 243, 244
social institutions, evolution of, 32–33
socialism: capitalism as alternative to, 50; competition of, with capitalism, 316–17, 325; definition of, 4n.4; economic reform of, 314–15, 316 (*see also* free economy, transition from socialism to); establishment of, by revolution, 310; material hardships of scientists under, 338–39; negative side effects of science under, 342–43; political reform of, 311, 312, 334–36, 343–44; role of intelligentsia in, 325–26; science as servant of, 325, 329–34; scientific basis of, 325; totalitarian, 310–11; transition to free economy from (*see* free economy, transition from socialism to); types of, 44–45; war economy of, 313–15, 316. *See also* Communism; Communist part(y)(ies) (Soviet and Eastern European); market socialism; Marxism
———, classical: coherence of, 12; combining, with capitalism, 26–27, 45; shortages under, 10; social discipline under, 21. *See also* Communism; Communist part(y)(ies) (Soviet and Eastern European); Marxism
social order, challenge of public debate to, 233
social organization: plant and animal domestication as factor in, 374–75, 380–81, 384; Polynesian, 357
social science, materialistic explanations in, 211
social welfare, role in economic transition, 65–67
society: background understandings of our relations to, 216, 217–18, 219, 220; legal foundation of, 235–36; metaphysical foundation of, 235, 236, 238; public space of (*see* public sphere); tribal, 236–38 (*see also*

hunter-gatherer tribes). See also human societies
Society Islands, 357, 358, 359
Socrates, 323, 324
soft budget constraint syndrome, 20, 21n, 23, 46–47
Solemn League and Covenant (1643), 92–93
Solomon, King, 98, 102
Solomon Archipelago, 356
Solomon example (decision theory), 179
Solzhenitsyn, Alexander, 328
Song of Songs, 102
soul engineering, 325, 327
South Africa, 354, 377, 378, 379–80, 382
Southeast Asia, 356, 366, 373, 374–75
South Island (NZ), 357, 358, 359
Soviet Academy of Science, 340, 342–43, 343–44
Soviet Agricultural Academy, 329
Soviet man, new (*Homo sovieticus*), 325, 326, 327, 328, 329
Soviet Union, 3, 76; appearance of market socialism in, 5; and arms control agreements, 314–16, 355; competition of, with capitalist world, 316–17, 325; economic reform in, 314–15, 316 (*see also* free economy, transition from socialism to); end of, 312–13, 321; ethnic violence in, 312, 320, 354; failed coup in, 78, 79, 312; failure of market socialism in, 47, 48; and German reconstruction, 74; ideological conformity in, 329–31; inheritance in, from French Revolution, 311–12; material hardships of scientists in, 338–39; militarization of science in, 340–41, 345–46; military-industrial complex in, 313–15, 316, 340–41, 345–46, 347; negative side effects of science in, 342–43; 1989 constitution of, 335–36; nuclear weapons program of, 331–34, 337; political reform in, 311, 312, 334–36, 343–44; rebuilding of intelligentsia of, 327, 329; repression against science in, 283, 328; restructuring of, 1, 73, 79–80 (*see also* free economy, transition from socialism

to); role of intelligentsia in, 325–26; scientific philosophy in, 323, 325; size of scientific cadre of, 336–37; and space exploration, 346–48; state policy toward science in, 329–34; suspicion toward intelligentsia in, 326–27; technological proficiency of, 337; terror against intelligentsia in, 327–28; totalitarian socialism in, 310–11; war economy of, 313–15, 316; in WWII, 332, 349
space exploration, 309, 337, 346–48
"Space Race," 346
Spain, 92, 93
Spanish Conquest: capture of Cajamarca during, 355–56, 360–64; military technology of, 364, 366–67; political organization behind, 367; role of disease in, 365–66; strategic miscalculations of the defeated in, 367–68; superior information of victors in, 367, 368
Sparta, 238
specialization, social, 375
Spector, Mark, 289–90
speech, freedom of, and government control of science, 292–97
Spinoza, Baruch, 101
*Sputnik I* (satellite), 309, 328, 337, 346
stabilization, economic, program for, 55–60
Stakhanov, Aleksei, 329, 342
Stalin, Joseph, 26n.20, 44, 78, 79; on conditions for revolution, 310; economic policy of, 313; ideological conformity under, 329, 330; indoctrination program of, 327; and intelligentsia, 325–29; militarization of science under, 341; nuclear weapons program of, 331–34; totalitarianism of, 311
Stanford-Binet intelligence test, 354
Stanford University, 267–68, 269
*stare decisis* doctrine, 122
Star Wars missile defense program (SDI), 266, 315, 316, 347, 348n
state, the: and contracts with industry management, 13–14, 15, 16, 17–19,

23; in Polynesian societies, 358; recognition of private realm as distinct from, 248, 250; responsibility of, to public opinion, 222, 229–31; role of, in market socialism, 12–17; time dimension of, 241; as type of common space, 229

state ownership: assignment of property rights under, 19–20; breakup of infrastructure of, 320; budget constraints under, 20, 46–47; contracts between state and firm managers under, 13–14, 15, 16, 17, 23; economic decision making under, 7–8; as fatal defect of market socialism, 46; managerial revolt against, 320; post-Communist, 38; predominance of, 7, 24, 26; relationship between principal and agents under, 17–19; replacement of, with private enterprises, 63–64, 318; role of, in free economy, 60

status, pursuit of, 158

steel weapons, transformation of warfare by, 364

Stoic cosmopolis, 235

stone tool technology, 353, 356, 385

Strategic Defense Initiative ("Star Wars" — SDI), 266, 315, 316, 347, 348n

Stravinsky, Igor, 328

strikes, as obstacle to market reforms, 320

*The Structural Transformation of the Public Sphere* (Habermas), 222

subsidies, state, elimination of, 55–56

Sudan, 378, 379, 381

*The Sufficiency of the Spirits Teaching without Humane-learning* (How), 96

sunk costs, influence on decisions, 144–50

super-conducting supercollider, 265

supervision, principle of, 230–31, 232

Supreme Court, U.S., free-speech rulings of, 293, 296, 297

Supreme Soviet, 343

Sure Thing principle, 162

*Sur la révolution du globe terrestre* (Cuvier), 326

Switzerland, 264

Sydney, Australia, 366

symbolic understanding, as background to belief, 218, 219

symbolic utility, 150–63; distinction of, from other categories of utility, 181, 182–83; of dominant vs. cooperative actions, 189–90, 192–94, 195, 196–97; of moral behavior, 154–55, 158–59, 200–202; variation of decision values with, 180–81

symbolism: correlation of, with actions by principles, 138, 139–43, 150, 160, 200–201; as determinant of decision making, 150–63, 180–81, 200–202; distinguishing good from bad, 157–58

system design/engineering, 32

systems of scientific research, 286

taboos, and loss of material culture, 387–88

*Tamburlaine* (Marlowe), 99–100

Tamm, Igor, 331

Tany, Thomas, 100

Taoism, 182n

Tasmania, 353, 356; contact of, with Europeans, 386; technological primitivism of, 384–89

TASS, 348

taxation: concessions in, to private sector, 63; and economic stabilization, 56; and social specialization, 375

Taylor, F. M., 4

technology: limitations of, 111–12; Polynesian, 358; retardation of, by geographic isolation, 384–89; and sociopolitical organization, 375, 384; spread of, in Africa, 381; transformation of conquest by, 364–65, 366–67; variation of human societies in, 353. *See also* science

Temin, Howard, 294

temptation: costs of commitment as barrier to, 145–48; distancing oneself from, 149; facilitation of, by principles, 139; overcoming, 133, 136–44, 163; principles as barrier to, 126, 133, 137–44, 147–48

Tenochtitlan, Mexico, 368
thermodynamics, second law of, 321–22
third estate, 319
Third System/Third Road, 9, 11, 45; romantic version of, 48–50
Third World: demoralization in, 212n; development in, 81; environmental protection in, 81–82; trade with, 81–82
Thirty Years War, 105
Thompson, Benjamin, 328
time: background understandings of our relations to, 258, 259; divine, 239–40; foundation, 241; heroic, 238–39, 245; profane, 239, 240–42, 246, 248, 249, 251, 254, 257; shifts in consciousness about, 246, 247
time preference, in judging utility of rewards, 133–37, 135 (fig.)
Tito, Josip Broz, 7, 44
Tocqueville, Alexis de, 207, 212n
Tonga, 357, 358, 359, 366
topical common agency, 238
topical common space, 229
topography, effect on human societies, 359
Torres Straits, 383
trade: international agreements on, 81–82; liberalization of, 58; and naval power, 93; and political organization, 359; spread of domesticated plants by, 380
trade deficit, of market-socialist economies, 10, 11
tradition: founding moments of, 236–37, 238–39; modernity as loss of, 208–10, 214–15, 253–54, 255; in tribal society, 236–38
transportation, and animal domestication, 374
tribalism: founding moments of, 236–37, 238–39; traditional law of, 236–38. *See also* hunter-gatherer tribes
Truman, Harry S, 71
truth: distortion of, in scientific research, 288; emergence of, from discarded superstitions, 254–55; rational pursuit of, 322; scientific, 256, 258–59; search

of science for, 283, 284–88, 293, 295; understanding of, through principles, 167–68
tsarism: Bolsheviks as successor to, 326; support in, for science, 339–40
Tupolev, Andrei, 328
Turkmenistan, 342
Tushnet, Mark, 119n
Twentieth Party Congress (CPSU), 311, 334
"Two Cultures and the Scientific Revolution" (Snow), 295
Tyndale, William, 87–88

Ukrainian nationalism, 245
uncertainty, effect on symbolic utility, 161–62
uncertainty principle, 323
understanding: furthering of, by principles, 167–68; levels of, 218–19; unformulated, behind belief, 215–20, 255
unemployment, in economic transition, 66
United Kingdom. *See* Great Britain
United Nations, 309
universities: importance of, to economic growth, 268; monopoly of, on intellectual life, 96–97; political supervision of research at, 267–69; regulatory environment in, 270; scapegoating of, for economic decline, 269–70; status of biological sciences in, 278
University of California, Berkeley, 72
Upper Paleolithic European society, 353
Ustinov, Marshall, 314
utility: alteration of, by sunk costs, 144–46; alteration of, by symbolic value of action, 138, 139–40; causally expected, 173; conditional, 191, 198; conditional expected, maximization of, 171–81; distinctions among categories of, 181–83; of dominant vs. cooperative actions, 183–97; effects of reasons for action on, 190–91; estimation of, from principled grouping of actions, 138; evidentially expected, 172; measurement of, 162n; of moral behavior, 154–55, 158–59, 200–202; principles

as transmitters of, 163; symbolic, variation of decision values with, 180–81; of symbolic behavior, 150–63; time-preferenced estimates of, 133–37, 135 (fig.)
utopias, 323, 324
Uzbekistan, 342

Vanbrugh, Sir John, 106
Vavilov, Nikolai, 329, 330
verification, scientific, 284–88
Vietnam, 5, 37
viruses, cloning of, 272–73
von Braun, Werner, 346
Von Neumann, John, 163n.52, 187
V-2 rocket, 346

wages: disciplining of, 56; runaway, under market socialism, 46
*Wall Street Journal*, 302–3
Walrasian economics, 27–30
Walsingham, Sir Francis, 92
Walwyn, William, 96, 99, 100, 104–5
war capitalism, 339
war communism economy, 313, 338
War on Cancer, 266, 282
warfare, technological transformation of, 364–65. See also conflict; conquest
Warner, Michael: on emergence of public sphere, 222, 225–26, 233; on nature of public discussion, 232–33; on public scrutiny of government, 230–31
*We* (Zamyatin), 324
wealth, pursuit of, 158

weaponry: and technological primitivism, 385; transformation of warfare by, 364
Weber, Max, 207, 208, 211n, 260
Wiesner, Jerome, 335
wilderness, as political symbol, 98–99
Williams, Bernard, 158n.42
Williams, Roger, 104
Wilson, Robert, 129n, 194–95
Winstanley, Gerrard, 96, 97, 99, 100
Wittgenstein, Ludwig, 215, 216
women: biblical doctrine concerning, 101, 103–4; moral judgments of, 130
wood tool technology, 385
worker self-management, 48
World War I, 331, 365
World War II, 264–65, 275, 282, 284, 310–11, 313, 329, 331, 332, 341, 346, 348–49
worldwide proletarian revolution, doctrine of, 310
Writer, Clement, 99, 100
writing: development of, in Africa, 381; facilitation of conquest by, 367, 368
Wyatt, Sir Thomas, 102
Wyclif, John, 87

Yeltsin, Boris, 78, 316, 319, 320
Yugoslavia: appearance of market socialism in, 5; civil war in, 76, 80; and German reconstruction, 74; postsocialist transition in, 11; public ownership in, 7

Zamyatin, Evgeny, 324